A Preface to Romans

A PREFACE TO ROMANS

Notes on the Epistle in Its Literary and Cultural Setting

Christopher Bryan

OXFORD

UNIVERSITY PRESS

2000

OXFORD
UNIVERSITY PRESS

Oxford   New York
Athens   Auckland   Bangkok   Bogotá   Buenos Aires   Calcutta
Cape Town   Chennai   Dar es Salaam   Delhi   Florence   Hong Kong   Istanbul
Karachi   Kuala Lumpur   Madrid   Melbourne   Mexico City   Mumbai
Nairobi   Paris   São Paulo   Singapore   Taipei   Tokyo   Toronto   Warsaw

and associated companies in
Berlin   Ibadan

Copyright © 2000 by Christopher Bryan

Published by Oxford University Press, Inc.
198 Madison Avenue, New York, New York 10016

Oxford is a registered trademark of Oxford University Press

Library of Congress Cataloging-in-Publication Data
Bryan, Christopher, 1935–
A preface to Romans : notes on the Epistle in its literary and
cultural setting / Christopher Bryan.
p.   cm.
Includes bibliographical references
ISBN 0-19-513023-5
1. Bible. N.T.   Romans—Commentaries.   2. Bible. N.T. Romans—
Socio-rhetorical criticism.   I. Title.
BS2665.3.B75   1999
227'.1066—dc21   99-10412

1 3 5 7 9 8 6 4 2
Printed in the United States of America
on acid-free paper

In Memoriam
Mickey
1982–1997
Faithful, Loving, and Beloved Friend,
and a Very Fine Cat

ἡ δικαοσύνη σου ὡσεὶ ὄρη θεοῦ,
τὰ κρίματά σου ἄβυσσος πολλή
ἀνθρώπους καὶ κτήνη σώσεις, κύριε.
Ψαλμοι ΛΕ΄

Acknowledgments

My thanks to the Reverend Professor Reginald H. Fuller, Professor of New Testament at Virginia Theological Seminary, and the Reverend Dr. Richard Burridge, Dean of King's College, London, both of whom read the manuscript of *Preface to Romans* at critical stages in its writing, and made invaluable criticisms and suggestions, as well as offering much-needed encouragement. My thanks to Dr. James T. Dunkley, librarian at the School of Theology of the University of the South, who is everything that the ideal librarian should be and more. No request for a book or a document ever appears too obscure for him, nor does any bibliographical question, however footling, ever appear to disturb his good humor. He, too, read the manuscript at critical stages and saved me at various points from making a fool of myself. My thanks to the Reverend Dr. Ellen Bradshaw Aitken, Visiting Assistant Professor of New Testament at Harvard Divinity School, and Ms. Sue Ellen Armentrout, Reference Librarian at the University of the South: they, too, put me right about several important matters. My thanks to the Reverend Susan Bear (now Rector of Rolling Fork, Mississippi), the Reverend Gabriel Sinisi (now Rector of Verona, New Jersey), and Sherry Coulter, my research assistants over several years. All have assisted me, patiently and graciously, in more ways than I can name. My thanks to Cynthia Read, Senior Editor of the Oxford University Press, for encouragement over several years, and for retaining her good humor even when I missed my deadlines (which I invariably did), and also to Nina Sherwin and Bob Milks of the Oxford University Press, for their unfailing good humor and support.

There is, finally, no way adequately to thank Wendy Bryan, who has (yet again) patiently and good-naturedly put up with my scribbling for three years while this thing slowly struggled into shape. It is as much in her name as in my own that I dedicate the result to the memory of Mickey, our cat, a dear companion who was with us during the first months of my writing, but died before the end. This dedication too, like my former, presumes (as it is written) that

> Thy righteousness standeth like the strong mountains:
> Thy justice is like the great deep:
> Humankind and beast shalt thou save, O Lord.
> (Psalm 36.6)

Sewanee, Tennessee   C. B.
Ss. Simon and Jude, Apostles, 1998

Contents

Abbreviations and Short Titles   xiii

Prologue: Looking at Romans   3

    The Scope of the Inquiry   3

    The Purpose of the Inquiry   4

PART I   WHAT KIND OF TEXT IS ROMANS?

1. The Genre of the Letter to the Romans   11

    What Are We Talking About? The Significance of Genre   11

    Romans as a Greco-Roman Letter   12

    Romans as an Essay with the Heading "Greetings!"   15

    Romans as a Persuasive Discourse   18

    Romans as a Family Letter   29

    Romans as a Letter of Commendation   33

        Additional Note A. Patronage   34

2. The Letter to the Romans, the Jewish Scriptures, and the Law   42

    What Did Paul Mean by "the Scriptures"?   42

    What did Paul mean by "the Law"?   45

        Additional Note B. Hebrew Tôrâ and Greek Nomos   47

    How Did Paul Interpret the Scriptures?   50

PART II   LISTENING TO ROMANS

3. The Epistolary Opening (1.1–15)   57

    Additional Note C. Apostle   64

    Additional Note D. Grace   66

4. The Dissuasive (1.16–4.25): Against Dependence on Anything save the Justice and Mercy of God   67

    The Nature of the Gospel (1.16–17)   67

        Additional Note E. Honor and Shame   72

Additional Note F. Salvation   75

Additional Note G. The Salvation of Israel and the Healing of Creation   75

Additional Note H. Translating Dikaiosunē   76

God's "No!" to Injustice (1.18–32)   77

Additional Note I. Romans 1.18–32 and Genesis 1–3   82

Additional Note J. Glory   83

Additional Note K. On the Significance of 1.26b–27   84

Additional Note L. "Self-Control"   89

God's "No!" to Our Injustice (2.1–3.20)   91

Additional Note M. Sin   100

God's "Yes!" through Jesus the Messiah (3.21–31)   102

Additional Note N. 3.24–26 as a Pre-Pauline Formula   107

Additional Note O. On Translating Pistis Christou   108

Additional Note P. Propitiation   111

Additional Note Q. The Interpretation of Hilastērion at Romans 3.25
    as "Mercy Seat"   112

Additional Note R. The Meaning of Paresis at Romans 3.25   112

Additional Note S. The Distinction between Ek and Dia
    at Romans 3.30   113

The Example of Abraham (4.1–25)   114

Additional Note T. Problems in Translating Romans 4.1   118

5. Demonstration and Defense (5.1–11.36): Peace with God
   through Christ   120

Demonstration (5.1–21)   120

Additional Note U. The Meaning of Eph'hō[i] at Romans 5.12   128

Additional Note V. Solidarity   129

Defense 1. Does the Gospel Undermine the Commandment? (6.1–8.39)   133

Additional Note W. On Translating Romans 6.5   137

Additional Note X. Flesh   155

Additional Note Y. Spirit   156

Additional Note Z. Body   157

Defense 2. Does the Gospel Call in Question God's Faithfulness
    to the Promises? (9.1–11.36)   159

Additional Note AA. The Eight Privileges of Israel at Romans 9.4–5   169

Additional Note BB. On Translating Romans 9.5   170

Additional Note CC. "The End of the Law" at Romans 10.4   171

Additional Note DD. On the Interpretation of Romans 10.5–10   172

Additional Note EE. Ministry   184

Additional Note FF. Calvin's Understanding of Romans 9–11   186

Additional Note GG. Problems of Interpretation in Romans 11.15–16   187

Additional Note HH. The Mystery   188

Additional Note II. The Salvation of All Israel   189

Additional Note JJ. On Problems of Translating 11.30–31   193

6. Exhortation (12.1–15.13): An Invitation to the Christian Life   194
   Grounds for the Exhortation: The Proper Response to God's Mercies (12.1–2)   194
   Some Basic Principles for Life in the Church (12.3–13)   196
      Additional Note KK. Moderation   200
   Relations with the World at Large (12.14–13.14)   201
      Additional Note LL. Further Thoughts on "the Authorities"   208
      Additional Note MM. Public Servant   210
   Further Notes on Life in the Church: The Problem of the "Strong"
      and the "Weak" (14.1–15.13)   211
      Additional Note NN. Other Opinions about the "Strong" and the "Weak"   215
      Additional Note OO. The Ethnic Composition of the Roman Church   217

7. Epistolary Conclusion (15.14–16.23)   222
   Paul's Plans (15.14–33)   222
   Commendation of Phoebe (16.1–2)   225
   Greetings to God's Household (16.3–16)   226
   Paul in His Own Hand (16.17–20)   230
   Greetings from Paul's Colleagues (16.21–23)   232

Epilogue: Unscientific Postscripts   234
   Outsiders?   234
   Insiders   236
   Hope   237

General Bibliography   239

Index of Holy Scripture   263

Index of Other Ancient Authors and Sources   269

Index of Authors and Sources between 1000 and 1850   272

Index of Modern Authors and Sources   273

Index of Subjects   276

Abbreviations
and Short Titles

Full publication information on books cited here is given in the general bibliography, except for dictionaries, grammars, and collections of primary sources.

Commentaries on Romans and Galatians

Barrett, *Romans*	Barrett, C. K. *A Commentary on the Epistle to the Romans.*
Barth, *Romans*	Barth, Karl. *The Epistle to the Romans.*
Barth, *Shorter Romans*	Barth, Karl. *A Shorter Commentary on Romans.*
Bruce, *Galatians*	Bruce, F. F. *The Epistle of Paul to the Galatians: A Commentary on the Greek Text.*
Burton, *Galatians*	Burton, Ernest de Witt. *A Critical and Exegetical Commentary on the Epistle to the Galatians.*
Byrne, *Romans*	Byrne, Brendan, S.J. *Romans.* Sacra Pagina Series. Vol. 6.
Calvin, Romans	Calvin, Jean. *Commentary on the Epistle of Paul the Apostle to the Romans.*
Cranfield, *Romans*	Cranfield, C. E. B. *A Critical and Exegetical Commentary on the Epistle to the Romans.*
Dodd, *Romans*	Dodd, C. H. *The Epistle of Paul to the Romans.*
Dunn, *Romans*	Dunn, James D. G. *Romans.*
Fitzmyer, *Romans*	Fitzmyer, Joseph A., S.J. *Romans: A New Translation with Introduction and Commentary.*
Johnson, *Romans*	Johnson, Luke Timothy. *Reading Romans: A Literary and Theological Commentary.*
Käsemann, *Romans*	Käsemann, Ernst. *Commentary on Romans.*
Lagrange, *Romains*	Lagrange, M.-J. *Saint Paul: Épitre aux Romains.*
Leenhardt, Romans	Leenhardt, F-J. *The Epistle to the Romans. A Commentary.*
Luther, *Romans*	Luther, Martin. *Lectures on Romans.*
Martyn, *Galatians*	Martyn, J. Louis. *Galatians.*

Matera, *Galatians*	Matera, Frank J. *Galatians*.
Moo, *Romans*	Moo, Douglas J. *The Epistle to the Romans*.
Nygren, *Romans*	Nygren, Anders. *Commentary on Romans*.
Rhys, *Romans*	Rhys, Howard. *The Epistle to the Romans*.
Sanday and Headlam, *Romans*	Sanday, W., and A. C. Headlam. *A Critical and Exegetical Commentary on the Epistle to the Romans*.
Stuhlmacher, *Romans*	Stuhlmacher, Peter. *Paul's Letter to the Romans: A Commentary*.

Dictionaries, grammars, and collections of primary sources

ABD	Freedman, David Noel, ed., *The Anchor Bible Dictionary*. 6 vols. New York: Doubleday, 1992.
ASP	American Studies in Papyrology
BAGD	Bauer, Walter, William F. Arndt, F. Wilbur Gingrich, and Frederick W. Danker. *A Greek-English Lexicon of the New Testament and Other Early Christian Literature*. Chicago: University of Chicago Press, 1979.
BD	Blass, F., and A. Debrunner. *A Greek Grammar of the New Testament and Other Early Christian Literature*. Translated and revised by Robert W. Funk. Chicago: University of Chicago Press, 1961.
BDB	Brown, Francis, S. R. Driver, and Charles A Briggs. *A Hebrew and English Lexicon of the Old Testament*. Based on William Gesenius's *Lexicon*, translated by Edward Robinson. First edition reprinted with corrections. Oxford: Clarendon Press, 1953.
BSGRT	Bibliotheca scriptorum Graecorum et Romanorum Teubneriana.
CC, SL	*Corpus Christianorum: Series Latina*. Turnholt: Brepols, 1958–
Charlesworth, *Old Testament Pseudepigrapha* 1 and 2.	Charlesworth, James H., ed. *The Old Testament Pseudepigrapha*. 2 vols. New York: Doubleday, 1983–85.
CIG	Boeckh, A. *Corpus Inscriptionum Graecarum*. 1828–77.
CIL	*Corpus Inscriptionum Latinarum*. Berlin, 1963–.
CNT	Commentaire du Nouveau Testament.
CSEL	*Corpus Scriptorum Ecclesiasticorum Latinorum*. Urba, Charles F., and Joseph Zycha, eds.
Dittenberger, *Inscriptiones*	Dittenberger, Wilhelm, *Orientis Graeci Inscriptiones Selectae: Supplementum Sylloges Inscriptionum Graecarum*. 2 vols. Hildesheim: George Olms Verlag, 1970 (Leipzig: Hirzel,1903–5).
Dittenberger, *Sylloge*	Dittenberger, Wilhelm, *Sylloge Inscriptionum Graecarum*. 4 vols. Third edition, 1915–24.
GKC	Cowley, A. E. *Gesenius' Hebrew Grammar as edited and enlarged by the late E Kautzch*. Second edition, corrected. Oxford: Clarendon Press, 1976.

Kaibel	Kaibel, Georgius. *Comicorum Graecorum Fragmenta.* Berlin: Weidmann, 1958 (Berlin: Weidmann, 1899).
LEHC	Lust, J., E. Eynikel, and K. Hauspie, with the collaboration of G. Chamberlain. *A Greek-English Lexicon of the Septuagint.* Part 1. A–I. Stuttgart: Deautsche Bibelgeselschaft, 1992.
LS	Liddell, Henry George, and Robert Scott. *A Greek-English Lexicon.* Revised by Sir Henry Stuart Jones, Roderick McKenzie, and others. With Supplement. Edited by E. A. Barber, P. Maas, M. Scheller, and M. L. West. Oxford: Clarendon Press, 1968.
Mason, *GTRI*	Mason, Hugh J. *Greek Terms for Roman Institutions: A Lexicon and Analysis.* ASP 13. Toronto: Hakkert, 1974.
Migne, *Patrologiæ*	Migne, J.-P. *Patrologiæ Cursus Completus Omnium SS. Patrum, Doctorum, Scriptorumque Ecclesiasticorum sive Latinorum sive Graecorum.* Turnholt: Brepols.
Moule, *Idiom*	Moule, C. F. D. *An Idiom Book of New Testament Greek.* Cambridge: Cambridge University Press, 1953.
Moulton, *Grammar*	Moulton, J. H. *A Grammar of New Testament Greek.* Third edition. Edinburgh: Clark, 1908.
NDIEC	*New Documents Illustrating Early Christianity*
OCB	Metzger, Bruce, and Michael D. Coogan, eds. *The Oxford Companion to the Bible.* New York: Oxford University Press, 1993.
OCD	Hammond, N. G. L., and H. H. Scullard, eds. *The Oxford Classical Dictionary.* Oxford: Clarendon Press, 1970.
OED2	*Oxford English Dictionary, Second Edition.* 20 vols. Prepared by J. A. Simpson and E. S. C. Weiner. Oxford: Clarendon Press, 1989.
OLD	Glare, P. G. W., ed., *Oxford Latin Dictionary.* Oxford: Clarendon Press, 1982.
POxy	Grenfell, B. P., and A. S. Hunt. *The Oxyrhynchus Papyri.* Vols. 1–17. 1898–1927.
Pouilloux, *Inscriptions*	Pouilloux, Jean. *Choix d'inscriptions grecques: Textes, traductions et notes.* Bibliothèque de la faculté des lettres de Lyon 4. Paris: Société d'édition "Les belles lettres," 1960.
Rahner and Vorgrimler, *CTD*	Rahner, Karl, and Herbert Vorgrimler, gen. eds. *Concise Theological Dictionary.* Edited by Cornelius Ernst, O.P. Translated by Richard Strachan. Freiburg: Herder; London: Burns and Oates, 1965.
Smyth, *Grammar*	Smyth, Herbert Weir. *Greek Grammar.* Revised by Gordon M. Messing. Cambridge, Massachusetts: Harvard University Press, 1956.
Sparks, *Apocryphal Old Testament*	Sparks, H. F. D., ed. *The Apocryphal Old Testament.* Oxford: Clarendon Press, 1984.

Spicq, *Lexicon*	Spicq, Ceslas, O.P. *Theological Lexicon of the New Testament.* Translated and edited by James D. Ernest. Peabody, Massachusetts: Hendrickson, 1994.
Staab, *Pauluskommentare*	Staab, K. *Pauluskommentare aus der griechischen Kirche: Aus Katenhandschriften gesammelt und herausgegeben.* Neutestamentliche Abhandlungen 15. Münster: Aschendorff, 1933.
TDNT	Kittel, Gerhard (ed. vols. 1–5), and Gerhard Friedrich (ed. vols. 6–9), *Theological Dictionary of the New Testament.* 9 vols. Translated by Geoffrey W. Bromiley. Grand Rapids, Michigan: Eerdmans, 1964 [1933]–1974 [1973].
TLOT	Jenni, Ernst, and Claus Westermann, eds. *Theological Lexicon of the Old Testament.* 3 vols. Translated by Mark E. Biddle. Peabody, Massachusetts: Hendrickson, 1997.
Turner, *Style*	Turner, Nigel. *Style.* Vol. 4 of *A Grammar of New Testament Greek.* Edited by James Hope Moulton. 4 vols. Edinburgh: Clark, 1976.
Zerwick, *Biblical Greek*	Zerwick, Maximilian, S.J. *Biblical Greek: Illustrated by Examples.* SPIB 112. Adapted from the fourth Latin edition by Joseph Smith, S.J. Rome: Pontificio Instituto Biblico, 1963.

Other abbreviations

In biblical citations and citations from rabbinic literature I have used the customary abbreviations, as presented, for example, on pages xx–xxi of the OCB.

AB	Anchor Bible
AnBib	Analectica Biblica: Investigationes scientificae in res biblicas
ANRW	*Aufstieg und Niedergang der Römanischen Welt*
ARV	The Holy Bible: American Revised Version (1901)
ATR	*Anglican Theological Review*
Barth, *Church Dogmatics*	Barth, Karl. *Church Dogmatics.*
BEP	La Bibbia: edizioni paoline (1987)
BHT	Beiträge zur historischen Theologie
Bib	*Biblica*
BJ	La Sainte Bible: traduit en français sous la direction de L'École Biblique de Jérusalem (1955)
BNTC	Black's New Testament Commentaries.
BSGRT	Bibliotheca scriptorum Graecorum et Romanorum Teubneriana
CBQ	*Catholic Biblical Quarterly*
CGTC	Cambridge Greek Testament Commentary
Class. Phil.	*Classical Philology*
CQ	*Classical Quarterly*
CWS	Classics of Western Spirituality
DR	The Holy Bible translated from the Latin Vulgate: Douay-Rheims (1899 edition)

ExpTim	*Expository Times*
FilNeot	*Filologia neotestamentaria*
FRLANT	Forschungen zur Religion und Literatur des Alten und Neuen Testaments
HAB	*Harvard Alumni Bulletin*
HNT	Handbuch zum Neuen Testament
HUCA	*Hebrew Union College Annual*
ICC	The International Critical Commentary
LCC	Library of Christian Classics
LCL	Loeb Classical Library
LD	Lectio divina
LEC	Library of Early Christianity
JSNT	*Journal for the Study of the New Testament*
JSNTSup	Journal for the Study of the New Testament Supplement Series
Mek.	*Mekilta de-Rabbi Ishmael*
NAB	The New American Bible
NICNT	New International Commentary on the New Testament
NIGTC	New International Greek New Testament Commentary
NLH	*New Literary History*
NovT	*Novum Testamentum*
NRSV	The Holy Bible: New Revised Standard Version
NTS	*New Testament Studies*
PMert	*A Descriptive Catalogue of the Greek Papyri in the Collection of Wilfred Merton*
PSB	*Princeton Seminary Bulletin*
Rahlfs, *Septuaginta*	Rahlfs, Alfred, ed. *Septuaginta: Id est Vetus Testamentum graece iuxta LXX interpretes.* Stuttgart: Deutsche Bibelgeselschaft; Athens: Ἡ Ἑλληνικὴ Βιβλικὴ Ἑταιρία, 1936.
RB	*Rivista Biblica*
RSV	The Holy Bible: Revised Standard Version
RV	The Holy Bible: Revised Version (1881–85)
SBLSBS	Society of Biblical Literature Sources for Biblical Study
SC	Sources Chrétiennes
SCM	Student Christian Movement
SE	*Studia Evangelica*
SNTSMS	Society for New Testament Studies Monograph Series
SPAW	*Sitzungsberichte der preussischen Akademie der Wissenschaften*
SPCIC	*Studiorum paulinorum congressus internationalis catholicus 1961.* AnBib 17–18. Rome: Biblical Institute, 1963.
SPCK	Society for Promoting Christian Knowledge
SPIB	Scripta Pontificii Instituti Biblici
SPS	Sacra Pagina Series
SR	*Studies in Religion/Sciences Religeuses*

STR	*Sewanee Theological Review*
THNT	Theologischer Handkommentar zum Neuen Testament
TU	Texte und Untersuchungen (Berlin: Akademie Verlag)
Vg	Biblia Sacra Vulgata
WBC	Word Biblical Commentary
WC	World's Classics
WTJ	*Westminster Theological Journal*
WUNT	Wissenchaftliche Untersuchungen zum Neuen Testament
ZNW	Zeitschrift für die neutestamentliche Wissenschaft

A Preface to Romans

Prologue

Looking at Romans

The Scope of the Inquiry

This book is, among other things, an attempt to examine Saint Paul's Letter to the Romans in its literary and cultural setting. Originally I intended it to follow the pattern of my earlier study, *A Preface to Mark*:[1] that is to say, in the former of two parts I would try to show which literary type or genre would have been seen by Paul's contemporaries as exemplified in the Letter to the Romans, and in the latter, how Romans works as a piece of literature, and what we may understand from it of Paul's intentions and hopes. As with *A Preface to Mark,* and reflecting the fact that the literature that composes what we now call "the New Testament" was not created in a vacuum, the study as a whole was also to involve discussion of and comparison with other literature from Paul's time, place, and milieu—including, of course, other writings attributed to Paul.[2] As I look now at *A Preface to Romans* completed, I still hope that this describes, more or less, what I have written.

Yet Paul's Letter to the Romans is, obviously, a very different kind of text from the Gospel according to Mark. Mark, though it involves theological reflection, presents itself first of all as a narrative; Romans, though it implies a narrative, presents itself first of all as theological reflection. This difference has led to at least two equally obvious changes in my own style. First, the immediate challenge with which Romans faces any student is actually to follow its argument; therefore the second part of *A Preface to Romans* follows the biblical text much more closely—virtually line-by-line—than did the second part of *A Preface to Mark*. Second, unlike *A Preface to Mark, A Preface to Romans* is laden with additional notes. This is because it seemed

1. Christopher Bryan, *A Preface to Mark: Notes on the Gospel in Its Literary and Cultural Settings* (New York: Oxford University Press, 1993).

2. For the sake of argument, I assume throughout this study direct Pauline authorship of those letters normally attributed to him by contemporary scholars (that is, Romans, 1 and 2 Corinthians, Galatians, Philippians, 1 Thessalonians, and Philemon). Other Pauline literature I refer to with qualification, as representing at the very least how some early disciples understood and tried to reflect his teaching; similarly with traditions about Paul in Acts.

to me that many decisions made or assumed in the text needed explaining, and I could see no other way of furnishing those explanations, if the text itself were not to become intolerable—in particular, if I were not completely to obscure the thread of Paul's discourse.

The Purpose of the Inquiry

In academic terms, I approach texts first as a literary critic. My immediate interest is to ask how the work I am considering is likely to have been heard and understood by those who first encountered it; and since I do not suppose that the texts I am examining were composed by the totally incompetent, I suspect that that may have some bearing on the author's purpose. Despite the claims of some twentieth-century critics, I remain convinced that through authors' words it is possible to see something of their minds, and something of what they are trying to tell us. We all base our convictions on our own stories, and perhaps the reason that I think like this is, in the last analysis, because I too, in a small way, use words and make texts in order to tell stories and share ideas. I should be frustrated indeed if I believed that it were all finally a matter of luck or coincidence whether my readers received from my words anything at all of what I intended.

Equally, however, I concede that words need to be interpreted, and that any interpretation—and particularly any interpretation of an ancient text that was evidently *never* regarded as easy (see 2 Peter 3.15–16)—will be a construct, involving partly what the author intended and partly what we ourselves have brought: our histories, our cultures, our hopes, and our fears. You and I may listen to the same words on the same occasion, but the chances are we shall each learn something different from them, because we are not the same person. If the words are about something fairly limited in scope or significance, like the distance from Rome to Naples, the difference may not matter much. If it is about something more complex, arousing our emotions or our commitments, then the difference may be very great indeed. One value of critical scholarship—that is, of the best historical and literary understanding we can obtain of our texts—is that it affords us a measure of defense (I do not say a complete defense)[3] against interpretations that simply indulge our fantasies, our fears, or our desires.

Nothing here stated of texts in general is altered if the text in question is regarded as divinely inspired. In both Jewish and Christian tradition, it is precisely those texts that are inspired that require interpretation. That is why rabbinic legend tells of God studying Scripture each morning, and Moses receiving authoritative exegesis at Sinai (*b.'Abod. Zar.* 3b, 4b; *m.'Abot* 1.1). Such stories affirm an essential connection between the Bible and studying the Bible: there is no authoritative rev-

---

3. One reason that the defense is not complete is that what we call critical scholarship is itself a blend of various exegetical methods and ways of understanding—grammatical, philological, linguistic, contextual (text, other texts by the same author, or historical context), literary critical, and so on. Should one apply every possible method to every possible passage? Even if that were possible, it would be intolerable. Should one admit the reasons that one prefers one set of questions to another? Does one even *know* why one prefers one set of questions to another? Probably not! Is that a reason to despair? I don't think so. It is merely a reason not to take oneself too seriously.

elation without interpretation and inquiry. Another legend tells of God laughing with delight when the rabbis defeat him at exegesis (*b. B. Meṣ.* 59b)—acting, as Richard Hays puts it, for all the world like "a father deliberately losing a game of checkers to his young son." The implication is obvious: the rabbis "have succeeded in extracting from the text an interpretation that the Holy One, blessed be He, never intended at all."[4] If that is possible, then evidently the quest for a final or definitive interpretation of Scripture is an illusion. The old text in a new situation can always generate a new possibility.

We need therefore to concede that in the interpretation of texts, when we have done our duty by critical scholarship, then, if our quest to engage the text is serious, we must move beyond critical scholarship to the deliberate embrace of imagination and vision. We need to speak about our texts in the light of our perception of our own story—or, if we will, our own part of the text's story. Only there can we hope to learn anything that actually matters, even about what we have observed critically. Needless to say, it will be a risky business. But then, so is life. With literature as with life, the only way to avoid risk is to avoid the thing itself. Again, if the literature is not about anything very significant—such as that distance from Rome to Naples— the risk may not be very great: at most, a long wait in a railway station or a missed connection. If it is about something more complex—someone's struggle against injustice, or a quest for love or meaning—then the risk may be very great indeed. There is, Epictetus said, "a certain skill in hearing, even as there is in speaking" (*Discourses* 2.24.5). He spoke of the living, but what he said is true also of the dead. Not only as a matter of courtesy, but for our own sakes, we need to be careful how we listen to the dead and how we speak of them. As Alfredo Panzini said, *si possono vendicare*—"they can avenge themselves."[5] Anyone who doubts that should read a history of literary criticism. Such histories are chronicles of those who thought they sat in judgment on texts and authors greater than themselves, and who in retrospect are seen themselves to have been judged. This is a risky business. Perhaps we all, as literary critics, do no more than create our own poems by misreading the works of our formidable ancestors.[6] So what? I know, for it is a part of my own story, that some literary criticism— Coleridge on Shakespeare; Sayers, Williams, and Leonardi on Dante; Lewis on Milton— has led me to find joy, wisdom, and beauty in the texts it purported to discuss, and to hear music where I did not, or could not, hear it before. Other literary critisism has not. I grant that in the last analysis there can be no "explanation" of any utterance. There is only the utterance itself, and its effect on a mind and heart ready to receive it. Yet something of that readiness may be enhanced by deliberate attention, and it is possible, I think, to be helped to give that attention.

So, finally, why? Why am I bothering, not merely to try to understand, but to write a book and to inflict it upon the world? Is it because I am an academic, and that is what academics do? Well, yes, it is—partly, at any rate. Why pretend other-

---

4. Richard B. Hays, *Echoes of Scripture in the Letters of Paul* (New Haven: Yale University Press, 1989), 4.

5. Alfredo Panzini, *Il bacio di Lesbia* (Milan: Mondadori, 1937), 74.

6. I am here, of course, creating my own little poem by misreading Harold Bloom: see his *Anxiety of Influence* (New York: Oxford University Press, 1973), 94.

wise? Is it because I hope that through my effort someone will hear music where they did not hear it before? Yes, I think so. Why else write literary criticism? Yet why have the temerity to choose Romans? So many have already written on Romans—Origen, Saint John Chrysostom, Saint Augustine, Martin Luther, Karl Barth! Yet still, as Barth said, "The Epistle to the Romans waits."[7] For what? For *me*? For late twentieth-century, European, high-Anglican *me*? Well, yes, of course. Just as it waits for you and for everyone else. We each (even academics) respond as best we can. Will I then risk being judged for my temerity by Saint Paul, not to mention Origen, Chrysostom, Augustine, Luther, and Barth? Of course I will, and gladly, for I think it better to be judged by such as they than to live in a universe without judgment—and therefore without meaning or hope.

Bibliographical Note

One's embarrassment at presuming to write about Romans is not lessened by the fact that it has been particularly well served by commentators in the last twenty or so years. Among recent commentaries, I have found the following particularly useful (in alphabetical order), Brendan Byrne, S.J., *Romans*, Sacra Pagina Series 6 (Collegeville, Minnesota: Liturgical Press, 1996) (henceforth Byrne, *Romans*); C. E. B. Cranfield, *A Critical and Exegetical Commentary on the Epistle to the Romans*, ICC, 2 vols. (Edinburgh: Clark, 1975–79) (henceforth Cranfield, *Romans*); James D. G. Dunn, *Romans*, Word Biblical Commentary 38, 2 vols. (Dallas, Texas: Word Books, 1988) (henceforth Dunn, *Romans*); Joseph A. Fitzmyer, S.J., *Romans: A New Translation with Introduction and Commentary*, AB 33 (New York: Doubleday, 1993) (henceforth Fitzmyer, *Romans*); Ernst Käsemann, *Commentary on Romans*, trans. Geoffrey W. Bromiley (Grand Rapids, Michigan: Eerdmans, 1980) (henceforth Käsemann, *Romans*), Douglas J. Moo, *The Epistle to the Romans*, New International Commentary on the New Testament (Grand Rapids, Michigan: Eerdmans, 1996) (henceforth Moo, *Romans*).

Another book I would press upon any serious student of Romans is Karl Barth, *The Epistle to the Romans*, trans. Edwyn C. Hoskyns (London: Oxford University Press, 1933) (henceforth Barth, *Romans*). Barth's work is, of course, more of a meditation than a commentary, yet the reflections of this profound and acute student of the text are always stimulating, even where, I think, he got it wrong (in terms, that is, of what Paul may have intended); occasionally it appears to me that he got it quite startlingly right, at just the points where some of the more formal commentators go astray. I have, incidentally, in quoting Barth, taken one liberty. I have occasionally emended Sir Edwyn Hoskyns's magnificent translation to make its language about humanity more sexually inclusive. This is not something I do lightly since (apart from anything else) I disapprove of rewriting the past. In this case, since the prose was in any case a translation from German, and since I did not want to place *any* impediment that might be avoided between those who might be sensitive on these issues and Barth's thoughts (a desire of which, I think, Hoskyns would approve) I decided to do it.

Cristina Grenholm's essay, "The Process of the Interpretation of Romans," in *Society of Biblical Literature Seminar 1997 Papers* (Atlanta, Georgia: Scholars Press, 1997), 306–36, provides a humbling experience for those who choose to write about Romans (or, indeed, anything else), and useful questions for those who must read them.

---

7. Karl Barth, *The Epistle to the Romans*, trans. Edwyn C. Hoskyns (London: Oxford University Press, 1933), 2.

Transliteration

I have transliterated Greek and Hebrew words where they occur in my main text, following the system presented on pages xviii–xix of OCB. I do this not without reluctance, since I regard both the Greek and the Hebrew alphabets as beautiful, but such transliteration seems likely to make my work more generally useful. I have, however, left Greek and Hebrew words untransliterated where they so occur in dictionary entries or citations from other secondary sources.

PART I

WHAT KIND OF TEXT IS ROMANS?

The Genre of the Letter
to the Romans

What Are We Talking About? The Significance of Genre

"The first qualification for judging any piece of workmanship from a corkscrew to a cathedral is," observed C. S. Lewis, "to know *what* it is—what it was intended to do and how it is meant to be used."

> After that has been discovered the temperance reformer may decide that the cork-screw was made for a bad purpose, and the communist may think the same about the cathedral. But such questions come later. The first thing is to understand the object before you: as long as you think the corkscrew was meant for opening tins or the cathedral for entertaining tourists you can say nothing to the purpose about them.[1]

With that quotation I began my book *A Preface to Mark*, and with it, or, at least, with the question that it implies, I would begin any serious study of any piece of literature—particularly the literature of another age and culture.

Lewis was posing the question of what critics of the written word like to refer to as "genre." Why is genre important? Briefly, because it is a tool of meaning. When we look at posters outside a cinema and see one of them advertising "romantic comedy" while another offers "a tense thriller," we expect the movies in question to be somewhat different from each other, and we are generally right. If we know the genre of a work of art, we have an important clue as to what it is supposed to be about, and the manner in which we are expected to receive it. Of course it is true (as critics and commentators unwilling to pursue seriously the question of genre never tire of saying) that the church kept and treasured Romans because of its distinctive qualities, rather than its conformity to any particular rhetorical or literary canon.[2] In just the same way, the theater has continued to treasure Shakespeare's *Hamlet* rather than Thomas Kyd's *Spanish Tragedy* because of the distinctive qualities that Shakespeare

---

1. C. S. Lewis, *A Preface to Paradise Lost* (London: Oxford University Press, 1942), 1.
2. Thus Dunn, *Romans* 1.lix; cited approvingly by Moo, *Romans* 15.

brought to the conventions and expectations of Elizabethan historical tragedy. Nevertheless, we can be helped to understand *Hamlet* (and even, perhaps, better to appreciate its distinctive qualities) by knowing something of those conventions and expectations, and the same will be true, mutatis mutandis, of Romans.

What, then, is, or was, the Letter to the Romans?

Bibliographical Note

On the significance of genre, see Alistair Fowler, *Kinds of Literature: An Introduction to the Theory of Genres and Modes* (Oxford: Clarendon Press, 1982); also Fowler's earlier essay "The Life and Death of Literary Forms," in *New Directions in Literary History*, ed. Ralph Cohen (London: Routledge and Kegan Paul; Baltimore, Maryland: Johns Hopkins University Press, 1974), 77–105. See further, E. D. Hirsch, *Validity in Interpretation* (New Haven: Yale University Press, 1974), 68–126; René Wellek and Austin Warren, *Theory of Literature*, third ed. (Harmondsworth, Middlesex: Penguin, 1963), 18–19, 226–37. There is a good summary in Richard A. Burridge, *What Are the Gospels? A Comparison with Graeco-Roman Biography*, SNTSMS 70 (Cambridge: Cambridge University Press, 1992), 26–54; or, very briefly, see my *Preface to Mark*, 9–15, and literature there cited.

Romans as a Greco-Roman Letter

To begin at the beginning, Paul's Letter to the Romans is, of course, a letter. More precisely, it is a "Greco-Roman" or "Hellenistic" letter. The basic form of such letters was simple:

A *Salutation*: "From A to B, greeting"

The Body of the Letter, often (but not invariably) beginning with a prayer or good wish.

A *Closing Salutation*, usually with further good wishes.

By way of example, we may conveniently consider the following, which was written about 97–102/3 AD.[3] By great good fortune, we actually have the original manuscript, which is addressed (on the back): "To Sulpicia Lepidina, wife of Flavius Cerialis; from Severa" (*Sulpiciae Lepidinae Flavi Cerialis a Severa*).[4] Sulpicia Lepidina and Claudia Severa were both married to officers in the Roman army, stationed on the British frontier at Vindola, just south of Hadrian's Wall. Severa wrote inviting Lepidina to visit her on her birthday, which was on the third day before the Ides of September, that is, September 10. Her text perfectly demonstrates the basic form of the Greco-Roman letter, and I quote it in full:

| Claudia Severa to her | *Cl. Severa Lepidinae suae* |
| Lepidina, greetings. | *salutem.* |

---

3. Alan K. Bowman, *Life and Letters on the Roman Frontier: Vindolanda and Its People* (London: British Museum Press, 1994; New York: Routledge, 1998), 17.

4. For the source of this and all other primary sources cited, see General Bibliography, under Primary Sources.

On the third day before the Ides of September, sister, for the day of the celebration of my birthday, I give you a warm invitation to make sure that you come to us, to make the day more enjoyable for me by your arrival, if you come.	*iii idus septembres, soror, ad meum diem sollemnem natalem rogo libenter facias ut venias ad nos iucundiorem mihi diem interventu tuo factura si venies.*
My greetings to your Cerialis.[5] My Aelius[6] and my little son send you their greetings.	*Cerialem tuum saluta Aelius meus et filiolus salutant.*
I shall expect you, sister. Farewell, sister, my soul, as I may prosper, dearest one, and hail!	***Sperabo te soror.*** ***Vale, soror, anima mea*** ***ita valeam karissima*** ***et have!***[7]

In the Letter to the Romans, as in all the letters attributed to him in the New Testament, Paul follows this outline.

The form of a Greco-Roman letter, like all literary convention, could be varied in detail according to the intention and creativity of the author. In Claudia Severa's invitation, brief though it is, a wealth of feeling is conveyed by the addition of the single word "her" (*suae*) to the name of her addressee.[8] In the Pauline letters, such additions are almost an art form, a rhetorical device whereby the apostle encapsulates and rehearses themes that will dominate the letter as a whole. In Galatians, where he evidently thinks that his entire understanding of the gospel and his authority as an apostle are on trial, his opening words include a terse statement of that authority, and of its source: "Paul, an apostle, not from human commission nor by human authority, but through Jesus Christ and God the Father, who raised him from the dead, and all the members of God's family who are with me, to the churches of Galatia" (Gal. 1.1–2). The Philippians, by contrast, to whom he writes in affection and gratitude for their support, are addressed more simply: "Paul and Timothy, slaves of Jesus Christ, to all the saints in Christ Jesus who are in Philippi" (Phil. 1.1). The actual word of greeting is itself regularly extended by Paul, the normal Helle-

5. Flavius Cerialis was Sulpicia Lepidina's husband; he was prefect of the 9th Batavian cohort (Bowman, *Roman Frontier* 17, 25).

6. C. Aelius Brocchus was Claudia Severa's husband; he must have commanded another cohort in the area (Bowman, *Roman Frontier* 55).

7. The use of *have* (i.e., *ave*) at the end of a letter, though quite elegant, seems to be fairly unusual. *OLD* cites only Sallust, *Catilina* 35.6.

8. Compare Pliny the Younger, *Letters* 1.1, and passim.

nistic *chairein* (Latin, *salutem*: "Greetings") being changed to *charis* ("Grace"), and the characteristically Jewish *eirēnē* ("Peace") added.

In Claudia Severa's letter we should also notice the section in bold type. In the manuscript, this is written in a different hand from the rest. Certainly the hand is Claudia Severa's own. Having dictated the letter to her secretary, when it was complete, she took the pen herself, and added a personal note. Naturally this makes us think of passages in the Pauline correspondence such as Galatians 6.11–18 ("See with what large letters I am writing to you in my own hand") and 2 Thessalonians 3.17–18 ("I, Paul, write this greeting with my own hand"); but probably we should also compare Romans 16.17–20 ("I appeal to you"), noting that if we did not have the original of Claudia Severa's letter, there would be nothing in her words *alone* that would tell us explicitly that she wrote these sentences herself, rather than using her secretary.[9]

The Letter to the Romans is, then, a Greco-Roman letter. There were, however, many different kinds of Greco-Roman letters, as literary critics of the time were aware—letters of advice, of rebuke, of friendship, of consolation, of mediation, and so on. And, of course, a single letter might combine elements of more than one type—such, for example, as Plutarch's beautiful letter of consolation to his wife on the death of their daughter (*Consolation to My Wife* [*Moralia* 608–612a]), which combines elements of a letter of consolation with that subdivision of the letter of friendship that modern literary critics have identified as "the family letter."

So we must next ask, What *kind* of letter was Romans?

Bibliographical Note

For a convenient short discussion of the Hellenistic letter, see John L. White, "Ancient Greek Letters," in *Greco-Roman Literature and the New Testament: Selected Forms and Genres*, ed. David Aune, SBLSBS 21 (Atlanta, Georgia: Scholars Press, 1988), 85–105; also R. H. Hachforth and B. R. Rees, "Letters, Greek," and R. G. C. Levens, "Letters, Latin," in *OCD*, 598–99.

Among longer studies, useful and easily accessible are Stanley K. Stowers, *Letter Writing in Greco-Roman Antiquity*, LEC (Philadelphia: Westminster Press, 1986) and John L. White, *Light from Ancient Letters* (Philadelphia: Fortress Press, 1986). The latter provides a rich sample of texts with notes and translations, a substantial essay (189–224), and an excellent bibliography. Regarded by many as seminal are Heikki Koskenniemi, *Studien zur Idee und Phraseologie des griechischen Briefes bis 400 n. Chr.*, Annales Academiae scientiarum fennicae, Series B. 102.2. (Helsinki: Suomalainen Tiedeakatemia,1956), and Klaus Thraede, *Grundzüge griechisch-römischer Brieftopik*, Monographien zur klassischen Altertumswissenschaft 48 (Munich: Beck, 1970).

Selections from a number of the primary critical texts, with translations, are in Abraham Malherbe, "Ancient Epistolary Theorists," *Ohio Journal of Religious Studies* 55 (1977): 3–77 (reprinted with minor revisions as SBLSBS 19 [Atlanta, Georgia: Scholars Press, 1988]).

9. Harry Gamble raises the possibility that Paul wrote the whole of Romans 16.1–20ab in his own hand, with Tertius adding 16.21–23: see *The Textual History of the Letter to the Romans: A Study in Textual and Literary Criticism*, Texts and Documents 42 (Grand Rapids, Michigan: Eerdmans, 1977), 93–95.

On Claudia Severa's letter to Sulpicia Lepidina, see Alan K. Bowman and J. David Thomas, "New Texts from Vindola," *Brittania* 18 (1987): 125–42, especially 137–40; for background see further, Alan K. Bowman, *Life and Letters on the Roman Frontier: Vindolanda and Its People* (London: British Museum Press, 1994; New York: Routledge, 1998), especially 51–99.

For other nonliterary letters, see A. S. Hunt and C. C. Edgar, eds., *Select Papyri*, vol. 1, 268–395; G. H. R. Horsley, ed., *New Documents Illustrating Early Christianity: A Review of the Greek Inscriptions and Papyri published in 1976* (North Ryde, New South Wales: Ancient History Documentation Research Centre, Macquarie University, 1981), 51–66; White, *Light from Ancient Letters*, 23–186.

For aristocratic and consciously literary examples of the genre, one could hardly do better than the letters of Pliny the Younger, available in R. A. B. Mynors, *Pliny: Letters I–X.* (Oxford: Oxford University Press, 1963) (Latin text) or in Betty Radice, *The Letters of Pliny the Younger* (Harmondsworth, Middlesex: Penguin Books, 1963) (English translation). Also, Plutarch's *Consolation to His Wife* (*Moralia* 608–612a) is a jewel: text and translation in Philip H. De Lacy and Benedict Einarson, *Plutarch's Moralia*, Vol. 7, LCL (Cambridge, Massachusetts: Harvard University Press, 1959); translation in Donald Russell, *Plutarch: Selected Essays and Dialogues*, WC (Oxford: Oxford University Press, 1993), 297–303.

Romans as an Essay with the Heading "Greetings!"

As a step toward more exact description, we may begin by taking note of a group of texts, letters in form, that Martin Luther Stirewalt[10] has characterized as "Greek letter-essays," namely, Dionysius of Halicarnassus's *Letter to Gnaeus Pompeius*, 2 Maccabees, Plutarch's *Advice on Marriage* and *Quiet of Mind* (among his *Moralia*), and the church in Smyrna's account of *The Martyrdom of St. Polycarp*—none of them, it will be noted, very far removed in time from the composition of Paul's Letter to the Romans.[11] To this group we can easily add others, also from the period, notably Dionysius of Halicarnassus's *First and Second Letter to Ammaeus*, Lucian's *Nigrinus*, and also his splendid spoof *The Passing of Peregrinus*. These writings have in common a number of features to which Stirewalt points, notably, that each of them is presented as a letter, in each of them the letter setting seems to be authentic,[12] and each is also in some way ancillary to some other existing or projected utterance,

10. See Martin Luther Stirewalt Jr., "The Form and Function of the Greek Letter-Essay" in *The Romans Debate: Revised and Expanded Edition*, ed. Karl P. Donfried (Peabody, Massachusetts: Hendrickson, 1991), 147–71.

11. Stirewalt offers other examples, some of them removed by centuries from the composition of Romans. In considering the genre of a text, however, it is better to focus attention on examples that are close to it in time—ideally, within a century (three generations) before or after: see F. Gerald Downing, "À bas les Aristos: The Relevance of Higher Literature for the Understanding of the Earliest Christian Writings," *Novum Testamentum* 30.3 (1988): 212–30; also my *Preface to Mark* 19–20.

12. Stirewalt, "Letter-Essay" 163. The epistolary nature of 2 Maccabees presents, obviously, the most complex problem, owing to the addition of two other letters (1.1–10a, 1.10b–2.18) to the beginning, both urging Jews to celebrate the Feast of Dedication. Part, perhaps the greater part, of the author's own opening appears, however, to be preserved in 2.19–32. In any case, what the final editor has done is to leave us with a document that is still, in its overall shape, a "letter-essay"—so offering further evidence that such a form was considered by some to be proper.

either by the author himself (as, for example, *2 Ammaeus* 1–2), or by another (so 2 Maccabees 2:19–23; *Nigrinus* 8–9, 11).[13]

There is, Stirewalt observes, no evidence that the ancients themselves thought of the "letter-essay" as a genre. That is correct, so far as it goes. It would not, however, be correct to suggest therefore that they did not notice it as a phenomenon. The unknown critical genius known to history as "Demetrius" (who probably wrote at some time during the first century BC or the first century AD) was strongly of the opinion that among the proprieties to be observed by good letter writers was the matter of length (*megethos*), and this led him to speak scornfully of documents using the letter form and yet, in his opinion,

> over long and, moreover, somewhat stilted in expression. To be truthful, these are not letters, but essays [*suggrammata*] with the heading "Greetings!" as is the case with many of Plato's, and with that of Thucydides. . . . If one writes logical subtleties or questions of natural history in a letter, one is writing, certainly, but one is not writing a letter. The aim of a letter is to be affectionate in brief, and to lay out a simple subject in simple terms. . . . The one who utters sententious maxims and exhortations seems to be no longer talking familiarly in a letter but speaking with contrivance. . . . Heightening [of style] should not . . . be taken so far that we have an essay in the place of a letter, as with those of Aristotle to Alexander, and with that of Plato to Dion's friends. (*On Style*, 228, 231, 232, 234)

"Essays with the heading 'Greetings!'" is, surely, exactly what Stirewalt is talking about when he speaks of "letter-essays".

We may or may not accept Demetrius's views as to the correct length or the proper subjects and style for a letter. Clearly, many throughout antiquity did not, or we should not have possessed the documents we are considering. Demetrius himself was aware, no doubt, that in criticizing Thucydides, Aristotle, and Plato, he was taking on some formidable littérateurs. It remains, nonetheless, that in describing his dislike of "letter-essays," Demetrius pointed to a real difficulty in speaking of them as a genre. "Logical subtleties," "questions of natural history," "sententious maxims": the problem is that these *suggrammata* can actually take almost any literary form at all, given the letter framework. That is certainly true of the writings identified by Stirewalt. For all that they have features in common, they do not have *much* in common. One can hardly identify them as members of a family in the way that one can rather easily classify *bioi* ("lives") or epic poems. Thus 2 Maccabees, apart from its epistolary setting, is naturally classified as history. Plutarch's two essays can (as they were) appropriately be classified as *moralia* ("moral essays"). Dionysius has produced literary critical essays. The *Martyrdom of Polycarp* naturally fits in the genre known as *vita*, particularly that subspecies dealing with the "deaths of the famous" (*de exitus illustrium virorum*)—into which, of course, also fits Lucian's *The Passing of Peregrinus*. Lucian's *Nigrinus* would have been classified as protreptic—a "persuasive" document.

This variety is matched by the variety of ways in which the authors themselves refer to what they have written. Thus *The Martyrdom of Polycarp* is referred to once,

---

13. Stirewalt, "Letter-Essay" 169. Another example of such an ancillary document composed by the author himself—in this case a document promised but never actually written—may be provided by Josephus's proposal at the end of the *Antiquities* to "compose a summary account" of the Jewish war (*Ant.* 20. 267).

in its closing, as an *epistolē* ("a letter") (*Martyrdom of Polycarp*, 20.1). Plutarch, as I have noted, speaks of the *Advice on Marriage* as *kephalaia* ("a compendium") and declares that he is sending it to the newly wed Eurydice and Pollianus "as a gift" (*Moralia* 138).[14] The author of 2 Maccabees twice refers to his work as *epitomē* (2:26, 28). "Otherwise," as Stirewalt notes, "the only word used with any consistency by the writers themselves in reference to their letter-essays is the neutral word *logos*"[15]— which is really to say not much more than that they identified them as statements. Stirewalt himself suggests that the texts he examines are moving in the direction of the monograph,[16] and that may be correct; but of course the authors themselves and their contemporaries cannot have recognized this.

What then of Romans? It would surely have qualified for all of Demetrius's complaints about "essays with the heading 'Greetings!'" He would have regarded it as too long for a proper letter, and he would have noted that its "maxims and exhortations" resulted in a composition whose author was "no longer talking familiarly in a letter but speaking with contrivance."[17] Romans has, moreover, exactly the characteristics observed by Stirewalt: it appears to be a genuine letter to a particular place and situation, yet it is clearly ancillary to—and, more precisely, explanatory of— other utterances. It is this, actually, in two ways. First, it is explanatory of Paul's own preaching—what Paul himself refers to as "my gospel" (2.16). Second, that explanation is bound up with showing the relationship of "my gospel" to another utterance, namely, Jewish Scripture, the written manifestation of *Tôrâ*—"the Law." According to Paul, his gospel was foretold by Scripture and accords with Scripture, and so it both upholds and fulfills the Law (1.2, 3.21, 3.31, 10.4). This—as I shall try to show—is relentlessly argued from the beginning to the end of the letter. For the moment, a statistic may serve to make the point: Dietrich-Alex Koch, in a detailed analysis, points to fifty-one citations of Scripture in the Letter to the Romans, out of eighty-nine in the entire Pauline corpus.[18]

This combination of characteristics—that Romans is a genuine letter yet ancillary to other utterance—is particularly striking in light of the scholarly debate that raged for some time over whether Romans "was addressed to a concrete historical situation or was to be considered as an essentially nonhistorical *christianae religionis compendium*"[19]—in other words, whether Romans was intended to provide a general account of Paul's teaching or was addressed specifically to the situation in the Roman church. Recently, several critics, on grounds not connected with the question of genre, have suggested something of a "both-and" position: namely, that the letter is indeed a summary or compendium of Paul's views on certain subjects, and that it was sent by him because he thought it relevant to the Roman situation. Such a view

14. "Demetrius," characteristically, points out that *any* letter is "sent as a gift" (*On Style* 224).

15. *Letter-Essay* 167.

16. *Letter-Essay* 148.

17. Presumably he would have said the same about all Paul's extant letters except, perhaps, Philemon.

18. Dietrich-Alex Koch, *Die Schrift als Zeuge des Evangeliums: Untersuchungen zur Verwendung und zum Verständnis der Schrift bei Paulus*, BHT 69 (Tübingen: Mohr [Siebeck], 1986), 21–23.

19. Karl P. Donfried, "Preface 1991," in Donfried, *The Romans Debate: Revised*, xlix. I inclined myself for some time to the former of these two views: see my *Way of Freedom* (New York: Seabury, 1974), 11–15.

seems even more likely to be correct if Romans is indeed to be seen as an example of the "letter-essay" since, as we have seen, it is evident that Stirewalt's examples also combined general observation with particular intent.

We may grant, then, that Romans has characteristics in common with Stirewalt's "letter-essays" and Demetrius's "essays with the heading 'Greetings!'" Still, as we have noted, as a *generic* description this is useful only to a limited extent. It tells us nothing more than we would learn about a particular creative effort by being told that it was "a movie." Naturally, before we paid our money to go into the cinema, we would still want to know, "What kind of movie?" A "tense thriller"? Or a "romantic comedy"? Granted the evident connection of Romans with other "letter-essays, " our next task must be to look for a generic description that will fit the particular "essay" presented in Romans. The ancient literary critics were, in their own way, at least as interested in questions of genre as we are. Aristotle's *Poetics* and Horace's *Art of Poetry* are, for example, almost entirely concerned with different kinds of poetry, and what is proper for them.[20] It will, then, be particularly satisfying if we can find a description of Romans in terms that the ancients, too, might have recognized.

Bibliographical Note

On the "letter-essay" in antiquity, see Martin Luther Stirewalt Jr., "The Form and Function of the Greek Letter-Essay," in Karl P. Donfried, ed., *The Romans Debate: Revised and Expanded Edition* (Peabody, Massachusetts: Hendrickson, 1991), 147–71.

On the importance of close dating for the study of genre, see F. Gerald Downing, "À bas les Aristos: The Relevance of Higher Literature for the Understanding of the Earliest Christian Writings," *Novum Testamentum* 30.3 (1988): 212–30; also my *Preface to Mark* 19–20.

On the debate about the provenance of Romans, and its relevance or otherwise to the Roman situation, see the masterly summary by Karl P. Donfried, in "False Presuppositions in the Study of Romans," *CBQ* 36 (1974): 332–58; reprinted in Karl P. Donfried, ed., *The Romans Debate: Revised and Expanded Edition* (Peabody, Massachusetts: Hendrickson, 1991), 102–25; and literature there cited. Among critics who have taken a "both-and" position are W. Marxsen, *Introduction to the New Testament: An Approach to Its Problems*, trans. G. Buswell (Philadelphia: Fortress Press; Oxford: Basil Blackwell, 1968), 92–109; Fitzmyer, *Romans* 68–80, Moo, *Romans* 13–14, and Donfried himself in "False Presuppositions" 123–25.

Romans as a Persuasive Discourse

Among various suggestions that have been made, I find most promising an idea that I first came across in Stanley K. Stowers's invaluable little book *Letter Writing in Greco-Roman Antiquity*, subsequently developed by David Aune (in an essay) and further refined and developed by Anthony J. Guerra (in a monograph).[21] They suggest that

---

20. "We are to speak of poetry generally, and of its genres [*eidōn*]; the capability of each, the rules for constructing a plot for poetic excellence; also the number and nature of the parts of a poem, and likewise other matters that belong to the same inquiry, starting, naturally, from first principles" (Aristotle, *Poetics* 1447a); compare Horace, *The Art of Poetry* 1–9.

21. Stanley K. Stowers, *Letter Writing in Greco-Roman Antiquity* (Philadelphia: Westminster Press, 1986), 112–14; David Aune, "Romans as a *Logos Protreptikos*" in Donfried, *The Romans Debate: Revised*

what we have so far called the "essay" aspect of Romans is marked by various char-acteristics that would have led the ancients to refer to it as protreptic: a persuasive discourse or statement. In philosophical tradition, protreptic was a form of address associated with the choice of a particular philosophical school, or else with the choice of philosophy itself. Protreptic was used by philosophers to confirm believers and to convert outsiders, inquirers, or neophytes. Ever since Aristotle's *Protrepticus* there had been a tradition of sometimes putting such addresses into the form of letters—as, for example, Lucian's *Nigrinus*, to which I have already referred in discussing the "letter-essay."[22] Writers exhorted their auditors to the love of wisdom (*philosophia*), to the choice of a particular school, and to perseverance in the disciplines needed for advanced study. Philon of Larissa (about 160–80 BC) saw protreptic as "urging on to excellence [*aretē*]." He compared the work of the philosopher to that of a phy-sician, who must simultaneously persuade the sick to receive the treatment and re-fute the words of those who would counsel against it; similarly, protreptic must, on the one hand, demonstrate the usefulness of philosophy and, on the other, refute those who took it to pieces, made accusations against it, or otherwise spoke evil of it (cited in Stobaeus, *Anthologies* 2.7.2). To these elements of demonstration (*endeiktikos*) and refutation (*apelegmos*) we should add a third: frequently, such a work will in-volve personal appeal and exhortation (*parainesis*).[23]

It is not, I think, difficult to discern in Romans the main elements of protreptic discourse that I have identified—indeed, in some respects they are easier to distin-guish than in other texts, such as *Nigrinus*, that are regularly identified as protreptic. I will attempt a detailed consideration of these elements in my analysis of Romans (see pp. 57–233). For the present, let a simple description of the letter in outline suffice.

Following the epistolary opening (1.1–15), the first part of the document (1.16 to 4.25) is a dissuasive, or refutation (*apelegmos*). These chapters do *not* (in spite of many commentators to the contrary) seek to dissuade their hearers from the

278–96; Anthony J. Guerra, *Romans and the Apologetic Tradition: The Purpose, Genre, and Audience of Paul's Letter to the Romans*, SNTSMS 81 (Cambridge: Cambridge University Press, 1995).

22. Aristotle's *Protrepticus* (now no longer extant: references in Diogenes Laertius, *Lives of Emi-nent Philosophers* 5.22, and Stobaeus, *Anthologies* 4.32.21) evidently became an influential model for the genre. Cicero's *Hortensius* (also no longer extant) apparently imitated it and brought together many of its arguments in a dialogue. The *Hortensius* in its turn was to influence Augustine, and played a part in his first conversion, both positively (see *Confessions* 3.4) and negatively (3.5). By the first century AD, competition between different philosophical schools was such that production of *logoi protreptikoi* was "a growth industry" (Aune, "Romans as *Logos Protreptikos*" 283). Philo, perhaps not surprisingly, refers to Deuteronomy as Moses's protreptic (*On Husbandry* 78). By the second century the genre would be familiar enough for Lucian to parody it (in, e.g., *The Parasite*) as well as producing a more or less serious example of his own (*Nigrinus*); and Christian apologists of the period (perhaps deliberately following the example of Romans) naturally made use of it: see Guerra, *Romans and the Apologetic Tra-dition*, especially 12–21; compare Mark D. Jordan, "Ancient Philosophic Protreptic and the Problem of Persuasive Genres," *Rhetorica* 4 (1986): especially 310–14. Of course protreptic writing was not *only* associated with philosophy: Origen, for example, wrote a protreptic to martyrdom, and Galen to medi-cine: see Jordan, "Philosophic Protreptic," 312.

23. See Abraham Malherbe, *Moral Exhortation: A Greco-Roman Source Book*, LEC (Philadelphia: Westminster Press, 1986), passim, but especially 122–25; Jordan, "Philosophic Protreptic," 322; Guerra, *Romans and the Apologetic Tradition* 3–8.

unexamined pagan life, or from mere philosophy, or from non-Christian Judaism, none of these being positions that Paul could conceivably have imagined that his hearers in the church at Rome would want to defend. They seek, *on the basis of Scripture, to dissuade Paul's hearers from a view of God's relationship with the world or with Israel that would see it as ever at any time or in any situation founded on anything except God's justice and grace.* This is the point not only of the lengthy discussion of Abraham that concludes the section (3.27–4.25) but also of the entire denunciation of human sin (Jewish and gentile) that runs from 1.18 to 3.20, culminating at 3.21–26 with the affirmation of "God's justice[24] . . . manifested apart from Law, although the Law and the prophets bear witness to it" (3.21). In other words, Paul is claiming that what he himself calls "my gospel" (2.16)—namely, the proclamation of a God who, through the long-promised coming of the Messiah, has chosen to be gracious to all, Jew and gentile alike—manifests the justice of God that had been promised through the prophets and says nothing about that justice that was not implicit in the Law given to Israel from the beginning.

This dissuasive involves Paul in two specific additional denials: (1) Although at first sight it might seem so, the proclamation of God's universal graciousness does not strip Israel of her "special relationship" with God. The unshakable foundation of that relationship is evident in Israel's possession of the Law itself (3.1–4). (This is important, since if the graciousness of God did strip Israel of her privilege, then the universally gracious God would not be trustworthy, since God promised a special relationship to Israel.) (2) Although at first sight it might seem so, the God who is gracious to all is not therefore a God who is morally indifferent, so that in proclaiming such a God, Paul is *not* saying, in effect, "Let us do evil, that good may come"—a charge against his preaching that was evidently made, and that clearly stung him (3.5–8).

The second part of the letter (5.1–11.36) is a positive demonstration (*endeiktikos*) of God's justice and grace at work in the life of faith—a life lived "at peace with God, through our Lord Jesus Christ" (5.1). This demonstration involves defense, which means further reflection on the falsity of the two charges that Paul has already summarily denied. First, he considers the question of moral indifference (6.1–8.39). One who is "in Christ" no longer lives under the dominion of sin (6.14), has "died to the Law" (7.4), and is freed from "condemnation" (8.1). Far from leading, however, to a life of moral indifference (6.1, 15), this leads to being "led by the Spirit" (8.14), wherein we "put to death the deeds of the flesh" (8.13) on the basis of a new relationship, as "God's heirs and joint heirs with Christ" (8.17). Even suffering may be endured cheerfully (8.18, compare 5.1–5), for Christians know that nothing can finally separate them from "God's love in Christ Jesus" (8.39). Second (9.1–11.36), Paul considers the question of God's special relationship to Israel. Paul argues that the fulfillment of the Law in Christ (10.4), far from meaning that God has abandoned the promised special covenant relationship with Israel, means on the contrary that God is being faithful to *all* the promises, including the promises to Israel. Despite the disobedience of all—Jew and gentile—it is God's will finally "to have mercy upon all" (11.32).

---

24. On "justice" as the translation for *dikaiosunē*, additional note H.

The third part of the letter (12.1–15.13) is taken up with exhortation (*parainesis*)—an exhortation springing directly out of the demonstration that preceded it. Those who know that they live only "by the compassion[25] of God" (12.1) certainly cannot lead lives of moral indifference (still, perhaps, Paul is harping indirectly on that false charge that so irked him). Far from being "conformed to this world," those who live "by the compassion of God" will look to be "transformed" by the "renewal" of their minds (12.2–3). Within the life of the Christian community, this is going to mean mutual acceptance among those who feel called to fulfill the Law in one way and those who feel called to fulfill it in another (14.1–12). The basis of their actions will be plain: the example offered by Christ himself: "Welcome one another therefore, *as Christ has welcomed you*, for the glory of God" (15.7; compare 12.1, 15.2–3).

The remainder of the letter (15.14–16.23) is taken up with Paul's plans, his salutations, and a commendation.[26]

It is not, then, difficult to see the main elements of a protreptic discourse in the Letter to the Romans. Two other suggestions have, however, been made about the literary style of Romans, and since they have a bearing on the question of genre, we should now consider them.

First, W. Wuellner and George A. Kennedy have both suggested that Romans is to be understood as *epideictic* rhetoric—that is (in the technical terminology of classical rhetoric) speech that "has for its subject praise or censure" (Aristotle, *Rhetoric* 1.3.1358b; compare *Ad Herennium* 3.6.18; Quintilian 3.4.12–14).[27] "The apparent judgment, or role," Wuellner says, "which Paul expects the Romans to perform, is for them not to deliberate (which would require the deliberative or symbouletic genre . . .), nor to adjudicate (which would require the legal or forensic genre . . .), but to affirm the communal values which Paul and the Romans share in being agents of faith throughout the world. We expect therefore the use of the epideictic or demonstrative genre."[28] In terms of ancient formal rhetoric, however, *protropē* ("persuasion") and its opposite *apotropē* ("dissuasion") were actually the two main kinds of *deliberative* speech—that is, speech urging to specific action in a particular situation (*Ad Herennium* 1.2.2., 3.2.2.). Two points should be made in response to this. First, the contradiction is more apparent than real. Since, to a considerable extent, the choice

25. Greek, *oiktirmōn*; RSV and NRSV "mercies." See further, pages 194–95.

26. Some critics have contended that the whole of chapter 16 (and even 15 and 16) did not form part of Paul's original letter. The question has been well aired, and there is no need to repeat the arguments here. Suffice it to say that I agree with those who regard Romans 1.1 to 16.23 as a single composition, by Paul (except for 16.22, which is, as it states, a personal note from Paul's secretary Tertius) and addressed to the Roman church. In common with most critics, I also grant that the concluding doxology at 16.25–27 is a later, though not therefore inappropriate, addition. See Peter Lampe, "The Roman Christians of Romans 16," in Donfried, *The Romans Debate: Revised*, 216–30; Harry Gamble, *The Textual History of the Letter to the Romans*, Studies and Documents 42 (Grand Rapids, Michigan: Eerdmans, 1977) and literature there cited.

27. Wilhelm Wuellner, "Paul's Rhetoric of Argumentation in Romans: An Alternative to the Donfried-Karris Debate over Romans," CBQ 38 (1976): 330–51; reprinted in Donfried, *The Romans Debate: Revised* 128–146; George A. Kennedy, *New Testament Interpretation through Rhetorical Criticism* (Chapel Hill: University of North Carolina Press, 1984), 152–56.

28. Wuellner, "Paul's Rhetoric of Argumentation" 337 (134).

to which philosophic *logoi protreptikoi* sought to persuade was a choice of *values* and particular *attitudes* to the world, their rhetoric tended often to what formal rhetoric would have regarded as epideictic, and the Letter to the Romans is, in fact, no exception in this respect. Second, Paul's discussion of the relationship of the "weak" and the "strong" in Romans 14.1–15.13 gives every appearance of being addressed to a specific situation in which Paul did look for specific action. Here—at what was, after all, the climax of his address as the Romans heard it read to them—he was not merely asking them to "affirm communal values": quite clearly, he wanted them to do something about those values. Hence, when it came down to it, his closing rhetoric *was* deliberative.

We might make the further point, moreover, that what is formally epideictic rhetoric will often tend to the deliberative—not least because those who praise, say, kings or emperors are naturally inclined at times, while ostensibly praising them for virtues they already possess, in fact to be urging them to act in line with virtues that the orators hope they will cultivate. Quintilian noticed the phenomenon: "Will any one deny the title of *epideictic* to panegyric? But yet *panegyrics* are advisory in form and frequently discuss the interests of Greece [*Atqui formam suadendi habent et plerumque de utilitatem Graeciae loquuntur*]" (3.4.14, trans. H. E. Butler). Had Quintilian written a few years later, Pliny's *Panegyricus*, addressed to the emperor Trajan, could have afforded him an excellent Roman example of the same thing: "If approached as Emperor, he [Trajan] simply replied as consul. No magistrate had his rights or authority diminished" (*Panegyricus* 77). This is not in any way to make Pliny a cynic, or to detract from his evidently genuine admiration and affection for his Emperor; it is merely to note that he naturally (and sensibly) fostered, by complimenting, those behaviors that he wanted to encourage.

Second, at least since the publication of Rudolf Bultmann's dissertation,[29] it has been common to associate Romans with the diatribe. This is helpful, if "diatribe" is understood in accordance with ancient usage—which, unfortunately, has not always been the case. In connection with the kind of literature we are considering, the word "diatribe" (*diatribē* ["a way of passing the time," "an occupation"]) is properly used either with reference to the activity of teaching in a school, or to a text recording that activity, such as Epictetus's *Discourses*—records of his lectures, noted down "so far as possible in his own words" by his student Arrian.[30] By extension, "diatribe" is also applied to texts using the rhetorical and pedagogical styles that characterized educational activity, such as the texts published by Dio Chrysostom (for example, *Discourse* 14, *On Slavery and Freedom*) and Plutarch (for example, the essays *On Curiosity* and *Concerning Talkativeness*, in *Moralia* 502b–523b—the latter a delight-

---

29. Rudolf Bultmann, *Der Stil der paulinischen Predigt und die kynisch-stoische Diatribe*, FRLANT 13, (Göttingen: Vandenhoeck and Ruprecht, 1910).

30. It is worth noting that the *only* characteristic that distinguishes Arrian's work from the "essays with the heading 'Greetings!'" that were discussed earlier is that the author's desire to preserve his teacher's discourses as separate pieces has meant that he presents us with what is clearly a collection rather than an "essay" or a summary. In every other way he conforms completely: the letter setting appears to be genuine, and he is concerned to refer to another piece of work—Epictetus's teaching— so as "to preserve for myself reminders in future days of his cast of mind and frankness of speech" (*Arrian to Lucius Gellius*: preface to Epictetus's *Discourses*).

ful piece whose only fault, ironically, is that it is far too long). As such, written diatribe has identifiable characteristics. It is generally concerned overall with a philosophical or moral issue (just, it should be noted, the sort of matters "Demetrius" regarded as unsuitable for a letter). Thus Epictetus's *Discourses* concern matters reflected in the following titles:

How Can We Act in Everything in a Manner Acceptable to the Gods? (1.13)

On Providence (1.16)

What Is the True Nature of the Good? (2.8)

That We Must Approach Everything with Circumspection (3.15)

On Freedom (4.1)

Similarly, Dio Chrysostom speaks philosophically and morally in *On Slavery and Freedom* (14). Evidently, as far as concerns subject matter, Paul's Letter to the Romans would be at home enough in company such as this.

Diatribe is distinguished not only by subject matter but also by marked characteristics of style. Frequently there is discussion with an imaginary partner:

Why should we be angry at the multitude?
"They are thieves and robbers."
What do you mean by "thieves and robbers"?
"They have gone astray in matters of good and evil."
Ought we, then, to be angry with them, or to pity them? Do but show them their error, and you will see how they will emend their faults; but, if they do not see it, they have nothing higher than their personal opinion to rely on.
"What, then? Ought not this thief or this adulterer to be put to death?"
By no means! But what you ought to be asking instead is . . . (Epictetus, *Discourses* 1.18.2b–5, trans. Elizabeth Carter, rev. Robin Hard)

This kind of thing is frequent in Epictetus, Dio Chrysostom, and in parts of Plutarch; and it inevitably reminds us of parts of the Letter to the Romans:

A true Jew is a Jew inwardly, and circumcision is of the heart, in the spirit, not in the letter; such a person receives not human praise, but God's.
"Then what advantage has the Jew? What profit is there in circumcision?"
Much every way. First, that to them were committed the oracles of God.
"What, then? If some were unfaithful, does their unfaithfulness bring to nothing the faithfulness of God?"
Heaven forbid! Let God be true, though all humankind a liar!—as it is written,

That thou mightest be justified in thy words,
And prevail when thou art judged. (Rom. 2.29–3.4)

So, in diatribe, it is regularly the task of the interlocutor to raise objections, offer false conclusions, and put difficult questions, while the teacher turns from his real audience to respond to such objections with direct, second-person discourse. Often this will be quite censorious in tone:

Be quiet, fellow! (Epictetus, *Discourses* 3.5.15)
Speak the truth, you wretch, and do not brag, or claim to be a philosopher! (2.13.23)

Similarly, Paul:

> "Why does God still find fault? Who can resist his will?"
> On the contrary, fellow, who are you, who are finding fault with God?
> (Rom. 9.19–20)

In Epictetus, as in Paul, false conclusions and suggestions may be set aside with a scornful cry:

> What, then, is the true nature of God? Flesh?
> By no means (*mē genoito*)!
> Land?
> By no means!
> Fame?
> By no means! (2.8.2–3; compare Rom. 3.4, 31, 6.2, 11.1)[31]

On the other hand, suggestions and conclusions held to be correct may be supported by citations from sources likely to be regarded as authoritative by those addressed. So in Epictetus there are allusions to Homer (for example, *Discourses* 3.1.38, citing *Odyssey* 1.37–39), Plato (for example, 3.1.19–20, loosely citing Plato, *Apology* 28e), and the rest of the "canon" of the *paideia*. In Paul, naturally, there are regular allusions and appeals to the Jewish Scriptures.

Some writers have a taste for personifying abstractions:

> Curiosity, it seems, takes no pleasure in stale evils. It needs them fresh and warm, it likes to see new tragedies, and has no enthusiasm for the cheerful or the comic. (Plutarch, *Curiosity*, *Moralia* 517f, trans. Donald Russell)

Similarly, Paul:

> Sin found its opportunity in the commandment, seduced me, and by means of the commandment killed me. . . . Thereby Sin exposed its true character: it used a good thing to bring about my death (Rom. 7.11, 13)

There is much sarcasm:

> "I am ill here," says one of the students, "and I want to go back home." What, were you never ill at home, then? Do you give no thought as to whether you are doing anything here that contributes to your improvement . . . ? (Epictetus, *Discourses*, 3.5.1. *To Those Who Leave because of Illness*)

So, again, Paul:

> Shall the thing formed say to the one that formed it, "Why have you made me thus?" Or does the potter have no authority over the clay . . . ? (Rom. 9.20–21)

Lists of virtues and vices occur—indeed, rather too often for my taste:

> It is this [the disappointment of our desires and the incurring of our aversions] that introduces disturbances, tumults, misfortunes and calamities; causes sorrow, lam-

---

31. According to some epistolary theorists, such direct, conversational style was, however, unsuitable in correspondence. "Demetrius" did not like it (*On Style* 226). Cicero was obviously prepared to use it in letters to his friends (compare *Letters to His Friends* 12.30.1). Julius Victor (appealing to Cicero's example) thought it acceptable in personal letters, but looked for rather more *severitas* in other types (*Art of Rhetoric* 27).

entation and envy; and makes us envious, jealous, and incapable of listening to reason. (*Discourses* 3.2.3, *What One Must Train in if One Is to Make Progress*; compare also 3.20.5–6; Dio Chrysostom, *Discourses* 4.93–94, 77/78.45)

In such company even Paul's (to my mind) somewhat wearisome vice list[32] sounds a little less odd:

filled with all manner of injustice, wickedness, ruthlessness, evil; full of envy, murder, strife, deceit, malignity, vicious gossips, public slanderers, hateful to God, insolent, arrogant, boastful, inventors of evil, disobedient to parents, foolish, faithless, heartless, merciless. (Rom. 1.29–31)

What is the purpose of all this vigor? Only indirectly is it polemic, since the teacher has little reason to suppose that any, in fact, but disciples and inquirers are actually listening. The purpose of such vigor is directly *pedagogical* and *persuasive*. By such language as this the student's attention is engaged and retained. This is the style in which the Letter to the Romans is written: a style designed, certainly, for criticizing the views of opponents, but, above all, for leading those who heard it to the truth— sometimes by correcting their assumptions or pretensions; a style not to be associated, as was at one time supposed, with public preaching to the masses,[33] but with the lecture hall, the classroom, and the school—in other words, with education and instruction; a style, therefore, eminently suited to *logos protreptikos*, which, as a genre, had precisely the same associations.

Thus I have found the three major elements of a typical persuasive or "protreptic" discourse—*Dissuasive, Demonstration and Defense,* and *Exhortation* —clearly present in the Letter to the Romans, and I have identified other stylistic features—notably the style of *diatribē*—consonant with that genre. There remains the question of purpose. Genre is a tool of meaning. We choose a genre because it suits what we want to say. *Logos protreptikos* was, I have said, a form of address associated with the choice of a particular philosophical school or with the choice of philosophy itself. Why then would Paul choose to present a defense of his gospel in this form?

Partly, of course, he may have acted in the light of Jewish precedent. The Wisdom of Solomon, which appears (as we shall see) to have influenced him in other respects, certainly seems to have protreptic features. More decisive, however, was perhaps something in the nature of the gospel itself as the ancient world, including Paul, would have perceived it. The ancients generally seem to have associated ultimate truth claims and demands for appropriate living with philosophy. So Seneca:

---

32. Not, it must be confessed, half so wearisome as Philo, who on one occasion has the gall to present us with a vice list of no less than 140 items (*On the Sacrifices of Abel and Cain* 32).

33. In his 1910 dissertation (see this chapter, page 22 and footnote 29), Rudolf Bultmann, as is well known, associated the diatribe with popular "preaching" to the masses, particularly by Stoics, so that "Cynic-Stoic diatribe" came to be regarded as virtually the name of a genre. In making such an association, Bultmann was reflecting the consensus of the best classical scholarship of his day. Unfortunately, those who succeeded Bultmann, instead of following his example and listening to what classical scholarship had to say, merely reproduced his views—and so failed to notice that classical scholarship had moved on. (Exactly the same thing happened, mutatis mutandis, to form-criticism. The early form-critics, Bultmann among them, used the work of those who were studying oral tradition. Later New Testament critics merely followed the early form-critics, and, again, carried on a conversation among themselves, oblivious to the work of Milman Parry, Albert Bates Lord, and others, who in the meanwhile had transformed our knowledge and understanding of the entire field.)

Who can doubt, my dear Lucilius, that life is the gift of the immortal gods, but that living well is the gift of philosophy? Hence the idea that our debt to philosophy is greater than our debt to the gods, in proportion as a good life is more of a benefit than mere life, would be regarded as correct, were not philosophy itself a boon which the gods have bestowed upon us. They have given the knowledge thereof to none, but the faculty of acquiring it they have given to all. . . .

[Philosophy's] sole function is to discover the truth about things divine and things human. From her side awe of the divine [*religio*][34] never departs, nor duty, nor justice, nor any of the whole company of virtues which cling together in close united fellowship. (*Letters* 90.3, trans. Richard M. Gummere, altered)

Hence joining a philosophical school involved many of the ideas, and even the emotions, that we associate with religious conversion. At this period, as Martin Hengel has pointed out, the most striking parallels to our understanding of vocation "occur pre-eminently where philosophy was laying a claim to truth."[35] So Lucian describes the effect of Nigrinus's teaching upon him in terms strikingly similar to those we might use to describe a religious conversion:

I took it all in with an eager, wide open soul, and at the moment I couldn't imagine what had come over me; I was all confused. At first I felt hurt because he had criticized what was dearest to me—wealth and money and reputation—and I all but cried over their downfall; and then I thought them paltry and ridiculous, and was glad to be looking up, as it were, out of the murky atmosphere of my past life to a clear sky and a great light. In consequence, I . . . by degrees grew sharper-sighted in my soul; which, all unawares, I had been carrying round in a purblind condition till then. (*Nigrinus* 4–5, trans. A. M. Harmon)

Likewise the reaction of Lucian's "unbeliever"—"you don't deign to notice us any more, you don't associate with us, and you don't join in our conversations: you have changed all of a sudden, and, in short, have a supercilious air" (*Nigrinus* 1)—is, granted that it is lighter in tone, almost a mirror image of the description given by 1 Peter of nonbelievers reacting to Christian converts: "They are surprised that you do not now join them in the same wild profligacy, and they abuse you" (1 Peter 4.4).

Hence Christianity (like Judaism) was for the ancients a confusing phenomenon. Insofar as it involved ritual and cult, it might naturally be described as *superstitio*—the usual Latin term for a foreign cult, and in the first century, disparaging: so, for example, Pliny, in his rescript to Hadrian about Christians in Bithynia (*Letters* 10.96.10).[36] On the other hand, insofar as Christianity presented itself as teaching doctrines *describing what is ultimately true and requiring appropriate activity*, it appeared

34. Latin *religio* refers fundamentally to a "feeling of constraint" in face of the supernatural, and hence a sense of the presence of supernatural power—"religious fear, awe" (see OLD, *religio* 1, 2, 3, 4, 5, 6, 7, 10).

35. Martin Hengel, *The Charismatic Leader and His Followers*, trans. James C. G. Greig (Edinburgh: Clark, 1981), 27; see 28–33. Also Jordan, "Philosophical Protreptic," 333.

36. Also Tacitus (*Annals* 15:44) and Suetonius (*Nero* 16.2). Many Roman authors regarded Judaism also as *superstitio*: see Cicero (*Flac.* 67), Horace (*Sat.* 1.9.69–71, 2.3.281–95), and Juvenal (*Sat.* 14. 99, 104). *Superstitio* (in distinction from *religio*) involved an essentially *inappropriate* response to the divine. It was therefore generally perceived as destructive of family life and inimical to Roman order.

to be a philosophical school. This, no doubt, was precisely the point. Paul's purpose in Romans was to persuade his hearers to a favorable view of his beliefs about God and God's promise—"my gospel." By using the protreptic form, he immediately declared to his hearers that he regarded what he was presenting as a witness to ultimate truth, "the power of God for salvation," in response to which no "reasonable service" was possible other than total obedience, the presentation of one's whole being "as a living sacrifice." So Wisdom and philosophy come together (compare 1 Corinthians 1.22–25).

I believe it was also the case that Paul's *logos* was slanted in particular toward divisions and parties that he knew existed in the church at Rome. To be more precise, I suspect he discerned at least two groups in the Roman church at whom he sought to aim his discourse. First were some—mostly but not necessarily all of Jewish descent—who had accepted Jesus as Messiah, but who believed that Paul's admission of uncircumcised gentiles to full fellowship on the basis of faith in Jesus was an abandonment of God's Law; who saw in Paul's gospel of "grace for all" both an implicit denial of Israel's calling and a proclamation of moral indifference. Second were those—mostly but not necessarily all of gentile origin—who resented the claims of the former group and felt, or claimed to feel, superior to those who were so preoccupied with questions of law and obedience.[37] A strategic reason for Paul's undertaking to address these groups is not difficult to see. He hoped for support from the Roman congregations for his projected mission to the West (15.23–24); evidently, the more generally his gospel was understood and accepted among them, the more broadly and soundly based that support would be. Yet finally, we may be sure, it was more than a matter of strategy. Paul was convinced that an approach to the gospel that founded it on *anything* other than the justice and grace of God available for all who would put their trust in the Son of God amounted in fact to rejection of the gospel. "You who want to be justified by the Law," he wrote on another occasion, "have cut yourselves off from Christ: you have fallen away from grace" (Gal. 5.4; compare 1.6–9). Equally, Paul was convinced that those who did accept that gospel were committed by it to emulating the grace by which they were saved: "Welcome one another, therefore, just as Christ has welcomed you, for the glory of God" (Rom. 15.7). In other words, not simply strategy but the thing itself was at stake. Hence the vigor—and the abiding importance—of his protreptic.

I believe I have done enough to show that the main part of the Letter to the Romans would have been regarded by contemporaries as a persuasive or "protreptic" discourse. No doubt those same contemporaries would also have thought it very Jewish (totally involved with "questions about words and names and your own law" [Acts 18.15]), and, if they were like Galen something over a century later, they might have said that while Paul's "philosophy" could lead in its adherents to behavior "not inferior to that of genuine philosophers" (*Summary of Plato's Republic. Fragment*), yet it was full of "talk of undemonstrated laws" (*On the Pulse* 2.4). Nevertheless, in broad terms, they would not have been in any doubt about what Paul was trying to do. He was, of sorts, a "philosopher," seeking to persuade hearers to his particular "school."

37. On the ethnic composition of the Roman church, see further, additional note OO.

I have noted, however, that letters, like other literary genres, might combine elements of more than one type—and this, in fact, appears to be the case in Romans. To be precise, we may plausibly identify elements of at least two other types, "the family letter," and the letter of commendation.

Bibliographical Note

On protreptic generally, see Abraham Malherbe, *Moral Exhortation: A Greco-Roman Source Book.* LEC (Philadelphia: Westminster Press, 1986), passim, but especially 122–25; see further Mark D. Jordan, "Ancient Philosophic Protreptic and the Problem of Persuasive Genres," in *Rhetorica* 4 (1986): 309–33; also the summary in Anthony J. Guerra, *Romans and the Apologetic Tradition: The Purpose, Genre, and Audience of Paul's Letter*, SNTSMS 81 (Cambridge: Cambridge University Press, 1995), 3–8.

On Romans as protreptic, *honoris causa*, one should mention Klaus Berger, who was, so far as I know, the first modern New Testament scholar to make the connection: see Berger, *Formegeschichte des Neuen Testament* (Heidelberg: Quelle und Meyer, 1984), 217; "Hellenistische Gattungen im Neuen Testament," in *ANRW*, 2.25.2 (Berlin: de Gruyter, 1984), 1140. See further Stanley K. Stowers, *Letter Writing in Greco-Roman Antiquity* 112–14; David E. Aune, "Romans as a *Logos Protreptikos*," in Donfried, *Romans Debate: Revised*, 278–96; and Ira J. Jolivet Jr., "An Argument from the Letter and Intent of the Law as the Primary Argumentative Strategy in Romans," in *The Rhetorical Analysis of Scripture: Essays from the 1995 London Conference*, ed. Stanley E. Porter and Thomas H. Olbricht, JSNTSS 146 (Sheffield, England: Sheffield Academic Press, 1997): 309–34. By far the fullest and most carefully argued statement of the case so far is, however, Guerra's *Romans and the Apologetic Tradition*. Guerra criticizes Aune's vagueness as to the degree to which Romans intends to address the actual situation in Rome and notes how lack of clarity in this respect blinds Aune to the protreptic function of Romans 9–11 (9–12, 170). Stanley E. Porter has recently presented significant reasons for caution about the currently fashionable procedure of examining Pauline letter structure in terms of the canons of ancient rhetoric: see "Paul of Tarsus and His Letters," in *Handbook of Classical Rhetoric in the Hellenistic Period, 330 B.C.–A.D. 400*, ed. Stanley E. Porter (Leiden: Brill, 1997), 533–86. With regard to Romans as protreptic (560–61, 568–69), therefore, he, too, is critical of Aune ("it is difficult to see in what sense [Romans] is a speech" [560]); on the other hand, he concedes that Guerra *has* made the case for Romans as a protreptic letter (568–69).

On Romans as employing epideictic rhetoric, see Wilhelm Wuellner, "Paul's Rhetoric of Argumentation in Romans: An Alternative to the Donfried-Karris Debate over Romans," *CBQ* 38 (1976): 330–51; reprinted in Donfried, *Romans Debate: Revised*, 128–146; George A. Kennedy, *New Testament Interpretation through Rhetorical Criticism* (Chapel Hill: University of North Carolina Press, 1984), 152–56; see also Andrew T. Lincoln, "From Wrath to Justification: Tradition, Gospel, and Audience in the Theology of Romans 1.18–4.25," in *Pauline Theology*, vol. 3, *Romans*, ed. David M. Hay and E. Elizabeth Johnson (Minneapolis: Fortress Press, 1995), 134. On links between epideictic and deliberative rhetoric, see D. A. G. Hinks, "*Tria Genera Causarum*," *Classical Quarterly* 30 (1936): 170–76, especially 173–76.

On the diatribe see Joseph Souilhe, *Épictète Entretiens*, Collections des universites de France (Paris: Société d'edition "Les belles lettres," 1975); John Glucker, *Antiochus and the Late Academy*, Hypomnemata 56 (Göttingen: Vandehoeck and Ruprecht, 1978), 159–66; and Stanley K. Stowers, *The Diatribe and Paul's Letter to the Romans*, SBLDS 57 (Chico, California: Scholars Press, 1981). A useful short summary of current classical scholarship in this area and its relationship to the New Testament is provided by Stowers, "The Diatribe," in *Greco-Roman Literature and the New Testament: Selected Forms and Genres*, ed. David E. Aune, SBLDS 2 (Atlanta, Georgia: Scholars Press, 1988), 71–83.

On "lists of virtues and vices," see Malherbe, *Moral Exhortation*, 138–41; there are also useful references to primary material in John T. Fitzgerald, "Virtue/Vice Lists," in *ABD* 6.857–59.

On protreptic features in Wisdom, see J. M. Reese, *Hellenistic Influence on the Book of Wisdom and Its Consequences* (Rome: Pontifical Biblical Institute, 1970), especially 117–21.

On the integrity of Romans, see Harry Gamble, *The Textual History of the Letter to the Romans: A Study in Textual and Literary Criticism*, Texts and Documents 42 (Grand Rapids, Michigan: Eerdmans, 1977). Gamble's careful study of the history of the text has persuaded the majority of recent commentators that Romans 1.1–16.24 is substantially the letter that Paul sent to Rome. On the question of Romans 16 in particular, see also the discussion in Peter Lampe, "The Roman Christians of Romans 16," in Donfried, *Romans Debate: Revised*, 216–21.

Romans as a Family Letter

The "family letter" is a subspecies that the ancient epistolary theorists themselves seem not to have recognized—although they well might have, as a type parallel to the letter of friendship, and designed for upholding the relationships and good feelings of a household. The kind of social group to which I here refer by the English word "household" (Greek, *oikia*; Latin, *familia*) would, it should be noted, have been a quite complex patronal structure including slaves, freedpersons, servants, and so on. In other words, it would have been a much more complicated and extensive group than is normally implied by the English word "family." It would therefore probably have been better if the letters of which we are speaking had been categorized as "household letters" rather than "family letters." The latter phrase has by now, however, been sanctioned through usage, and to avoid confusion I do not change it.

That the ancient epistolary theorists did not recognize the family letter was probably because they were largely confined to the traditional Greek view that literate culture worthy of critical discussion (not to mention serious affection worthy to be called "friendship" [Greek, *philia*; Latin, *amicitia*]) could occur only among free adult males.[38] Evidently, human nature did not wait upon theory, as is illustrated not only by Plutarch's *Consolation* but also by Claudia Severa's *To Lepidina*, which is both literate and friendly. Similarly, the Egyptian papyri in fact preserve for us a number of what we can only categorize as family letters, so that at this point we are obliged either to abandon the material or to admit the inadequacy of the ancient categories.

Three obvious characteristics mark the family letter. First, and fundamental, is its purpose. Family letters are, as we have said, letters designed in one way or another to uphold the relationships and good feelings of a household. They generally identify the recipient as a family member (father, mother, brother, sister). Many

---

38. Stowers, *Letter Writing* 71. For the same debate as late as the Renaissance, see Guy Fitch Lytle's essay on "Friendship and Patronage in Renaissance Europe," in F. W. Kent, Patricia Simons, and J. C. Eade, *Patronage, Art, and Society in Renaissance Italy* (Oxford: Clarendon, 1987), especially 52–53, and literature there cited.

contain some type of prayer or wish for the well-being of the recipient. Other typical features are similar to those common in letters of friendship—such as information about the situation of the sender, and anxiety over separation.[39] These elements are present in the following brief note, written at some time during the reign of Augustus:

> Heraklas to Horos and Tachonis, greetings and good health.
>
> I am worried about you. Since we have been on duty we have been sailing in the boat for eight days. With the gods' will, we shall be on board ship in three days. As for the child, watch him as you would an oil lamp, for I worry about you . . . [the rest of the text is not clear and has several lacunae]. (Heraklas, *To Horos and Tachonis*, trans. G. H. R. Horsley, altered)

The same elements are also present in Romans, which, had it been totally lost save for the following fragments, would surely have been classed as a family letter:

> Paul [. . .] to all the [. . .] beloved [. . .]
>
> First, I thank my God [. . .] for all of you [. . .] without ceasing I mention you always in my prayers, asking that by God's will I may at last succeed in coming to you. For I long to see you [. . .]. I want you to know, brothers, that I have often intended to come to you, but thus far have been prevented [. . .]. (1.1, 7, 8–10, 13)

In addition to greeting the addressee, from the mid-first century BC onwards, writers of the family letter often salute various people who are named at the end of the letter. The phenomenon is well illustrated by the following two letters, one from the second century:

> Apollinarius to Taesis, his mother and lady, many greetings.
>
> Before all else I pray for your health. I myself am well, and make supplication for you before the gods of this place. I want you to know, mother, that I arrived in Rome in good health on the 25th of the month Pachon and was posted to Misenum, though I have not yet learned the name of my company, for I had not yet gone to Misenum at the time of writing this letter. I beg you then, mother, look after yourself and do not worry about me, for I have come to a fine place. Please write me a letter about your welfare and that of my brothers and of all your folk. And whenever I find a messenger I will write to you. Never will I be slow to write. I salute [*aspazomai*] heartily my brothers and Apollinarius and his children and Karalas and his children. I salute Ptolomaeus and Ptolemais and Heraclous and her children. I salute all who love you, each by name. I pray for your health. (Appolinarius, *To Taesis*, trans. A. S. Hunt and C. C. Edgar)

---

39. Compare, for example, the following letter of friendship, written practically at the same time as Romans: "Chairas to his dearest Dionysius, many greetings, and good health always. When I received your letter, I was extremely happy, as if I had actually been at home again, for without that there is nothing [i.e., presumably, "there's place like home"]. No need to write you a big 'thank you,' for it's to those who are not friends that one says 'thank you' with words. I am sure that I am continuing calmly, and I am sure that if not able to give something equivalent, I will be able to give some little thing for your affection (*philostorgia*) towards me. . . . Goodbye, and remember what I have said. [Year] 5 of the lord Nero, the month of Germanicus 1 [i.e., 29 August 58]" (Chairas, *To Dionysios the Physician*, trans. John L. White).

and another from the third century:

> Aurelius Dius to Aurelius Horion, my sweetest father, many greetings.
>
> I make supplication for you every day before the gods of this place.
>
> Now don't be uneasy, father, about my studies. I am working hard, and taking relaxation. I shall do very well.
>
> I salute [*aspazomai*] my mother Tamiea and my sister Tnepherous and my sister Philous. I salute also my brother Patermouthis and my sister Thermouthis. I salute also my brother Heracl[. . .] and my brother Kollouchis. I salute my father Melanus and my mother Timpesouris and her son. Gaia salutes [*aspazaitai* (read *aspazetai*)] you all. My father Horion and Thermouthis salute you all. I pray for your health, father. (*Dius to Aurelius Horion. P.* Oxy. 1296, trans. A. S. Hunt and C. C. Edgar, altered)

It would be difficult indeed not to be reminded by all this of Romans 16:

> Salute [*aspasasthe*] Prisca and Aquila. . . . Salute my beloved Epaenetus. . . . Salute Mary. . . . Salute Adronicus and Junia, my kin. . . . Salute Ampliatus my beloved . . . and my beloved Stachys. . . . Salute my kin Herodion.
>
> The grace of our Lord Jesus Christ be with you. Timothy . . . salutes [*aspazetai*] you; so do Lucius and Jason and Sosipater, my kin. . . . Gaius, who is my host . . . salutes you. Erastus . . . and our brother Quartus salute you. (Rom. 16.3, 5, 6, 7, 8, 9, 10, 21, 23)

The Letter to the Romans, then, includes the major elements of the family letter, as critics have identified them. What, then, of its purpose? In what sense is Romans designed, as we have said is true of family letters in general, "to uphold the relationships and good feelings of a household"? It was true, of course, as Pseudo-Demetrius noted, that those in prominent positions might on occasion write, for example, something in the style of a letter of friendship to those they did not know personally, as a matter of tact. "They do so, not because they are close friends . . . but because they think that nobody will refuse them when they write in a friendly manner, but will rather submit and heed what they are writing" (*Epistolary Types* 1). It is surely the case, however, that in Paul we are dealing with something deeper than diplomacy. The response to our question leads us, in fact, to Paul's understanding of the church. Christians, for Paul, *are* a household: they are "members of the household of the faith" (Gal. 6.10; compare Eph. 2.19), and although he does not use those actual words in Romans, the concept is everywhere present. Christians claim Abraham as their father (Rom. 4.16), yet their relationship to one another is closer than that, for

> all who are led by the Spirit of God are children of God. For you did not receive a spirit of slavery to fall back into fear, but you have received a spirit of adoption [*huiothesia*, "adoption as a son"]. When we cry "Abba! Father!" it is that very spirit bearing witness with our spirit that we are children of God, and if children then heirs, heirs of God and joint heirs with Christ. (8.14–17)

Naturally, therefore, Paul repeatedly addresses the Roman Christians as his "brothers and sisters" (*adelphoi*: literally, "brethren") (1.13, 7.1, 8.12, 10.1, 12.1, 15.30, 16.17); and that, of course, is how he assumes they think of each other (14.10, 15). "In love of your brothers and sisters" (*philadelphia*: literally, "love of the brethren"), he says, "show one another affectionate kindness" (12.10). The word group involved in "affectionate kindness" (*philostorgein* and its cognates) is common in Greek of the period to denote warmth of feeling and is evidently appropriate to tenderness within families—although, of course, not only that.[40] That Paul therefore set his protreptic within the framework of a family letter both confirms and is confirmed by his understanding of the church. If he is successful—if he can clear away misunderstandings about his teaching and his gospel, and gain the Romans' support in his work—then he will have helped to uphold the relationships and good feelings of a household: the household of God. Even more is this the case if in so doing he can address and bring to mutual tolerance rival groups within that household at Rome.

At the same time, Paul's view of the church as "the household of God" implicitly supports—and even demands—his basic purpose in Romans, which is, as I have said, *to dissuade his hearers from a view of God's relationship with the world or with Israel that would see it as ever at any time or in any situation founded on anything except God's justice and grace*. Whatever else the Greco-Roman household was, it was hardly an egalitarian institution. Members of the household were all, finally, dependent upon the goodwill of the head, the *patronus* (or, occasionally, the *patrona*)—legally and, to a considerable extent, in practice. Within the household itself no doubt there were other distinctions—the wife above freedpersons, freedpersons above slaves, some slaves above other slaves, and so on—but all such distinctions fade into relative insignificance before *that* distinction, for the household has only one head. To think, then, of the church as God's household is to use a profoundly nonegalitarian image for what turns out to be a profoundly egalitarian end. No doubt there are real differences within the church—Jew and gentile, slave and free, men and women, not to mention "gifts that differ according to the grace given to us" (12.6)—but all such differences fade into utter insignificance before that which unites us in the household, which is that we are "one body in Christ" (12.5) and hence belong to him. "Who are you to pass judgment on someone else's household slave?" (14.4) We all, whatever our nature or gifts, are finally dependent upon one thing, which is the goodwill of our Lord—*God's grace and God's justice*.[41]

Bibliographical Note

On family letters, see White, *Light from Ancient Letters* 196–97, Stowers, *Letter Writing* 71–76, 177–78, and literature there cited.

On the Greco-Roman household, see Paul Veyne, "The Roman Empire," in *A History of Private Life*, ed. Philippe Ariès and Georges Duby, ed. Paul Veyne, trans. Arthur Goldhammer, vol. 1, *From Pagan Rome to Byzantium* (Cambridge, Massachusetts: Harvard University Press, 1987), especially 6–115, and K. R. Bradley, *Discovering the Roman Family* (New York: Oxford University Press, 1991). Also useful is H. O. Maier, *The Social Setting of the*

---

40. Thus, for example, Plutarch, *Consolation to My Wife, Moralia* 608, 609; *On the Intelligence of Animals, Moralia* 962a; Lucian, *The Tyrant* 1. For *philostorgia* used of affection between friends, see the example on, page 30, footnote 39.

41. In exactly the same spirit, Matthew 18.21–35 also uses the image of members of the community of Christ as slaves in an imperial household, and bases upon it a requirement for continuing mutual forgiveness.

Ministry as Reflected in the Writings of Hermas, Clement, and Ignatius, Dissertations SR 1 (Waterloo, Ontario: Wilfred Laurier University Press, 1991), 15–28. Maier, in particular, offers evidence of the role of the "household" in relation to ancient groups other than the household itself, in particular mystery religions, philosophical schools, Greco-Roman associations, and the Synagogue (18–24).

Romans as a Letter of Commendation

According to Pseudo-Demetrius (an epistolary theorist who wrote some time between 200 BC and AD 300) "the commendatory [*sustatikos*] type" of letter is one that we write on behalf of one person to another, mixing in praise, at the same time also speaking of those who had previously been unacquainted as though they were now acquainted. In the following manner:

> So-and-so, who is conveying this letter to you, has been tested by us and is loved on account of his trustworthiness. You will do well if you deem him worthy of a welcome both for my sake and his, and indeed for your own. For you will not be sorry if you entrust to him, in any matter you wish, either words or deeds of a confidential nature. Indeed, you, too, will praise him to others when you see how useful he can be in everything. (*Epistolary Types* 2)

To judge from the papyri, such letters were quite often of "mixed" type, combining commendation with elements of, say, a letter of friendship; this is hardly surprising, since the basis for the commendation is generally the good relationship of the writer with both parties. The following, both written in the first century AD, are typical:

> Apollonius to Sarapion the strategus and gymnasiarch, many greetings. And good health always.
>
> Isodorus, the one who is delivering this letter, is from my household. I ask you to consider him as introduced to you, and if he comes to you for anything, do it for him for my sake. If you do this, I will be indebted to you. Whatever you wish to signify, I will do without delay.
> Take care of yourself so that you may be in good health.
> Farewell. (*Apollonius to Sarapion*. P. *Merton* 62, trans. Stanley K. Stowers)

The appeal to friendship is even clearer in the following, and the one introduced is also presented as a friend, rather than a member of the writer's household:

> Heracles to his dearest Musaeus, greetings.
>
> I request you to regard as introduced to you Dioscorus, who will deliver the letter to you; he is a very close friend of mine. By doing this, you will be conferring a favour on me.
>
> Farewell. Pharmuthi 13 (?). (*Heracles to Musaeus*, trans. B. R. Rees)

There are references to letters of commendation in Paul's correspondence (1 Cor. 16.3, 2 Cor. 3.1–2)—which is hardly surprising, in view of the importance of travel in Paul's mission, and the continuing need for hospitality for himself and his fellow workers. The beginning of Romans 16, however, gives us the thing itself and, aside from its Christian content and the fact that it is better written, it reads like an exercise based on Pseudo-Demetrius's outline:

> I commend to you our sister Phoebe, who is deacon [*diakonos*] of the church at Cenchreae, so that you may welcome her in the Lord as is fitting for the saints, and help her in whatever she may require from you, for she has been a patron [*prostatis*] of many, and of myself as well. (16.1–2)

Phoebe is to be welcomed on three, and probably four, grounds. First, she is "our sister," which is to say that she is already a member of the family. Second, she is "deacon [*diakonos*] of the church at Cenchreae," the form of Paul's expression suggesting that he understands by *diakonos* here a particular office, commanding respect among Christians.[42] Third, she is *prostatis*—that is, benefactor, or patron—"of many, *and of myself*." In first-century Greco-Roman society, to declare someone your benefactor or patron was to make a very serious claim indeed about their status in relation to you. By using that word, Paul declared himself Phoebe's client and her protégé.[43] As for the fourth ground, Pseudo-Demetrius's model, the letters of Apollonius and Heracles, and numerous other surviving examples of commendatory letters indicate they were to be delivered by those whom they commended. Was Phoebe, then, to deliver the Letter to the Romans? Paul does not say so, and we cannot be sure. But it is likely. If she were, then that Paul trusted her with such an office for such a document speaks more of his view of her than do even the words of his commendation.

Bibliographical Note

On letters of commendation, see further White, *Light from Ancient Letters* 193–94; Stowers, *Letter Writing in Greco-Roman Antiquity* 153–65, 178, and literature there cited.

Additional Note A. Patronage

No one who does not understand the institution known to the Romans as *clientela* (that is, "the relationship, status, or position of a client" or, in a transferred sense, "protection, guardianship")[44] will understand very much of how Greco-Roman society worked. There is, indeed, some question as to how far the specifically Roman form of the institution penetrated the Eastern Empire, and its terminology (*patronus, cliens, beneficium,* and so on) are not much found there; on the other hand, it undoubtedly had some influence, and in any case, the entire culture of "saviors," "benefactors," and relationships of interdependency that was characteristic of the Eastern Mediterranean had obvious points of contact with Roman *clientela*. We are, as Frederick W. Danker has observed (and, to some extent, demonstrated) dealing with "a depth structural reality that breaks into various thematic patterns and comes to linguistic expression in numerous modes and forms."[45] Virtually the whole of society was structured on the basis of what has been called "evergetism"[46]—that is, the

---

42. On Phoebe as *diakonos* see additional note EE.

43. On patronage, see additional note A.

44. *OLD, clientela* 1, 3.

45. Frederick W. Danker, *Benefactor: Epigraphic Study of a Graeco-Roman and New Testament Semantic Field* (St. Louis: Clayton, 1982), 27.

46. E.g., Paul Veyne, "The Roman Empire," in *A History of Private Life,* gen. eds. Philippe Ariès and Georges Duby, ed. Paul Veyne, trans. Arthur Goldhammer (Cambridge, Massachusetts: Harvard University Press, 1987), 107.

relationship between a patron or benefactor, whose role (as a matter of honor) was to convey protection, favor, and other types of "benevolence" to a client, and the client, whose proper role (as a matter of honor) was, in return, to render support, loyalty, praise, and other appropriate marks of "obligation" to the benefactor. The wealthy and powerful gained honor by the extent of their patronage and the number and well-being of their clients, while clients gained honor by the nobility and generosity of their patrons.

Nor was this understanding confined to gentiles. We have only to recall the terms in which Job speaks of himself as a just man:

> If I have withheld anything that the poor desired,
>   or have caused the eyes of the widow to fail,
> or have eaten my morsel alone,
>   and the orphan has not eaten from it—
> for from my youth I reared the orphan like a father,
>   and from my mother's womb I guided the widow—
> if I have seen anyone perish for lack of clothing,
>   or a poor person without covering,
> whose loins have not blessed me,
>   and who was not warmed with the fleece of my sheep . . .
> then let my shoulder blade fall from my shoulder,
>   and let my arm be broken in its socket. (Job 31.16–22; compare Sirach 31.5–11)

A significant issue in parables such as the Rich Fool (Luke 12.16–20, *Gos. Thos* 63) and Dives and Lazarus (Luke 16.19–31) is the failure of each protagonist to act honorably—that is, to use his wealth for the good of the community. The rich fool simply regards his wealth as something he has for himself. When we hear of the beggar at Dives's gate "desiring the crumbs," the first-century listener will have expected Dives to act as his patron. That the beggar was left to the street dogs makes plain—and, indeed, emphasizes—Dives's failure to act honorably. What Dives ought to have done is made clear by Jesus on another occasion, where he says, "[W]hen you give a banquet, invite the poor, the crippled, the lame, and the blind. And you will be blessed, because they cannot repay you, for you will be repaid at the resurrection of the righteous" (Luke 14.13–14)—clearly envisaging the *patronus* or *patrona* of an extended Greco-Roman household who will not merely have at table those from whom he or she can expect support or other advantage, but who (like Job) will invite the genuinely needy.

A really wealthy person might be patron of a whole city or endow public works. So Pliny the Younger speaks of benefactions to his beloved Comum (*Letters* 1.8, 4.13, 5.7, 7.18). In return the city would show its *obligatio* by conferring titles on the patron and putting up statues and memorial inscriptions, as Comum did for Pliny (*CIL* 5.5262, 5263). Evidently Pliny also took very seriously his responsibility toward individuals who sought or depended on his patronage. He supported numerous aspirants to office (3.2, 4.4), as well as being generous to more humble people who were dependent upon him—such as his aging nurse, on whom he bestowed a small farm (6.3), and a valued freedman, for whom he funded a holiday abroad to improve his health (5.19).

Benefactions to a city would require considerable wealth, since they would normally include activities such as providing roads or public buildings, adorning public buildings, constructing public utilities, or subsidizing the grain supply in times of shortage, either by bringing ships carrying grain to one's particular city, or by making grain available for sale at less than the market price (all attested to in the Ephesian epigraphic material; see, for example, *BMI* 449, 450, 452, 455). It has been argued that such evergetism as this—such evergetism as was shown by benefactors like Pliny—was the economic glue that held the Roman Empire together, and when the system began to disappear—when the wealthy, in particular, no longer sought the "honor" and "praise" that came from being "benefactors," but instead started (like the Rich Fool) to be satisfied to invest their wealth purely in personal acquisition—then the empire began to collapse.

Be that as it may, the sources bearing witness to the system are everywhere. There is the mass of inscriptions and other references honoring imperial and local "benefactors" and "saviors" for the benefits they have granted (for example, Dittenberger, *Inscriptiones* 2.458)[47] and promising to bestow future honors on such benefactors so that it may be known (as an inscription from the mid-second century BC has it) "that the people both praise and honor those who are noble and good [*kalous kai agathous*]" (*BMI* 420). There are Jewish writers such as Philo, who appears to speak without hesitation of "our savior and benefactor Augustus" (*ho sōtēr kai euergetēs Sebastos*) (*Flaccus* 74; cf. Josephus, *Jewish War* 3.459). There are the philosophical discourses of writers such as Seneca explaining at (somewhat tedious) length the ethics of benefaction and obligation (*On Benefits*, in the *Moral Essays*). There are the streams of commendations in letters such as those of the younger Pliny (*Letters* 3.2, 3.8, and 4.4). Pliny provides us with the viewpoint of someone high on the social scale who took his responsibilities very seriously. More lowly viewpoints are to be found in the papyri—such, for example, as the *Deferential Greetings to Patron* sent at some time during the first or second century AD: "greetings, and that you may always remain in good health in your whole person for long years to come, since your good genius allowed us to greet you with respect and salute you" (trans. G. H. R. Horsley). There are the witty (and often cruel) references to the relationships of patrons and clients in Martial (for example, *Epigrams* 1.99, 108; 2.5, 13, 18; 5.44, 47; 10.24; 12.18, 29, 40 [cited later]) and Juvenal (for example, *Satire* 1). All point to a system that dominated the entire spectrum of relationships, both private and public, from the relationship of Rome itself with its "client" states to the relationships within each individual household, with the head of the household himself "patron" of all other members—which in practice meant an extended network of wife, children, freedpersons, and slaves. It was a system that included the universal patronal power of the emperor, the power exercised by powerful and aristocratic senators on behalf of their protégés, the protection and gifts they might all offer to their plebeian "clients," and the virtually unbreakable chains of obligation and duty that bound freedpersons to the families that had once owned them.

There are, of course, parallels to the ancient systems in modern society. We are all familiar with the notion of special interest groups that work together for mutual benefit. Even as I write, British newspapers are full of a story about what is being referred to as "the Hong Kong club" at the British Foreign Office—a group of highly

---

47. See pages 37–38.

placed and influential figures in the government service who are said to have been offended by the blunt fashion in which Christopher Patten, the last British governor of Hong Kong, criticized certain aspects of the British hand-over of Hong Kong to China, and who are therefore alleged to be out to cause him trouble.[48] The parallels with Greco-Roman systems of obligation break down, however, at a crucial point. In modern Western society, such systems must be discreet, and if brought to light are invariably sources of embarrassment to those involved in them, being regarded as by their nature subversive of that openness which is (at least in theory) the modern Western democratic ideal. The words and phrases by which we refer to such systems ("the old-boy network," *mafiosi*, "clique," "club," and so on) suggest that we generally perceive them as at best ludicrous, at worst sinister. In Greco-Roman society, by contrast, such systems were matters of *honor* for those involved in them. Patron and client alike *boasted* of their connections, the benefits springing from them, and the duties owed. Thus we, as we read the letters of Pliny the younger, are inclined to be slightly critical of him for mentioning at all—and still worse, describing at length!—the gifts he has given and the personal kindness he has bestowed. But that, as Betty Radice points out, is entirely to misunderstand "the Roman attitude to *officia* and *beneficia*; for services rendered and kindness bestowed, the giver had every right to expect in return society's approbation and a suitable gratitude in the recipient."[49] To criticize Pliny in this respect is, in short, totally to misunderstand ancient conceptions of honor.[50]

In the same context we may usefully compare the following decree of the corporation of Greek citizens of Asia, in reply to a letter from the proconsul proposing that they honor the emperor's birthday:

> Providence, which governs the course of our lives, has shown attention and goodness and has provided for the most perfect good for life by bringing forth Augustus, whom it has filled with virtue in order to make him a benefactor of humanity. So to us and to those with u[s it has sent a savior] who has put an end to war and set [all things] in order: Caesar, [by his appearing,] has realized the hopes of our ancestors . . . not only has he surpassed earlier benefactors of humanity, but he leaves no

48. *The Sunday Times* (London) 3 August 1997, 1.1, column 2. The same column also cites a source speaking of "the Hong Kong mafia at the Foreign Office." The root of the dispute was that Patten had criticized on ethical grounds earlier negotiations that had taken place between Great Britain and China regarding the future of Hong Kong.

49. *The Letters of Pliny the Younger* [London: Penguin, 1963], 23. Interestingly enough, a writer even as late as Jane Austen still understood the game perfectly. The joke with the nauseating Mr. Collins in *Pride and Prejudice* is not that he speaks of his debt to his patroness: that would be his duty. The joke is that to boast of *such* a patron does him no honor: her manners are appalling, her intelligence minimal, and she lacks either justice or compassion. Moreover, the things about her of which he boasts— such as the architecture of her house, and its cost—are not examples of benevolence at all, but of self-indulgence. This is not, of course, to suggest that notions of patronage had undergone no development since the classical period: see again Lytle, "Friendship and Patronage." Nevertheless, the degree of continuity is manifest and remarkable. For all the generations that separated them from her, Paul's contemporaries would have understood Jane Austen's joke.

50. On honor and shame, see additional note E. Of course, while it was the duty of the client to be grateful for favors received, when it came to speaking of your *own* generosity, even in a "patronage" society it was possible to overdo it, as Martial wittily reminds us: see *Epigrams* 5.52.

hope to those of the future that they might surpass him. The god's [birthday] was for the world the beginning of the good news [*euangeli(ōn)*] that he brought. (in Dittenberger, *Inscriptiones* 2.458)

As Jean Rouffiac pointed out, "Doubtless this text would not have needed much adjustment for a Christian fifty years later to have been able to apply it to Christ. . . . The idea that a 'good news' began for the world with the birth of Augustus is one of the most remarkable points of contact between our inscription and the NT, because no word received the imprint of Christianity more profoundly than the word *evangel*."[51] At the basis of these connections lies the fact that the relationship of benefactors and those obligated to them was such a pervasive fact of all social life as to be the natural way to symbolize any relationship of power and dependency, whether religious or political.

In a patriarchal society, most "patronage" (the word itself indicates its origins) was naturally exercised by men, but by the first century of the Christian era it was by no means impossible for women to exercise "patronage" too. The claim still occasionally heard—that "women could not take on legal functions"—is simply mistaken. Thus, an Egyptian papyrus from 142 BC shows a woman being appointed legal *prostasis* for her son.[52] A small but significant number of women are mentioned on coins as benefactors and officials, and as receiving municipal honors. At Pompeii, a woman called Eumachia made her money by a brick manufacturing business. She provided cash for a major building, which she donated to a workingman's association, and she held the title *sacerdos publica* ("priest of the people") (*CIL* 10.810–13; compare 816). Ramsay MacMullen has estimated, on the basis of a survey of rescript addresses, that possibly "a tenth of the protectors and donors that *collegia* sought out were women."[53]

Naturally, the system of patronage and clientage affected the young Christian church, too—and in two ways, perhaps, that are particularly relevant to the study of Paul's Letter to the Romans.

First, we should note that a number of recently published studies point to the leading role played in the expansion of Christianity by upper-class benefactors who gave their support within and on behalf of the Christian community (compare Luke

---

51. Jean Rouffiac, *Recherches sur les caractères du grec dans le Nouveau Testament d'après les Inscriptions de Priène* [Paris: Leroux, 1911], 73–74.

52. Published by Orsolina Montevecchi, in "Una donna 'prostatis' del figlio minorenne in un papiro del IIa," *Aegyptus* 61 (1981): 103–15: the document in question is particularly striking since it is the first witness to the term *prostatis* in Egyptian papyri, and the first anywhere "in which this term may be applied to a woman in what appears to be a legal a sense" (106); on the parallel with Rom. 16.1–2, see 106.

53. Ramsay MacMullen, "Women in Public in the Roman Empire," *Historia* 29 (1980): 211. Under Roman law, Yan Thomas sees the unifying principle as that "women were legally incapacitated not in their own right but only when it came to representing others" ("The Division of the Sexes in Roman Law," in Georges Duby and Michelle Perrot, gen. eds., *A History of Women in the West*, vol. 1, *From Ancient Goddesses to Christian Saints*, ed. Pauline Schmidt Pantel, trans. Arthur Goldhammer (Cambridge, Massachusetts: Belknap-Harvard University Press, 1992), 88; even this, however, is open to question: see Richard A. Baumann, *Woman and Politics in Ancient Rome* (London: Routledge, 1992); also Roy Bowen Ward, "Why Unnatural? The Tradition behind Romans 1.26–27," *HTR* 90.3 (1997): 280, and literature there cited.

8.3; Acts 16.14–15; Romans 16.3–5, 23; 1 Corinthians 1.11 [?]; Phil. 4.2).[54] The patron or patroness of a church was in general someone of high social standing and considerable means, and the owner of a house sufficiently large for the church to gather in it. That Paul speaks of Phoebe as patroness (*prostatis*) "to many, and also to me" suggests just such a role for her in the church at Cenchreae. In the light of this, the tendency of translations like the RSV to render *prostasis* by "helper" (or even worse, in the NEB, by "a friend") is rightly characterized by Robert Jewett as "preposterous."[55]

Second, Bruce M. Winter has argued that early Christians were in general taught to play a part as benefactors of their societies at large, even if society slandered them and, indeed, partly as a means of countering that slander,

> so that, though they malign you as evildoers, they may see your noble works [*ergōn kalōn*] and glorify God when he comes to judge. Accept the authority of every human institution, whether of the emperor as supreme, or governors, as sent by him to punish those who do wrong and praise those who do good [*agathopoiōn*]; for it is God's will that by doing good [*agathopoiountas*] you should silence the ignorance of the foolish. (1 Peter 2.12–15)

The phrase "to do good [*to agathon poiein*]" appears linked to public benefaction and service in a number of inscriptions: thus, for example, the people of Athens are found praising a certain Menalaus, saying that "because he is a good man and does whatever good he can [*kai poiei hoti dunatai agathon*] for the people of Athens . . . it is resolved that Menalaus be considered a benefactor" (*SIG* 174).[56] Thus, it is possible that Christian obligation to public service was a part of the issue in the exhortation to "do good" at Romans 13.3 (on which see further, pages 206–207), and Erastus, referred to in Romans 16.23, may be an example of such a benefactor (see further, page 283).

Such commitment to the earthly (and pagan) *politeia* is, at first glance, surprising on the part of Christians in a society where they regarded themselves as pilgrims and sojourners whose real citizenship (*politeuma*) was in heaven. But we should understand their commitment first, as Winter has suggested,[57] in the light of the ancient prophetic injunctions to exiles who, even as they looked for future deliverance, were nevertheless told to "seek the welfare of the city where I have sent you into exile" (Jer. 29.7); and second, in connection with dominical injunctions, such as that in Matthew to "let your light so shine before others that they may see your noble works [*kala erga*], and give glory to your father in heaven" (Matt. 5.16). We may notice that in the passage from 1 Peter cited earlier it is, in fact, precisely *in*

---

54. See, for example, Wayne A. Meeks, *The First Urban Christians: The Social World of the Apostle Paul* (New Haven: Yale University Press, 1983), 51–63; Jerome Murphy-O'Connor, *St. Paul's Corinth: Texts and Archaeology*, Good News Studies 6 (Wilmington, Delaware: Glazier, 1983), 153–66.

55. Robert Jewett, "Paul, Phoebe, and the Spanish Mission," in *The Social World of Formative Christianity and Judaism: Essays in Tribute to Howard Clark Kee*, ed. Jacob Neusner, Ernest S. Frerichs, Peter Borgen, and Richard Horsley (Philadelphia: Fortress Press, 1988), 150.

56. Cited, with other material, in Bruce M. Winter, *Seek the Welfare of the City: Christians as Benefactors and Citizens*, First Century Christians in the Graeco-Roman World (Carlisle, England: Paternoster Press; Grand Rapids, Michigan: Eerdmans, 1994), 35.

57. Winter, *Seek the Welfare* 1, 18.

view of their future hope that the author exhorts believers to perform what even those who traduce them will have to recognize as "noble works." Thus nascent Christianity, like ancient Judaism before it, kept eschatological and social concerns bound together.

Third, if Paul had in mind at Romans 13.3–4 to encourage individual members of the Church who had means to act as benefactors to the city, it is possible (though not certain) that at 13.8 ("Owe no one anything") he had in mind another agenda connected with patronage—this time one in which he did *not* wish to encourage members of the Roman church: namely, the role of client. "Owe no one anything" (13.8) (compare 1 Thessalonians 4.11–12, "work with your hands, as we directed you, so that you may behave properly toward outsiders and be dependent on no one")[58] may well have a lot to do with concern for Christian public image. Being someone's client could, according to normal convention, mean days spent in idleness, flattering the whims and ego of a rich patron—an aspect of the institution that Christians were certainly not alone in criticizing (e.g., Epictetus, *Discourses* 4.1.177). Contemporary satires regularly mock the fawning activities of clients, as in the following bitter self-mockery of Martial:

> *Mentiris: credo. recitas mala carmine: laudo*
> *cantas, canto. bibis, Pontiliane: bibo*
> *pedis: dissimulo. gemma vis ludere: vincor*
> *res una est sine me quam facies: et taceo*
> You lie: I believe you. You recite bad poems: I praise them.
> You sing: I sing. You drink, Pontilianus: I drink.
> You fart, I pretend not to notice. You want to play chequers: I lose.
> There's one thing you do without me: and I'm silent [about that]. (*Epigrams* 12.40)

Paul would not, one suspects, want Christians to be open to the same kind of criticism or mockery. Therefore, believers were not to be personally obligated to benefactors. This might, on the surface, appear to contradict Paul's own acceptance of Phoebe as his patroness at 16.1–2, but the contradiction would be formal, not substantial. Evidently, such insolent patronage as the satirists mock would be something entirely different from the apostle's (and the church's) accepting the protection and assistance of committed believers directly for the work of the gospel, which appears to be what is being spoken of at 16.1–2.

Bibliographical Note

On patronage in general see John H. Elliott, "Patronage and Clientage," with bibliography, in *The Social Sciences and New Testament Interpretation*, ed. Richard Rohrbaugh (Peabody, Massachusetts: Hendrickson, 1996), 144–56; John E. Stambaugh and David L. Balch, *The New Testament in Its Social Environment* (Philadelphia: Westminster Press, 1986), 63–64; and Frederick W. Danker, *Benefactor: Epigraphic Study of a Graeco-Roman and New Testament Semantic Field* (St. Louis: Clayton, 1982). See further Paul Veyne, "The Roman Empire" in

---

58. It may be patronage/clientage of this type, rather than eschatological frenzy, that lies behind the situations addressed by 1 Thessalonians 5.14 and 2 Thessalonians 3.6–13. Compare Winter, *Seek the Welfare* 51–53.

A History of Private Life, gen. eds. Philippe Ariès and Georges Duby, ed. Paul Veyne, trans. Arthur Goldhammer (Cambridge, Massachusetts: Harvard University Press, 1987), 95–115; also *NDIEC* 4 (1987): 239–44, where G. H. R. Horsley draws attention to a number of Greek inscriptions and papyri relating to the exercise of patronage by women; on which see also Orsolina Montevecchi, "Una donna 'prostatis' del figlio minorenne in un papiro dell IIa," *Aegyptus* 61 (1981): 103–15.

On the part played by patrons and benefactors in the expansion of Christianity, see Bengst Holmberg, *Paul and Power: The Structure of Authority in the Primitive Church as Reflected in the Pauline Epistles* (Philadelphia: Fortress Press, 1978), 103–6; Wayne A. Meeks, *The First Urban Christians: The Social World of the Apostle Paul* (New Haven: Yale University Press, 1983), 51–73, 135, 137; Jerome Murphy-O'Connor, *St. Paul's Corinth: Texts and Archaeology* (Wilmington: Delaware: Glazier, 1983), 153–66; Stambaugh and Balch, *New Testament in Its Social Environment* 114–16, 140–41.

On the case for supposing that Christians were urged to play their part as benefactors of their societies, see Bruce M. Winters, *Seek the Welfare of the City: Christians as Benefactors and Citizens, First Century Christians in the Graeco-Roman World* (Carlisle, England: Paternoster Press; Grand Rapids, Michigan: Eerdmans, 1994). Winters's views, though running counter to much received wisdom about early Christian communities, are carefully argued and, in my opinion, for the most part convincingly.

The Letter to the Romans, the Jewish Scriptures, and the Law

According to Paul, his "gospel" was foretold by Scripture and accords with Scripture, and so both upholds and fulfills the Law (1.2, 3.21, 3.31, 10.4). This, as I intend to show, is argued from the beginning to the end of Romans. Before attempting that demonstration, it will be useful, however, to reflect on three preliminary questions.

What Did Paul Mean by "the Scriptures"?

Loosely, Paul meant by "the Scriptures" what Christians have come to mean when they speak of the "Old Testament."[1] These were the only Scriptures Paul had, and there is no evidence that he envisaged any others. They are, of course, *Jewish* Scriptures. In discussing Paul's handling of them in his letters, it is not, however, correct to speak of them as "Hebrew Scriptures" or "the Hebrew Bible." Paul read and wrestled with his Bible in Greek. That is not to say that he did not understand Hebrew: it is simply to point out that as far as his letters are concerned, it is the rhetoric and cadences of what is generally known as the Septuagint (that is, the Bible of Greek-speaking Judaism) in which he is soaked, and which in their turn drench his thinking, his rhetoric, and his symbolic universe. It is the rhetoric of the Septuagint, therefore, that we must consider, if we are to approach him.

The term "Septuagint" and the description here given of its sense are not, it should be noted, themselves beyond controversy. A number of scholars would prefer to refer to the (supposed) original Greek translation of any given book of the Hebrew Bible as the "Old Greek," reserving the term "Septuagint" either for the collection of transla-

---

1. Paul seems to use the singular ("Scripture" [*graphē*]) when appealing to *particular* passages: see Rom. 4.3, 9.17, 10.11, 11.2; Gal. 3.8, 3.22 (presumably referring to LXX Deut. 27.26, cited at 3.10), and 4.30. At other times—indeed, most frequently—when referring to such passages he speaks of what "is written" (*gegraptai* or *egraphē*: e.g., Rom. 1.17, 2.24, 3.4, 10, 4.17, 4.23, 8.36, 9.13, 9.33, 10.15, 11.8, 26, 12.19, 14.11, 15.3, 15.9, 15.21; 1 Cor. 1.19, etc.). He seems to use the plural ("Scriptures" [*graphai*]) when appealing to the *whole* (Rom. 1.2, 15.4; 1 Cor. 15.3, 4). Otherwise the distinction between "Scripture" and "Scriptures" appears to have no significance.

tions that eventually found its place in the great codices of the fourth and fifth centuries, or else, like the purist Jerome, for the Greek Pentateuch (*In Michaeam* 2.9 [*CC, SL*, 76.446–47]). Some would doubt whether the "Septuagint," as an accepted complete translation (with additions) of the entire Hebrew Scriptures, even existed in Paul's time. For my present purpose, I believe there are enough obvious connections between Paul's scriptural allusions and the documents that have come to form what we know as the Septuagint for the designation to be useful—granted that we remember that any particular Pauline allusion to Greek Scripture, if it varies from Septuagint texts known to us, *may* involve either Paul's own translation, or his creative interpretation, or his inaccuracy of memory, or his citation of a textual variant otherwise no longer extant.[2]

I have spoken of Paul being "soaked" and "drenched" in the rhetoric of the Septuagint, and I intend the metaphors to be forceful. I am sometimes asked whether I think it really possible that Paul had in mind, and that his hearers would have had in mind, all the subtle echoes of Scripture that I, and other exegetes, suggest in our analyses. My response is, "Yes, I do. Paul, certainly. The more attentive and better informed among his hearers, very probably." Indeed, I think it certain that we *miss* many allusions that would have been obvious to them, simply because the Septuagint does not— and in the nature of the case cannot—have the same place in our universe of significant discourse as it had in theirs. Limping lame-footed after them with our concordances and our commentaries we must, nonetheless, do the best we can. As Richard Hays has pointed out, "We will have great difficulty understanding Paul, the pious first-century Jew, unless we seek to situate his discourse appropriately in what Hollander calls the 'cave of resonant signification' that enveloped him: Scripture."[3]

Hays's citation of John Hollander, a literary critic, is a useful reminder that the phenomenon we are considering is hardly confined to biblical studies. Those who heard the opening of Lucan's *Civil War* (the poet Lucan being, be it noted, Paul's exact contemporary):

> *Bella per Emathios plus quam ciuilia campos*
> *iusque datum sceleri canimus*, . . .
> Wars worse than civil, fought through Ematha's fields,
> And justice given over to crime, we sing . . . (1.1–2)

were evidently expected to recall the opening to Virgil's *Aeneid*:

> *Arma virumque cano*, . . .
> Arms and the man I sing, . . . (1.1)

2. See, e.g., Paul Lamarche, S.J., "The Septuagint: Bible of the Earliest Christians," in *The Bible through the Ages*, dir. Charles Kannengiesser and Pamela Bright, vol. 1, *The Bible in Greek Christian Antiquity*, ed. and trans. Paul M. Blowers (based on *Bible de tous les temps*, vol. 1, *Le monde grec ancien et la Bible*, ed. Claude Mondésert) (Notre Dame, Indiana: University of Notre Dame Press, 1997), 15–33.

3. Richard B. Hays, *Echoes of Scripture in the Letters of Paul* (New Haven: Yale University Press, 1989), 21. Useful general background to this question is provided by Michael Fishbane, *Biblical Interpretaton in Ancient Israel* (Oxford: Clarendon Press, 1985); or (more briefly) "Inner Biblical Exegesis: Types and Strategies of Interpretation in Ancient Israel," in *Midrash and Literature*, ed. Geoffrey H. Hartmann and Sanford Budick (New Haven: Yale University Press, 1986), 19–37; see also James L. Kugel and Rowan A. Greer, *Early Biblical Interpretation* (Philadelphia: Westminster Press, 1986), and Jacob Neusner, *What Is Midrash?* (Philadelphia: Fortress Press, 1987).

Much of the irony in Lucan's extraordinary dismembered epic—what he referred to as his *opus immensum* ("measureless work") (1.68)—would be missed by an audience that was not familiar with what Virgil had already referred to as his *maius opus* ("greater work") (7.45).

Ronald Martin, commenting on echoes of Cato's *Origins* that appear to mark the opening chapter of Tacitus's *Agricola*, reminds us, "It must be remembered that a Roman author, writing for an educated public that shared a closely knit cultural and literary heritage, could employ reminiscences and resonances of language in the knowledge that many of his readers would be conscious of the emphasis that these overtones were intended to give."[4] Doubtless the greater part of Paul's audience were not so well educated as Tacitus's or Lucan's. In the matter we are considering, however, that is more than compensated for by the fact that the Scriptures to which Paul alluded were sacred to them, and they heard them regularly.[5]

Needless to say, the wording of Paul's quotations and allusions sits, by modern standards, somewhat loosely to his source, but here again, as Christopher D. Stanley has shown, falls within boundaries evidently considered perfectly acceptable by his contemporaries.[6] In Stanley's careful survey of a wide range of literature, both Jewish and gentile, passages cited from other authors were regularly found "either quoted verbatim or altered according to the needs of the author." Ways of adapting the text included

> omitting unnecessary or problematic materials (usually the most common approach), adding words to the text to clarify its intended meaning, substituting more appropriate expressions for words or phrases considered unclear or troublesome in some way, adjusting the grammar of the quotation to suit the linguistic requirements of the new context, and altering the word order . . . Quotations are normally introduced one at a time as needed, each with its own citation formula, but occasionally two or more . . . will be adduced *seriatim* in support of a single point. In a few

4. Ronald Martin, *Tacitus* (London: Bristol Classical Press, 1981), 16, 41; see further the note in R. M. Ogilvie and Sir Ian Richmond, eds., *Cornelii Taciti: de Vita Agricolae* (Oxford: Clarendon Press, 1967), 126, on *Agricola* 1.1.

5. A parallel from popular culture may be offered by Chariton's romantic novel *Callirhoe*, with its repeated allusions to traditions about Aphrodite and to Homer. Despite reservations of some recent critics, I believe that this work was designed for entertainment: to judge by the manuscript evidence it was remarkably popular, and it was certainly jeered at by some among the literati for being lowbrow (see Philostratus, *Letters* 66). On the other hand, entertainment (or, as our forebears would have said, "delight") was not necessarily opposed to "instruction." By constantly echoing Greek literary tradition, particularly in descriptions of his heroine, Chariton reinforces, and evidently intends to reinforce, values that were basic to him and, presumably, his readers, such as the celebration of Greek identity and history, and the affirmation of Greek culture and religion—perhaps consciously over against the ever-evident, and ever-increasing, dominance of Rome. See Douglas E. Edwards, *Religion and Power: Pagans, Jews, and Christians in the Greek Near East* (New York: Oxford University Press, 1996) (though one may not be entirely persuaded by all the details of his attempt to locate *Callirhoe* exactly in the period of Trajan–Hadrian); also Glen W. Bowerstock, *Fiction as History: Nero to Julian* (Berkeley: University of California Press, 1994).

6. Christopher D. Stanley, *Paul and the Language of Scripture: Citation Techniques in the Pauline Epistles and Contemporary Literature*, SNTSMS 74 (Cambridge: Cambridge University Press, 1992), 227–367.

instances verses have been combined back-to-back or even merged together. . . . In the great majority of cases it can be demonstrated with confidence that this adapting and combining of texts took place under the influence of the author's own literary or pastoral agenda.

Such wide-ranging consensus on such a common literary practice must, as Stanley says, be considered strong evidence for an ethos wherein "incorporating interpretative elements into the wording of a quotation was considered a normal and acceptable means of advancing one's argument."[7]

Finally, it should be borne in mind that the Greek Bible itself, like the Hebrew texts upon which it is largely based, was subject during our period to a good deal of what Shemaryahu Talmon has called "controlled freedom of textual variation." That is to say, while the scope of variations within the textual traditions is *relatively* restricted, so that "major divergencies which intrinsically affect the sense are extremely rare," still, a "limited flux of the textual transmission of the Bible appears to be a legitimate and accepted phenomenon of ancient scribal tradition and not a matter which resulted from sheer incompetence or professional laxity."[8] Hence, we can never ignore the possibility that even a unique reading in Paul, while it may be the result of his having translated the Hebrew for himself, or his creative interpretation, or his faulty memory, *may* also be the result of his having used a form of the text otherwise lost to us.

The reasons for this freedom, both in citation and in manuscript tradition, are probably to be found in the nature of manuscript culture itself. It is not merely that such a culture is still close to orality (though that is a factor) but rather that, as Stanley says, since

> no single manuscript could ever claim to have preserved the precise and unalterable wording of the original composition . . . the application of a rudimentary form of 'textual criticism' (albeit of a highly subjective nature) was a *sine qua non* for the use of any ancient manuscript, especially where a reader had been exposed to differing copies of the same work over the course of a lifetime. In other words, the physical realia of the manuscripts would have encouraged not a reverence for the wording of this or that exemplar, but rather a critical attitude toward the text of every individual manuscript.[9]

What Did Paul Mean by "the Law"?

I began this chapter by saying that according to Paul, his "gospel" was foretold by the Scriptures and accords with the Scriptures, and so both upholds and fulfills the Law (*nomos*)[10] (1.2, 3.21, 3.31, 10.4). Paul's understanding of and attitude to the

---

7. Stanley, *Paul and the Language of Scripture* 337.

8. Shemaryahu Talmon, "Textual Study of the Bible: A New Outlook," in *Qumran and the History of the Biblical Text*, ed. Frank Moore Cross and Shemaryahu Talmon (Cambridge, Massachusetts: Harvard University Press, 1975), 326.

9. Stanley, *Paul and the Language of Scripture* 355.

10. Greek *nomos* renders Hebrew *tôrâ* (EVV usually "law") in the overwhelming majority of cases in the LXX. On its appropriateness as a translation, see additional note B on Hebrew *tôrâ* and Greek *nomos*.

Law is undoubtedly somewhat complicated, and perhaps not always entirely clear to us—although not, I think, either as complicated, or as obscure, or as contradictory, as has sometimes been made out.[11] This is, again, a matter upon which I shall be touching at various points in my examination of Romans.[12] For the present, let it suffice to lay out what I see to be Paul's basic position.

While there are occasions where precisely what Paul has in mind by *nomos* is open to discussion (for example, Rom. 3.27a, 7.21, 23), it is clear that at key points he uses the word unambiguously to refer either to the totality or to a part of the revelation and commandment given by God to Moses at Sinai—the Mosaic Law. So in Galatians he speaks of the Law "which came four hundred and thirty years later" than the promise to Abraham (Gal. 3.17; compare Rom. 5.13, 20). It is also clear that possession of that Law, more than anything else, was for Paul (as for the later rabbis) what gave Israel its identity as a peculiar people, God's own possession. Thus Paul's division of the world into those who are "apart from the Law" and those who are "under the Law" (Rom.1.12) evidently corresponds to the world's division between gentiles and Jews. Gentiles, by definition, are those "who do not possess the Law" (see Rom. 2.12–17; compare 9.4, 30–31, 1 Cor. 9.19–21, Eph. 2.14–16). Israel's possession of the Law is an essential part of Israel's story, and the world's nonpossession of it is an essential part of the world's story.

At the same time—and generally in related contexts—it is also clear that there is for Paul a relationship amounting to an identity between "the Law" and "the Scriptures." He commonly uses *nomos* in reference to some part of Scripture (such as the Psalms, at Rom. 3.19). Thus he can on occasion simply quote or allude to the Scriptures, and then go on at once to say that this is what "the Law" says (Rom. 3.10–19, 7.1–3, Gal. 4.21–31; compare Gal. 3.10, citing LXX Deut. 27.26). "The Scriptures," in short, are "the Law written."

To what end? In the coming of the Messiah, God's justice, which is the only basis on which we may stand before God, has been revealed to us "apart from" Law—that is, God's justice "manifested through the faith of Jesus Christ" (3.21–22). Nevertheless, *"the Law and the prophets bear witness to it"* (Rom. 3.21; compare Gal. 3.8). The Law is God's witness, to instruct and to guide. The Law also teaches us our real situation apart from Christ, for "through the Law comes the knowledge of [our] sin" (3.20; compare 4.15, 5.13, 7.7, Gal. 3.10). This is because the Law is not only God's witness but also embodies God's command. With our knowledge of that command comes the knowledge that we do not obey it (2.17–29, 5.13, 7.7–11). It is true that Paul at one time describes himself as having been "as to righteousness under the law, 'blameless'" (Phil. 3.6)—but that is clearly his record of how he saw himself before he came to know Jesus Christ (compare Gal. 1.14). Nothing could make clearer the

---

11. E.g., E. P. Sanders, *Paul, the Law, and the Jewish People* (Philadelphia: Fortress Press, 1983), 192–99; Heikki Räisänen, *Paul and the Law* (Tubingen: Mohr [Siebeck], 1983; reprint Philadelphia: Fortress Press, 1986), 94–109; also "Paul, God, and Israel: Romans 9–11 in Recent Research," in *The Social World of Formative Christianity and Judaism*, ed. Jacob Neusner, Ernest S. Frerichs, Peter Borgen, and Richard Horsley (Philadelphia: Fortress Press, 1988), 196–206, especially 195–96.

12. See especially pages 94–100, 105–7, 133–93.

sense of irony with which Paul now views this stage of his life, and the "righteousness" to which it led, than his close linkage of it with his role as a persecutor of the church (compare Gal. 1.13.)[13]

Hence, what the Law is not and cannot be is in itself the *basis* of our standing before God (8.3; compare 7.7–25, Phil. 3.3–9). On the contrary, as Paul wrote to the Galatians, the Law was "added" to the promise to Abraham, not to place a new condition on that promise but to be our *paidagōgos* (that is, one in charge of someone who is not of age)[14] until the Messiah came—by showing us, negatively as well as positively, that the only basis of our justification before God would indeed be God's own justice and faithfulness toward us (Gal. 3.19, 23–24; compare Rom. 10.2–5). When, therefore, in writing to the Romans, Paul faced the rhetorical question, "Are we then overthrowing the Law by our talk of 'faith'"? the answer was inevitable: "By no means! Rather, we are upholding the Law!" (3.31).

It will be evident from the foregoing that I do not find it necessary to suppose, as do Hans Hübner and others,[15] that between writing Galatians and Romans Paul had what amounted to a complete change of mind about the Law, with Galatians representing an essentially negative view and Romans a more positive. Certainly I grant there are differences of emphasis in the two letters, but these are more than adequately explained by the difference of situation. There is not the slightest evidence anywhere in Paul's writing that he ever considered obedience to the Law as in itself anything but a good thing. The effort to attain that obedience is faulted, as E. P. Sanders points out, "only when it seems to threaten the exclusiveness of salvation by faith in Christ"—precisely, of course, what is at issue in Galatians.[16]

Additional Note B. Hebrew *Tôrâ* and Greek *Nomos*

The Hebrew word *tôrâ* centers around notions such as "teaching" or "instruction." Quite how the Hebrew verb *yrh* came to develop this meaning—hiphil, "to teach," whence *tôrâ*, "teaching"—is in itself a still-unsolved etymological puzzle. Wellhausen's view that it originated in the throwing (*yrh*) of lots for divine guidance is now gen-

---

13. Cranfield aptly compares Phil. 3.6 with the words of the rich young man when Jesus reminded him of the commandments: "Teacher, I have kept all these since my youth" (Mark 10.20). Such "righteousness" is evidently an illusion (Cranfield, *Romans* 2.847–48).

14. The word *paidagōgos* has no modern English equivalent. Certainly it did not mean "pedagogue" in our sense (OED2, "pedagogue," n. 2). Views of the role and what it might involve varied greatly (see, e.g., Plato, *Lysis* 208c, cf. 223a–b; Quintillian, *Institutio Oratoria* 1.1.8; Clement of Alexandria, *The Rich Man's Salvation* 9). Yet the one essential characteristic of all *paidagōgoi*—and this and this alone is surely the point of Paul's metaphor—is that (like "baby-sitters") they were put in charge of those not deemed to be of age or mature enough to be in charge of themselves (cf. *Lysis* 209a, c). In Paul's view those who have been brought to Christ have (or ought to have) "come of age." See James D. G. Dunn, *Jesus, Paul, and the Law: Studies in Mark and Galatians* (London: SPCK; Louisville, Kentucky: Westminster-John Knox Press, 1990), 250, 262 note 42, and literature there cited.

15. Hans Hübner, *Law in Paul's Thought*, J. C. G. Greig, trans. (Edinburgh: Clark, 1984).

16. E. P. Sanders, *Paul and Palestinian Judaism: A Comparison of Patterns of Religion* (London: SCM Press, 1977), 550. For further reflection on Paul's essentially positive attitude to the Law, see N. T. Wright, *The Climax of the Covenant: Christ and the Law in Pauline Theology* (Edinburgh: Clark, 1991), especially (as regards Galatians) 137–74, 214–15.

erally rejected. The currently favored view seems to be Gesenius's proposal to derive it from *yrh* in the sense of "extend the finger in order to indicate the way" (compare Prov. 6.13, Ps. 45.5, and possibly Gen. 46.28).[17]

Be that as it may, in the overwhelming majority of cases the translators of the LXX chose to render Hebrew *tôrâ* by Greek *nomos*, a word generally understood to center around notions of "usage," "custom," "law," "statute," and "ordinance."[18] Their decision has not lacked its modern critics. "It must first be stated," Solomon Schechter wrote in *Some Aspects of Rabbinic Theology*,

> that the term *Law* or *Nomos* is not a correct rendering of the Hebrew word *Torah*. The legalistic element, which might rightly be called the Law, represents only one side of the Torah. To the Jew the word *Torah* means a teaching or instruction of any kind.[19]

In agreement with Schechter, C. H. Dodd pointed out in his influential study *The Bible and the Greeks* that "the natural Greek equivalent of תּוֹרָה in the more general sense would have been something like διδαχή [teaching], διδασκαλία [instruction] . . . but such words are never used."[20] On the other hand,

> the rendering of תּוֹרָה by νόμος is thoroughly misleading, and it is to be regretted that the English versions followed the LXX (*via* the Vulgate) in so many cases. But while the translation is often misleading as a representation of the original meaning, it is most instructive in its bearing upon Hellenistic Judaism. It is clear that for the Jews of Egypt in the Hellenistic period the developed meaning of תּוֹרָה as a code of religious observance, a "law" for a religious community, was the normal and regulative meaning, and they made this meaning cover the whole use of the word in the Old Testament. Thus the prophetic type of religion was obscured, and the Biblical revelation was conceived in a hard, legalistic way.[21]

Since Paul followed the LXX usage, more than one critic has seen elements of his theology as a direct consequence of this misunderstanding, and has portrayed him either as an unwitting victim of the LXX's mistake and the consequent mistakes of Hellenistic Judaism,[22] or as himself a culpable troublemaker.[23]

The LXX translators were, however, a good deal closer to the world of the Hebrew Bible and ancient Judaism than we are, and in making judgments about the quality of their work we should exercise caution. Schechter's and Dodd's view of

---

17. See G. Liedke and C. Petersen, "תּוֹרָה *Tôrâ*: instruction," in *TDOT* 3.1415, and literature there cited.

18. LS νόμος. For Wellhausen's view, see, e.g., BDB, תּוֹרָה יָרָה; W. Gutbrod, "νόμος," B 7, in *TDNT* 4.1044–46.

19. Solomon Schechter, *Some Aspects of Rabbinic Theology* (New York: Macmillan, 1909), 117; see the whole section, 116–26.

20. C. H. Dodd, *The Bible and the Greeks* (London: Hodder and Stoughton, 1935), 32; see the whole section, 25–41.

21. Dodd, *The Bible and the Greeks* 33–34.

22. So Hans Joachim Schoeps, *Paul*, Harold Knight, trans. (Philadelphia: Westminster Press, 1961), 29, 213.

23. Pinchas Lapide, in Pinchas Lapide and P. Stuhlemacher, *Paul: Rabbi and Apostle* (Minneapolis: Augsburg Press, 1984), 39.

nomos is itself open to criticism. Thus Stephen Westhold[24] has argued that there are numerous contexts in the Hebrew Scriptures where the Hebrew *tôrâ* is, in fact, most adequately rendered by *nomos* or "Law" rather than "teaching" (for example, Gen. 26.5; Exod. 12.49, 16.28, 26.46; Isa. 24.5; Jer. 32.23; Ps. 105.45), and that these contexts include the Deuteronomist's usage (Deut. 4.8, 30.10, 32.46; Josh. 1.7, 24.26; 1 Kings 2.3; 2 Kings 17.13).[25] "That the scope of 'the *torah* of Moses' was later extended, becoming a title for the whole of the Pentateuch, is," he suggests, "a natural development; and, naturally, the Greek followed suit and spoke of the Pentateuch as *ho nomos*." But "it is not clear why Hellenistic Judaism should be more legalistic for that reason."[26]

Adele Reinhartz[27] has explored the meaning of *nomos* in Philo's *Exposition of the Law*. Here, she argues, "the purely legal aspect is subordinated to the instructional aspect." From this, she concludes, "contrary to Schoeps, the mere use of *nomos* to translate *torah* does not in itself point to an accidental or deliberate misrepresentation of *torah* on the part of Hellenistic Jewish writers, and quite possibly did not even lead to misunderstanding of *torah* on the part of their Hellenistic Jewish readers."[28]

We need always to bear in mind that neither etymology nor previous usage are in themselves secure guides to the meaning of words in any language. Words take their meanings—and frequently take new meanings—from the contexts in which they are used. It is perfectly clear—and to do them justice, neither Schechter or Dodd was unaware of this fact or attempted to ignore it—that the biblical, Mosaic *tôrâ*, taken as a whole, partakes by its nature *both* of instruction and guidance, *and* of command.[29] Once a single word was used to cover that whole *tôrâ*—whether it was the word *tôrâ* itself, or *nomos*, or English "Law"—the word so used had in fact *become* a word meaning both "instruction and guidance" and "command," and the thoughtful (and we may surely grant Paul that) will have been aware of that. Regardless of whatever other associations *nomos* may have had for Paul, it is clear, as we have seen, that the *nomos* of Israel did, in his view, involve elements both of guidance and teaching (Rom. 3.21, Gal. 3.8), and of command (Rom. 2.17–29, 5.13, 7.7–11). All other considerations are, in fact, irrelevant.

For what it is worth we may note, however, at least two other factors that may have influenced the LXX translators in their choice of *nomos*:

1. *Nomos* was a term originally rooted in divine sanctions, and retained something of that sense. As Hermann Kleinknecht pointed out, "Even the written Law of the νόμος is still an expression of the will of the deity which holds sway over the city (Aristotle, *Politics* 3.16. 1287a, 28ff., cf. Plato, *Laws* 4.712b). This rootage in

---

24. Stephen Westerholm, "Torah, Nomos, and Law: A Question of 'Meaning,'" *SR* 15 (1986): 327–36.
25. Westerholm, "Torah, Nomos, and Law" 333–35.
26. Westerholm, "Torah, Nomos, and Law" 335.
27. Adele Reinhartz, "The Meaning of Nomos in Philo's Exposition of the Law," *SR* 15 (1986): 337–45.
28. Reinhartz, "Meaning of Nomos in Philo" 345.
29. See Walter Breuggemann, *Theology of the Old Testament: Testimony, Dispute, Advocacy* (Minneapolis: Fortress Press, 1997), 580, 581–82.

the divine sphere, which always persists, gives to the Greek νόμος concept its characteristic value and its true strength";[30] it also, presumably, made it a peculiarly appropriate word with which to speak of the *tôrâ* of the God of Israel.

2. We gain at times an impression from the work of Dodd in particular that he was to some extent embarrassed by the very notion of Law—as if it were in itself something to be avoided in a truly "religious" experience. His talk of "law" for a religious community slipped perhaps just a little too easily into talk of "hard" legalism, naturally the opposite of truly "prophetic" religion. By contrast, as Paul Lamarche points out, "before excesses and abuses were recognized, law was originally for ancient civilizations a marvelous discovery, guaranteeing harmony and peace in human relations."[31] At the time of the Septuagint, therefore, *nomos*, law, might well have been seen as encapsulating a *vital* element of the Hebrew concept of *tôrâ*—indeed, an aspect of the "teaching" that was characteristic of the covenant relationship between God and God's people.

How Did Paul Interpret the Scriptures?

There are those among modern critics who would accuse Paul and his contemporaries of attempting to do little more than seize upon texts that seemed to fit what they wanted to say and press them into service, regardless of their context or original significance.[32] Certainly this is to misunderstand them. Of course, neither Paul nor his contemporaries used or conceived of the principles of what we call historical criticism. But to suggest, therefore, that they did not exercise rational thought upon the texts and traditions they examined, or approach them with critical intelligence, is false. Critical intelligence can work on a text in many ways, as the Qumran commentaries, the rabbinic interpretative principles (for example, *t. Sanh.* 7.11), and the careful discussions in Tyconius's *Book of Rules* all make clear—not to mention the interpretative and evaluative principles that had long been articulated by Greek and Roman rhetoricians and grammarians.[33]

What is the greatest single difference between the way in which the ancients received traditions about the past and our post-Enlightenment way of receiving them? Perhaps it lies precisely in our concern to ask that question: for that, in fact, is exactly what the ancients did *not* do. They, on the contrary, in general assumed that their texts and traditions were by and about people who were much the same as themselves.

30. Hermann Kleinknecht, "νόμος," A 2, in *TDNT* 4.1025.

31. Lamarche, "The Septuagint" 26.

32. Some of the points to be made here about early exegesis were, incidentally, also made in my article "The Preachers and the Critics: Thoughts on Historical Criticism," *ATR* 74.1 (1992): 37–53.

33. How far the rabbinic interpretative principles and those of the Greco-Roman literary critics should be seen as distinct is not entirely clear. While no one (I imagine) would question the independence of spirit that breathes through the substance of the rabbinic handling of Scripture, a case can be made that formally and terminologically it was influenced by the Greco-Roman rhetoricians and grammarians. See further David Daube, "Rabbinic Methods of Interpretation and Hellenistic Rhetoric," *HUCA* 22 (1949): 259–65; "Alexandrian Methods of Interpretation and the Rabbis," in *Festschrift H. Lewald* (Basel: Helbing and Lichtenholm, 1953), 27–44. For a different view, see Saul Liebermann, *Hellenism in Jewish Palestine* (New York: Jewish Theological Seminary, 1962), 56–68.

The point was powerfully made over sixty years ago by the great Homer scholar Milman Parry in an essay on "The Historical Method in Literary Criticism."[34]

> When one trained in this method, while still staying in the past, turns his eyes back to his own time, he cannot prevent a certain feeling of fear—not for the fact that he has become a ghost in the past, but because of what he sees in the person of his living self. For in the past, where his ghostly self is, he finds that men do the opposite of what he has been doing: they by their literature turn the past into the present, making it the mirror for themselves, and as a result the past as it is expressed in their literature has a hold upon them which shows up the flimsiness of the hold which our past literature has upon ourselves.

Parry then illustrates this by referring to a passage from Robert Wood's *Essay on the Genius of Homer*, published in 1767.

> There is a famous passage in the twelfth book of the *Iliad* in which Sarpedon, the ally of the Trojans, calls upon his friend Glaucus to follow him to the assault on the Greek Wall: "If after escaping this war we were to become ageless and deathless, then would I not fight myself in the front ranks, nor urge you into the battle which gives men glory. But there are hazards of death beyond counting which stand above us, and which no man can escape or dodge. So let us go forward: which shall give glory to some man, or some man will give glory to us". . . .
>
> Robert Wood says that in 1762, at the end of the Seven Years' War, being then Under-Secretary of State, he was directed to wait upon the President of the Council, Lord Granville, a few days before he died, with the preliminary articles of the Treaty of Paris. "I found him so languid that I proposed postponing my business for another time; but he insisted that I should stay, saying it could not prolong his life to neglect his duty, and repeating the following passage out of Sarpedon's speech, he dwelled with particular emphasis on the third line, 'Then would I not fight myself in the front ranks', which called to his mind the distinguished part he had taken in public affairs." And then Lord Granville recited to himself in Greek the lines which I just gave you in translation.[35]

Parry's point was this: because of his training in historical method, he himself undoubtedly read those verses with an understanding that Lord Granville could never have had. Parry knew, for example, that for those who first sang and heard Sarpedon's words, they were an assertion in heroic terms of their own way of life—they offered, indeed, a sanction and an ideal for it. They saw no important distinction between Sarpedon's words and deeds and the kinds of words and deeds to which they aspired themselves. They had not the slightest interest in putting themselves into other times and surroundings, nor did they desire to learn "how things really were," but they treated the past as a mirror for themselves. Hence, its hold on them was enormously powerful. Their histories were a part of them. That is how Homer was heard for centuries and that, mutatis mutandis, was how Lord Granville was still hearing him 2,500 years later. Therefore, as Parry pointed out, Granville was in a sense closer to the

---

34. Milman Parry, "The Historical Method in Literary Criticism," in *The Making of Homeric Verse: The Collected Papers of Milman Parry*, ed. Adam Parry (New York: Oxford University Press, 1987), 408–13; reprinted from *HAB* 38 (1936): 778–82.

35. Parry, "Historical Method" 410–11 (779–80).

text as the ancients would have received it than was Parry himself, for all Parry's scholarship—*and partly because of it.*

Parry goes on to make some very interesting points about the limitations and problems of the historical-critical method for our appreciation of ancient texts, but those are not my concern here.[36] My concern here is that Parry put his finger on precisely the way in which the ancients in general—and hence Paul in particular—received and understood texts and traditions about the past. It is not, as we have said, that they did not exercise critical reason upon them. It is certainly not that they were all literalists: Saint Augustine, for example, was quite well aware that not all scriptural accounts could be taken literally (see *The Literal Meaning of Genesis* 4.1–2, 8–9).[37] It is not that they did not think that some narratives were true and others false, or that they would not have thought it important to tell even a true story *right*: it is, as we shall see, precisely the concern to tell Israel's story right (according, of course, to Paul's view of it) that is one of the driving forces behind the Letter to the Romans. But it *is* true that in general ancient readers and critics did not regard the past as essentially different from the present.[38] Hence the attitude of many ancient historians to their task: history, as well as being entertaining and true, was useful because it taught moral lessons:

> The statesman must read the historians attentively because . . . it is most essential that the statesman, the man who chooses to conduct public affairs, should be acquainted with measures and successes and failures, which happen not only in accordance with reasonable expectation, but also at times contrary thereto, to both men and states . . . [I]t is the man with the widest knowledge of what has happened to others who will best carry out his own undertakings, and, as far as is possible, safely, who will not be unduly elated in the hour of success, while every reverse he will bear nobly because of the fact that even in his successes he was never unaware of the possibility of a change to the opposite fortune. (Dio Chrysostom, *Discourses* 18.9, trans. J. W. Cohoon)[39]

36. Parry's comments finally relate, of course, to the *limitations* of the historical-critical method, not to the method itself; and views such as his, as well as elements of other twentieth-century critique, lie behind the very brief rationale of my own work given in the prologue. If I chose a single work to place directly alongside Parry's essay it would not, however, be anything from formal criticism or philosophy, but a work of fiction: Charles Williams's extraordinary novel *The Place of the Lion* (London: Faber and Faber, 1931) remains the most powerful statement known to me of the dangerous illusion involved in attempting to treat the past *merely* as the past.

37. So, incidentally, were Thomas Aquinas (see *Summa Theologica* 1.70.1, reply to objection 2) and John Calvin (*Commentary on Genesis* 1.16). Literalism seems, in fact, like the historical-critical method itself, to be a phenomenon of the Enlightenment, unknown (and perhaps impossible) before the dominance of print technology.

38. All this has, incidentally, an important bearing on our use of the ancient critics of Paul himself—notably the church fathers. Because they were not, in general, interested in asking the same questions that we want to ask, their interpretative work is of limited value for us. Nonetheless, the Greek fathers in particular were studying documents written in their own language and still representing, more or less, their own culture; we need therefore always to take seriously their insights as to language and rhetoric.

39. For similar sentiments see also Thucydides, *History of the Peleponnesian War* 1.22.3–4. This view of history came to be virtually dominant among Roman historians. See Arnaldo Momigliano, *Studies in Historiography* (London: Weidenfeld and Nicolson, 1966), especially 211–20 on Greek historiography; also *Latin Historians*, ed. T. A. Dorey (New York: Basic, 1966), especially F. W. Walbank, "Polybius" (39–63), and P. G. Walsh, "Livy" (115–42).

But speaking generally, the main lesson to be learned from this history by any who care to peruse it is that those who conform to the will of God, and do not venture to transgress laws that have been excellently laid down, prosper in all things beyond belief, and for their reward are offered by God felicity; whereas, in proportion as they depart from the strict observance of these laws, things else practicable become impracticable, and whatever imaginary good thing they strive to do ends in irretrievable disasters. (Josephus, *Jewish Antiquities* 1.14, trans. H. St. J. Thackeray)[40]

Mutatis mutandis, precisely the same is true of a sacred text. As Rowan A. Greer has noted, "Pagan, Jew and Christian were united in assuming the general correlation of sacred texts with the beliefs and practices of religious communities. Scripture represented the authority for those beliefs and practices, but at the same time the religious convictions of the community unveiled the true meaning of Scripture."[41] In other words, the sacred text offers one a sanction and an ideal for one's own belief, one's own hope, one's own way of life. The difference, therefore, between what we would now call "Christian" interpretation of the Bible (and hence of the Law) and other interpretations (such as that of the Pharisees or Qumran)—the difference, if we will, between various forms of "oral *tôrâ*"[42]—was not a difference of opinion about the nature of sacred texts, or about the particular methods that might be appropriate for dealing with them, or about the function of biblical interpretations, but purely about the particular thrust of the interpretation in question. *The particular thrust of Christian interpretation was that it understood the Bible and the written Law—and thereby, Israel's story—in its Christian (and in what therefore, according to Christians, had to be its true) sense.*[43] *At the same time, the Bible's authority was taken for granted, not only in*

---

40. Josephus, it should be said, is faithful to this program throughout his entire opus, notably in his consideration of the destruction of the Temple. His answer to the question "How could a faithful God have let this happen?" is clear: the destruction of Solomon's temple and the destruction of Herod's are parallel. As God once used Nebuchadnezzar to punish the sins of Israel, so now God has used Vespasian and Titus—a parallel Josephus is prepared to take so far as to assert that the dates of the two burnings corresponded (*Jewish War* 6.250, 267), and even to compare himself, implicitly, to Jeremiah (5.391–94).

41. James L. Kugel and Rowan A. Greer, *Early Biblical Interpretation* (Philadelphia: Westminster Press, 1986), 126.

42. From Paul's point of view the comparison of his work to other types of "oral *tôrâ* (*tôrâ še-bĕ-'al-peh*)" (cf. Josephus, *Ant.* 13.297) is not inapt. From the point of view of later Christianity it was to break down, in that the letters of Paul themselves were to become for those who accepted them "Scripture"—authoritative texts requiring interpretation, alongside (but not replacing) the Scriptures that they had originally interpreted.

43. This concern with the "true sense" of the Scripture leads Boaz Cohen and Ira J. Olivet Jr. (from very different points of view) to see in Romans the deliberate use of a Greco-Roman argumentative strategy based on distinguishing "the letter" from "the intent" of a law: thus Cicero, who observes that if a dispute is perceived "to turn on written documents," then there are "five forms" that it can take, one of which is "that there is a variance between the actual words and the intent of the author . . . [Such a dispute] is said to be concerned with the letter and the intent (*de scripto et de sententia*)" (*On Invention* 1.13, trans. H. M. Hubbell) (see Cohen, *Jewish and Roman Law: A Comparative Study* [New York: Jewish Theological Seminary of America, 1966], 1.31–64; Jolivet, "An Argument from the Letter and Intent of the Law as the Primary Argumentative Strategy in Romans," in *The Rhetorical Analysis of Scripture: Essays from the 1995 London Conference*, ed. Stanley E. Porter and Thomas H. Olbricht, JSNTSS 146 [Sheffield, England: Sheffield Academic Press, 1997], 309–34). Bearing in mind antiquity's general attitude to and use of texts regarded as authoritative (not only Jewish *midrash*, but also pagan interpretations of Homer), I am not convinced that such a precise hypothesis is necessary, or even likely, for Paul's use of Scripture in Romans (or elsewhere).

the fact that it was constantly referred to but more importantly in that its categories were used to interpret Christ and the significance of Christ—his life, death, and resurrection. [44]

So it is for Paul. The Scriptures tell the story of Israel. That story, in Paul's view, constantly prefigures the church of Paul's own day, and the church is supposed to learn from it. "Now these things happened to them as a warning, but they were written down for our instruction . . . " (1 Cor. 10.11; compare 6).[45] Nothing could illustrate more plainly than 1 Corinthians 10.1–13 the ancient assumption that the past was a mirror for the present. For Paul and his readers alike, that assumption is a commonplace, a datum. It is clear that Paul knows that much of what he writes to the Corinthians will be controversial for his hearers: it is equally clear that he sees absolutely nothing controversial about this. So—"whatever was written in former days was written for our instruction, that by steadfastness, and by the encouragement of the Scriptures, we might have hope" (Rom. 15.4; compare 4.23–24). Paul is therefore concerned to draw a picture of the church that is in essential continuity with the story of the ancient People of God and fulfills God's purpose for this people. When Paul speaks of the "good news" being "according to the Scripture," what he is saying is above all *that it accords with and continues the story (the story told right!) of God's dealing with Israel—the story of God's call, and God's promise, the story of Adam, Abraham, the call of Moses, the Exodus, the giving of the Law, David, the prophets, and the exile.* This is generally the basis of Paul's approach to the Bible, and it is in particular the basis of his approach in the Letter to the Romans.

44. See further N. T. Wright, *Christian Origins and the Question of God*, vol. 1, *The New Testament and the People of God* (London: SPCK, 1993, 2nd ed.), 378–417; also Jacques Guillet, S.J., "The Role of the Bible in the Birth of the Church," in *The Bible through the Ages*, dir. Charles Kannengiesser and Pamela Bright, vol. 1, *The Bible in Greek Christian Antiquity*, ed. and trans. Paul M. Blowers (based on *Bible de tous les temps*, vol. 1, *Le monde grec ancien et la Bible*, ed. C. Mondésert) (Notre Dame, Indiana: University of Notre Dame Press, 1997), 34–48; Ellen Bradshaw Aitken, "τά δρώμενα καί τά λεγόμενα: The Eucharistic Memory of Jesus' Words in First Corinthians," *HTR* 90.4 (1997): 359–70.

45. Compare, then, not surprisingly, 1 Cor. 9.10; also 2 Tim. 3.16.

PART II

LISTENING TO ROMANS

3

The Epistolary Opening (1.1–15)

Paul comes before the believers at Rome as **slave of the Messiah, Jesus** (1.1). (Throughout what follows, the use of **boldface** type in the main text [not footnotes] is intended to indicate a quotation from the part of Romans under discussion. *Italic boldface* indicates that Paul is citing or alluding to the LXX.) For those attuned to the Scriptures, the word **slave** at once ties Paul to the Jewish and scriptural tradition of those who belong to God (compare LXX Judg. 2.8, 4 Kingd. 18.12, Jer. 7.25, Isa. 49.3).[1] The notion of being "slave of the god" (though not common) is also occasionally found in pagan contexts. Lucius Apuleius, after his deliverance by the grace of Isis, rejoices that he has begun to be "slave to the goddess" and is in his turn exhorted to accept willingly "the yoke of service" (*Metamorphoses* 11.15).

Still it is striking that slavery is the metaphor with which Paul chose to present himself to believers at the heart of the empire. He might have chosen "citizenship"—citizenship of heaven—as he did on another occasion (Phil. 3.20), but on this occasion he chose slavery (compare Phil. 1.1; Gal. 1.10, 6.17). Why?

The essence of slavery was *ownership*. Slavery, according to the jurist Florentinus, was "an institution of the *ius gentium* whereby someone is subject to the *dominium* of another" (*Digest* 1. 5.4.1). Certainly we must not romanticize slavery, and certainly the ancients did not. Jew and gentile alike regularly agreed that to be a slave was the worst life imaginable. But that did not alter the fact that some slaves actually found the system working to their advantage. A slave or freedman of the emperor would

---

1. In all these cases the LXX uses *doulos* to render Hebrew '*ebed*—a term designating essentially a relationship of subservience to another, which can be anything from "slave" (e.g., Exod. 21.2, 32) to "[paid] worker" (e.g., Job 7.2) (see further Claus Westermann, "עֶבֶד, '*ebed*, servant," in *TLOT* 2.819–32). Evidently dependent on this scriptural tradition, and quite apart from Paul, there is also, of course, a general New Testament tradition of speaking in these terms of our relation to God: see for example Matt. 6.24 and parallels, Luke 12.42–46, Rev. 1.1, 7.3, 19.5, all of which use *doulos* or its cognates. This tradition tends to be hidden in English versions, which usually translate *doulos* and its cognates by "servant" and its cognates (see, however, NAB, NRSV margin).

be no one in himself, but in certain circumstances he might give orders to a patrician and expect to be obeyed. As Dale B. Martin points out,

> though the institution of slavery was severely oppressive, some slaves were able to manipulate it to become rather powerful persons with a certain degree of informal status in society, compared, at least, to the majority of the people of the empire, who were, though free, poor and powerless. For this small but significant minority of slaves, slavery represented an avenue to influence and was therefore, remarkable as it usually sounds to modern ears, a means of social mobility.[2]

The key to security and even to a measure of (derived) authority among others was to be *in a favorable relationship with the right master or mistress*.

Hence, though slavery was usually a metaphor for drudgery, it could also be a metaphor for salvation—as it clearly was on occasion for Jew and pagan alike. Paul, then, *belongs* to Christ: "he belongs to his Lord and his Lord answers for him," as Karl Barth put it;[3] and so, Paul will stress, must all who would find wholeness. What is to be considered here is not bondage versus liberty, for at the level at which Paul intends to speak, *everyone* must belong to something or someone, and there can be no question of belonging to oneself. The operative question is, therefore, To whom or to what will you belong? So in his letter to the Galatians Paul had declared himself unconcerned by the hostility of his enemies because he bore "the marks [*stigmata*] of Jesus in my body," by which *stigmata* he presumably referred to the scars and wounds he had received in Jesus' service as in effect the tattoos or brand of a slave—Christ's slave, and therefore one who was free in respect of all others (Gal. 6.17).

Doubtless all this, like the institution of slavery itself, was much easier for the ancients to grasp and even take for granted than it is for us, since they lived in a "patronage" society where virtually *everyone's* sense of dependence on someone else at some level was constantly reinforced.[4]

The opening sections of the letter (1.18–4.25) will then be a *dissuasive*; and the dissuasive will be concerned with our willingness (or not) to acknowledge our utter dependence on the justice and grace of God—in other words, our willingness (or not) to be in bondage *to God*. The alternative to that bondage is not liberty, but bondage of another kind, bondage to the wrong thing. According to Paul, those who refuse to "honor," "serve," or "acknowledge" the Creator (1.21, 25, 28) simply find themselves worshiping and serving "the creature" (1.24, 26, 28) and hence "under the power of sin" (3.9).

So later, in the course of his *demonstration* of God's justice and grace in the life of the believer (5.1–11.36), Paul will ask his hearers: "Do you not know that if you present yourselves to anyone as obedient slaves, you are slaves to the one you obey,

---

2. Dale B. Martin, *Slavery as Salvation: The Metaphor of Slavery in Pauline Christianity* (New Haven: Yale University Press, 1990), xiii; see further, especially 1–49, 61–62; also S. S. Bartchy, *First Century Slavery and the Interpretation of 1 Corinthians 7:21*, SBLDS 11 (Missoula, Montana: Scholars Press, 1973), especially 114–120. On Greco-Roman slavery in general, see Yvon Thébert, "The Slave," in *The Romans*, ed. Andrea Giardina, trans. Lydia G. Cochrane (Chicago: University of Chicago Press, 1993), 138–74, and literature there cited.

3. Barth, *Romans* 10.

4. On patronage, see additional note A.

either of sin, which leads to death, or of obedience, which leads to righteousness?" (6.16).

Finally, in his *exhortation* he will beg them to "present" themselves as "a living sacrifice" (12.1) to God, since they, like Paul himself (and here he will come full circle), *belong* to the Messiah—"whether we live or die, we are the Lord's" (14.8). As he wrote on another occasion to the Corinthians, "Whoever was free when called is a slave of Christ. You were bought for a price!" (1 Cor. 7.22–23).

Paul, then, belongs to the **Messiah, Jesus** (*christos Iēsous*) (1.1)—that is, to Jesus, who is God's anointed. It is sometimes suggested that here and elsewhere (1.6, 8; 3.22; 5.1, 15, 17, 21; 13.14; 15.6) Paul uses *christos* ("anointed") as little more than a double name, inherited from earlier Christian tradition.[5] There is, it is claimed, no specific allusion intended to *the* anointing—that is, to messiahship. Paul was writing (the argument goes) for gentiles, and for them the notion of Jesus as "Lord" (*kurios*) was much more likely to be comprehensible than the specifically Jewish notion of Jesus as "Messiah." I am not convinced. It is perfectly clear that Paul does know what *christos* can mean, and on occasion refers to it (9.5). At Romans 1.2–4 in particular, he is about to speak of the gospel as "promised beforehand through [God's] prophets in holy Scriptures," and then to use language that *specifically* identifies "Jesus the Messiah our Lord" with one "born of David's seed according to the flesh." The notion that scarcely a breath earlier he is using the same words without any sense of these allusions appears to me extraordinarily unlikely. Ernst Käsemann says the very least that must be said: the order of the words in 1.1 ("Christ Jesus" rather than "Jesus Christ") seems likely to "recall the original Messianic significance, of which Paul is certainly aware though he does not emphasize it."[6]

Jewish hopes for the "anointed" were neither consistent nor universal. There were indeed those who spoke of the fulfillment of God's purposes and promise without any mention at all of an "anointed," such as, apparently, the authors of the *Aramaic Apocalypse*, which recently came to light among the Dead Sea Scrolls (4Q246). Those, however, who did speak of God's anointed used the symbol in many different ways, from the royal "Lord's anointed" of the *Psalms of Solomon* (for example, 17.32, 18.1.5.7), to the dual "anointed ones" of other Dead Sea Scrolls, such as the *Rule of the Congregation*, wherein the royal "anointed" is to be subordinate to the priest and the sons of Aaron (1Q28a [1QSa] 2.12–22).[7] Yet one thing may be said

5. See, for example, Krister Stendahl, "Qumran and Supersessionism—and the Road Not Taken," *PSB* 19.2 (1998): 136.

6. Käsemann, *Romans* 5.

7. The *Psalms of Solomon*, most probably presenting first-century Pharisaic tradition, offer classic witness to a royal, Davidic messianic tradition, centering on the establishment of a kingdom of peace, justice, and faithful obedience to Torah, wherein Israel would return from exile, order be restored in the land of Israel, and the gentiles would come to worship. Forms of this tradition appear to be represented among the Dead Sea Scrolls by, for example, the *Rule of War* (4Q285, fr. 5). Such traditions seem also to have played a part at the time of the Jewish War (compare Josephus, *Jewish War* 2.434, 444; 4.510, 573–75), and in the rebellion of Bar Kosiba, also known as Bar Kochba ("Son of a Star"), who styled himself "Simon, Prince of Israel." The idea of *two* "anointeds" (compare Zech. 4.11–14) appears in the Dead Sea Scrolls, and perhaps also in *The Testament of the Twelve Patriarchs* (*T. Simeon* 7.2, *T. Jud.* 21.1–5). The superiority of the priestly anointed is, of course, typical of Qumran: see Helmer Ringgren, *The Faith of Qumran* (New York: Crossroad, 1995), 167–82.

with certainty: however variously understood, the presence of an "anointed" in texts of the period always speaks in some way of the fulfillment of God's purposes and promises to Israel—and so, inevitably, it does here. And *that* is essential to Paul's purposes.

Paul is also one **called to be an apostle**—called, that is, to be the representative[8] of Christ—and therefore **set apart**, that is, consecrated, **for the good news** [*euaggelion*] **of God**. *Euaggelion* was a word that had its place in the ritual of empire: imperial decrees would speak thus of the birth of an heir to the imperial house or the accession of a new emperor.[9] Yet again, for those familiar with the Scriptures, the cognate verb *euaggelizein* was associated with "good news" of an even greater ruler:

> Get you up to a high mountain,
>   You, bringing good news to [*euaggelizomenos*] Zion!
> Lift up your voice with strength,
>   You, bringing good news to [*euaggelizomenos*] Jerusalem!
> Lift it up, do not fear.
>   I said to the cities of Judah,
> "Behold, your God!" . . .
> As a shepherd he shall feed his flock,
>   and with his arm he shall gather his lambs,
>   and he will encourage those that are with young
>   (LXX Isa. 40.9, 11; compare 52.7, 60.6, 61.1; Joel 3.5;[10] Ps. 95.2 [MT 96.2])

Though no doubt his language will have resonated with those who were familiar with the language of imperial "good news," it is the biblical "good news" that most concerns Paul here—a **good news of God**.

Of course, such good news is at one with God's promise and God's call for it was, as Paul continues, **promised beforehand through** God's **prophets in holy Scriptures** (1.2). Here, already, Paul throws down the gauntlet to any among his hearers who would see "his gospel" as undermining God's promise. On the contrary, it *is* what was promised, for it concerns God's **son**,

> **born of David's seed**
>   **according to the flesh,**
> **and designated Son of God in power**
>   **according to the Spirit of holiness**
> **by resurrection of the dead,**
> **Jesus the Messiah our Lord** (1.3–4)

Most students agree that Paul is here quoting, perhaps from a credal or liturgical source that he knew was familiar and acceptable to the Roman church. There are uncertainties as to the meaning of some of the phrases, and the extent to which Paul has added his own words of expansion and interpretation is also disputed: yet clearly, as

---

8. On "apostle," see additional note C.

9. See the decree of the Greek citizens of Asia honoring the emperor's birthday, cited in additional note A.

10. The verse corresponds in the MT; the MT does not, however, have anything corresponding to LXX Joel 3.5 *euaggelizomenoi*.

it stands, the passage says yet again that what God's people had hoped for from the seed of David is here, not as dream, but "in power."[11]

It is also clear that the mark of that hope realized was, as it had to be, **resurrection of the dead**—the plural form of **the dead** reflecting the conviction that the single resurrection of Christ that had already taken place carried within it the coming resurrection of all. As Paul reminded the Corinthians on another occasion,

> Christ has been raised from the dead, the first fruits of those who have died. For since death came through a human being, the resurrection of the dead has also come through a human being; for as in Adam all die, so also in Christ will all be made alive. (1 Cor. 15.20b–22)

This means that *already* Paul and the Roman Christians are living at the beginning of the new age, the age of God's promise, the age of **Jesus the Messiah our Lord, through whom we have received grace and apostleship** (1.4b–5a).

Grace and apostleship were what Paul **received** on the Damascus road. He received **grace** (*charis*—that is, "favor," "kindness," "gracious care")[12] inasmuch as he was forgiven, even though he had been a persecutor of the church (1 Cor. 15.8–10); and he received **apostleship**[13] inasmuch as he was commissioned **for the obedience of faith for the sake of Jesus' name among all the nations** (1.5b; compare 2 Cor. 5.18; 1 Cor. 15.9–11; Gal. 1.13–16; 1 Tim. 1.12–13; Acts 9.5–6, 13–15)—commissioned, be it noted, not just to go to God's ancient people, Israel after the flesh, but to *all* the nations, **among whom are also you,**[14] called to belong to Jesus Christ (1.6)—that is, to be Christ's "slaves," just as Paul is. It is therefore to **all God's beloved in Rome, who are called to be saints** (that is, called to be God's own, set apart and consecrated for God) (1.7a)—that Paul bids **grace and peace:**[15] the "grace" and the "peace" that overwhelmed him on the Damascus road, the grace and peace that can come to them only from **God our Father and the Lord Jesus Christ** (1.7b).

---

11. Among reasons for supposing that 1.3–4 involve allusion to a pre-Pauline formula rather than free Pauline composition are the following: (1) these verses contain the only reference in Paul's generally acknowledged letters to Jesus as "Son of David" (but compare 2 Tim. 2.8); (2) they contain the only Pauline use of the verb *horizein* ("appoint, designate, declare," BAGD, ὁρίζω, 1.b); (3) they associate Jesus' sonship with the resurrection (elsewhere only at Acts 13.33, citing LXX Ps. 2.7), but do not speak of Christ's death, which is surprising if Paul is composing freely; (4) they use the Semitic-sounding phrase "Spirit of holiness" (*pneuma hagiōsunēs*) which does not occur in the LXX and has no parallel in Paul, although it is anticipated (in Hebrew) in the MT (e.g., *rûaḥ qādēšēkā*, Ps. 51.13, *rûaḥ qādēšw*, Isa. 63.10–11 [twice] [all translated *to pneuma to hagion* in the LXX]) and the Dead Sea Scrolls (e.g., *Rule of the Community* [1QS 4.21]), and is found in Greek in *Testaments of the Twelve Patriarchs* (*T. Levi* 18.11). Such a combination of characteristics makes it possible, and even probable, that Paul is using the language of an already existing formula, although, as Cranfield points out, "hardly as certain as it is sometimes assumed to be" (*Romans* 1.57). In any case, the beginning of the formula and possible Pauline additions to it remain areas of debate.

12. On "grace," see additional note D.

13. Or perhaps, with Chrysostom, we should understand this as an example of hendiadys—"the grace of apostleship": in which case, Paul is asserting that he became an apostle through no deserving on his part, but simply through the favor of his master (compare 1 Cor. 15.9–10) (see Chrysostom, *Homilies on the Epistle to the Romans* 1. 2).

14. On the possible significance of this phrase with regard to Paul's understanding of the composition of the Roman church, see additional note OO.

15. On "grace and peace," see further, additional note D.

What does Paul mean by **faith** (*pistis*)? *Pistis* and its cognates (*pisteuein* [have faith], *pistos* [faithful]) in general usage seem to have spoken of conviction, persuasion, assent, and commitment. In relationships, they connoted qualities such as fidelity, faithfulness, and trust.[16] It is, moreover, important to note (since we have no English word that will do precisely the same) that the noun (*pistis*) and the adjective (*pistos*) could and regularly did carry *both* an objective *and* a subjective sense: that is to say, they could speak both of trust *in* someone and of trust*worthiness*, of having faith *in* someone and of keeping faith *with* someone.[17] It is only from the context that we can tell which part of the word's significance is uppermost in a speaker's mind at any given moment, and sometimes it is not clear.

For Paul, too, the word *pistis* and its cognates evidently had to do with assent and commitment, and in relation to God Paul understood by it at least the kind of trust and faithfulness that was displayed by Abraham when he "had faith" in God (LXX Gen. 15.6)—a story that he will examine at some length (4.1–24) and that was obviously important for him (compare Gal. 3.6).

Here, however, he speaks of **the obedience of faith** (1.5). Is that "the obedience that belongs to faith" (subjective genitive) or "the obedience that is marked by faith or consists of faith" (qualifying, adjectival, or explanatory genitive)? Paul does not distinguish clearly, and there is no need for us to attempt such distinction. What matters is that in Paul's understanding (whatever rumors the Romans may have heard about him) **faith** and **obedience** go together (compare 10.16–17). Faithful hope leads to faithful action. That is the hint he is dropping, and that, we may suspect, is the reason for his choice of this relatively unusual phrase;[18] otherwise, he might simply have said that he had received grace and apostleship "to bring about faith."

Paul has offered his salutation, and in doing so has already laid the foundation of his argument. But he is addressing his family, the household of God, and, therefore, as their brother, he brings them before God in prayer, thanking his **God through Jesus Messiah for all of** them (1.8). He gives thanks first for their **faith, spoken of throughout the entire world**—which is doubtless good rhetoric, for "from speaking of the person of our hearers goodwill is secured . . . if we show in what esteem they are held" (*Ad Herrenium* 1.5.7.)—and also promises that **without ceasing** he mentions them **always**

---

16. Neither the LXX nor secular Greek lacks examples of *pistis* and its cognates used in connection with religion. In the LXX, we have, notably, Genesis 15.6, Exodus 14.31, and Habakkuk 2.4. In secular Greek we might cite Plutarch, *Consolation to His Wife*, *Moralia* 612a: "since this [the hope of our departed child] is harder to disbelieve [*apistein*] than to believe [*pisteuein*], let us keep our outward conduct as the laws command" (trans. Philip H. De Lacy and Benedict Einarson), or Lucian, *Alexander the False Prophet* 38: "If any atheist or Christian or Epicurean has come to spy upon the rites, let him be off, and let those who believe [*pisteuontes*] in the God perform the mysteries, under the blessing of heaven" (trans. A. M. Harmon). Yet in neither the LXX nor secular Greek did *pistis* ever have the religious significance that it came to have in Paul and the Fourth Evangelist, and hence (through their influence, presumably) in Christianity. The word group seems, indeed, to have been most prominent in the field of rhetoric, and James L. Kinneavy may well be correct in his suggestion that it is in the political and judicial "persuasion" of the Greco-Roman world, rather than either the LXX or pagan religion, that we should see the main source for the breadth and extent of Christian usage: see Kinneavy, *Greek Rhetorical Origins of Christian Faith: An Inquiry* (New York: Oxford University Press, 1987), passim.

17. BAGD, πίστις, 1.a, 2; LS, πίστις 1.1, 2.

18. It occurs again in the concluding (deutero-Pauline) doxology: see Rom. 16.26.

in his **prayers** (1.8–10). As a good brother, he desires their presence—**longs to see them**—expecting that they and he will benefit from this exchange (1:11–12).

Perhaps, as some among the Jewish believers at Rome may have doubted Paul's faithfulness to the promises of God, so some among the gentile believers may have thought that the apostle to the gentiles would come to Rome expecting to take them over. On the contrary, Paul says, though he comes to **impart to you some spiritual gift** (*charisma*)[19] **to strengthen you**, still, what that means is that **we may be mutually strengthened by each other's faith, yours and mine** (1.11–12).

I do not want you to be unaware, brothers and sisters, **that I have often intended to come to you** (1.13a). This—**I do not want you to be unaware** (*ou thelō de humas agnoein*)—is a form Paul often uses when he wants to make something that he considers important absolutely clear (compare 11.25; also 1 Thess. 4.13, 1 Cor. 10.1, 12.1, and 2 Cor. 1.8). It is, then, with a solemn expression of "epistolary disclosure" that he now addresses his Roman audience as fellow members of the family of God, his **brothers** and sisters. There is a particular reason that he wants **some harvest** at Rome **as in the rest of the gentile world** (1.13b).[20] It is because, as the grace of God is for all, so Paul, as "apostle to the gentiles" (11.13) is **under obligation** to all, **to both Greeks and to barbarians, to both wise and to foolish** (1.14).

Both parts of Paul's expression *could* have been understood as compassing all humanity, including the Jews; and some of Paul's contemporaries would have regarded the two phrases as virtually equivalent. For Paul, in this context, they evidently declare the universality of his commitment to the gentile world. What city could better symbolize that universality than Rome, *princeps urbium?* Here, wrote Tacitus scornfully, "all things hideous and shameful from every part of the world meet and become popular" (*Annals* 15.44.4). For Tacitus, that is Rome's condemnation; for Paul, it is precisely the opportunity: **so I am also eager to preach the gospel to you who are in Rome** (1.15).

If it is indeed the case that Paul knows the Roman church to be divided and weakened by factional infighting, by claims to superiority of one group over another, then he has already undermined all such claims. The gospel by which they stand is God's, and those who are Christ's *belong* to Christ. There is implied therefore already the question that Paul will later pose explicitly to those who would create or nourish disputes: "Who are you to pass judgment on someone else's household slave [*oiketēn*]?" (14.4).[21]

Rhetorically, then, Paul's opening is by no means divorced from the rest of his argument. Granted his hope that at least some among the believers at Rome would

---

19. Paul uses the word *charisma* ("gift") several times in Romans, to refer to God's gift to us in Jesus Christ (5.15, 16, 6.23), to refer to God's special gifts to Israel (11.29), or to refer to particular endowments given by God to individual members of the Church (12.6). Here (1.11) the sense intended does not seem to be quite the same as in any of the foregoing. Rather, it seems to speak of a particular (undefined) "blessing or benefit to be bestowed on the Christians in Rome by God through Paul's presence" (Cranfield, *Romans* 1.79): compare 15.29.

20. On the possible significance of this phrase as regards Paul's understanding of the ethnic composition of the Roman church, see additional note OO.

21. Despite the usual translation "servant" (KJV, DR, RSV, NEB, NRSV, NAB), it is evident that the *oiketēs*, too, was normally a slave: see LS, οἰκέτης; BAGD, οἰκέτης.

be moved to endorse his gospel, and so to bring him on his way and support his mission in the west, then he has laid grounds for his acceptance by them. In the manner of a good speaker he has given them a chance to see something of his ethos (character), and invited them to give him and the gospel he serves a hearing.

His opening address began, and has now ended, with reference to **the gospel** for which he is **set apart** (1.1, 1.15)—and **the gospel** is the rhetorical hook by means of which he will now (1.16) move to his main argument.

Additional Note C. Apostle

Apostolos ("apostle") is cognate with the verb *apostellein* ("send, dispatch"), and in general usage had a wide variety of meanings from, occasionally, that of "ambassador, delegate, or messenger" (Herodotus, *History* 1.21; LXX 3 Kingd. 14.6), through "sending out" (Josephus, *Ant.* 17.300) and "naval expedition" (Dittenberger, *Sylloge* 305, 50), to "passport" (POxy. 1271).

The occurrence of *apostolos* in 3 Kingdoms 14.6 is an LXX *hapax*, although the verb *apostellein* is widely used in the LXX of the commissioning and authority of prophets (e.g., LXX Isa. 6.8), generally translating MT Hebrew *šlḥ*. Only this latter usage prepares us at all for the weight that the word comes to bear in the New Testament generally, and Paul in particular. According to Luke, Jesus "called his disciples, and having chosen twelve from among them, he named them apostles [*apostoloi*]" (6.13), but New Testament usage is hardly limited to the twelve. Paul speaks of "all the apostles," whom he clearly distinguishes from "the twelve" (1 Cor. 15.5, 7), and frequently, of course, as in Romans, of himself as *apostolos*, personally commissioned by Christ (1.1; compare 1 Cor. 1.1, 15.9, 2 Cor. 1.1, Gal. 1.1). Later in Romans (16.7) Paul will use the word in yet another sense, in which it was also used generally by the early church, of those who were commissioned by the church, or even by a particular church, for some task (so also Phil. 2.25; compare Acts 14.4–14, *Didache* 11.3–6).[22]

To explain this density, commentators have understandably fallen back on a connection with ideas that were later to crystallize into rabbinic concepts of the *šālîaḥ*, that is, the "authorized representative or agent"—concepts aptly summarized in the well-known rabbinic dictum, "one's agent is as oneself" (*m. Ber.* 5.5; compare Mark 9.37b; Matt. 10.40; Luke 9.48; John 5.30–36, 6.39–40, 7.16–18, 17.18). Other critics doubt the connection, in view of the lateness of sources that use the term, and the lack of missionary emphasis in the rabbis.[23]

Be that as it may, we may note at least two characteristics that Paul appears to associate with his apostolate:

22. Spicq, *Lexicon* 1.186–94.
23. In favor of the connection, see Cranfield, *Romans* 1.52–53; Fitzmyer, *Romans* 232; against the connection, see Moo, *Romans* 41–42. For a very full, balanced, and careful discussion of the whole subject, see further C. K. Barrett, "Shaliach and Apostle" in *Donum Gentilicium: New Testament Studies in Honour of David Daube*, ed. E. Bammel, C. K. Barrett, and W. D. Davies (Oxford: Clarendon Press, 1978), 88–102; also R. W. Herron Jr., "The Origins of the New Testament Apostolate," *WTJ* 45 (1983): 101–31.

1. It involves his being "set apart for the good news of God" (1.1), and is with a view to "the obedience of faith among all the nations" (1.5) (see page 62). In other words, he is "apostle to the gentiles" (11.13; compare Gal. 1.16). As such, he views his apostolate as *diakonia*, a "ministry," that is, a sacred task of one who "goes between" God and humankind as a representative, agent, or attendant.[24]

2. In 2 Corinthians Paul unburdens himself to the Corinthians at some length about the nature of the "ministry of [God's] justice" (2 Cor.3.9, compare 3.6), which is his in view of his being an "apostle of Christ Jesus" (1 Cor. 1.1, 2 Cor.1.1). He writes,

> God was reconciling the world to himself in Christ, not counting their trespasses against them, and entrusting to us the message of reconciliation. So we are ambassadors [*presbeuomen*] on behalf of Christ, as if God were appealing through us. We implore you on behalf of Christ, be reconciled to God. (2 Cor. 5.19–20)

The ambassadorial language here (particularly the word *presbeuomen*) has long been recognized, and commentators have normally associated it with the notion of the imperial legate, or else, within Judaism, with that of an envoy sent by the Sanhedrin or the High Priest to distant synagogues with authority to convey decrees and judgments.[25]

Anthony Bash, however, as the result of an examination of the epigraphic evidence,[26] suggests that Paul and his readers would have been more likely to have in mind Greco-Roman thought about the kind of embassies that were on occasion sent between one community and another to appeal for peace in a dispute—a complex of ideas that Paul linked with Hellenistic-Jewish ideas about Moses as mediator and reconciler (compare 2 Cor. 2.14–3.18).[27] The irony in Paul using such a metaphor for his work would be this: Greco-Roman embassies seeking peace were normally sent by the weaker party to the stronger (for example, Luke 14.32). They involved ritual self-abasement and humility on the part of the ambassadors, and, by implication, on the part of those who sent them, along with supplication. Therefore, in effect, Paul would have been saying that through his ministry as God's ambassador, God was being suppliant to humanity, and God was accepting self-abasement for the sake of peace.

As J. Lionel North has indicated in a short but important review, it may be possible to produce literary evidence that does not entirely bear out Bash's view of an ambassador as derived from the inscriptions—that is, the ambassador as one who represents the weaker party (North cites, for example, Philo, *Life of Moses* 1.258);[28]

---

24. On "ministry," see additional note EE.

25. For example, Victor Paul Furnish, *II Corinthians*, AB 32a (Garden City, New York: Doubleday, 1984), 339; Paul Barnett, *The Second Epistle to the Corinthians*, NICNT (Grand Rapids, Michigan: Eerdmans, 1997), 309–10.

26. Anthony Bash, *Ambassadors for Christ: An Exploration of the Language of the New Testament*, WUNT 92 (Tübingen: Mohr [Siebeck], 1997), 55–80.

27. Josephus, *Antiquities* 2.334–37, 3.315, Philo, *Moses* 2.166; see Bush, *Ambassadors for Christ* 101–3.

28. J. Lionel North, in *JTS* 49.1 (1998): 278–81, especially 280. Of course, North's examples (as he admits) themselves need examination: thus at *Life of Moses* 1.258, *does* Philo think (as North seems to imply) that it was entirely clear, from the beginning of the episode, that Moses was the stronger party addressing the weaker? Evidently Philo did not think it was clear to Sihon, since he tells how Sihon at once "went on to the attack thinking to win an immediate victory" (*Life of Moses* 1.258).

and there remain, of course, the imperial and Jewish connections of the ambassadorial concept that evidently were also current, at least in some circles, and with which, as we have observed, commentators have been accustomed to connect 2 Corinthians 5.19–20. It remains that Bash's is an interesting and challenging suggestion, and—the epigraphic evidence at least serves to make this clear—certainly represents what must have been a *possible* way of understanding Paul. It is a suggestion that does, of course, make the Pauline notion of the apostolate into something somewhat scandalous: but then, as Bash points out, that scandal is in marked conformity to the scandal of the cross as Paul describes it (compare 1 Cor. 1.21–25),[29] not to mention his description of the apostolic ministry (2 Cor. 10–13, especially 12.9–10).

Additional Note D. Grace

The basis of the meaning of *charis* ("grace") is its relationship to its cognate *chairein*—"to rejoice." *Charis*, "grace," "graciousness," or "charm," is essentially what *causes* joy: hence, it naturally becomes "grace" in the transferred sense of "favor" or "kindness." Although not a key religious or philosophical term in classical antiquity, it was already used of the "favor" or "kindness" of the gods (for example, Euripides, *Bacchae* 535), and in later antiquity it is frequently used of the "favor" of a ruler, and so frequently in inscriptions: for example, an inscription of AD 68 speaks of what is bestowed "by the grace of the god Claudius [*tou theou Klaudiou chariti*]" (Dittenberger, *Inscriptiones* 2.669 §4). In the LXX, *charis* is the usual translation of Hebrew *ḥēn*—which likewise means "grace" in the sense both of "favor" in the eyes of a superior (its chief theological sense) and "charm," or "attractiveness."[30]

In view of Paul's description of himself and others as *belonging* to Jesus Christ, it is not irrelevant to note that *charis* and its cognates (and *ḥēn*) have natural associations with the world of patronage and obligation: "favor" is invariably a gift given by the greater to the less, by the patron to the dependent. In Romans, *charis* and its cognates are key words, *charis* alone occurring no less than twenty-four times. The particular "favor" to which it refers in Romans is, of course, God's undeserved love and faithfulness toward us, revealed and effected in Jesus Christ.

In this connection, particularly striking is the way in which Paul regularly transforms the conventional epistolary greeting *chairein* into the distinctive combination *charis kai eirēnē* ("grace and peace") (Rom. 1.7, 1 Thess. 1.1, Gal. 1.3, Phil. 1.2, 1 Cor. 1.3, 2 Cor. 1.2, Philem. 3). "Peace" was commonly used in Jewish epistolary greetings (for example, LXX Dan. 4.37c), sometimes in combination with another noun (for example, "mercy and peace" [2 Bar. 78.2]); but in any case, as Cranfield says, "*charis* and *eirēnē* together well express the sum of the evangelical blessings" (*Romans* 1.72), *charis* speaking of God's gracious favor toward us in Jesus Christ, and *eirēnē* of the wholeness and harmony—particularly, here, the wholeness of our restored relationship with God—bestowed on us through that favor.[31]

29. Bash, *Ambassadors for Christ* 109–10.
30. See H. J. Stoebe, "חנן ḥnn, to be gracious," in *TLOT* 1.439–47.
31. See Spicq, *Lexicon* 3.500–506; see further Hans Conzelmann and Walther Zimmerli, "χαίρω, χαρά, συγχαίρω, χάρις, κτλ.," in *TDNT* 9.359–402.

4

The Dissuasive (1.16–4.25)

*Against Dependence on Anything save the
Justive and Mercy of God*

The Nature of the Gospel (1.16–17)

Why must Paul preach to all in Rome, barbarian or Greek? **For,** he says—the conjunction clearly linking what he will now say to what has gone before—just as a true philosopher was "not ashamed to confess poverty" (Lucian, *Nigrinus* 14),[1] so Paul is **not ashamed of the gospel** (1.16). Yet with Paul this is something more than the paradox of boldness in confessing something that others might think ridiculous or humiliating—in fact, he is very proud of the gospel (compare 1 Cor. 1.30). It is also something more than an example of that rhetorical understatement whereby, "when saying that we . . . possess some exceptional advantage, so as to avoid the impression of arrogance, we moderate and soften the expression of it" (*Ad Herrenium* 4.38). Who, according to Isaiah, will be "ashamed" in the hour when God reigns openly? *Those who have forsaken God:*

> For they shall be ashamed
>   at their idols, which they desired,
> and they shall be ashamed at their sacred gardens, on which
>   they set their hearts. (LXX Isa. 1.29)

By contrast, the faithful psalmist says,

> Then I will *not* be ashamed
>   when I observe all your commandments. (LXX Ps. 118.6 [MT 119.6])

It is shame before God's judgment, shame when God's promises are fulfilled and God's glory is seen, of which Paul speaks here—and speaks in the present tense, for in his view the promise has come (1.2). For those familiar with the Greek Bible a whole battery of texts linked the idea of "being put to shame" with unfaithfulness to the God of Israel, and at the same time declared that those who continued faithful would

---

1. The same word in a similar context occurs in Lucian's spoof of protreptic: "'Do you not blush to call yourself a parasite?' 'Not at all! I should be ashamed not to speak it out'" (*The Parasite* 2).

not be ashamed, just as their forebears had not been ashamed.[2] In a society peculiarly sensitive to questions of honor and shame (as by our standards was all ancient society, Jewish and pagan alike)[3]—where, in particular, to avoid being finally "shamed" by God might well mean to experience "dishonor" and "shame" in the world now (Mark 13.13, compare 8.38; Acts 5.41; 2 Tim. 1.8; also Sophocles, *Antigone* 72, 77, 97, 450–70)—such vocabulary will have been peculiarly noticeable. It is in this context that the force of Paul's claim becomes apparent.

Paul is not "ashamed" of the gospel, first, because **it is God's power for salvation.** "It's like this," Koko says to the Mikado: "When your Majesty says, 'Let a thing be done,' it's as good as done—practically, it *is* done—because your majesty's will is law."[4] The ancients would doubtless have taken W. S. Gilbert's words more seriously then he did. When Caesar declared this one raised to the senatorial class, and that one condemned to exile, the word was the act. Those named *were* what they were declared to be. Yet even the emperor was only a man, whereas the word of the gospel is God's. So Paul does not say that the gospel is *about* God's saving power, it *is* God's saving power.

> For as rain or snow comes down from heaven and does not return
> until it drenches the earth,
> and makes it bring forth and bud, and it gives seed to the sower
> and bread for eating,
> thus shall be my word that goes forth from my mouth,
> it shall not return until it completes what I will. (LXX Isa. 55.10–11)

> By the word of the Lord the heavens were established,
> and by the breath of his mouth all their power. (LXX Ps. 32.6 [MT 33.6])

> And God said . . . and it was so. (LXX Gen. 1.6, 9)

The gospel is God's power **to salvation** (1.16). What does Paul mean by "salvation" (*sōtēria*)? *Sōtēria* in general (together with its cognates, *sōzō* [save], *sōtēr* [savior], and *sōtērios* [saving, salutary]) has to do with "deliverance from whatever oppresses" or "preservation."[5] More precisely, for one who wrote in the Jewish tradition, "salvation" meant deliverance and preservation by God, and in the last analysis *that* meant the restoration of Israel and the healing of creation. This is the essence of Jewish hope and Jewish promise in every type of early Judaism known to us, from Genesis to Qumran.[6]

To whom does this salvation come? According to Paul, **to everyone who has faith,** or (as the NAB has it) "who believes" (compare KJV). Those, incidentally,

---

2. Compare, for example, LXX Isa. 1.29, 28.16 (to which Paul will appeal in Rom. 9.33), 50.7–8 (presumably in mind at Rom. 8.31–39), 53.4; LXX Jer. 2.36, 9.9, LXX Ps. 24.2, 20 (MT 25.2, 20), 34.6 (MT 34.6); also LXX Ps. 21.6 (MT 22.6). One might also point to LXX Psalm 43.10: "thou hast put us to shame"—where the Psalmist is evidently frustrated because the scheme does not appear to be working: "[W]e have *not* forgotten thee, and we have *not* been unfaithful to thy covenant" (LXX Ps. 44.18). Paul will quote this Psalm also in the same passage where he appears to echo Isa. 50.7–8.

3. On "honor" and "shame," see additional note E.

4. W. S. Gilbert, *The Mikado: or The Town of Titipu*, act 2.

5. On "salvation," see additional note F.

6. On the salvation of Israel and the healing of the Creation, see additional note G.

who read the Bible only in English have been and surely still are exposed to massive possibilities for misunderstanding and confusion by the persistent habit of rendering Greek *pistis* and its cognates into English by *various* English words at different points throughout the text: "faith" or "faithfulness," "belief," and "trust," together with *their* cognates, according to the preference of the translator.

The initiative in salvation is God's, and **faith** (*pistis*) is the response God seeks. For Paul, as we have noted,[7] **faith** and its cognates had to do with commitment, trust, and faithfulness. Doubtless Anders Nygren and others have been right to point out that such "faith" is itself God's gift, since freedom to have it arises only through an encounter with God's grace,[8] but that is hardly Paul's point here. Paul's point here is that faith, faithfulness and trust such as Abraham's—*in God alone* and therefore not, by implication, in something else such as circumcision or Jewish privilege—that kind of faith is the sign that God's power to save is at work in the human heart.

This gift is **to the Jew first, and also to the Greek**. God's grace is for all, but the honor of priority remains a Jewish honor, for those whom God has called are neither forsaken nor forgotten. Later, Paul will say more of this privilege, of its glory and its limitations (9.1–11.36; compare 4.1–25); for the moment, he is simply laying down basic positions: the gift is to the Jew first, and also to the Greek.

Paul is not "ashamed" of the gospel, second, because **in it God's justice** [*dikaiosunē*: RSV "righteousness"][9] **is being revealed** (1.17). What is **justice**? Greek *dikaiosunē*—and, incidentally, the Hebrew *ṣedeq* and *ṣĕdāqâ* that it commonly translates in the LXX—is essentially a communal and forensic word. It has to do with covenant, with the fulfillment of obligation, with responsibility to others, with right behavior toward all (whether human or divine) with whom we are in a relationship—in a word, with much of what we mean by "loyalty." Thus Plutarch has his brother Lamprias place *dikaiosunē* with *philia* (friendship) among the "social virtues," and notes that even God's justice can only be manifested in relationship with others, since "justice, favor, and goodness have no function in relation to oneself or to a part of oneself, but only in relation to others" (*Oracles in Decline*, *Moralia* 423d, Donald Russell, trans.). The Jewish texts reflect a similar understanding. Josephus says of the High Priest Simon that he was "surnamed the Just [*ho dikaios*] because of his piety toward God and his benevolence toward his countrymen" (*Ant.* 12.43). The LXX consistently shows God's justice manifesting itself in *faithfulness*—in particular,

---

7. See page 62, and footnotes 16 and 17.

8. "It is the gospel which is primary, which creates faith and awakens it in us. When one hears the gospel and is conquered by it, that is faith" (Anders Nygren, *Commentary on Romans* [Philadelphia: Muhlenberg Press, 1949], 78).

9. On my decision to translate *dikaiosunē* by English "justice," rather than "righteousness," see additional note H. On the meaning of *dikaiosunē* and its cognates, see further Spicq, *Lexicon*, 1.318–47; also Gottfried Quell and Gottlob Schrenk, "δίκη, δίκαιος, δικαιοσύνη, δικαιόω κτλ.," in *TDNT* 2.174–225; on the Hebrew background, see K. Koch, "צדק, *ṣdq*, to be communally faithful, beneficial," in *TLOT* 2.1046–62; note also Walter Brueggemann, *Theology of the Old Testament* (Minneapolis: Fortress Press, 1997), 130–35. For a very full discussion of Paul's use, see J. A. Ziesler, *The Meaning of Righteousness in Paul: A Linguistic and Theological Inquiry*, SNTSMS 20 (Cambridge: Cambridge University Press, 1972). On Zeisler's possible overemphasis in distinguishing Paul's use of the verb from his use of the noun and the adjective, see N. M. Watson's important review of Ziesler in *NTS* 20 (1974): 217–28.

faithfulness toward Israel, both in giving her "*just* commands" (*dikaiōmata*) (LXX Deut. 4.8), and in vindicating her cause, God being therefore both just (*dikaios*) and a savior (*sōtēr*) (LXX Isa. 45.21 compare Rom. 3.26)—acting, in other words, as Israel's faithful benefactor. In an honor-shame society[10] such faithfulness is, needless to say, bound up also with personal honor, and the distinction between *iustitia salutifera* and action for the vindication of one's name would not, perhaps, be readily apparent.

It will surely therefore have seemed natural to Paul's hearers that the quality of justice in God should be manifested **from faith to faith** (*ek pisteōs eis pistin*) (1.17b), for where else should "justice"—right behavior in relationships—show itself if not in "faith"—faithfulness and trust? So much we may say fairly simply; and at this point in the letter, perhaps, that was all that Paul wanted his audience to hear. Certainly, if at this point we try to pin him down more precisely, matters become complicated. What did he mean by "from faith to faith"? Was he saying that God's justice "starts from faith and ends in faith," as the New English Bible suggests? Or that it "is based on faith and addressed to faith" as the margin suggests? Did he mean "from the faith of the Law to the faith of the Gospel," as Tertullian claimed (*Against Marcion* 5.13)? Or "from the faith of the preachers to the faith of the hearers," as Augustine suggested (*On the Spirit and the Letter* 11.18)? Or was he saying that "Unto faith is revealed that which God reveals from his faithfulness," as Barth thought (*Romans* 41)? It is not clear.

Paul goes on to illustrate his words by a quotation from the prophet Habakkuk: **as it is written, "the just shall live by faith"** [*ek pisteōs*][11] (1.17c, citing LXX Hab. 2.4). This particular verse seems to have been regarded as important by several among those who interpreted Israel's traditions,[12] and in view of its original setting in the prophet—it forms the climax to a passionate reflection on the delay of God's eschatological justice (Hab. 1.1–2.5)—to quote it here in connection with the manifestation of that justice was certainly appropriate.

But again, there are problems—does Paul mean us to understand that the just will live on the basis of *their* faithfulness, as the Hebrew text apparently[13] says (see

---

10. On "honor" and "shame," see additional note E.

11. This (as opposed to something like "The one who is just by faith shall live") is the most obvious way of translating the Greek of 1.17b, as well as being closer than its alternative to the Hebrew original. It is therefore preferred by most of the major translations (KJV, DR, RV, NRSV, BJ, BEP), and I think rightly (but contrast RSV, NEB). Arguments for the alternative translation tend to suggest that it fits better with Paul's theology; but we do well to base our understanding of Paul's theology on what he seems to say, rather than straining what he seems to say on the basis of what we conceive to be his theology. In any case, as will be evident from what I have said above, there is no particular problem in reconciling the obvious translation of this passage with the argument of the rest of the letter.

12. Besides being cited by Paul himself here and at Gal. 3.11, it is also cited by the author of Hebrews at Heb. 10.38, and in the *Habakkuk Pesher* (1QpHab. 8.1–3) (where it is understood, incidentally, in a sense about as remote from Paul's as could be imagined: "Interpreted, this concerns all those who observe the Law in the House of Judah, whom God will deliver from the House of Judgment because of their suffering [or, possibly, work], and because of their faith in the Teacher of Righteousness" [trans. Geza Vermes]), and later at *b.Mak.* 24a (at the climax of a discussion of the Law, where its [implied] interpretation appears quite close to Paul's).

13. So the recent English versions: see NRSV, NAB. It is interesting to note, however, that in a closely (and in my view, convincingly) argued essay published in 1980, J. Gerald Janzen suggested that the intended antecedent of the third-person masculine pronoun suffix attached to the word '*ĕmûnâ*

MT Hab. 2.4b)? Or does he mean that the just will live on the basis of *God's* faithfulness, as the Septuagint seems to have said (see LXX Hab. 2.4b)?[14] Unfortunately, this also is not clear, for while Paul has broadly quoted the Septuagint, he has omitted the crucial word "my" (*mou*) that qualifies "faith," and so has provided us with a text that could be understood in either sense.

"There's a double meaning in that!" cries Shakespeare's Benedick in response to Beatrice's avowal that she did not wish to call him to dinner, and our best response to this Pauline ambiguity would be the same (*Much Ado About Nothing* 2.3). The ancients, even as late as the seventeenth century, were not only untroubled by ambiguity, they looked for it and relished it when they found it (see "Demetrius," *On Style* 99–101). Indeed, the entire method of allegorical interpretation developed at Pergamum during the first and second centuries BC (which pagans like the Stoic Crates of Mallos used to interpret Homer, and Jews like Philo and Christians like Origen subsequently used to interpret the Bible), depended on the assumption that words could, and when properly used often did, mean more than one thing at a time.[15] In the Middle Ages, entire works such as *Pearl*, *The Romaunt of the Rose*, and Dante's *Commedia* were to be created on the basis of the same assumption. Many of the best moments of Elizabethan drama (including, incidentally, the scene in which Benedick has just participated) were likewise to depend on whole series of double meanings and ambiguities.

There is, then, no reason to treat Paul as if he were an exception to this. He is about to tell us of a divine faithfulness that no human faithlessness can overthrow;

("faith") in Habakkuk 2.4 is not *ṣaddîq* ("the righteous one") but *ḥāzôn* ("vision")—the rhetorical vector running throughout the entire passage 2.2–4: see "Habakkuk 2:2–4 in the Light of Recent Philological Advances," *HTR* 73.1–2 (1980): 53–78. If Janzen is correct, then, as he observed, "one can appreciate that the LXX rendering 'my faithfulness,' while missing the precise rhetorical connections and grammatical reference of the pronoun, did in essence construe it properly, that is, as referring to that on which the *ṣaddîq*, the righteous one, may confidently rely" (61). I am grateful to my friend and colleague Rebecca Abts Wright, professor of Old Testament at the University of the South, for drawing my attention to Janzen's essay.

14. Codex Alexandrinus places *mou* before *ek pisteōs* (see LXX margin), but Rahlfs is almost certainly correct in following the majority of the manuscripts (which place *mou* after *pisteōs*) in his preferred text. See Dietrich-Alex Koch, "Der Text von Hab. 2.4b in der Septuaginta und im Neuen Testament," *ZNW* 76 (1985): 68–85.

15. There are, of course, examples of allegorical interpretations of Homeric poetry to be found as early as the sixth and fifth centuries. This approach was not encouraged, however, by either Plato or Aristotle: Plato spoke of *huponoia*, "hidden meaning," and raised the problem of distinguishing between what is an example of this and what isn't (*Republic* 2.378.d). Stoics of the Hellenistic period, by contrast, found in allegorical interpretation a convenient way to express their philosophical views. On the allegorical method of interpreting texts in classical antiquity, see George A. Kennedy, "Language and Meaning in Archaic and Classical Greece," and George A. Kennedy and Doreen C. Innes, "Hellenistic Literary and Philosophic Scholarship," in George A. Kennedy, ed., *The Cambridge History of Literary Criticism*, vol. 1 (Cambridge: Cambridge University Press, 1989), 85–86, 209–10, 215. See further Rudolph Pfeiffer, *History of Classical Scholarship from the Beginning to the End of the Hellenistic Age* (Oxford: Oxford University Press, 1968), 9–10, 240; J. Tate, "On the History of Allegorism," *CQ* 28 (1934): 105–14. On patristic scriptural interpretation, see Henri de Lubac, *Medieval Exegesis*, vol. 1, *The Four Senses of Scripture*, Mark Sebank, trans. (Grand Rapids, Michigan: Eerdmans, Edinburgh: Clark, 1998), especially 117–59.

he is also about to speak of the human faith that God seeks in response. In the last analysis, as Karl Barth said, "Whether we say *of the faithfulness of God* or 'of human faith', both are the same. The form in which the prophet's words have been handed down already points in both directions. . . . Where the faithfulness of God encounters human fidelity, there is manifested God's righteousness."[16]

Northrop Frye comments acidly but appositely: "I once read a book on the language of children which remarked that children seem endlessly fascinated by the fact that a word can have more than one meaning. The authors should have added that they ought to keep this fascination all their lives: if they lose it when they grow up they're not maturing, just degenerating."[17] At least the better educated in Paul's audience (as in Shakespeare's) will have had that fascination, for it will have been part of their education.

Additional Note E. Honor and Shame

The Greco-Roman world was what we call an "honor-shame" society: that is to say, it was a society in which the getting and protection of honor was of prime importance to individuals and to groups. What is this "honor"? "Honor" (Greek: *timē*, Latin: *honor, dignitas, fama, existimatio*) can be described as a combination of the worth that you have in your own eyes *together with* the worth that you have in the eyes of whomever is important to you—normally your family, your friends, your patrons, your dependents, the legitimate rulers and so on; but perhaps in special circumstances someone else—the gods, for example, as in the case of Sophocles' Antigone, who thinks it "noble" (*kalos*) to die, rather than "hold in dishonor [*atimasas*] the things that the gods honor," and so defies Creon, her king, in order to bury her brother, thinking no suffering greater than "an ignoble death" (Sophocles, *Antigone* 72, 77, 97; compare 450–70). We are still moving in essentially the same circle of ideas four centuries later when Luke tells us how Peter and the apostles, having been told by the Sanhedrin not to speak in the name of Jesus, first reply, "We must obey God rather than any human authority," and then, on being flogged for their contumacy, leave rejoicing "that they were considered worthy to suffer dishonor [*atimasthēnai*] for the sake of the name" (see Acts 4.18–19, 5.29, 40–41).

As with vocation, both "inner" and "outer" honor are necessary. If you claim honor for yourself, but everyone who is important to you thinks you dishonorable, you will appear to be a fool. On the other hand, in Shakespeare's *Macbeth*, Macbeth's problem might well be described by saying that from the beginning, while he is prepared to act (by murdering his king) so as to receive honor from those around him (that is, to receive the crown of Scotland), he is troubled because he knows in his heart that he will not deserve that honor—in other words, because he is fundamentally an honorable man, what he is about to do makes him feel shame (*Macbeth* 1.7.1–35). Lady Macbeth seems at first to have no such problem (1.4.41–53, 7.54–59), which makes her, in terms of an honor-shame society, shameless.

---

16. Barth, *Romans* 42; see also *Shorter Romans* 22–23.

17. Northrop Frye, *Northrop Frye on Shakespeare*, ed. Robert Sandler (New Haven: Yale University Press, 1986), 6.

It should be noted therefore that shame (Greek: *atimia, aischunē, aidōs*; Latin: *pudor, rubor, confusio*), although it is not, of course, something anyone wants, is not in itself something bad. On the contrary, it is a healthy reaction, like feeling pain if one's hand touches something hot. Shame is what a healthy person *ought* to feel when experiencing disgrace or acting disgracefully, and there is evidently something wrong with someone who does not feel it in such circumstances. Thus, for Suetonius, it was an obvious sign of Caligula's unfitness to rule that he felt no shame over behaving in an unworthy fashion: indeed, says Suetonius, he even boasted of his "shamelessness" (*adiatrepsia*—literally, "refusal to be turned aside from anything") (*Caligula* 29.1). For Horace, celebrating the *pax Augusti*, it is a cause for joy that not only *Fides et Pax* ("faith and peace") but also *Honos Pudorque* ("honor and shame") have returned (*Carmen Saeculare* 57)—and Horace himself was adapting what was already a poetic commonplace in the time of Euripides, namely, that in times of moral decline, shame departs from a decadent world (for example, *Medea* 439–40). "Shame," in other words, is connected with proper modesty.

The basic honor-shame model is then:

Positive		Negative	
Honor /	*Shame*	*Dishonor /*	*Shamelessness*
Active: quest for, or aggressive defense of, honor —tends to be male	Passive: nurturing and cherishing of honor; —tends to be female	Active: aggressive in pursuit of (say) power without honor— tends to be male	Passive: content with dishonor— tends to be female

Naturally, since Greco-Roman society was patriarchal, the normal role for a man was to be *aggressive* and *active* in pursuing honor, and the normal role of a woman was by her *modesty* to defend it: so, for example, Plutarch, *On Marriage, Moralia* 138a–146a (especially 140c [18], 141d–e [25 and 26], 142c–d [31]). This was normal, but not invariable, for there are also cases where women (invariably to rectify the *dishonorable* behavior of the men around them) were approved for being *active* and *aggressive* in protecting honor: see, again, Plutarch, *Virtues in Women, Moralia* 242e–263c (for example, "The Cian Women" [especially 245a–245c], "The Persian Women" [246a] and "Valeria and Cloelia" [250a–f]), and Pliny the Younger, *Letters* 3.16, on the heroism of Arria, wife of Caecina Paetus (also Martial, *Epigrams* 1.13 on the same subject). The Jewish heroine, Judith, likewise acts aggressively to rectify the disgraceful behavior of the Jewish men (Jth. 8.11–27). (We might note, incidentally, that Plutarch, for all his patriarchy, expects modesty in the husband, too, and does not see how a husband can expect his wife to learn what he does not manifest. Such a man is "in no way different from one who orders his wife to fight to the death against enemies to whom he himself has already surrendered" [*On Marriage* 145a]).

That the concept of honor and shame plays an important part in the discourse and thinking of the Letter to the Romans has been pointed out by a number of scholars,[18] and is most clearly evidenced by the regular occurrence of the vocabulary of honor and shame; such as cognates of *timē* ("honor") (1.24, 26; 2.7, 10, 23; 9.21; 12.10; 13.7), *kauchēsis* ("boasting," that is, "claiming honor") (2.17, 23; 3.27; 4.2; 5.2, 3, 11; 15.17), and *aischunē* ("shame") (1.16, 27; 5.5; 6.21; 9.33; 10.11).

What, then, is its significance?

"Honor," I have said, can be described as a combination of the worth that you have in your own eyes *together with* the worth that you have in the eyes of whomever is important to you. Who, then, is the "significant other" for Paul? As I have indicated,[19] there can be no doubt as to the answer to that question: it is not to be "ashamed" before God that Paul seeks above all. On the other hand, as we have already seen, and as will continue to emerge as we examine later stages of the letter, while Paul's view of what is "honorable" does have certain features that we may identify as characteristically Christian—notably its concern that personal behavior shall "build up" the community rather than the individual[20]—nevertheless, Paul's view also has a good deal in common with what many among his contemporaries, Jew and pagan alike, would have regarded as "honorable." Even the "characteristically Christian" concern to build up the community should not be regarded as something *alien* to the thought of Paul's contemporaries: the ancients had, after all, a deep sense of communal solidarity.[21] It was a Roman, not a Jew or a Christian, who declared *dulce et decorum est pro patria mori*—"it is sweet and fitting to die for the fatherland" (Horace, *Odes* 3.2.13)—and was thereby regarded as stating what was, or ought to be, a commonplace. In short, not for nothing does Paul counsel those who follow Jesus in Rome to take thought **for what is *noble in the sight of all*** (10.17; compare Phil. 4.8–9). In many respects, as we shall see, the church as Paul believes it should be is also the ideal Hellenistic community.[22]

Bibliographical Note

Regarding ancient conceptions of honor and shame, a good general introduction is provided by Halvor Moxnes, "Honor and Shame," in *The Social Sciences and New Testament Interpretation*, ed. Richard L. Rohrbaugh (Peabody, Massachusetts: Hendrickson, 1996), 19–40, which also offers a useful bibliography. It is unfortunate that some work in this area has been marred by an uncritical application to ancient societies of the results of research on modern societies. Thus, there is useful material in Bruce J. Malina, *The New Testament World: Insights from Cultural Anthropology* (Lousiville, Kentucky: Westminster / John Knox Press, 1993) (for example, 28–62), but the book suffers as a whole from the weakness just mentioned, as well as from the author's insistence on drawing generally tendentious and inappropriate comparisons between what he calls "Mediterranean preferences" and "emerging U.S. preferences" (for example, 56–58).

Specifically in reference to Romans, Halvor Moxnes, "Honor, Shame, and the Outside World in Paul's Letter to the Romans" (in Jacob Neusner, Ernest S. Frerichs, Peter Borgen, and Richard Horsely, eds., *The Social World of Formative Christianity and Judaism: Essays in*

18. For example, Moxnes, "Honor, Shame, and the Outside World in Romans," 210, 217 note 15.
19. See pages 67–68.
20. See page 198.
21. On communal solidarity in the ancient world, see pages 124–26, and additional note V.
22. See pages 196–200.

Tribute to Howard Clark Kee [Philadelphia: Fortress Press, 1988], 207–18) makes some good points, although his view of Romans 1.18–32 as lacking concern with civic virtue appears to me to be mistaken: contrast page 81.

An excellent background and basis for further literary study is provided by Douglas L. Cairns's careful examination of the relevant material in ancient Greek literature, *Aidōs: The Psychology and Ethics of Honour and Shame in Ancient Greek Literature* (Oxford: Clarendon Press, 1993).

Additional Note F. Salvation

Sōṭēria ("salvation") (together with its cognates, *sōzō* [save], *sōṭēr* [savior], and *sōṭērios* [saving, salutary]) has in general to do with "deliverance from whatever oppresses" or "preservation." Thus physicians and even medicines are commonly "saviors." A second-century BC inscription at Samos honors the physician Diodorus, who had cared for many

> and was the cause of their salvation [*paraitios egeneto tēs sōṭērias autōn*]. . . . He placed the common salvation [*tēs koinēs sōṭērias*] above all fatigue and all expense. (Pouilloux, *Inscriptions* 3.14, lines 17, 32)

Sōṭēria and its cognates also are often used during our period in reference to sovereigns, notably the Roman emperor: thus, even a Jewish writer such as Philo appears to speak without hesitation of "our savior and benefactor Augustus" (*ho sōṭēr kai euergetēs Sebastos*) (*Flaccus* 74; cf. Josephus, *Jewish War* 3.459).

Sōṭēria and its cognates have broadly the same meanings in the LXX as in secular Greek, commonly translating Hebrew *yasa*, which has the sense of "being set in a wide space, or at liberty" (for example, Judges 13.5). For the LXX, nevertheless, it remains that the only real source of "salvation" is God, as is repeatedly stressed in the psalms and the prophets (LXX Ps. 3.8 [compare 3.2], 34.3 [MT 35.3], Isa. 21.2, Jer. 3.23; see also Exod. 14.13). That is the dominant association that carries over into its use in the New Testament generally, and Paul in particular (although there are, of course, also examples of the word in its secular sense: for example, Acts 23.24).[23]

Additional Note G. The Salvation of Israel and the Healing of Creation

A close connection between the promise to Israel and the healing of creation is integral to the scriptural tradition. As early as Genesis, the commandments to Adam and the blessing of Abraham and Abraham's seed correspond with each other—indeed, the command to Adam has virtually *become* the promise to Abraham's seed, so that (by implication) that seed is the true humanity, and its land the new Eden (compare Gen. 1.28 with 12.2–3; 17.2, 6–8; 22.18; 26.3; 26.24; 35.11, 48.3.)

Most important for my present purpose, this view also clearly continued to be prominent in later Judaism. So Daniel, *Jubilees*, and the *Testaments of the Twelve*

---

23. See further Spicq, *Lexicon* 3.344–57; also Georg Fohrer and Werner Foerster, "σῴζω, σωτηρία, σωτήρ, σωτήριος," in *TDNT* 7.965–1023.

Patriarchs all link Israel with Adam, and the nations with the beasts over whom Adam rules (Dan. 7.1–27; *Jub.* 3.30–31, 15.25–27, 19.15–31, 22.10–14; *T. Levi* 18.10).

The messianic hope, where it occurs, is closely linked with the foregoing. Israel's true anointed king has focused upon him the hopes and aspirations of the nation; hence, he, like the nation, is God's child and he, like the nation, is Son of Man, destined to rule the nations (*2 Apoc. Bar.* 30.1; 2 [4] Esdras 14.9; *b. ḥag.* 14a). Naturally, the promises to the anointed are closely linked to those to Abraham:

> May his name endure for ever,
>   his fame continue as long as the sun.
> May all nations be blessed in him;
>   may they pronounce him happy. (Psalm 72.17)

Parallel to this is the development of Israel's understanding of the Divine Wisdom, by which the world was made (Prov. 8.22–31): increasingly the Law becomes identified with Wisdom, and with God's Spirit. The Law shows one how to be human, and so those who follow it (i.e., Israel) are taking on Adam's role (Sirach 17.11, 19.20, 24.1–34, 38.34, 39.1–11; 2 Baruch 3.9–4.4). Out of all the world, Philo says, it is those who keep the Law alone who are "in a true sense human beings [*tous pros alētheian anthrōpous*]" (*The Special Laws* 1.303).

Bibliographical Note

In general, see N. T. Wright, *The New Testament and the People of God: Christian Origins and the Question of God*, vol. 1 (London: SPCK 1992; Philadelphia: Fortress Press, 1993), 21–26. On the link between Wisdom, Creation, and Torah, see Martin Hengel, *Judaism and Hellenism: Studies in Their Encounter in Palestine during the Early Hellenistic Period*. John Bowden, trans., 2 vols. (London: SCM Press, 1974), 1.153–75.

Additional Note H. Translating *Dikaiosunē*

After some hesitation I have chosen to render *dikaiosunē* in English by "justice" and hence *dikaiosunē theou* by "God's justice" (with which compare Vg, *justitia Dei*; BJ, *la justice de Dieu*; BEP, *la giustizia di Dio*). "God's righteousness" (or something like that) has, of course, been usual in English versions (so KJV, RV, ARV, RSV, NRSV, REB; but contrast Douay-Rheims [probably under the influence of Jerome's Latin] and NEB [which alternates between "justice" and "God's way of righting wrong"]).

Translating *dikaiosunē* as "justice" has the outstanding advantage that one can then fairly satisfactorily render its cognates by English cognates, notably *dikaios* ("just"), *dikaiōma* ("just deed" or "just requirement," "just command" [the most common LXX sense]), *dikaioō* ("justify" ["acquit"]), *dikaiōsis* ("justification"), and *dikē* ("just penalty," or "Justice" personified).

The usual objection to "justice" as a translation for *dikaiosunē* is that it is tied in common understanding to ideas of "retributive" or "distributive" justice. While this may have been true until recently, contemporary popular views of legal processes such as those that have recently engaged the European Court or the United States Supreme Court seem to me quite commonly to involve the notion of *saving* justice for individuals, and the *protection* of rights. This is evidently the central issue with those, for example, who seek "justice" for unfairly dismissed workers, the unborn, or the poor. I therefore suggest that this objection to "justice" as a translation for *dikaiosunē*, though it still needs to be considered (see BJ 1492, note c), no longer has the force it had. In any case, to talk as if Paul (or we) might conceivably regard "saving justice" and "retributive justice" as unconnected, or opposed, is absurd: see LXX Isaiah 63 or LXX Psalm 75.8–10 [MT Ps. 76.9–11a].

The second great advantage of the word "justice" as a translation for *dikaiosunē*—and Hebrew *ṣedeq* and *ṣĕdāqâ*—is that, like those words, it invariably speaks of something social.[24] "Justice" (or "injustice") is evidently something that takes place between people, and as Lamprias said, *dikaiosunē* has "no function in relation to oneself or to a part of oneself, but only in relation to others" (Plutarch, *Oracles in Decline*, [*Moralia* 423d]).

The word "righteousness," by contrast, besides being associated in many minds with "*self*-righteousness" (among the very last things Paul would have intended) also (and perhaps therefore) tends in contemporary English to be associated with purely *individual* merit (likewise among the last things Paul would have intended). Thus, it is quite striking that in defining English usage of "righteousness," the alternatives to "justice" suggested by *OED2* are, "uprightness, rectitude; conformity of life to the requirements of the divine or moral law; virtue, integrity"—all words and phrases that could be used of someone in solitude. Especially is this true of "virtue," the disastrous translation for *dikaiosunē* proposed by the original English version of BJ.

God's "No!" to Injustice (1.18–32)

So the gospel is faithful, for it declares faithfully two fundamental truths: that the Lord is powerful to save everyone, Jew and Greek, according to the promise, and that the Lord is just, faithful to the promise. Those two truths about the gospel, must, however, be understood in connection with a third: **for God's wrath is revealed from heaven against all the impiety and injustice of humanity—of those who by their injustice suppress the truth** (1.18). Perhaps for some among the Jewish believers in Jesus who first heard Paul's letter, this third affirmation came as something of a surprise. Did not Paul's "gospel" notion of a God who would save all, Jew and Greek alike, regardless of the yoke of Torah, imply a God who did not care about sin? Was not that precisely why they objected to it? Yet here Paul was speaking of God's anger, God's passionate "No!" to human sin, in language as severe as they might have used themselves![25]

---

24. See my discussion of Romans 1.17, pages 69–70, and the literature cited in footnote 9.

25. Certainly Paul's setting the revelation of God's wrath in parallel with the revelation of God's power for salvation and God's justice has caused later interpreters some headaches: see the convenient summary in Steve Finamore, "The Gospel and the Wrath of God in Romans 1," in *Understanding, Studying, and Reading: New Testament Essays in Honour of John Ashton*, JSNTSS 153, Christopher Rowland and Crispin H. T. Fletcher-Lewis, eds. (Sheffield, England: Sheffield Academic Press, 1998), 140–45, and literature there cited. The key to the problem is not to forget that for Paul the consummation of that revelation is the cross (3.25): "In [Christ's] death God's necessary wrath has done with sinners" (Barth, *Shorter Romans* 46). Finamore himself makes an interesting use of René Girard's anthropological theory of mimesis to exegete Romans 1: the gospel, "acknowledges, even declares, the innocence of Jesus," whom the culture regards as guilty—and thereby, Finamore suggests, reveals "the founding lie, the misrepresentation of the violence at the root of all culture. . . . The gospel is revelation in that it confronts us with the truth about ourselves and our victims" (148).

The Wisdom of Solomon had spoken powerfully of gentile unbelief and disobedience, contrasting it with the faith that God seeks:

> For all who were ignorant of God were foolish by nature;
> and they were unable from the good things that are seen to know him who exists,
> nor did they recognize the craftsman while paying heed to his works. . . .

> For from the greatness and beauty of the created things [*ktismatōn*]
> comes a corresponding perception of their creator. . . .
> Yet again, not even they are to be excused;
> for if they had the power to know so much
> that they could investigate the world,
> how did they fail to find sooner the Lord of these things? (Wisd. of Sol. 13.1, 5, 9)

Paul's language is reminiscent of the Wisdom of Solomon, but his indictment is wider and more severe. The writer of Wisdom accused the gentiles of culpable ignorance. Paul, speaking not merely of gentiles but of **all the impiety and injustice of humanity,** declares that disobedient humanity as a whole[26] was *not* ignorant. On the contrary, they *knew.* **For what can be known about God is plain to them, because God has shown it to them. For from the creation of the world** [*apo ktiseōs kosmou*][27] God's invisible nature, namely, his eternal power and divinity, has been clearly visible, being understood in the things that have been made (1.19–20a).

In giving this additional twist to his accusation—that is, in declaring that humanity was *not* ignorant—Paul has in mind not only the Wisdom of Solomon (which, as we shall see, seems to lie in the background of much that follows) but also Genesis 1 to 3. At a later point in the letter Paul will indeed speak specifically of Adam (5.12–21); here the reminiscence is indirect and allusive, but, in my view, inescapable.[28] According to Genesis, the truth about God was "plain" to Adam, who knew God but was willing, nonetheless, to credit the serpent's lie. Seeking to be "like God, knowing good and evil" (Gen. 3.5), Adam submitted himself to a creature over whom he was meant to rule (compare Gen. 1.26–28). So it is of humanity "in Adam" (compare 1. Cor. 15.22) that we must say,

they are without excuse [*anapologētous*], **for even though they knew God, they did not glorify** [*edoxasan*] **him as God or give thanks to him, but they became futile in their thinking and their senseless heart was darkened. Claiming to be wise, they became fools and changed** [*ēllaxan*] **the glory** [*doxan*][29] **of the incor-**

---

26. On the implication that *all* are involved in this indictment, see additional note I.

27. The translation preserves something of the ambiguity of the original *apo ktiseōs kosmou.* Most modern commentators think that Paul intended *apo* in a temporal sense, i.e., "ever since" (compare 2 Cor. 8.10, 9.2), and that by *ktisis* he meant "act of creation." So they render the phrase by something unambiguous such as the RSV's "Ever since the creation of the world." In view of what follows, I suspect this *was* the sense uppermost in Paul's mind. Grammatically, however, it is possible to understand *apo* as speaking of origin, cause, or source, and *ktisis* as "created order" or "what is created." So we could render *apo ktiseōs kosmou* by "from the created order of the world" or words to that effect. Despite the frequent claims of theologians arguing on the basis of later disputes, there is no particular reason to believe that Paul would have denied that insight, either: compare Psalm 19.1–4 (LXX Psalm 18.1–4), Wisd of Sol. 13.1,5. Once again, there is no reason not to allow Paul a double meaning, and, indeed, every reason to so do.

28. On the relationship of Romans 1.18–32 to the Creation story, see additional note I.

29. On "glory," see additional note J.

ruptible God for the likeness [*homoiōmati*] of corruptible humanity, of birds, of four-footed beasts, and of creeping things. (1.20b–23)

Paul's language here is partly the language of popular Hellenistic philosophy (as was that of the Wisdom of Solomon), but also reminds us of the language with which the LXX in various places speaks of Israel's falls from grace.

Thus, there are evident reminiscences of the psalmist describing the episode of the golden calf: "[T]hey changed [*ēllaxanto*] their glory [*doxan*] for the likeness [*homoiōmati*] of a calf eating hay" (LXX Ps. 105.20 [MT 106.20]), and also of Jeremiah's language describing Israel's idolatry in his day: "[M]y people have changed [*ēllaxato*] their glory [*doxan*] for that which does not profit" (LXX Jer. 2.11). It was surely, as Brendan Byrne suggests, a deliberate irony on Paul's part to describe the apostasy of humankind in language that recalled, for the biblically alert, Israel's apostasy—so indicating the essential connection between them.[30]

There follows a catalogue of human disobedience that is similar to much written at this period by pagan and Jew alike, but is, again, notably reminiscent of the Book of Wisdom, both in its content and in its understanding of the basis of human evil. As for the *content* of human disobedience, Wisdom says,

> Afterward, it was not enough for them to err about the knowledge of God, . . .
> they no longer keep either their lives or their marriages pure,
> but they either treacherously kill one another, or grieve one
> another by adultery,
> and all is a raging riot of blood and murder, theft and deceit,
> corruption, faithlessness, tumult, perjury,
> confusion over what is good, forgetfulness of favors,
> pollution of idols, sex perversion,
> disorder in marriage, adultery, and debauchery. (Wisd. of Sol. 14.22–26;
> compare Rom. 1.24–32)

As for the *basis* of this disobedience:

> the worship of idols not to be named
> is the beginning and cause and end of every evil. (Wisd. of Sol. 14.27)

For Paul, too, the root cause of every evil is the apostasy and rebellion he has described;[31] in other words, all *other* forms of disobedience are merely symptoms of the basic disobedience, which is apostasy—signs that those who have chosen to abandon God receive what they have chosen. Paul says this three times,[32] each time, however (by means of a verbal play that is sometimes more obvious in his Greek than in our English translations), "making the punishment fit the crime."[33]

---

30. Byrne, *Romans* 67–68.

31. So, by contrast, Philo says, "[W]here honor is rendered to the God who IS, the whole company of the other virtues must follow in its train" (*On the Virtues* 181). The entire passage 175–83 is, as it happens, filled with ideas and expressions that resonate with the discourse of Romans.

32. On the punctuation of 1.22–32, see Morna D. Hooker, "A Further Note on Romans 1," in *NTS* 13 (1966–67): 181–83; compare Byrne, *Romans* 63, 67–72; Cranfield, *Romans* 1.105, 123; Nestle–Aland 27th edition; contrast Sanday and Headlam, *Romans* 40, 46.

33. Hooker, "Further Note" 182.

First, for Paul as for the writer of the Wisdom of Solomon (and other Jewish writers, see *Letter of Aristeas* 138–52; *Sybelline Oracles* 3.586–600), there is an evident connection between idolatry and sexual immorality:

> Claiming to be wise, they became fools, and changed the glory [*doxan*] of the incorruptible God for the likeness of corruptible humanity, of birds, of four-footed beasts, and of creeping things: *therefore* God gave them up in the desires of their hearts to impurity, that their bodies should be dishonored [*atimazesthai*] among themselves. (1.22–24)

The verbal play here lies in the contrast between *doxa* (glory—that is, the good estimate others have of one) and *atimia* (dishonor) (represented by its cognate, *atimazō*). This particular verbal contrast is quite common, occurring not only in Paul (see also 1 Cor. 11.14–15, 15.43; 2 Cor. 6.8), but elsewhere (compare in the LXX Isa. 10.16, 22.18; Hos. 4.7; Hab. 2.16; Prov. 3.35, 11.16; Sirach 3.10, 5.13, 29.6b). It is, of course, entirely of a piece with the ancients' general understanding of honor and shame.[34]

The perceived connection between idolatry and sexual immorality is also manifest in Paul's second statement, where the play on words is obvious even in English:

> They actually exchanged [*metēllaxan*] the truth about God for a lie and worshipped and served the creature rather than the Creator who is blessed for ever, Amen!— *for this very reason*, God gave them up to dishonorable passion: so their women exchanged [*metēllaxan*] the natural use to that which is against nature, and so likewise the men gave up natural relations with women and were consumed with passion for one another, men committing shameless acts with men, and receiving in their own persons the due penalty for their error. (1.25–27)[35]

Paul's third and climactic statement, however, widens and deepens the picture, offering in diatribe style a "list of vices"[36] that focuses not on the "warm" sins of sexual weakness, but on something evidently more cruel, the so-called "cold" sins of strength:

> And since they did not approve [*ouk edokimasen*] of acknowledging God, God gave them up to a reprobate [*adokimon*] mind and to improper conduct. They were filled with all manner of injustice, wickedness, ruthlessness, evil; full of envy, murder, strife, deceit, malignity, vicious gossips, public slanderers, hateful to God,[37] insolent, arrogant, boastful, inventors of evil, disobedient to parents, foolish, faithless, heartless, merciless. (1.28–31)

Against these last, in a final rhetorical flourish, Paul pronounces his ultimate condemnation, that **knowing the judgment of God, that those who do such things are worthy of death, they not only do them, but applaud those who do them** (1.32).

---

34. On "honor" and "shame," see additional note E.
35. On the significance of 1.26–27, see additional note K.
36. See pages 24–25.
37. Such is the normal sense of *theostugēs* (see LS, θεοστυγής); in that sense it was understood here by Jerome (*deo odibiles*), and possibly (despite BAGD, θεοστυγής) by Clement of Rome (see *1 Clem.* 35.5–6); so (again, despite BAGD, θεοστυγής) there seems to be no particular reason that an active sense, "hating God," should "seem preferable."

Habit breeds character, and the true punishment of those who indulge the cold and cruel sins is to become as cold and cruel as their deeds.

Paul was hardly, of course, the only writer to notice this. Tacitus, in his own way, points to the same phenomenon, telling of a stage in the Roman civil war when "the victors had come to disregard the difference between right and wrong so completely that a common soldier declared that he had killed his brother in the last battle *and actually asked the generals for a reward*" (*Histories* 3.51, trans. Clifford H. Moore).

It is sometimes suggested that in his account of human "shame" in 1.24–32 Paul speaks only of private morality.[38] This is manifestly not true. On the contrary, the "cold" sins that he lists in 1.29–31 were correctly characterized by C. H. Dodd as "anti-social vices,"[39] beginning as they do from **injustice** (*a-dikia*—the opposite of fulfilling one's obligations toward others), proceeding by way of **wickedness** (*ponēria*—"vice," "knavery," "baseness," "cowardice,")[40] and **ruthlessness** (*pleonexia*— as Dodd noted, "the characteristic vice of the tyrant . . . the man who will pursue his own interests with complete disregard for the rights of others and for all considerations of humanity"),[41] and concluding with those who, knowing **that those who do such things are worthy of death, not only do them, but applaud those who do them** (those, that is, who by condoning and praising the vicious actions of others "are actually making a deliberate contribution to the setting up of a public opinion favorable to vice").[42] All this is precisely opposite to the behavior required of those who will meet the civic obligations that Paul will later lay out in Romans 12.14–13.7, where believers are to take **thought for what is *noble in the sight of all*** (12.17b), being properly **subject to the governing authorities** (13.1a), paying **respect to whom respect** is due and **honor to whom honor** (13.7b), and so in their turn receiving honor as good citizens (13.3).[43]

The scheme of priorities here implied was, incidentally, to be worked out in detail in later Christian writing, including not only formal theology but more popular observation. Thus, for example, in Dante's *Commedia*, those guilty of sins of incontinence, such as lust and gluttony, find their place in the upper circles of Hell, even (except for heresy) outside the walls of the city of Dis (*Inferno*, cantos 5–9), whereas *within* Dis are those guilty of sins of violence (cantos 12–14), and far below them, in the pit of Malboge, those who have practiced fraud, or treachery. Among those guilty of treachery we find further divisions: first are those guilty of fraud against those who did not trust them (cantos 18–24); then, lower down, those who have been guilty of

---

38. So, for example, Halvor Moxnes, "Honor, Shame, and the Outside World in Romans," in Jacob Neusner, Ernest S. Frerichs, Peter Borgen, and Richard Horsely, eds., *The Social World of Formative Christianity and Judaism: Essays in Tribute to Howard Clark Kee* (Philadelphia: Fortress Press, 1988), 212–16.

39. Dodd, *Romans* 27.

40. LS, πονηρία, BAGD, πονηρία;

41. Dodd, *Romans* 27.

42. Cranfield, *Romans* 135: "So, for example, to excuse or gloss over the use of torture by security forces or the cruel injustices of racial discrimination and oppression, while not being involved in them directly, is to help to cloak monstrous evil with an appearance of respectability and so to contribute most effectively to its firmer entrenchment" (ibid.)

43. See pages 201–208.

treachery toward those who *did* trust them—toward their kin, their country, their guests; and then, lowest of all, those who have betrayed their lords and benefactors (cantos 32–34).

Again, akin to the Pauline principle of matching the punishment to the crime, the deeper in the *Inferno* Dante goes, and the "colder" the crimes to be punished, the colder the punishment, until, at the lowest point of all,

> Lo'imperador del doloroso regno
>   da mezzo il petto uscia fuor della ghiaccia. . . .
> The Emperor of the doleful realm
> at mid-breast stood forth from the ice. . . . (*Inferno* 34.28–29)

So in 1.18–32 Paul presents a picture of human disorder, dominated by the passions and utterly lacking that self-control (*egkrateia*) which was the ancient ideal—pagan and Jewish alike.[44] It is, however, a *general* picture. We can hardly emphasize too strongly that throughout this part of his argument Paul is not condemning anyone in particular, nor, indeed, is he talking about individual behavior at all. As we have noted, from 1.18 onward (**all the impiety and injustice of humanity**) it is the plight of the race of which he speaks. In Paul's view, whatever the merits of individuals, humankind as a whole has **from the creation of the world** (1.20) possessed knowledge of God, and therefore humankind as a whole is subject to God's **wrath**—God's passionate "No!"—for its rejection of that knowledge.

It is also important to notice that in the particular vices he lists, both private and civic, Paul is not being controversial; indeed, he is being positively commonplace. As we have observed, he could reasonably expect that any serious Jew, and most Romans and Greeks, would be in general agreement with him.[45] To be controversial at this point would be, in fact, to defeat his entire rhetorical purpose, which is to create among his hearers *pathos*, a frisson of disgust and revulsion at the errors of the world. The act of judgment implicit in that reaction prepares them for the next step in Paul's argument.

Additional Note I. Romans 1.18–32 and Genesis 1–3

It is evident that the creation story continued to play a considerable part in Jewish and Christian thinking during the early years of the Christian era (see, for example, Wisd. of Sol. 2.23–24; 2 (4) Ezra 4.30–32; Mark 1.12–13;[46] Luke 3.38; 1 Tim. 2.13–14; *Jub.*3.28–32; *Life of Adam and Eve*; 2 *Apoc. Bar.* 54.13–22) as well as in Paul's

---

44. On "self-control," see additional note L.

45. The one point at which at which this statement needs some qualification (though not much) is with regard to 1.26–27. See further, additional note K.

46. See my *Preface to Mark*, 141–43; also Ernest Best, *The Temptation and the Passion: The Markan Soteriology*, second edition (Cambridge: Cambridge University Press, 1990), xvi–xvii, 6–7; Petr Pokorný, "The Temptation Stories and Their Intention," NTS 20 (1973–74): 120–22; Eduard Schweizer, *The Good News According to Mark*, trans. Donald H. Madvig (Richmond: John Knox Press, 1970), 42–43; also (cautiously) Susan R. Garrett, *The Temptations of Jesus in Mark's Gospel* (Grand Rapids, Michigan: Eerdmans, 1998), 58 (and further literature cited there in footnote 19), and Morna D. Hooker, *The Gospel According to Mark* (London: Black, 1991), 50.

own thinking (Rom. 5.12–21; 1 Cor. 15.21–22, 45; 2 Cor. 11.3). With regard therefore to Romans 1.19–32, I find it hard to take seriously the still quite commonly made suggestion[47] that, in telling the story of those who, seeking to be wise, became fools, and served the creature rather than the creator, Paul could possibly *not* have had somewhat in mind thoughts of the primeval story of those who also sought to be "as gods, knowing good and evil" (LXX Gen. 3.5), who chose therefore to do what the serpent said rather than what God said, and were cast by that choice from honor to dishonor. I find it equally hard to imagine that Paul would not have expected at least the more biblically literate among his hearers to have similar thoughts.

In Paul's view, when properly understood, "the things that have been made" are, in their claim and their call, pointers to God and (therefore) to our own creatureliness: "They have been this from the very beginning and for everyone to the extent that, in face of them, one can become aware of dependence on one's creator and limitation by one's Lord, not by rational deduction but existentially and immediately" (Käsemann).[48]

Closely connected with this is a second issue, much disputed. Despite Paul's explicit statement that he is speaking of God's "wrath" against "all the impiety and injustice [*adikian*] of humanity" (1.18), the view persists among some students of Romans that the Jews cannot be implicated in 1.18–32 because "Paul appeals to God's creational revelation as the standard by which these people are to be judged" whereas "the Jews are judged by God, according to Paul, on the basis of their possession of the law."[49] This entirely overlooks that fact that in Paul's view Israel, too, is "in Adam" (3.20, 23; 5.12–14, 20; compare 1 Cor. 15.22)—something that was not changed by the call of Abraham. Hence, although at this point in his rhetoric Paul only speaks in general terms, still it is evident that the group he has in mind—that is, the group that does not glorify God as God—is the group he also will have in mind at 3.23 when he speaks of those who "fall short" of God's glory: namely, "all"—"for there is," as he will then say, "no distinction; for all have sinned, and come short of God's glory" (3.22b–23).

Additional Note J. Glory

The word *doxa* ("glory") in secular Greek most commonly means "opinion" or "judgment," hence, "the opinion others have of one, estimation, repute" and hence, in good sense, "honor, glory";[50] in the LXX it was regularly used to translate Hebrew *kābôd*, connected with *kbd*, literally "be heavy, weighty," hence meaning the kind of

---

47. See, for example, Fitzmyer, *Romans* 274, 283–84. Contrast Morna D. Hooker, "Adam in Romans 1," *NTS* 6 (1959–69): 297–306; also A. J. M. Wedderburn, "Adam in Paul's Letter to the Romans," in *Studia Biblica 1978*, vol. 3, JSNTSup (1980): 413–30; Richard H. Bell, *No one seeks for God: An Exegetical and Theological Study of Romans 1.18–3.20*, WUNT 106 (Siebeck: Mohr, 1999), 24, and footnote 22.

48. Käsemann, *Romans* 41–42.

49. Edward Adams, "Abraham's Faith and Gentile Disobedience: Textual Links between Romans 1 and 4," *JSNT* 65 [1997]: 48–49.

50. LS, δόξα II, III; see also Spicq, *Lexicon* 1.362–79.

"weightiness" that causes esteem, or respect, and so "honor, glory."[51] Thus used, the Greek word underwent a remarkable extension of meaning: the whole earth is full of God's *doxa* (LXX Isa. 6.3), and the *doxa* of God can appear (LXX Exod.16.10). Being the "radiant power of [God's] Being, as it were the external glorious manifestation of His mysterious holiness, it extends all over the earth"[52] and is too brilliant for mortals to look upon (LXX Exod. 33.18–22, Deut. 5.24, Isa. 6).

There is always, as Spicq says, "a touch of luminescence"[53] about God's *doxa* in the LXX, and God's *doxa* gives that luminosity, moreover, to whatever it illuminates: so the face of Moses shone when he returned from speaking with God (LXX Exod. 34.29–35).

Hellenistic Jewish writers in general (for example, Philo and Josephus) seem not much affected by this biblical extension of meaning. Paul, however, *is* affected by it, and not only in Romans: in 2 Corinthians, for example, he strikingly takes up the tradition of Moses returning from speaking with God in terms of the "extraordinary glory" (*huperballousēs doxēs*) of the new covenant (2 Cor. 3.7–11; see also 2 Cor. 4.4–6, 7.23). Humanity in general, however, is estranged from God's glory by sin (Rom. 1.23) and so is deprived of the enriching and enhancing power of that glory: hence, as Paul will say later, we "fall short of the glory of God" (3.23)—that very glory which, by being what it is, would also be our glory.

Additional Note K. On the Significance of 1.26b–27

Pious Judaism abhorred the type of behavior that we characterize as "homosexual" (see, for example, *The Letter of Aristeas* 152; *Sybelline Oracles* 3.596; Josephus, *Against Apion* 2.199, 273, 275; Philo, *On Abraham* 135–37). In taking this attitude, however, Judaism was not necessarily different from the world around it. Thus, it is mistaken to claim, as does John Boswell, that in ancient Roman society generally, "Romans were quite open about homosexual feelings and gay relationships were 'public' in the sense of being frankly acknowledged and generally accepted."[54] There was, in fact, no single Greco-Roman attitude to homosexuality, any more than there is at present a single European or American attitude to it. As it happens, in Greek and Latin there was not even a *word* for "homosexuality"—the earliest recorded use, even in English, according to *OED2*, was in C. G. Chaddock's translation of Krafft-Ebing's *Psychopathia Sexualis* (3.255) (1892).

The question at issue in the Greco-Roman world at the beginning of the Common Era was very largely one of activity or passivity, of penetrating or being pen-

---

51. BDB, בָּבַד vb., כָּבוֹד n.m. See further Claus Westermann, "כבד *kbd*, to be heavy," in *TLOT* 2.590–602.

52. Th. C. Vriezen, *An Outline of Old Testament Theology*, second edition revised and enlarged (Oxford: Oxford University Press, 1970), 299.

53. Spicq, *Lexicon* 1.366.

54. John Boswell, *Christianity, Social Tolerance, and Homosexuality: Gay People in Western Europe from the Beginning of the Christian Era to the Fourteenth Century* (Chicago: University of Chicago Press, 1980) 22, note 42. See further, and contrast, Martti Nissinen, *Homoeroticism in the Biblical World: A Historical Perspective* (Minneapolis: Fortress Press, 1998), 69–88, especially 79–88.

etrated. In general, it seems likely that the average "Roman in the street" disapproved of what we call male homosexual behavior between free adult males, because it was perceived as disgusting for such a male to submit to the woman's role (*viri muliebria pati*: for example, Sallust, *Cat.*13.3; Tacitus, *Annals* 11.36 [see also Philo, *On Abraham* 135–36])—which is to say, it was disgusting for the male to abandon masculine *egkrateia* ("self-control").[55] Certainly, we gain the impression of such general disapproval from the rhetoric and innuendo of Cicero—a rhetoric that was calculated, of course, to appeal to just such "Romans in the street" (for example, *On Behalf of Milo* 21.55; *Philippics* 2.77). Among those of Greek culture, the matter seems to have been more generally (and hotly) debated. Probably Plutarch's *Of Love* is not unrepresentative: it describes a conversation in which his father took part, and involves a whole range of strongly expressed views both for and against male homosexual love (*Moralia* 748e–771e).

This granted, it remains that Wayne Meeks's dictum is broadly correct: "On the whole, . . . the sexual purity for which Pauline Christians strive in an impure world is defined mostly in terms of values that are widely affirmed by the larger society."[56] Meeks justifiably points to the way in which the Greek popular romances habitually turn on the utter faithfulness of the hero and heroine to each other, even through terrible adversities and temptations, from which they always, of course, emerge with virtue untarnished and faithfulness uncompromised. Think of *Callirhoe*! Meeks also points to the number of graves that praise married women because they were *monandros* or *univira*.[57] Significant in this context is also Josephus's description of Jewish sexual mores:

> The Law recognizes no sexual connections, except the natural [*kata phusin*] union of man and wife, and that only for the procreation of children. Sodomy it abhors, and punishes any guilty of such assault with death. (*Against Apion* 2.199, trans. H. St. J. Thackeray)

The whole point here is that Josephus is engaged in apologia: throughout this entire section (2.190–219) it is evident that he is describing aspects of Judaism of which he takes it for granted his respectable Greco-Roman readers will approve.

At Romans 1.26b–27 Paul is, then, speaking in a typically Jewish fashion, and perhaps even a typically first-century fashion, when he describes what we call "male homosexual relations" as *planē*, an "error"—that is, literally, a "wandering," a "roaming," a "going astray," and so, by transference, a "wandering" from the path of truth, a "deceit," a "delusion," or an "error"[58]—and as *para phusin*, "against na-

---

55. On self control, see additional note L. See also Nissinen, *Homoeroticism* 129–30.

56. Wayne Meeks, *The First Urban Christians: The Social World of the Apostle Paul* (New Haven: Yale University Press), 101. As regards homoeroticism, by contrast, Nissinen is able to quote a catena of classical critiques that lead him to the view that in general "sex between men was also viewed negatively in the Greco-Roman world at the beginning of the Common Era. Homosexual or bisexual behavior was not generally condemned in every form, but its specific characteristics were criticized again and again" (*Homoeroticism*, 87; see 79–88).

57. *First Urban Christians* 228, note 135. See further Ramsay MacMullen, "Roman Attitudes to Greek Love," *Historia* 31 (1982): 484–502; T. P. Wiseman, *Catullus and His World: A Reappraisal* (Cambridge: Cambridge University Press, 1985), 10–14 and literature there cited.

58. See LS, πλάνη; BAGD, πλάνη.

ture."[59] The latter phrase, which Josephus also uses when speaking of homosexuality (*Against Apion* 2. 273, 275; see also Philo, *On Abraham* 135–37), probably although not certainly[60] represents an appropriation of popular Stoicism, though Jews and Stoics would generally have meant something different by "nature." For Paul, Philo, and Josephus, "against nature" in such a context as this would mean "against the divine order, and hence contrary to God's commandment." All three would regard homosexual acts as an interruption of the ordinary course of nature, and in this connection (that is, with regard to sexual activity) all three regard that "ordinary course" as instituted by God.

It will be noted that I began my discussion in the preceding paragraph by speaking of Paul's description of "what we call 'male homosexual relations.'" I say *male* because it is not, actually, entirely clear that Paul discusses female homosexual relations at all. Certainly many commentators (including patristic commentators such as John Chrysostom [*Homilies on the Epistle to the Romans* 4.1 (Migne, PG 60.417)]) have seen and continue to see such a reference in Romans 1.26; but while Paul does talk there of women "changing the natural use for that which is against nature," it is noticeable that he does not actually say (as he does of men) that they "burned in their desire toward *one another*." Granted the centrality of the question of *egkrateia* for the ancients, it is therefore perfectly possible, as Bernadette Brooten has suggested,[61] that what he

59. See BAGD, παρά 3.6; Smyth, *Grammar* §1676, 1692.3.a; BD §§236.2; see also Stobaeus, *Anthologies* 2.7.7a. On *phusis* generally, see Helmut Koester, φύσις, φυσικός, φυσικῶς," in *TDNT* 9.251–77.

60. It is also possible to argue for a Platonic connection: thus, according to the *Timaeus* genital activity for the purpose of creation is *kata phusin* (41a–d; compare *Laws* 636c): see Roy Bowen Ward, "Why Unnatural? The Tradition behind Romans 1:26–27," *HTR* 90.3 (1997): 263–84, especially 264–69. But in any case the ancients were just as capable of being eclectic as we are. See also Nissinen, *Homoeroticism* 105–13.

61. Bernadette Brooten, "Patristic Interpretations of Romans 1.26," *Studia Biblica XVIII*, ed. E. A. Livingston (Kalamazoo, Michigan: Cistercian Publications, 1985) 287–88. Brooten cites scholia in two manuscripts of Clement of Alexander (*Paidogus* 8.501–2, note 9: GCS 12.331,6–8) and a passage in Augustine (*On Marriage and Concupiscence* 20.35 [CSEL 42.289]) as evidence of patristic interpretations of Romans 1.26 that referred it to "unnatural heterosexual intercourse" (287). Fitzmyer flatly rejects her view of the passage from Augustine (*Romans* 287). My own suspicion is that the section in question is not quite so clear as either of them implies. Augustine writes of "a part of the body that is not meant for generative purposes" that "if someone should use even his own wife in it, it is against nature [*contra naturam*] and scandalous." He continues,

in sum [*denique*], previously the same apostle said concerning women, "for their women changed the natural use into that which is against nature [*contra naturam*];" then concerning men that they worked that which is shameful by abandoning the natural use of women. Therefore, by this name, i.e., "the natural use," conjugal union is not praised, but [thereby] are indicated scandalous deeds more unclean and criminal than deeds even with women that are unlawful, but nevertheless follow natural use.

As he quoted Romans 1.26, *was* Augustine still thinking of the "scandalous" use between married couples to which he had just referred? or was he already moving back to thoughts about same-sex relationships, as well as "natural" adultery and "natural" relationships with prostitutes—subjects that had occupied him earlier in the section, and to which he seems to return at its conclusion? *Denique*, which appears to link the quotation from Paul to what immediately preceded it, and the fact that the quotation itself, involving the phrase *contra naturam*, actually echoes what preceded it, suggest on rhetorical grounds the former, so I incline to think Brooten is right. It remains, Augustine's intention has in mind by "women changing the natural use to that which is against nature" at 1.26b are not what we call "lesbian" sexual relations at all, but what might have been regarded by some in Paul's day as "unnatural" ways of women having sex with *men*— perhaps, in particular, women taking an "active" as opposed to a "passive" role (compare Ovid, according to whom experienced women knew "a thousand positions [*mille figuras*]" [*Art of Love* 2.679]; and Epictetus, [*Discourses* 3.1.27–37], who speaks with contempt of men who, to please women, transform themselves into women; compare also Plutarch, *On Marriage* 5, 18, and, 46 [*Moralia* 139a, 140c–d, 144e–f]). In that case, the word "likewise" (*homoiōs*) with which Paul links the respective charges against men and women in this passage does not mean "this case also involves same-sex relations," but "this case also involves men abandoning *egkrateia*."[62]

(The phrase *para phusin*, together with its opposite, *kata phusin* ["in accordance with nature"], can, of course, be used in other connections without such burdens of theological and philosophical baggage. Paul himself so uses both phrases at Romans 11.21–24, in a metaphor from arboriculture wherein, with regard to the grafting of a wild olive onto a cultivated olive, he speaks of it as *para phusin*, not because it should not happen, or because it is against God's will—in the context, it manifestly *is* God's will—but because it is, nonetheless, an interruption of the ordinary course of nature, insofar as nature is normally and humanly observed.)

So much for the act itself. What of the question of responsibility? We should note that the ancients in general—and, as it happens, Paul in particular—appear to have made no distinction between homosexual behavior as deliberate choice, and as arising from a psychological orientation whose nature and cause remains to this day (so far as I know) something of a mystery—as therefore, for some, an inclination both unchosen and unavoidable. Certainly, as Byrne has pointed out, "Any modern assessment of the issue in which scripture plays a part must clearly take this gap between ancient and modern thinking into consideration."[63]

As students of Paul, however, we may also incline to ask, What might Paul or any of his contemporaries have thought of homosexuality if they *had* been made aware of that distinction? In considering such a question we must be careful that it does not slide into a version of, "What would first-century people have thought if they had not been first-century people?"—in other words, a question without meaning—but that does not mean that the question itself, though finally unanswerable, is illegitimate.

A number of considerations appear to be relevant:

First, granted that Paul clearly did regard homosexual behavior as *planē* and *para phusin*, it is also clear that he does not in any sense regard it as *the* human problem. For Paul, evidently—as for all serious Jews—the essential and fundamental sin of humankind is refusal to glorify God as God: in a word, apostasy (1.18–23). All other sins, for Paul, are merely symptoms of this sin. That is the point of his repeated *paredōken* ("he handed them over") in the latter part of the first chapter of Romans—

---

in this detail is not completely clear—and, granted his purpose was to argue that *any* sexual activity not intended for procreation was illicit, there was no particular reason why it should be.

62. On women taking "the man's part" in heterosexual acts, see Ward, "Why Unnatural?" 282–84.

63. Byrne, *Romans* 70.

and that *paredōken* clearly includes "being handed" over to the sexual conduct of which he speaks in 1.26–27.

Second, even though Paul includes what we call homosexual behavior within his list of the symptoms of human rebellion, it is evident that he hardly regards it as the most serious even of those. The climax of his discussion of the results of human rebellion against God is, as we have noted, the list of "cold" sins, sins of "strength," in 1.28–31—"murder, strife, deceit, malignity, vicious gossips, public slanderers, haters of God, insolent, haughty, boasters, inventors of evil . . . faithless, heartless, ruthless." These he sees as the most destructive sins, and it is only of these that he says those who commit them are "worthy of death" (1.32).

Third, granted that Paul regarded (and might have continued to regard) male homosexual behavior as *planē* and *para phusin*, that hardly puts the homosexual person in a different position from that of any other human being since in Paul's view we *all* "have sinned" (or, as we might perhaps more precisely translate on this occasion, "have gone astray")[64] and "fallen short of the glory of God" (Rom. 3.23). Nor would the fact that for some the homosexual inclination was unchosen and unavoidable put such persons in a position different from anyone else, since, again, it is also evident that in Paul's view sin *in itself*, so far as the individual is concerned, is in the present age a thing unchosen and unavoidable. "I do not understand my own actions. For I do not do what I want, but I do the very thing I hate. Now if I do what I do not want, I agree that the Law is noble. So then it is no longer I that do it, but sin that dwells within me" (7.15). That, according to Paul, is the lot of humankind "in Adam," and there is no avoiding it. "Through the Law comes the knowledge of sin" (3.20b).

Fourth, we should note that besides the contrast between what Paul regards as sexual behavior *para phusin* and that which was (by implication) *kata phusin* ("according to nature" see, for example, 1 Cor. 7. 2–6), he writes about various other alternative states of being—male and female, slave and free, Greek and barbarian, Jew and gentile, "weak" and "strong." There is no doubt that he does not consider these pairs, whether they are anyone's "fault" or not, as being actually the same as each other, or as necessarily representing options that are of equal value or equally proper. He imagines being asked, for example, "What advantage has the Jew? Or what is the value of circumcision?" (Rom. 3.1), and his answer is clear, "Much in every way!" (3.2). In disputes about opinions between the "weak" and the "strong" it is, again, evident that he does consider it better, in itself, to be "strong" rather than "weak" (see 14.14). Given Paul's insistence on the reality of these distinctions (and given his probable understanding of Gen. 1.27–28, 2.18–25 [compare 1 Cor. 7.2, 10–11]), it is difficult to conceive of him under any circumstances regarding homosexuality as simply a God-given alternative to heterosexuality. He would probably have continued to claim that faithful, lifelong union between and a man and a woman is the only God-given "norm" for human beings.

On the other hand, even though, in the pairings I have identified, Paul does not necessarily regard both opinions or positions as of equal value, or equally soundly

---

64. On this as the meaning of biblical words for "sin," see additional note M.

based, his message to both groups is invariably the same: "[W]elcome one another, as Christ has welcomed you, for the glory of God." "Who are you to pass judgment on someone else's household slave? It is before their own master that they stand or fall; and they will be upheld, for the master is able to make them stand" (14.4). The basis for this acceptance is clear: that in the matter of the only pairing that really matters—namely, that between those who "honor God as God," of whom there are, according to Paul, "none . . . , no not one" (3.12), and those who have "refused" such honor, and so fallen short of the glory of God, in which company are "all" (3.23)—God has chosen to accept the disadvantaged group, "as a gift by his grace through the redemption that is in Christ Jesus" (3.24; compare 11.32).

Given, then, the awareness that, as we have noted, neither Paul nor his contemporaries had—namely, that of a distinction between homosexual behavior as deliberate choice, and homosexual behavior as arising from an unavoidable psychological orientation—the proper way actually to *apply* the biblical norm to those individuals who happen to have a homosexual orientation would remain, presumably, a matter for pastoral consideration.[65]

No doubt those who see homosexuality as a problem for the church will continue so to see it, and this is not the place to attempt the process of "discernment and decision making"[66] that such a problem will require. It is, however, my view that no proposed "solution" (whether "liberal" or "conservative") can possibly claim to be Pauline if it does not pay attention to the considerations listed above, for they are closely related to the essence of Paul's theology, and to his claim in Romans—which is, as we have said, that no human being can finally stand before God on *any* basis, save that of the justice and mercy of God. That is perhaps another way of saying that such a solution cannot be Pauline if it is not, in Paul's sense, "according to the Scriptures."

Additional Note L. "Self-Control"

Classically, *egkrateia* ("self-control") and its related state *karteria* ("endurance"), together with their opposites *akrasia* ("lack of self-control") and *malakia* ("softness" or "luxury"), had been described in Aristotle's *Nicomachean Ethics* (7.1.1–10.5 [1145a–1152a]). In our period the necessity for *egkrateia* in a complete human being was a commonplace among Jews and non-Jews alike: compare, from the pagan side, Epictetus, asserting what true philosophers ought to teach their fellows, "persuading them most of all, and above all else, that we are born with a natural sense of fellowship, and that self-control [*egkrateia*] is good"(*Discourses* 2.20.13: *Against Epicureans*

---

65. With the distinction I am making here, compare Joseph Monti on the need to distinguish between "ethical norms" and "moral rules": "Arguments about sexual morality often confuse ethical norms and moral rules, and by collapsing the distance between them offer little guidance to their proper role and function. Correcting this mistake will advance the moral rhetoric of the church in actual practice" (*Arguing about Sex: The Rhetoric of Christian Sexual Morality* [Albany, New York: State University of New York Press, 1995], 117).

66. I borrow the phrase from the title to Luke Timothy Johnson's useful trio of essays on this very subject, *Discernment and Decision Making in the Church* in STR 39.4 (1996): 352–84.

and Academics); and from the Jewish side, the hero Eleazar defying the tyranny of Antiochus: "I will not play you false, O Law my teacher; I will not forswear you, beloved self-control [*egkrateia*]; I will not shame you, philosophic reason, nor will I deny you, venerable priesthood and knowledge of the Law" (4 Macc. 5.33–35; see also *Letter of Aristeas* 278; Josephus, *Jewish War* 2.120, 138 [of the Essenes]). When Quintillian, in the Preface to his *Institutio Oratora*, speaks of the necessity for the orator to be a good person, the first three qualities that spring naturally to his mind are *iustitia, fortitudo,* and *temperantia*—justice, courage, and self-control (1.Pr.9,12).

Paul himself uses the word *egkrateia* in his list of the fruits of the Spirit at Galatians 5.23, and it forms part of the Lucan summary of his teaching at Acts 24.25. He does not use it in Romans; but the *idea* is clearly present at various points (see, for example, 5.3–4, 7.7–25)—and was, indeed, at this period, virtually inescapable, if one was to speak about virtue or virtuous persons.

It was not, of course, that Hellenistic thinkers did not recognize that people had needs, or even that pleasures could have value, but they were generally convinced that healthy human beings would be in control of these things, rather than the things in control of them: "Now of appetites and pleasures," Aristotle had said, "some belong to the class of things generically noble and good—for some pleasant things are by nature worthy of choice . . . but yet there is an excess even in them. . . . There is no wickedness, then, with regard to these objects, for the reason named, viz., because each of them is by nature a thing worthy of choice for its own sake; yet excesses in respect of them are bad and to be avoided" (*Nicomachean Ethics* 7.4.5 [1148a–1148b], trans. Sir David Ross).

There is evidently a sense in which *egkrateia* was perceived as an essentially masculine virtue: but that did not mean that women—or even slaves—could not achieve it: the object of *egkrateia* was, after all, not mastery over anyone else, but *self*-control. Plutarch's *Virtues in Women* is full of stories of women who display *egkrateia*—frequently when the men around them lack it. Similarly, in his *Consolation* to his wife on the death of their daughter, he compliments her upon her self-control in grief—and nothing could make clearer, incidentally, than this piece, that *egkrateia* did not involve the denial of feelings. In a Christian context, *egkrateia* is largely the issue in St. Perpetua's words as she prepared for martyrdom and says, "I became a man [*facta sum masculus*]" (*The Passion of Saints Perpetua and Felicity* 10.7): she means that in union with Jesus Christ she has achieved self-control, and therefore no one (including the men in her family) can have any power over her—that is, the *real* her, the inner her. When she deals with her father ("[Father,] can you call this jug by anything other than its true name?" "Certainly not!" "Well, I am the same. I cannot call myself by anything other than what I am: a Christian"), she is speaking and acting exactly as Epictetus would have approved, even if he might not have thought much of her actual beliefs. Thus, according to Epictetus, when the tyrant tells a philosopher to say what the philosopher believes is untrue, the philosopher should respond with

> not a word, for [the philosopher says,] This is under my control.
> "But I will chain you up!" [says the tyrant].
> What's that? Chain me up? My leg you can put in a chain, but my moral purpose not even Zeus can overcome.

"I will throw you into prison!"
My paltry body rather!
"I will behead you!"
Well, when did I ever claim that my neck could not be severed?
(*Discourses* 1.1.23–24, *Of the Things Which Are Under Our Control and Which Are Not Under Our Control*).

Behavior like Perpetua's was exactly the kind of thing that led the pagan philosopher Galen to say that Christians seemed able to act like philosophers, even if they didn't seem to think like them (*Summary of Plato's Republic*).

Bibliographical Note

On self-control, particularly as contrasted with "barbarian" behavior, see Edith Hall, *Inventing the Barbarian: Greek Self-Definition through Tragedy* (Oxford: Clarendon Press, 1989), especially 79–84, 125–33; also Stanley K. Stowers, A *Rereading of Romans: Justice, Jews, and Gentiles* (New Haven: Yale University Press, 1994), 47–65. On the relevance of *egkrateia* to Romans, Stowers, *Rereading Romans* 66–82, contains much that is helpful, although I do not accept Stowers's view of the recipients in mind throughout Romans.

God's "No!" to Our Injustice (2.1–3.20)

Therefore you, sir (*ō anthrōpe*)—the somewhat scornful use of the vocative of *anthrōpos* in philosophical dialogue ("You sir!" "Sirrah!") (also at 2.3 and 9.20) is far too well established not to have struck Paul's hearers (compare, for example, Epictetus, *Dissertations* 2.23.36–37, 4.9.5–6, 4.13.10). In Paul's discourse doubtless *anthrōpos* carries a certain additional irony in its being set against "the judgment of God" at 2.3 and "God" at 9.20, so that Paul's hearers would also have heard in it something of the implications of "mere mortal"—**you, sir, are without excuse** [*anapologētos*], **whoever you are when you judge another; for in passing judgment on another you condemn yourself, because you, the judge, are doing the very same things** (2.1).[67]

---

67. Barth's comment on "in passing judgment on another you condemn yourself" was as follows:

Whenever thou dost erect thyself upon a pedestal, thou doest wrong; whensoever thou sayest "I" or "we" or "it is so", thou dost exchange the glory of the incorruptible for the image of the corruptible (1.23). . . . The removal of thyself from the burden of the world by some pretended insight or vision does but press the burden of the world more heavily upon thee than upon any other. By striding ahead of others, even though it be for their assistance, as though the secret of God were known to thee, thou dost manifest thyself ignorant of God's secret; for by thy removal from thy fellows thou dost render thyself incapable of assisting even the most helpless among them. By beholding folly as the folly of others, thine own folly cries out to heaven. (*Romans* 56)

As will be obvious from my own comments on this passage, I do not think that this (at this point) was what Paul was getting at. I think Paul was making a much simpler point. Nevertheless, if ever there was an example of a new poem arising out of creative misreading of a text, this is it. I quote it, not because I think it wide of the mark, but because, as a general observation, and even as a general observation about Romans, I think it magnificent.

Here, it is crucial that we recognize not merely the diatribe form, with which Paul opens this section, but its function. Paul addresses an imaginary dialogue partner.[68] Tactfully (for the moment) Paul is somewhat vague about just who his partner might be. This somewhat oblique approach means that the person he addresses *could* be a philosophically minded gentile; or perhaps a gentile who had turned to Jesus Christ; or perhaps again a Jew; or perhaps even a Jew like some of Paul's hearers—a Jew who had added belief in Jesus as Messiah to an original belief in Israel's covenant status and the necessity of the Law. *Precisely* what sort of person Paul's hearers are to imagine will emerge only as the conversation continues. For the moment, he makes a simple point: **whoever you are,** if you condemn another while **doing the very same things,** you also **condemn yourself**.

Now—whatever particular kind of person is supposed to fit this brief portrait— the portrait is also clearly something of a caricature, at least as far as anyone in Paul's *real* audience is concerned. Not for one moment need we suppose Paul imagined that among his good listeners in the Roman church, Jewish *or* gentile by origin, there were some who were personally rushing into the riot of evil he had just described and needed to be confronted with the consequences of that debauch. But they would all have known perfectly well the position of someone—**whoever** he or she was— who did **judge another**, and yet did **the very same things**. In short, Paul was presenting them with a topos that they would have recognized at once: "It really doesn't much matter what you *say*, if you don't *do*. In fact, the better you *talk*, the worse things are if you don't live up to it." Epictetus, in his own way, makes exactly the same point to *his* imaginary dialogue partner:

> What is making progress, then? The person who has read many treatises by Chrysippus? Why, does Virtue consist in having gained a thorough knowledge of Chrysippus? . . . For if you are acting in harmony with nature, give me evidence of that, and I will say that you are making progress; but if you are acting out of harmony, be on your way! Do not merely comment on these treatises . . . ! (*Discourses* 1.4.6,15)

We know, Paul says, **that God's judgment on those who do such things is in accordance with truth** (2.2). Well, of course. Any right-minded person ought to know that. **Do you then suppose, sir, whoever you are, that when you judge those who do such things, and yet do them yourself, you will escape the judgment of God?** (2.3) Obviously, anyone who supposed such a thing would be mad.

---

68. In terms of rhetorical technique, in this section of his argument (2.1–3.20) Paul alternates between passages of *synkrisis* ("comparison") (2.12–16, 2.25–29), and passages of dialogue with the imaginary objector (2.1–11, 2.17–24, 3.1–9), concluding with a lengthy series of authoritative citations (3.10–18). So much we may say in general terms. Beyond that, we need to concede that in the dialogue passages, and also below at 3.27–4.1, while *precisely* what was understood to be said by the dialogue partner and what was understood to be said by Paul was doubtless clear to Paul himself, and was probably made clear to whoever was authorized to deliver Romans, it is by no means always clear to us. We can only make our best guess, conceding, as Robert L. Brawley points out, "the lack of methodological controls for identifying different speakers in a diatribe" ("Multivocality in Romans 4," in *Society of Biblical Literature 1997 Seminar Papers* [Atlanta, Georgia: Scholars Press, 1997], 295, footnote 32, citing an unpublished review of Stowers, *Rereading Romans*, by Richard Hays).

Yet Paul continues to hammer away at the point. Would not to think and behave in such a way be to **presume on the riches of** God's **kindness** [*chrēstotētos*][69]
and forbearance and patience [*makrothumias*] (2.4a)? Wouldn't such a person know
that such **kindness** and **patience** was always **meant to lead to repentance** (2.4b)?
The psalmist had pleaded with God to overlook his sins on the grounds of God's
"compassion [*tōn oiktirmōn*]" and by appeal to God's "mercies [*ta eleē*]" (LXX Ps. 24
[MT 25].6–7)—but he had also clearly offered amendment of life (vv. 15, 20). By
contrast, would not such stubborn persistence as this merely be storing up for itself
wrath on the **day of wrath** (2.5)?

Of course, no one among Paul's hearers could or would disagree with any of this.
The Book of Wisdom had used the very same arguments to speak of God's "patience"
with the gentiles (Wisd. of Sol. 11.23b, 12.8–11). But Paul now goes a little further.
There will be tribulation and distress for every human being who does evil, the
Jew first and also the Greek, but glory and honor and peace for every one that
does good, the Jew first and also the Greek. For there is no partiality with God
(2.9–11). Obedience is obedience, Paul says, and disobedience is disobedience,
whoever does it: what is sauce for the gentile goose is sauce for the Jewish gander
(contrast Wisd. of Sol. 12.20–22; Ps. Sol. 18.4).

This, for some among Paul's audience, might be a little more painful, but still
they could scarcely argue. Sirach said exactly the same thing: "The Lord is judge,
and with him there is no partiality" (35.12)—and merely followed Deuteronomy and
the Psalmist: "For the Lord your God is God of Gods and Lord of Lords . . . who is
not partial and by no means takes a bribe" (LXX Deut. 10.17; see also 2 Chron. 19.7);
"You render to each according to his works" (LXX Ps. 61.13 [MT 62.13]). Had not
the prophet Amos said that precisely *because* of Israel's privileged position, the Lord's
anger was the more severe against her when she transgressed?

> But you I knew out of all the families of the earth;
> therefore I will exact justice upon you for all your sins. (LXX Amos 3.2)

Now throughout this tirade—throughout what Paul has already said, and what
he is about to say—we who are influenced by Luther (and no serious modern Christian of whatever denomination can [or even should] avoid being influenced by Luther
to some extent) have an enormous and constant temptation to try to find some "gospel" in it—to claim, for example, that the "work" about which Paul is talking is "faith,"
or "looking for God's salvation." But that, if we wish to follow Paul's argument, is
precisely what we must not do. What Paul says from 2.1 to 2.29 must be taken in its
plain and obvious sense, for he is talking about **judgment** (*krima, krinein*: see also 2.1
[3 times], 2, 3 [twice], 12, 16); and what he is saying is that God's **judgment** of everyone is based on *deeds*, not status, or race, or privilege, or anything else. **All who have**
sinned—all who have acted in ways that miss or go astray from God's will[70]—**with-**
out the Law will perish without the Law, and all who have sinned under the Law

---

69. References to God's *chrēstotēs*, or to God as *chrēstos*, are also present in the LXX Psalms: see,
e.g., LXX Ps. 30.20 [MT 31.19], 85.5 [MT 86.5], 99.5 [100.5], 118.68 [119.68].

70. On "sin" and its cognates, see additional note M.

will be judged by the Law. For it is not the hearers of the Law who are just before God, but the doers of the Law who will be justified (2:12–13).

Sometimes even gentiles get it right. What then? **When gentiles that do not have the Law do by nature the things of the Law, they, not having the Law, are the Law to themselves, in that they show that what the Law requires is written on their hearts, while their conscience [*suneidēsis*][71] also bears witness and their conflicting thoughts accuse them, or perhaps** even **excuse them on that day when, according to my gospel, God judges human secrets by the Messiah Jesus** (2.14–16). This is the first time in the entire tirade that Paul has mentioned Jesus or the gospel, and there is a grim irony in it. "My gospel," he is pointing out, "takes sin and obedience, and believes God takes sin and obedience, just as seriously as you do." Sin is sin, and doing justice is doing justice, whether you are a Jew or a gentile, and whether you believe in Jesus Christ or not.

So Paul moves to his second direct address to his imaginary partner, and now at last we learn something more about who the partner is: **you call yourself a Jew and rely upon the Law and boast about God** (2.17). You know **God's will and determine what is best because you are instructed in the Law** (2.18).

Other Jewish writers spoke of such privileges for Israel. So, for example, an author writing some time after the destruction of Jerusalem by the Romans in 70:

> In you we have put our trust, because, behold, your Law is with us,
> and we know we do not fall as long as we keep your statutes.
> We shall always be blessed; at least, we did not mingle with the nations.
> For we are all a people of the Name;
> we, who received one Law from the One.
> And that Law which is among us will help us,
> And that excellent wisdom which is in us will support us. (*2 Apoc. Bar.* 48.22–24, trans. A. F. J. Klijn)

So you are sure that you are a guide to the blind, a light to those who are in darkness, a corrector of the foolish, a teacher of children, having in the Law the embodiment of knowledge and truth (2.20). Had not the prophet said

> I the Lord God called you in justice . . .
> and I gave you to be a covenant for the people,
> to be a light for the nations,
> to open the eyes of the blind,
> to lead forth from their bonds the prisoners,
> and from the prison house those who sit in darkness. (LXX Isa. 42.6–7)

---

71. As C. A. Pierce demonstrated in his seminal work *Conscience in the New Testament* (London: SCM Press, 1955) the word *suneidēsis* and its cognates are used "again and again, throughout the range of Greek writing as a whole—not in literature only—from the sixth century B.C. to the seventh century A.D. . . . It is in fact an 'everyday' group of words expressing a commonplace idea—truly popular, and belonging rather to 'folk wisdom' than to 'popular philosophy'—or rather, second-hand philosophical jargon" (16–17). Despite the suggestions of some critics, there is therefore no reason to connect Paul's use of the word at Romans 2.15 with Stoicism. He simply uses it in its usual sense of "moral consciousness" or "conscience" (LS, συνείδησις; BAGD, συνείδησις 2)—of "knowledge-shared-with-oneself" of having done good or ill.

What then? Paul puts a series of questions,

> **You then that teach others, will you not teach yourself? While you preach against stealing, do you steal? You that forbid adultery, do you commit adultery? You that abhor idols, do you rob shrines? You that boast in the Law, do you dishonor God by breaking the Law?**—as it is written, **The name of God is blasphemed among the gentiles because of you**. (citing LXX Isa. 52.5) (2.21–24)

Paul quotes the Septuagint text of Isaiah but alters its implication. In the Septuagint, "because of you" speaks of what has been done to the exiled people of God by their gentile enemies; Paul hears the phrase speaking of Israel's own transgressions that have led to her continuing exile, and to the scandal caused thereby among the gentiles (Deut. 28.15–68, 31.16–21; compare Ezek. 36.17–20).

Here Paul has touched upon central commands of the Law—theft, adultery, idolatry,[72] and blasphemy of the name of God (2.21b–24). Again, of course, he does not imagine that his hearers are themselves busily engaged in doing these things. His point, even now, is quite simple. His "Jew" is an obvious caricature, but his hearers all know perfectly well what *must* be the position of any Jews who boast of their reliance on the Law and their relation to God and yet answer "Yes" to such questions as Paul is putting. Had not the psalmist said it?

> Why do you recount my statutes,
>   and take my covenant upon your mouth?
> You hated discipline [*paideian*],
>   and cast my words behind you.
> If you saw a thief, you were in league with him,
>   and you cast your lot with adulterers. . . .
> These things you did and I was silent;
>   You assumed, in lawless fashion, that I was like you:
> I will convict you,
>   and I will show you to yourself, face to face.
> Understand these things, you that forget God,
>   lest he snatch you away, and there be none to deliver. (LXX Ps. 49.16–18, 21–22
>   [MT 50.16–18, 21–22])

Circumcision is indeed of value if you obey the Law, but if you break the Law, your circumcision becomes uncircumcision (2.25). For,

> Behold the days are coming, says the Lord,
>   when I shall come in visitation against all the circumcised for their
> uncircumcision . . .

---

72. Although the general direction of Paul's argument is, I think, clear, precisely what he intends by the third of his questions—"You that abhor idols, do you rob shrines?" (2.22b)—remains uncertain. The most sensible suggestion seems to be that he is thinking of Jewish merchants profiting by disposing of valuable artifacts stolen from pagan shrines (or else by reusing precious metals that had been part of them) on the pretext that, since pagan gods do not exist, objects dedicated to them have no owner. Such behavior would be against *tôrâ* (compare Deut. 7.25–26), as well, incidentally, as being generally contrary to pagan mores (e.g., Plato, *Republic* 344b). See Gottlob Schrenk, "ἱεροσυλέω, ἱερόσυλος," in *TDNT* 3. 255–57, especially 256; see further J. Duncan M. Derrett, "'You Abominate False Gods; but Do You Rob Shrines?' Rom 2.22b," *NTS* 40.4 (1994): 558–71.

the whole house of Israel are uncircumcised in their heart. (LXX Jer. 9.24–25 [MT Jer. 9.25–26])

If therefore one who is uncircumcised keeps the just requirements [*dikaiōmata*] of the Law, will not his uncircumcision be reckoned [*logisthēsetai*] as circumcision? and will not the one who is by nature uncircumcised but keeps the Law condemn you who have the written code and circumcision, but break the Law? . . . One is a Jew who is one inwardly, and real circumcision is of the heart, spiritual and not literal. Such a person receives not human praise, but God's (2.26–27, 29).[73]

We must not by any device drag "gospel" into all this because if we do, we entirely lose Paul's rhetoric. In one sense, of course, he was deadly serious; but in another, as a rhetorician, he was playing a game. It was open to his imaginary partner (or, indeed, his Jewish listeners in the congregation at Rome) to say at any point during his tirade, "*Of course* we do not keep the Law properly all the time. Sometimes, no doubt, we all live like gentiles. But God's justice means that God is faithful to us, even when we fail God. You have said nothing of God's mercy. Even for sins as terrible as those you mention, there is always a place for repentance." For a striking example of this, the imaginary partner might have pointed to Manasseh, the king of Israel whose sins were so grievous that they brought about the destruction of his people: yet even he, when he repented, was accepted (see 2 Chron. 33.10–16; Pr. of Man.). As a twentieth-century Jewish writer, Michael Wyschogrod, points out,

> Every Jew knows, or should know, that if God were to pay him what he deserves, neither more nor less, he would be lost. His only chance depends upon the mercy of God. If God decides to overlook his sorry record and to bestow mercy rather than justice on him, then he has a chance. But certainly not otherwise.
>
> So the Jew does not claim to be "justified" by works of the law but rather by the mercy of God.[74]

All that, presumably, was as obvious to Paul as it is to us—as also would have been Paul's response to it, in effect, "Thank you. Then you concede that for our salvation we Jews do not finally 'rely upon the Law' at all, and never have. We rely on God's

---

73. The contrast between outward circumcision and inward circumcision (circumcision of the heart) is, of course, familiar both in biblical and later Judaism (Lev. 26.41; Deut. 10.16, 30.6; Jer. 4.4, 9.25–26; Ezek. 44.7, 9; 1 QS 5.5; 1QH 2.18; 1QpHab 11.13; *Jub.* 1.23; Philo, *On the Special Laws* 1.304–6; *On the Migration of Abraham* 92–93); hence I do not find Cohen's and Jolivet's hypothesis (see page 53, footnote 43) necessary. On the other hand, there is a notable shift in Paul's usage. In many of the preceding passages (though not Philo) the circumcised heart will be a mark of the true Jew in the future: for Paul, as for Philo, it is the mark of the true Jew now—but perhaps for a different reason. Philo is generally not interested in eschatology. Paul, by contrast, is deeply interested, but for Paul the first stage in the fulfillment of the eschatological promise is already here (which is not, of course, to say that for Paul, too, the completion of that fulfillment is not still in the future: see 3.30, 8.18–25, 13.11–14). The only other parallel to Paul's use of the "inward circumcision" image in the present tense of which I am aware is the beautiful passage in the *Odes of Solomon* 11.1–3—which is also certainly Christian.

74. Michael Wyschogrod, "The Impact of Dialogue with Christianity on My Self-Understanding as a Jew," in *Die Hebräische Bibel und ihre zweifache Nachgeschichte, Festschrift für Rolf Rendtorff zum 65 (Geburtstag:* Neukirchener Verlag, 1990), 731.

justice and God's grace. That is what 'my gospel' teaches." Or, as he put it on another occasion to Peter, "If you, being a Jew, live like a gentile and not like a Jew, how can you compel the gentiles to live like Jews? We ourselves, who are Jews by birth and not gentile sinners, we know that one is not justified by works of Law, but through faith in Jesus Christ" (Gal.2.14–16).[75]

For the moment, however, Paul allows no such appeal. He insists on pursuing the logic of one who will **rely on the Law** (2.17), and presents, in diatribe style, the following dialogue, beginning with a question evidently put by his partner, who at this point has become his critic: **"Then what advantage has the Jew? Or what is the value of circumcision?"** (3.1). The question is understandable enough and may well represent one of the actual challenges that Paul had received, debating this question with Jewish believers in Christ who were frustrated by his logic, yet unable to get past it.[76] "Since you are so clever, perhaps *you* could tell *me* why there is any point in being a Jew?"

The dialogue (which in the letter's original delivery could easily have been brought out for Paul's hearers by the properly prepared reader) continues as follows:

Paul: **Much in every way! To begin with, Jews are entrusted with the oracles of God** (3.2). Certainly Paul does not intend this lightly. The "oracles of God [*ta logia tou theou*]," according to the psalmist, are "the counsel of the most high"—in rebellion against which Israel is merely "in darkness and the shadow of death . . . in poverty and iron" (LXX Ps. 106.10–11 [MT. 107.10–11]; see also Josephus, *War* 6.310–13; Philo, *On the Contemplative Life* 25; *On Rewards and Punishments* 1.1). In a word, Israel's privilege, as she had always claimed, was that she *knew*. She thanked God for

> announcing his word to Jacob,
>   his statutes and ordinances to Israel;
> he did not do thus with every nation,
>   and he did not reveal his ordinances to them (LXX Ps. 147.8–9 [MT Ps.147.19–20])

Some of the implications of this privilege Paul will spell out later (see 9.4–5); for the moment, he passes to his partner's next question.

Partner: **Then what if some were unfaithful? Does their faithlessness nullify the faithfulness of God?** (3.3). Granted the gift, and the promises it implied, was Paul then implying that God had not remained faithful to those promises? Was not

---

75. I here follow P46 and Alexandrinus in omitting *de* at Galatians 2.16. The point at issue in Galatians is surely that it is *because* Peter is a Jew that Paul expects him to understand that "one is not justified by works of the Law," not *in spite* of his being a Jew (so, correctly, KJV and BEP; but contrast DR, RV, ARV, RSV, NEB, NAB, NRSV, BJ). In fact, even if we do retain *de*, the KJV and BEP translations are defensible, since the particle *de* itself is often used as a simple connective, without necessarily implying contrast [see BAGD, δέ]: see Michael Winger, *By What Law? The Meaning of Νόμος in the Letters of Paul* (Atlanta, Georgia: Scholars Press, 1992), 132–33.

76. Indeed, throughout this entire dialogue, I gain the impression that the "Jewish objector" becomes something less of a caricature, and something more the voice of serious objections that Paul might actually have heard and tried to answer. As evidence for this, I would point to the fact (repeatedly noted above) that the questions raised here are all questions that Paul will, in fact, reflect on further, and at some length, in later parts of the letter.

that the implication of Paul's claim that sinful Jews were no better off than sinful gentiles?

Paul: **By no means!** (3.4a). The very suggestion that God is unfaithful is dismissed by Paul in true diatribe fashion—*mē genoito!*: literally, "Let it not be so!" **Let God be true, though every human being a liar!** (3.4b). That God is **true** (*alēthēs*: that is, truthful, reliable) will remain evident, whatever may be the degree of human treachery. Precisely how it is that God in dealing with Israel remains faithful will be spelled out by Paul later (9–11); for the present, he is content to remind his opponent of Scripture: **as it is written, *That thou mayst be justified in thy words, and prevail when thou art judged*** (3.4c; compare LXX Ps. 50.1, 6 [MT 51.intro. and 4]). Even King David, guilty of adultery and murder, knew that in his confession of sin God's justice would be manifest and that in judgment God would triumph.

Partner: **But if our injustice makes manifest God's justice, what shall we say? That God is unjust in inflicting wrath?** (*I speak*, Paul observes in an aside, evidently embarrassed by the expression about God's "injustice" that he has allowed his partner to use, *in a human way*) (3.5).

Paul: **By no means! For then how could God judge the world?** (3.6). The suggestion that God might be unjust is dismissed as abruptly as was the suggestion that God might be unfaithful. It was (and remains) fundamental to Judaism that judgment was the prerogative of God, that judgment was the manifestation of God's justice, and that God will judge:

> For lo, the Lord as fire will come,
>   and his chariots as a hurricane,
> to render punishment [*ekdikēsin*: that is, the exaction of justice] in wrath,
>   and utter casting off, by a flame of fire.
> For by the fire of the Lord all the land will be judged,
>   and all flesh by his sword. (LXX Isa. 66.15–16; compare Joel 3.12; Ps. 93.2 [MT 94.2])

This, too, Paul will reflect on at greater length in 9–11, but for the moment he is content to refuse the suggestion and then to allow his partner to put another question.

Partner: **But if through my falsehood God's truthfulness abounds to his glory, why am I still being condemned as a sinner? And why not do evil that good may come?** (3.7–8a). Again, Paul will later consider this challenge at greater length and explain what he sees as its error (6.1–22); for the present, he simply notes that some people accuse him of teaching exactly this—**as some people slanderously charge us with saying**—and rejects it: **Their condemnation is just** (3.8b).

Partner (*continuing*): **What then follows? Are we Jews at a disadvantage?** (3.9a)[77] Is *that* the implication of what Paul is saying? Perhaps it would be better not to have

---

77. There are a number of difficulties with 3.9a—the text, the punctuation of the text, and the voice of the verb. The above follows the preferred reading and the punctuation of Nestle-Aland 27. The verb, *proechometha*, is a middle-passive form. It seems most natural to take it as passive (BAGD, προέχω 3) (so Fitzmyer, *Romans* 330–31), and this way of reading also appears, in the context, to make perfectly good sense. The majority of commentators, however, read *proechometha* as middle with an active sense, "Do we have an advantage?"—a meaning not found elsewhere for the middle of *proechō* (see BAGD, προέχω 2).

known the Law at all?—a view that Paul himself will feel bound to consider seriously at a later point (7.7–25). Here, again, for the moment he is content simply to deny it. **Not at all,** Paul has not said that Jews are at any *disadvantage,* **for we have already charged that** *all,* **Jews and Greek alike, are under the power of sin** (3.9b).

Strictly speaking, perhaps, Paul has not yet made this charge. What he *has* shown is that according to the Law, which his critics claim to value so highly, as well as according to "his gospel," God takes sin very seriously, whether it is gentile sin or Jewish sin; and he may, I think, reasonably be supposed to have sufficient respect for his critics' honesty to know that, while doubtless scarcely conceding that they were involved in the riot of evil he had described for their edification, still they would admit, if pressed, that their lives were not spotless. In any case, he proceeds to make his charge now, with a series of quotations from the Scripture carefully chosen to point not only to the *universality* but also to the **power of** human **sin, as it is written,**

> *There is none who is righteous,* **not even one.** (echoing and amplifying LXX Eccles. [MT Qoh.] 7.20)
> *No one has understanding; no one searches for God;*
> *All have turned aside, together they have gone wrong;*
> *no one does good, not even one.* (alluding to LXX Ps. 13 [MT 14].2–3; closely paralleled in Ps. 52 [MT 53].1b, 3)
> *Their throat is an open grave,*
> *they use their tongues to deceive.* (LXX 5.10b)
> *The venom of asps is under their lips.* (LXX Ps. 139 [MT 140].4b)
> *Their mouth is full of cursing and bitterness.* (echoing LXX Ps. 9.28 [MT Ps.10.7])
> *Their feet are swift to shed blood,*
> *In their paths are ruin and misery,*
> *and the way of peace they do not know.* (adapting LXX Isa. 59.7–8a)
> *There is no fear of God before their eyes.* (LXX Ps. 35 [MT 36].2b) (3.10–18)

Did Paul compose this group of *testimonia*[78] himself, or did he use an already existing list, perhaps liturgical in origin? It is impossible to know, but in any case Fitzmyer is surely right in observing that the group "is hardly a composition of Paul put together ad hoc during his dictation of the letter."[79] It may well be, as Leander Keck has argued, that Paul's reflection on the position of humankind apart from the justice and mercy of God was based (in combination with his own experience of Christ) on traditions such as these, so that in a sense more than rhetorical or even logical, what he had so far said (1.18–3.9) found its culmination here.[80]

78. The name for this literary form appears to derive from Cyprian's treatise *Ad Quirinium: Testimoniorum libri tres* (CSEL 3.1, 35–184), an anti-Jewish polemic that proceeded by gleaning various Old Testament passages to use against the Jews. The form itself is, however, evidently much older than Cyprian. It occurs in the Qumran literature, and therefore was evidently Jewish and pre-Christian: see *Testimonies* (4Q175 [4QTestim]), which resembles Romans 3.10–20 in that it not only strings together a series of quotations from Scripture, but also concludes with a quotation to which is added an interpretation.

79. Fitzmyer, *Romans* 334.

80. Leander E. Keck, "The Function of Romans 3.10–18: Observations and Suggestions," in *God's Christ and His People: Studies in Honour of Nils Alstrup Dahl,* ed. J. Jervell and Wayne A. Meeks (Oslo: Universitetsforlaget, 1977), 141–57.

Had someone once pointed out to Paul that the bulk of the *testimonia* he cited seemed to be aimed against gentiles? If so, Paul would have none of it. On the contrary—**Now we know that whatever the Law says, it speaks to those who are under the Law, so that every mouth may be silenced and the whole world may be held accountable to God** (3.19). Paul had, moreover, a final passage for his auditors to consider—the words of David himself: **For *no human being will be justified in his sight*** by deeds prescribed by the Law (*ex ergōn nomou*—literally, "through works of the Law" [also at 3.28 and 9.32, and the singular form at 2.15]) (3.20a). Despite some recent debate, "deeds prescribed by the Law"—that is, deeds performed in conscious obedience to God's commandments—is evidently the meaning of the phrase *ex ergōn nomou*, which, although it is not found either in the Old Testament or later rabbinic witings, does occur in the Qumran literature.[81] Paul's allusion here was to LXX Psalm 142 (MT Psalm 143), and it was peculiarly apt:

> Lord . . . do not enter into judgment with your slave,
> for none living shall be justified in your sight.

It would be hard to think of a passage that made better the point Paul was making than David's lament (according to the tradition) over the disloyalty and ruin of his own family, "when his son is persecuting him" (LXX Ps. 142.1). Evidently **no human being**, not even David, is justified **by deeds prescribed by the Law**. What the Law tells us is the truth about ourselves, **since through the Law comes the knowledge of** our **sin** (3:20b).

Additional Note M. Sin

(a) *The General Concept*

Hamartia ("sin") and its cognates (*hamartanō*: "to sin"; *hamartēma →hamartia; hamartōlos*: "sinner") were originally words to do with archery or the javelin, and spoke of "missing one's mark." Thus, for example, Homer had told how Diomedes threw his spear at Dolon and "missed deliberately" (*Iliad* 10.372). But the word group is also found in general use in connection with failing in one's purpose, or of intellectual error, perhaps through defective education: so, for example, Plutarch, criticizing the Stoics for believing "the ignorant person [*ton amathē*] to be quite wrong [*hamartōlon einai*] in all things" (*On Listening to the Poets*, Moralia 25c; compare Philo, *That Every Good Man is Free* 132).

From the beginning, however, these words also sometimes carried the sense of *transgressing*—against divinity, custom, or law. Thus, again, in Homer, the old warrior Phoenix reminded Achilles that by propitiatory rites even the gods may be turned from wrath "when any one transgresses and goes astray [*hamartē*]" (*Iliad* 9.501); nearer

---

81. Thus in the document titled *More Precepts of the Torah* (4Q394–99 [4QMMTa–f] the phrase *ma'ase hattorah* ("deeds of the law") occurs in connection with talk of *sdqh* ("justice"), and the citing of Gen. 15.6 (compare Romans 4.2); see also *Florilegium* 1.7 (4Q174 [4QFlor]), and the *Rule of the Community* 5.21, 6.18 (1QS).

to our own period, we find common usage of *hamartōlos estō* in curses on violators of graves (for example, *CIG* 3.4307, 4259).

It was, then, in accordance with its already established meanings that in the LXX the *hamart-* word group was used most often to translate Hebrew *ḥaṭṭā't*, which also sometimes meant simply "miss the target" (for example, MT Judg. 20.16; compare LXX *diamartanontes*), but was also frequently used with the implication "offend against God" (MT Exod. 32.30; compare LXX *hēmartēkate hamartian megalēn*: "you have sinned a great sin")—including, incidentally, offenses committed in ignorance (for example, MT Lev. 5.15, compare LXX *hamartē[i] akousiōs*). It is perfectly clear, therefore, that while both *ḥaṭṭā't* and *hamartia* and their cognates can have religious significance, neither of them is essentially a religious word—something that is true, incidentally, of other Hebrew words for "sin," *'āwōn* (meaning something twisted or distorted, deviating from the norm) and *peša'* (meaning "rebellion"), both of which are also often rendered in the LXX by *hamartia* and it cognates. We might appropriately compare the range of meanings possible for English "err" and its cognates—all the way from Robert Southey's "The arrows . . . err not from their aim" (*Thalaba the Destroyer* 1.42), through Sir Benjamin Brodie's "It seems to me that the best writers . . . have erred in considering the mind too abstractedly" (*Psychological Inquiries* 1.2.42), to "we have erred and strayed from thy ways like lost sheep" (*Book of Common Prayer* 1662).

All this sets *hamartia* and the Hebrew words it can render in sharp contrast to their most common English translation, "sin"—which has become almost exclusively a religious word. For this reason, indeed, I considered rendering *hamartia* and its cognates throughout my own translation by "err" and its cognates: that I have not done so is because the tradition of using the English "sin" for *hamartia* seems now so firmly established as to render any attempt to change it merely a cause for confusion.

Pauline usage of *hamartia* and its cognates follows the general pattern of the LXX. As we shall see, however, in two particular respects Paul's understanding of sin appears to be qualified by reflections that are particularly characteristic of the post-biblical period.

1. A number of deuterocanonical and extracanonical books see a connection between the Genesis fall story and the problems of human disobedience (for example, Wisd. of Sol. 2.23–24; Ecclus. 25.24; 2 [4] Esdras 7.116–18; *Jub.* 3.23–25; *Enoch* 30.17; *Life of Adam and Eve* [Greek] 14.1–3, [Latin] 44.1–5); Paul evidently moves within the realm of such speculation (Rom. 5.12–21; 1 Cor. 15.21, 45–50; 2 Cor. 11.3).

2. Particularly in the Dead Sea Scrolls, although also in other Jewish post-biblical literature, there is discernible a tendency to speak not merely of particular sins, but of sin as a "power" dominating human lives; and in this connection there is also an interest in the "spirit of holiness " that will repair the broken relationship between God and humanity and restore "the glory of Adam" (*Rule of the Community*: 1QS 4. 20–23). Paul evidently moves in this field of discourse also (Rom. 7.7–25).

(b) Sin Committed in Ignorance

Sin committed in ignorance is a category of which the ancients were certainly aware. Actions performed with good intentions, such as Neoptolemus robbing Philoctetes of his bow, may still be *hamartia*, and need to be atoned (see Sophocles, *Philoctetes* 1221–26). The Old Testament was also aware of this possibility, and the Law offered specific remedies. While the precise relationship between sin- and guilt-offering, and the situations that necessitate them, are not entirely clear, it is clear that both are concerned with nondeliberate offenses: "if anyone sins, doing any of the things which the Lord has commanded not to be done, and does not know it [*kai ouk egnō*]" (LXX Lev. 5.17; compare 5.3). (Deliberate offenses are quite another matter. Crimes against the neighbor are dealt with by punishments not involving sacrifice, while rebellion against God [sin with "a high hand" (LXX *en cheiri huperēphanias*)] cannot be atoned by sacrifice at all: "[B]ecause of having despised the word of the Lord and broken his commandment, that soul shall be utterly destroyed, its sin shall be upon it" [LXX Num. 15.31]).

Some moderns seem to have difficulty taking seriously the notion of sin committed in ignorance, yet in our own century, at a *corporate* and *communal* level, it is easy to see its results in, for example, the racism of Nazi Germany, apartheid South Africa, or the United States, or the religious and social bigotry of Northern Ireland, Israel, or the Balkans. Those enslaved to these forms of bigotry may be (and frequently seem to be) utterly convinced that they are "right," and so, in Pauline terms, we might suggest that such sin cannot be "counted" against them in the fullest sense—that is to say, it is not reckoned against them as deliberate rebellion against God's Law. Nonetheless, as Paul observed, such sin still has its dominion: it "reigns"—which is to say, its disastrous consequences remain and will continue to remain, for others, for its perpetrators, and for their children.

Likewise, the disastrous effects of unconscious sin upon the *individual* psyche have been highlighted by some twentieth-century analysis. As Victor White pointed out, the

> deliberate sinner, who acts with full knowledge and consent, is at least acting as a human being; to act otherwise . . . without consciousness and responsibility, is to act infra-humanly. . . . It is true that only deliberate choice can separate us from the love of God and bring about the final loss of God: and it is true that only such deliberate sin is a necessary matter for the sacrament of penance. But emphasis on this can too easily blind us to the full reality of sin, which, according to Aquinas and the older theologians, may occur not only from the informed consent of the will, but also when intelligence and will should intervene but do not do so.[82]

White further notes the ancients' connection of much that we know as "guilt" with their concept of "shame [*verecundia*]," and cites Aquinas, *Summa* 1–2.44.

God's "Yes!" through Jesus the Messiah (3.21–31)

But now something new has happened. **God's justice has been manifested to us apart from Law, although the Law and the prophets bear witness to it—God's**

---

82. Victor White, "Guilt: Theological and Psychological," in *Christian Essays in Psychiatry*, ed. Philip Mairet (New York: Philosophical Library, 1956),165–66, citing Aquinas, *Summa Theologica* 1–2.74.3–6.

justice manifested **through the faith of Jesus Christ** [*dia pisteōs Iēsou Christou*][83] **for all who have faith** (3.21–22; compare 1.17). Inasmuch as Jesus Christ is faithful, insofar as we hazard our faith in response, there God's justice is seen. What, exactly, brought about this state of affairs? In Paul's view, it was brought about when Jesus died outside Jerusalem, becoming a "curse for us," and rose for the justification of those who trust in him. As Paul wrote on another occasion,

> Christ redeemed us from the curse of the Law by becoming a curse for us—as it is written, "Cursed is everyone who hangs on a tree"—in order that in Christ Jesus the blessing of Abraham might come to the Gentiles [this being, in Paul's view, the original promise: see Gen. 12:3b], so that we might receive the promise of the Spirit through faith. (Gal. 3.13–14)

So now he writes to the Romans: **For there is no distinction; for all have sinned and come short of the glory of God, being justified** [*dikaioumenoi*] **by his grace as a gift, through the redemption** [*apolutrōseōs*] **that is in Christ Jesus: whom God set forth to be a propitiation, or a Mercy Seat** [*hilastērion*], **by his** own **blood, through faith** [*dia pisteōs*] (3:22b–25a). God's response to our disobedience was the faithful obedience of Jesus Christ on the cross—in his own blood.

It is possible, though by no means certain, that Paul was here adapting for the purposes of his argument a formula already familiar to Jewish believers,[84] which would certainly have been a piece of rhetorical tact on his part; in any case, the three metaphors that now fly past us like changing images on a screen enable him to make his point with a force that has echoed through the centuries.

The first metaphor—**justified**—is about law and judgment: the dominant metaphor, as we observed, of Romans 2.1–3.20. Those standing before the judge are guilty, and by the criterion of judgment alone their doom is sealed. But now it is the judge who provides the solution for their plight: **by his grace, as a gift** they are **justified**.

"Justify" (Greek: *dikaioō*) means "to treat as just," or, more simply, "to acquit." For Paul, "justification" (*dikaiōsis*) is God's declaration that we are not condemned, even though we are sinners; and through that declaration we are holy ("set apart for God"), for by it we are set in a positive relationship with the One who is Holy. The believer is, in Luther's phrase, *simul iustus et peccator*.[85] This, as Karl Rahner finely observed, is "God's justice, that in fact divinises us, [being] an unmerited gift of God's incalculable favor"[86]—and this is the justification that is brought about **through the redemption that is in Christ Jesus**.

---

83. On "the faith of Jesus Christ," see additional note O.

84. On 3.24–26 as a pre-Pauline formula, see additional note N.

85. See, for example, Jaroslav Pelikan, ed., *Luther's Works*, vol. 26, *Lectures on Galatians* (1535) *Chapters 1–4* (Saint Louis, Missouri: Concordia, 1963) 232, and note 49.

86. Rahner was commenting on Luther's formula, and his observation is worth recording in its entirety: one "should not spread out one's justice before God. One should rather from day to day accept God's justice, which in fact divinises us, as an unmerited gift of God's incalculable favor. If one wants to express this by saying that one is always and of oneself a poor sinner and always someone justified by God's grace as long as one does not close oneself to this grace of God by disbelief and lack of love, then one is quite at liberty to do so" (from *Theological Investigations* 6 [London: Darton, Longman and Todd, 1969]), 230.

Redemption (*apolutrōsis*) is a metaphor from the slave market, but has roots in Scripture. The cognate verbs *apolutroō* and *lutroō* (both meaning "obtain release on payment of a ransom") are used in the LXX to speak of God's redemption of Israel from Egypt (for example, Exod. 6.6,[87] Deut. 7.8[88]) and from Babylon (Isa. 51.11). "Redemption" speaks therefore of those who have been handed over, or fallen, into the power of something they cannot control—the dominant metaphor of Romans 1.18–32, which, as we saw, repeatedly speaks of humankind "handed over" into the power of sin. Perhaps the word redemption speaks also, implicitly, of the *cost* of deliverance from such a power—a cost that in this case will be borne by the deliverer.[89]

Finally, **propitiation** (RSV "expiation," NRSV "sacrifice of atonement") involves a metaphor from the cult. Greek *hilastērion* appears to be a neuter noun formed from the (somewhat rare) adjective *hilastērios*, meaning "propitiatory" or "offered in propitiation."[90] In the LXX this noun occurs regularly—and in the context of very important passages—in connection with the **mercy seat** in the temple (LXX Exod. 25.18–22 [MT Exod. 25.19–22], 31.7, 35.12, 38.5–8 [MT 37.6–9]; Lev. 16.2–15; Num. 7.89). Since this seems to have become an accepted usage in Greek-speaking Judaism of the early Christian era (see Heb. 9.5; Philo, *Cher.* 25; *Life of Moses* 2.95, 97; *Flight* 100), there seems little reason to question that Paul, too, will have used it in this way, and that so he expects it to be heard. As Fitzmyer has put it, the expression will "depict Christ as the new 'mercy seat,' represented or displayed by the Father as a means of expiating or wiping away the sins of humanity, indeed as the place of the presence of God, of his revelation, and of his expiating power."[91]

If there was one thing in Judaism that was evidently forbidden to uncircumcised gentiles, it was to come anywhere near the Holy of Holies, the place of the Mercy Seat, where once a year the High Priest entered to make atonement by the sprinkling of blood (Lev. 16.14–16). There was therefore in the present context a peculiar poignancy in Paul's seeing Christ himself as a true Mercy Seat, set forth by God the Father for Jews and gentiles to approach together—and that, not by the blood of animal victims, but **by his** own **blood**, the blood of the Messiah.

Trito-Isaiah had depicted powerfully the tension between, on the one hand, God's holiness, outraged by the sin of the world, for "from the nations no man was with me, and I trod them down in wrath," and by the sin of Israel, who "disobeyed and enraged his holy spirit" (LXX Isa. 63.3,10), and, on the other hand, God's yearning to be gracious to his people, saying, "Are they not my people? Children who will

---

87. Translating Hebrew *g'l*: "to set free or redeem," with the underlying thought of acting the part of kin; see J. J. Stamm, "אל‎, *g'l*," in *TLOT* 1.291.

88. Translating Hebrew *pdh*: "to set free or redeem," with the underlying thought of payment; see J. J. Stamm, "פדה‎, *pdh*," in *TLOT* 2.969.

89. In view of the LXX usage, Cranfield is surely correct to say that this possibility cannot be ruled out (*Romans* 1.206); but contrast J. Cambier, S.D.B., *L'Évangile de Dieu selon l'Épître aux Romains: Exégèse et théologie biblique*, vol. 1, *L'Évangile de la justice et de la grâce*. Studia Neotestamentica, Studia 3 (Bruges: Desclée de Brouwer, 1967), 84.

90. On propitiation, see additional note P.

91. Fitzmyer, *Romans* 350. On the Interpretation of *hilastērion* at Romans 3.25 as "Mercy Seat," see additional note Q.

not disobey?" (LXX Isa. 63.8). Paul now speaks of the resolution of that tension on the cross, where the one who will be Immanuel, God with us, is **set forth** bound to his people even though that binding brings him to death.

On what basis is Christ so **set forth**? It is **through faith** (*dia pisteōs*). God's faith? Christ's faith? Our faith? Yes, of course, to all. Rooted in the faithfulness of God, the faithfulness of Jesus Christ invites our faithfulness in return: indeed, there is nothing else we can offer, no other basis on which we can stand with regard to God. Paul, as a good rhetorician, has brought us full circle. In this "gospel," as he said from the beginning, "God's justice is revealed from faith for faith; as it is written, 'the just shall live by faith'" (1.17).

More precisely now, however, Paul points out that the cross **was for the manifestation of God's justice, by passing over** [*paresis*][92] **former sins in his divine forbearance**, as the Book of Wisdom had said. But it was also **for the manifestation of God's justice at the present time, so that he might both be just**—holy and righteous, still uttering the divine "No!" to all that is contrary to Love—**and justify** us—acquit us, set us free. And on what basis would it do that? By the divine Love itself paying the terrible price of our alienation from Love—**by the faith of Jesus**—through Jesus' faithfulness, even to death, by which we may seek to be faithful in return (3.25b–26).

To grasp Paul's argument, it is perhaps as important here to be clear what he is *not* doing as to see what he *is* doing. He is not presenting theodicy. He is not explaining evil. He is not explaining God's ways. Indeed, he is not *explaining* anything. He is merely describing a relationship, as he understands it. In the face of those who understand their relationship to the God of Israel to be based on their knowledge of and obedience to the Law—in short, on their own justice—he is simply saying that, on the contrary, their relationship to God is based (as the Law said) on *God's* justice, which is God's loyalty to them; and that saving justice, that loyalty to them, is what has now been manifested in the faithfulness of Jesus Christ, faithful unto death.

Following these crucial assertions (3:21–26) another dialogue again provides implicit "refutation" (*elenchos*) of the "reliance-on-Law" position (3:27–31); but this time tactfully designed, somewhat in the Socratic manner, so that the dialogue partner now seems to be coming to the correct opinion. Indeed, in this part of the conversation it appears to be Paul himself who is putting questions, which, far from being awkward, are rather a teacher's invitations, giving the student an opportunity to show that the lesson has been learned. (Again, the question and answer style could easily have been brought out in delivery by a properly prepared reader.)

PAUL: **What then**, in view of all that we've said, of **"boasting [*kauchēsis*]"**? (contrast 2.17!)

PARTNER: **It's excluded!**

PAUL: **On the basis of what Law [*nomou*]? Of works?**

PARTNER: **No, but on the basis of a Law of faith** [*nomou pisteōs*]. (3.27)

---

92. On the meaning of *paresis* at 3.25, see additional note R.

The contrast that Paul here makes between a "Law of works" and a "Law of faith" is, I think, *not* a contrast between Jewish Law and some other law or "principle," or between the Jewish Law and faith. It is a contrast between the Jewish Law understood as a basis in itself of human standing before God, and the Jewish Law understood as a witness to God's faithfulness and mercy.[93] What is at issue is mistaking the signpost for the thing to which it points, or confusing the riverbed with the river. Paul's contrast is about telling the story wrongly (according, of course, to his view of it), as opposed to telling it right. Wrongly understood, Paul believes, the Law of Moses *becomes* a Law of works. Rightly understood, it is the Law of faith.

Even a Law of works will eventually exclude "boasting," in its own way, for our works will fail, and our end will be despair: "What good is it to us, if an eternal age has been promised to us, but we have done deeds that bring death?" (2 [4] Esdras 7.119). But when the Law is read rightly, as God's Law, the Law of faith, "boasting" is excluded on quite other and more gracious grounds: it is excluded because **we are reckoning that a person is justified through faith, apart from works of Law** (3.28), so there is nothing we need boast about—unless, of course, as Paul will note later, we choose to "boast" in our hope for God's grace (5.2, 11; compare 1 Cor. 1.31; also Jer. 9.23–24).

But now Paul wishes to indicate to his "student" another way to see the truth—a way that is rooted deep in the very Law of which they are speaking. So he puts another question.

PAUL: **Or is God the God of Jews only? Is God *not* the God of gentiles also?**

PARTNER: **Indeed, of the gentiles also, for** [*recalling the Shema*] **'God is one'** [compare LXX Deut. 6.4] **who will justify the circumcised by** [*ek*] **faith—and the uncircumcised through** [*dia*][94] **faith!** (3.30)

In order to see the importance of this observation in its context, we need perhaps to remind ourselves of the particular significance of Jewish monotheism at this period. It was not, as perhaps for some gentile philosophers, simply a matter of argument or speculation about the divine. It was, as N. T. Wright has put it, a "fighting doctrine,"[95] and it was involved in warfare on two fronts. On the one hand, its assertion of the *One* God who had created all things well stood against paganism, which attempted to deify the created order, or forces within it. On the other hand—and this is most important for our present consideration—its assertion of the One God who created *all* things well stood against dualism, which rejected the goodness of the created order, or parts of it. If God's saving justice is limited to Jews, then there is, so to speak, a "no-go" area for God in the universe, and Jewish monotheism is overthrown. Only the "Law of faith," with its assertion of the universality of God's

---

93. See Cranfield, *Romans* 1.219–20; Dunn, *Romans* 1.185–86. Hence, in my view, the RSV and NAB's procedure of translating *nomos* in 3.27 as "principle," and then returning to "law" in 3.28, is unhelpful. (Even worse was the NEB, which appeared at 3.27 to have given up on Paul altogether, and simply offered a wild paraphrase.) For a different opinion, however, see Fitzmyer, *Romans* 131, and (more nuanced) Moo, *Romans* 247–50; compare BAGD νόμος 1.

94. On the distinction between *ek* and *dia* at 3.30, see additional note S.

95. N. T. Wright, *Climax of Covenant* 125.

saving justice, accords truly with Jewish monotheism, and hence with the basis of the Law.

PAUL: **Are we then overthrowing the Law** by our talk of **"faith"?**

PARTNER (*who is beginning to sound more and more like his teacher*): **By no means! Rather, we're upholding the Law!** (3.31)

"[T]he Law," as Käsemann says, "does not contradict the righteousness of faith; it summons us to it."[96]

Additional Note N. 3.24–26 as a Pre-Pauline Formula

Among the reasons for supposing 3.24–26 to be making use of a pre-Pauline formula, the most important seem to be

1. the somewhat awkward use of the participle *dikaioumenoi* ("being justified") to introduce the formula;
2. the vocabulary that, in Paul's writings, occurs only in these verses: namely, *hilastērion* ("propitiation"), *paresis* ("passing over"), *endeixis* ("manifestation"), and *progegonotōn* ("former") (perfect participle of *proginesthai* ["to happen beforehand"]); and
3. certain phrases appear to be "redundantly repeated" (Fitzmyer):[97] namely, "as a gift" (*dōrean*) and "by his grace" (*tē(i) autou chariti*) occurring together at 3.24 (an evident tautology), and "as a manifestation of God's justice," occurring twice in 3.25–26.

Those who believe that Paul has adopted a pre-Pauline formula generally agree that he has modified it, nevertheless, by introducing at least three phrases,

1. "by his grace" (3.24),
2. "through faith" (3.25), and
3. "for the manifestation of God's justice at the present time" (3.26)—the last phrase expressing, Fitzmyer suggests, "God's purpose in the eschatological 'now.'"[98]

Cranfield, on the other hand, thinks that in "the construction of a paragraph as vital and central to [Paul's] whole argument as this is," the process of composition thus envisaged is extremely unlikely. He considers it "very much more probable that these verses are Paul's own independent and careful composition."[99]

Bibliographical Note

For further discussions of this question, see John Piper, "The Demonstration of the Righteousness of God in Romans 3:25, 26," *JSNT* 7 (1980): 2–32, especially 4–10: Piper con-

---

96. Käsemann, *Romans* 105.
97. Fitzmyer, *Romans* 342.
98. Fitzmyer, *Romans* 343.
99. Cranfield, *Romans* 1.200, note 1.

cludes that "even if Paul was using tradition here . . . he presents theological sentences which to an especially high degree he has made his own'" (9, citing Otto Kuss); also Douglas A. Campbell, *The Rhetoric of Righteousness in Romans 3.21–26*, JSNTSS 65 (Sheffield, England: Sheffield Academic Press, 1992), 37–57, who, after an examination of the various considerations generally cited in favor of form-critical hypotheses concerning Romans 3.24–26a, comes to the conclusion that *none* of them is soundly based. Still to be read with profit, from a somewhat different viewpoint, is J. Cambier, S.D.B., *L'Évangile de Dieu selon l'Épître aux Romains: Exégèse et théologie biblique*, vol. 1, *L'Évangile de la justice et de la grâce*. Studia Neotestamentica, Studia 3 (Bruges: Desclée de Brouwer, 1967), 73–79.

Additional Note O. On Translating *Pistis Christou*

In translating *dia pisteōs Iēsou Christou* "through the faith of Jesus Christ" (3.22) I have more or less followed the KJV and DR, which, by means of what is admittedly now an archaic English usage (see *OED2*, "Faith" n. 1.1.a), retain something of the ambiguity of the Greek original (and, incidentally, of the Vulgate), as opposed to the quite *un*ambiguous "by faith in Jesus Christ" that is, more or less, represented in other major versions (for example, RV, ARV, RSV, NEB, NAB, NRSV, JB, BEP; note, however, RV, ARV, and NRSV margins).

In doing anything at all with this phrase one enters a battle zone—it is at present perhaps the single most hotly contested question in the interpretation of the entire letter. The question at issue is, Is the genitive that follows *pistis* subjective ("Christ's faith") or objective[100] ("faith in Christ")? Is Paul saying (3.22) that God's justice has been manifested to us through Christ's faithfulness, or though our faith in Christ? Details of the present state of the question are available in all the major commentaries and in many articles, and there is no point in repeating them here.[101] I simply note, therefore, some issues that have seemed to me, if not decisive, at least significant enough to sway my decision for the present.

1. Whatever critics on either side of the question may say, the phrase *is* ambiguous and clearly always was: this applies not only to its use here, but also at 3.26, Galatians 2.16, 20, 3.22, and Philippians 3.9 (compare also Ephesians 3.12). In all these cases it is entirely possible to translate the phrase either way. (Also ambiguous, incidentally, is *pistis tou euaggeliou* at Philippians 1.27, where "standing together side by side for the faith of the gospel [*tē pistei tou euaggeliou*]" has been variously understood to mean "the faithfulness that belongs to the gospel" [subjective] or "the faith that the gospel gives" [also subjective], or "faith in the gospel" [objective], or any of them—without, as it happens, causing any controversy.)[102]

---

100. Douglas A. Campbell prefers to refer to this as the "traditionalist" view, since *pistuein* does not actually take a direct object: see "False Presuppositions" 715, footnote 5.

101. See the bibliographical note at the end of additional note O.

102. On Philippians 1.27, contrast, for example, Wilhelm Michaelis's interpretation, *"den Glauben an das Evangelium"* ("faith in the gospel") (objective) in *Der Brief des Paulus an die Philipper*, THNT 11 (Leipzig: Deichertsche Verlagbuchhandlung, 1935), 28–29, with that of Jean-François Collange, *"l'Evangile de la foi"* ("faith's Gospel") (subjective) in *L'Épitre de Saint Paul aux Philippiens* (Neuchâtel: Delachaux et Niestlé, 1973), 69–70.

In admitting such ambiguity the grammarians (even while tending in the present case to come down on the "objective" side) have in general been a good deal more forthright than the commentators. "The division of the genitive into objective, subjective, etc., is really only an attempt to set off several special types among the manifold possibilities of the general function of the adnominal genitive, which is to denote a relationship."[103] "The genitive with substantives denotes in general a connection or dependence between two words. . . . The same construction may often be placed under more than one of the different classes . . . and the connection between the two substantives is often so loose that it is difficult to include with precision all cases under specific grammatical classes."[104]

2. Whatever (again) critics on either side of the question may say, it seems perfectly evident that *either* way of translating *pistis Christou* can be squared with what else we know (or think we know) of Paul's theology—as J. D. G. Dunn, notably, concedes.[105] The clearest evidence for that is the number of the intelligent and learned on both sides of the question who are clearly persuaded that they have so squared it—without, so far as can be seen, differing widely from each other as to what that theology involves.

In this context, I should perhaps note that I am not impressed by the "anti-subjective" argument that Paul does not talk elsewhere of "the faithfulness of Christ": in fact,

1. Paul (notoriously) does not talk much about the incarnate Lord at all,
2. he seems to use this particular expression in contexts where he is discussing the relationship of believers to the Law; and in that connection he makes use of several ideas and expressions that he does not use elsewhere—most notably, "justification," and
3. in any case, since Paul saw in Jesus Christ the "mind" that all believers should seek [Phil. 2.3], presumably one could hardly claim that the idea that Christ was faithful would have been alien to Paul's thinking.

Granted that Paul appears to have been capable of being clear when he wanted to be, I am constrained, in view of the foregoing, to ask myself whether the question at issue was really important for him. Again, it is a grammarian who seems to point in the right direction: "it is important," Nigel Turner says, "not to sacrifice fullness of interpretation to an over precise analysis of syntax. *There is no reason why a genitive in the author's mind may not have been both subjective and objective.*"[106]

The ancients, as I have already said, were not nearly so troubled by ambiguity as we are—indeed, they relished it. Critics who refuse to take that seriously are simply failing to face the realities of ancient usage. My suspicion is that for Paul and his contemporaries the expression "the faith of Christ" had approximately the same kind and degree of ambiguity as exists in our English expression "the love of God." If we

103. BD § 163.
104. Smyth, *Grammar* § 1295; compare Turner, *Syntax* 210–12, and Moule, *Idiom* 40, 203.
105. J. D. G. Dunn, "Once More, ΠΙΣΤΙΣ ΧΡΙΣΤΟΥ," in *Society of Biblical Literature 1991 Seminar Papers*, ed. E. H. Lovering (Atlanta, Georgia: Scholars Press, 1991), 744.
106. Turner, *Syntax* 210, my italics.

ask people to do something "for the love of God," do we mean them to do it "because God loves them" or because "they love God"? We mean, I think, something of both: we mean to suggest that a relationship of love exists between them and God—God for them, and they for God—and on the grounds of that relationship we beseech them to act. Mutatis mutandis,[107] there seems every reason to suppose that the effect of the phrase *pistis Christou*—"faith of Christ"—on those who first heard it would have been somewhat similar. "Quite apart from Torah," Paul is saying, "(although Torah bears witness to it) God's justice is now being manifested through and by means of the relationship of faithfulness that exists between us and God's Messiah, whose faithfulness to God and to us enables our faithfulness in return—and hence (in union with him) our restored relationship to God."

Bibliographical Note

The literature on this question seems almost endless. The following, however, probably represent most of the main points that are being made as the question stands at present:

On the "objective" side, see J. D. G. Dunn, "Once More, ΠΙΣΤΙΣ ΧΡΙΣΤΟΥ" in *Society of Biblical Literature 1991 Seminar Papers*, ed. E. H. Lovering (Atlanta, Georgia: Scholars Press, 1991), 730–44; Brian Dodd, "Romans 1:17—A *Crux Interpretum* for the Πίστις Χριστοῦ Debate?" *JBL* 114 (1995): 470–73; also the major commentators: Cranfield, *Romans* 1.203; Byrne, *Romans* 130; Dunn, *Romans* 1.166–67; Fitzmyer, *Romans* 345–46; Moo, *Romans* 224–26. Also to be placed in the "objective" category is A. J. Hultgren, "The *Pistis Christou* Formulation in Paul," *NovT* 22 (1980): 148–63—though with some interesting qualifications.

On the "subjective" side, see Marcus Barth, "The Faith of the Messiah," in *HeyJ* 10 (1969): 363–70; Luke Timothy Johnson, "Romans 3.21–26 and the Faith of Jesus," in *CBQ* 44 (1982): 77–90; Morna D. Hooker, "ΠΙΣΤΙΣ ΧΡΙΣΤΟΥ," *NTS* 35 (1989): 321–42; S. K. Stowers, "ΕΚ ΠΙΣΤΕΩΣ and ΔΙΑ ΠΙΣΤΕΩΣ in Romans 3.30," *JBL* 108 (1989): 665–74 (which also takes the view that *ek* and *dia* are normally used by Paul to refer to Jews and Gentiles, respectively);[108] Richard B. Hays, "ΠΙΣΤΙΣ and Pauline Theology," in *SBL 1991 Seminar Papers* 714–29; Douglas A. Campbell, *Rhetoric of Righteousness* 58–69, 204–13, 214–18; "Romans 1:17—A *Crux Interpretum* for the Πίστις Χριστοῦ Debate," *JBL* 113 (1994): 265–85; and "False Presuppositions in the ΠΙΣΤΙΣ ΧΡΙΣΤΟΥ Debate: A Response to Brian Dodd," *JBL* 116 (1997): 713–19.

As indicated earlier, recent major commentaries on Romans have mostly come down on the "objective" side. One exception is Luke Timothy Johnson, who in his *Reading Romans: A Literary and Theological Commentary* (New York: Crossroad, 1997), 58–61, continues to hold to the "subjective" view defended in his 1982 *CBQ* paper (cited above). Interestingly enough, at least two recent major commentaries on Galatians (commentaries, it may be said, that in several other important questions by no means agree with each other) agree in preferring the "subjective" interpretation of *pistis Christou*: see Matera, *Galatians* 100–102; and Martyn, *Galatians* 251, 263–75, and especially 271–73.

On approaching the problem of linguistic ambiguity generally, Douglas L. Cairns's preliminary discussion of *aidōs* provides an excellent model: see his *Aidōs: The Psychology and Ethics of Honour and Shame in Ancient Greek Literature* (Oxford: Clarendon Press, 1993),

---

107. Of course, I am aware that the parallel between the two phrases is not exact.
108. On the significance of *ek* and *dia* at Romans 3.30, see additional note S.

1–4. On ambiguity specifically in biblical literature, see G. B. Caird, *The Language and Imagery of the Bible* (London: Duckworth, 1980) 95–108 (Caird himself, as it happens, took the "objective" view of *pistis Christou*: see 99). Also relevant here is my own discussion of Paul's use of Habakkuk 2.4 at Romans 1.17: see pages 70–72, and the literature cited in footnote 15.

Additional Note P. Propitiation

In an influential essay published in 1931, C. H. Dodd[109] argued that LXX usage of *hilaskesthai* and its cognates did not carry the notion of propitiating, averting, or appeasing wrath—a notion that is generally agreed to be present in pagan usage—but spoke merely, from the human side, of the *expiation* of guilt (that is, of a means of doing away with or extinguishing guilt), or, from the divine, of God's gracious and forgiving mercy.

Whether, even in terms of English usage, Dodd's distinction can be maintained, is not clear: *OED2* uses "to offer or serve as a propitiation for" as one way of explaining "expiate" (see *expiate* 3), and "expiation" as one way of explaining "propitiation" (see *propitiation* 1)! In any case, however, it is simply not true that the idea of God's wrath is absent from LXX usage of *hilaskesthai*, whether that wrath is explicitly named—as, for example, on the occasion of Moses' prayer at LXX Exod. 32.12–14: "'Cease from thy fierce wrath [*tēs orgēs tou thumou sou*]' . . . and the Lord was propitiated [*hilasthē*] concerning the evil which he said he would do to his people" (compare LXX Dan. 9.16–19, Lam. 3.42–43)—or implicit, as at LXX 4 Kingd. 24.2–4 (MT 2 Kings 24.2–4).

Certainly we may concede that since God is perfectly just, the wrath of God in the LXX (and, of course, the Hebrew Scriptures upon which it is based), unlike the wrath of pagan gods or human wrath, is neither capricious, irrational, or vindictive. God's wrath is God's passionate "No!" to our injustice. Nor need it be questioned that in averting that wrath, it is God, in the LXX, who takes the initiative. None of this changes the fact that in the LXX as much as in pagan usage, the idea of averting wrath is generally present. Similarly, if we attempt to remove this idea from Paul's usage in Romans, then we strip his rhetoric of much of its force: since he started from God's "wrath," in describing the human problem (1.18), it is surely essential that we allow him his "means of averting wrath" as a way of describing its solution at 3.25.

Bibliographical Note

Evidently seminal in this debate is C. H. Dodd, "ἱλάσκεσθαι, its cognates, derivatives and synonyms in the Septuagint," in *JTS* 32 (1931): 352–60. The most important response to Dodd was probably that by L. Morris, "The Use of ἱλάσκεσθαι etc. in Biblical Greek," in *ET* 62 (1950–51): 227–33. See further, however, D. Hill, "Greek Words and Hebrew Meanings: Studies in the Semantics of Soteriological Terms (Cambridge: Cambridge University Press, 1967), 23–36; also G. H. R. Horsley, *New Documents Illustrating Early Christianity: A Review of the Greek Inscriptions and Papyri Published in 1976* (North Ride, New South Wales: Macquarie University, 1981), 2–25.

---

109. C. H. Dodd, "Ἱλάσκεσθαι, Its Cognates, Derivatives and Synonyms in the Septuagint," in *JTS* 32 (1931): 352–60.

Additional Note Q. The Interpretation of *Hilastērion* at Romans 3.25 as "Mercy Seat"

The main objections to translating *hilastērion* at Romans 3.25 as "Mercy Seat" have been as follows:

1. that, unlike its usage in the LXX, it is here anarthrous. But LXX *hilastērion* has the definite article when it clearly refers to *the* Mercy Seat, that is, the known, historical Mercy Seat in the Temple at Jerusalem (the one exception is LXX Exod. 25.17, where, however, the addition of *epithema* likewise removes *hilastērion* from the possibility of general interpretation). Paul's usage is, by contrast, evidently metaphorical. He is not saying that Jesus was set forth by God as *that* Mercy Seat, which would be absurd; Paul is saying that Jesus was set forth by God as *a* Mercy Seat, just as he will later describe Jesus as sent by God as *a* sin offering (*peri hamartias*) (8.3) (see chapter 5, footnote 51). Among the ancient critics, notably Origen perceived the connection with the Mercy Seat at 3.24 and did not perceive the fact that *hilastērion* was anarthrous as a possible objection to that perception: indeed, he does not seem even to have noticed it (*Commentary on Romans* 5.5 [Scherer 156–63]).

2. that the implied comparison is too difficult. Thus Cranfield claims that,

> While it is an understandable paradox to refer to Christ as being at the same time both priest and victim, to represent him as being the place of sprinkling as well as the victim is surely excessively harsh and confusing . . . . there seems to be something essentially improbable in the thought of Paul's likening Christ . . . to something which was only an inanimate piece of temple furniture.[110]

This, with all respect to a great commentator, is simply a description of his own limitations. How can my true love's lips be rubies? How can my heart turn to water? How can Juliet be the sun? How can Jesus be a stone? *All* metaphor is harsh and confusing, until you get it: then it is illuminating. In the present case, we may profitably contrast Karl Barth:

> The analogy with Jesus is particularly appropriate because the Mercy Seat is no more than a particular, though very significant, place. By the express counsel of God, Jesus has been appointed from eternity as the place of propitiation above which God dwells and from which He speaks; now, however, He occupies a position in time, in history, and in our presence . . . just as in the Old Testament the *Kapporeth* covered the testimonies of God as well as marked their presence, so here the Kingdom of God, His atoning activity, and the dawn of the day of redemption (3.24) are in Jesus covered as well as displayed. Jesus is presented to us unmistakably as the Christ, but his Messiahship is also presented to us as a sharply defined paradox. It is a matter for faith only. The propitiation occurs at the place of propitiation—only by blood, whereby we are solemnly reminded that God gives life only though death.[111]

Additional Note R. The Meaning of *Paresis* at Romans 3.25

This somewhat unusual word (it is a New Testament *hapax*, and does not occur at all in the LXX) has caused the commentators some difficulty. Should it be inter-

---

110. Cranfield, *Romans* 1.215.
111. Barth, *Romans* 105.

preted in relation to its cognate *pariēmi* ("pass over," "let go unpunished") (so Dionysius of Halicarnassus: "they did not get an absolute dismissal [*paresis*] of the charges" [*Roman Antiquities* 7.37.2], Dio Chrysostom: "a very few, however, have some relief [*paresis*] from God" [*Discourses* 30: *Charidimus* 19])?[112] Or should it be interpreted "remission," "pardon" (so the Vulgate: "*remissionem*" [Rom. 3.25])?[113]

It appears to me that the movement in meaning from "pass over" to "let go unpunished" and hence to "remit" or "pardon" is so easy and natural as to render the dispute almost meaningless. Thus, the same movement is observable in the cognate verb, which is also sometimes used of the remission of guilt, debt, or other obligation,[114] and a similar movement in Aramaic has apparently led to the alternative forms of the Lord's Prayer in the New Testament (Matt. 6.12, Luke 11.4). To insist on deciding where, precisely, we should locate Paul's usage in this movement is to insist on his making a distinction (1) that he probably was not making, and (2) concerning which, if he were making it, and it were important to him, he would undoubtedly have expressed himself differently.

Additional Note S. The Distinction between *Ek* and *Dia* at Romans 3.30

Most modern commentators follow Augustine in supposing the variation in pronouns (*ek* . . . *de* . . .) to be merely stylistic and literary (*quod non ad aliquam differentiam dictum est . . . sed ad varietatem locutionis*) (*On the Spirit and the Letter* 29.50). Yet, as Stowers has pointed out,[115] both Origen and Theodore of Mopsuesta sensed a real distinction, and their reasons are worth examining.

The passage "would seem to suggest," Origen said,

> that by believing in Jesus both the circumcised and the uncircumcised are saved— the former when they fulfill, as far as possible, the Law of Moses, the latter when they conduct themselves as citizens according to the liberty of Christ. Following that, let us ask in what consists the difference between the justification of the circumcised which comes 'by [*ek*] faith,' and the justification of the uncircumcised, which comes not 'by [*ek*] faith,' but 'through [*dia*] faith.'"

Very instructively, Origen then compared 1 Corinthians 11.12, where Paul speaks of woman created "out of the man" (*ek tou andros*) and man as created "through the woman" (*dia tēs gunaikos*) (Origen, *Commentary on Romans* 5.7 [Scherer 168–175]).

What is involved here is a manner of contrasting the prepositions *ek* and *dia* that was common in Greek texts of the period that dealt with questions of lineage and paternity, whether literally or metaphorically. Behind the contrast lies the ancient (Aristotelian) assumption (at this point held in common by Jews and gentiles) that in procreation men provided the generative spark and women the supportive nutrients and a place for the seed: thus men and women were related, so to speak, as

---

112. Compare BAGD, πάρεσις.
113. Compare LS, πάρεσις 3.
114. Compare LS, παρίημι 3.3.
115. See Stowers, *Rereading Romans* 237–40.

seed and soil. *Ek tou andros* ("out of the man") spoke of the essential generative role, *dia tēs guniakos* ("through a woman") of the instrumental and supportive role; and the former is, as we should expect at this period, regarded as superior to and more important than the latter.

Of course, Paul's use of this language at Romans 3.30 will have been metaphorical, and we have no need (nor is it possible) to press him on the details of his metaphor. Nevertheless, it seems entirely likely that Origen was correct in drawing attention to the parallel at 1 Corinthians 11.12, and that what Paul was hinting at here is simply what he says more plainly elsewhere, that Jewish participation (*ek pisteōs*) in the people of God is more ancient and deeply rooted than gentile (*dia pisteōs*): "the Jew first, and also the Greek" (2.9–10, 9.4–5, 11.17–24).

Similarly, though more briefly, Theodore of Mopsuestia said that, as regards the Jews, "granted that they were moved by other reasons to seek justification, nonetheless they could not attain to it save 'by faith' [*non poterant tamen eam consequi nisi ex fide*]; to the gentiles, on the other hand, these things pertain 'through faith' [*ad gentes autem pertinent illa per fidem*]" (*Commentary on Paul's Letter to the Romans* 3.30).

Similarly Calvin suggested we might understand Paul as saying "that the Jews are justified *by* faith, because they are born as the heirs of grace, while the right of adoption is transmitted to them from the fathers, but that the Gentiles are justified *through* faith, because the covenant comes to them from outside" (my italics).[116]

Bibliographical Note

On ancient understandings of the roles of the sexes in procreation, see Giulia Sissa, "The Sexual Philosophies of Plato and Aristotle," in *A History of Women in the West: From Ancient Goddesses to Christian Saints*, Pauline Schmitt Pantel, ed., Arthur Goldhammer, trans. (Cambridge, Massachusetts: Harvard University Press), 46–81, and literature there cited.

The Example of Abraham (4.1–25)

But then the dialogue partner puts a new question: **"What then shall we say that Abraham, our forefather according to the flesh, found?"** (4.1).[117] The partner is not changing the subject. The talk has been of Law, and the falsity of regarding obedience to the Law as the basis of our standing before God. In Philo, Josephus, and other writers representative of early Judaism, Abraham is the great convert, the proselyte par excellence, who turned from the paganism into which he was born to serve the living and true God. But the traditions they hand on seem often to suggest that Abraham's keeping of the Law *was* the basis of his standing. So, for example, ben Sira:

> Abraham was the great father of a multitude of nations,
>   and no one has been found like him in glory;
> he kept the Law of the Most High,
>   and was taken into covenant with him;

116. Calvin, *Romans* 80.
117. On problems connected with translating 4.1, see additional note T.

he established the covenant in his flesh,
    and when he was tested he was found faithful.
Therefore the Lord assured him with an oath
    that he would be blessed through his posterity;
that he would multiply him like the dust of the earth,
    and exalt his posterity like the stars,
and cause them to inherit from sea to sea,
    and from the River to the ends of the earth. (Sirach 44.19–21)

So the testament of dying Mattathias to his sons:

Remember the works of the fathers which they did in their generations; and receive great honor and an everlasting name. Was not Abraham found faithful when he was tested, and it was reckoned to him as righteousness?" (1 Macc. 2.51–52)

and so Philo:

Abraham, then, filled with zeal for piety, the highest and greatest of virtues, was eager to follow God and to be obedient to his commands. . . . Under the force of an oracle which bade him leave his country and kinfolk and seek a new home, thinking that quickness in executing the command was as good as full accomplishment, he hastened eagerly to obey. (*On Abraham* 60, 61, trans. F. H. Colson)

In Philo's description, Abraham's keeping of the Law reminds us, indeed, somewhat of the Law keeping that Paul has earlier suggested gentiles might occasionally achieve (compare 2.14–16): which is to say, Abraham was obedient,

not taught by written words, but unwritten nature gave him the zeal to follow where wholesome and untainted impulse led him. . . . Such was the life of the first, the founder of the nation, one who obeyed the Law, some will say, but rather, as our discourse has shown, himself a law [*nomos autos ōn*] and an unwritten statute. (*On Abraham* 275–76, trans. F. H. Colson) [118]

It is therefore essential that Paul and his partner in dialogue consider the *paradeigma* ("example") of Abraham, for, as the partner points out, **if Abraham was justified on the basis of his works, he does have something to boast about.**

But not, interrupts Paul at once, **in God's sight!**[119] The story must be told right! **For what does the Scripture say?** (4.2–3a).

There follows what James D. G. Dunn has called "one of the finest examples of Jewish midrash available to us from this era."[120] Paul begins by quoting Genesis: **Abraham had faith in [*episteusen*] God, and that was credited to him—reckoned to his account—[*elogisthē*] as justice** (4.3b, citing LXX Gen. 15.6). Paul's point is that here in Genesis, whatever the later traditions may say, there is no mention of Abraham's "works." Only his faith, apparently, is "placed to his account."[121]

---

118. See further Philo, *On the Virtues* 211–19 (see especially 219: "[Abraham] is the standard of nobility for all proselytes"); also Josephus, *Jewish Antiquities* 1.154–57, 161, 167.

119. The text is a little awkward, but the above seems likely to represent its intention (see Cranfield, *Romans* 1.225, 228; Moo, *Romans* 260–61).

120. Dunn, *Romans* 1.197.

121. "Reckon, credit, place to one's account" (*logizomai*) was a word whose associations were often with accountancy and business (see LS λογίζομαι) as Paul is obviously aware. He is not, of course,

> Now to one who works, his wages are not credited to him as a gift, but as his due; to one who does not work, but has faith in the One who justifies the ungodly, his faith is credited to him as justice. (4.4–5)

In so expressing himself, Paul was taking something of a risk with his Jewish hearers: for "you shall *not* justify the ungodly" was what God told them in the Law (LXX Exod. 23.7). If they had forgotten or not understood what Paul had said earlier about the meaning of Christ's death (3.23–26), then what he was saying now might confirm their worst fears—that his "gospel" undermined all justice. But it was a risk he must take. The entire thrust of his argument depended upon his claim that "all alike are under the power of sin" (3.9). If that were so, and if God were to "justify" anyone at all, then his hearers must be brought face-to-face with the essential paradox: *God, though just, justifies the ungodly*—and, even for the most pious among them, that paradox was their only hope of salvation.

What, again, does the Scripture say? **So also David pronounces a blessing upon the man to whom God credits [*logizetai*] justice apart from works:**

> *Blessed are those whose iniquities are forgiven, and whose sins are covered;*
> *blessed is the one to whom the Lord will by no means credit [ou mē logisētai] his sin.*
> (4.6–8, citing LXX Ps. 31.1–2a)

So much for the blessing of Abraham, the blessing of Israel. But Paul is about to go even further. He puts a question of his own. **We say that faith was credited to Abraham as justice. How then was it credited to him? Was it before, or after, he was circumcised?** (4.9b–10a). The answer is inevitable, for here Paul's weapon is simply the order of the narrative itself. **It was not before, but after he was circumcised (4.10b).** When Abraham's **faith** was **credited** to him **as justice,** he was not a proper Jew. In fact, to all intents and purposes, he was a gentile. Clearly, then, circumcision was not the basis of his acceptance. **He received circumcision as a sign or seal of the justification on the grounds of faith that was already his when he was uncircumcised (4.11a).**

What, then, was the purpose of his circumcision? **The purpose was to make him the father of all who have faith without being circumcised, and who thus** like him **have justification credited to them** on the basis of their faith—like the gentile believers—**and the father of the circumcised, who also follow in the footsteps of the faith which our father Abraham had before he was circumcised (4.11–12):** so affirming that God is still faithful to the promise to Israel, but in the very same expression again noticing that the promise was given before, so to speak, Israel was Israel, since it was given before Abraham was circumcised. **For it was not through the Law** that God made **the promise to Abraham and to his seed, that he should be heir of the world** [compare Gen. 12.3], **but through justification on the grounds of faith (4.13).**

Strictly, it might be said, the promise to Abraham's seed that it should inherit the earth is not found in Genesis. Nevertheless, the universal promise that "all the

---

the only writer to use such business themes metaphorically. Catullus dwells frequently on the idea of *foedus* ("contract") (e.g., *aeternum sanctae foedus amicitiae* "the eternal contract of a sacred love," *Poems* 109.6), with himself the honest partner who has been defrauded.

tribes of the earth should be blessed in you" (LXX Gen. 12.3), together with the promise of the land "to your seed" (LXX Gen. 13.15, 17.8) was generally extended in Jewish tradition to include the entire world (for example, Sirach 44.21, *Jub.* 19.21; compare *Bib. Ant.* 32.3).[122]

Paul has already established that all, Jew and Greek alike, are "under the power of sin." Therefore, inevitably, **if it is to be the adherents of the Law who are to be heirs, faith is null**—if that is the case, then the story of Abraham is obviously complete nonsense, since according to that story Abraham was *not* an adherent of the Law when he was told he would be an heir—and the promise is void—for who will ever be in a position to receive it? **For the Law brings wrath, and** only **where there is no Law** is there **no transgression** (4.15). But such a nightmare is, in fact, based on a false premise: for it is *not* to "adherents of the Law" that the promise was made, but to uncircumcised Abraham, who had faith: and **that is why we** (as Habbakkuk said) **live by faith** (*ek pisteōs*)—that is, on the basis of God's faithfulness to us, seeking our faithfulness in return, **so that the promise may rest on God's grace, and be sure to all Abraham's descendants, not only to the adherents of the Law but also to those who share the faith of Abraham, for he is the father of us all, as it is written, *I have made you the father of many nations*** (4.16–17a, citing LXX Gen. 17.5).

So Paul concludes his midrash—at the very least, a tour de force of quite extraordinary originality and imagination. By any standards it must be that: and yet perhaps the true brilliance of its achievement is missed if we do not see it against the situation that Paul was addressing. Those who were of Jewish descent in Paul's audience will presumably have been accustomed to see in the story of Abraham the great moment of separation in the world's history. Until Abraham, there were the nations; after Abraham there was one nation, God's chosen, heir to the Law and to the promise, and there were "the nations," without the Law, excluded from the promise. Paul has shown them an Abraham in whom they are robbed of nothing that they hoped for themselves, but in whom, now, they may also see hope for those others.

Paul's gentile hearers, on the other hand, in hearing Paul thus defend his gospel, are at the same time being asked to see themselves in a new light, as bound to God's ancient people. "Abraham is the father of us all" means that they can ignore neither Israel's history nor her hope, for it is actually a part of their history and their hope. The blessings in which they share are the blessings promised to Abraham's seed. "The Jew first" is more than just a primacy in time, it is a movement in the mystery of God's grace to all humankind. "The Jew first" means that Israel is the root, and therefore the gentile believers must remember—as, indeed, Paul will later directly challenge them to remember—"it is not you that support the root, but the root that supports you" (11.18).

Yet Paul has not quite finished. There is one more thing to be learned from the history of Abraham, and perhaps it is the most important thing at of all. Abraham was faithful **in the presence of the God in whom he had faith, who gives life to the**

---

122. The rabbinic tradition would later quote Rabbi Nehemiah (c. 150) as saying (in a passage whose argument is in some ways similar to Paul's), "Our father Abraham inherited both this world and the world beyond only as a reward for the faith with which he believed, as it is said, 'And he believed in the Lord,' etc. [Gen. 15.6]. . . . And thus it says, 'The Lord preserveth the faithful' [Ps. 31.24]" (*Mek. Exod.* 14.31) (trans. Jacob Z. Lauterbach, 1.253).

dead and calls into being the things that are not (4.17). It is God the creator with whom Abraham had to do—that same God the creator from whom Paul's story began, whose "invisible nature, namely, his eternal power and divinity" was from the creation of the world perceived in the things that had been made" (1.19–20a). For Abraham faith was not, apparently, easy. **In hope he believed against hope that he should become *the father of many nations*, as he had been told, *thus shall your seed be* (LXX Gen. 15.5). He did not weaken in faith when he beheld his own body which was as good as dead because he was about a hundred years old, or when he considered the barrenness of Sarah's womb (4.8–19).** He was surrounded by death's harbingers, yet unlike those who, "even though they knew God," were too mean to "honor him as God or give thanks to him" (1.21), **no unfaithfulness made Abraham waver concerning God's promise of God, but he was strengthened in faith as *he gave glory to God*, fully convinced that what God had promised, that God was able to do. And so it was *credited to him as justice* (4.20–22).**

For Paul, as for his hearers, the past is a mirror for the present. **The words *it was credited to him* were not written only for his sake, but for ours (4.23–24a).** That, of course, is why it is so important to tell the story right. **To us** also, Paul says, such faith **is going *to be reckoned*—to us who believe in the One who raised Jesus our Lord from the dead, who was handed over for our transgressions, and raised for our justification (4.24b–25).**

The story must be told right, but the story goes on. Those—Jew and gentile alike—who now place their reliance on nothing save the saving justice and grace of God are one with Abraham, **for he is the father of us all.** As they put their faith in nothing save the faithfulness of God manifested in the faithfulness of Jesus crucified and risen, they too, like Abraham, reverse the disobedience of rebellious humanity and give glory to God the creator; for it is, as Paul observed on another occasion to another group of believers, the very same God who in the beginning said, "Let light shine out of darkness" (compare LXX Gen. 1.1–3) who now shines in their hearts "to give the light of the knowledge of the glory of God in the face of Jesus Christ" (2 Cor. 4.6).

Bibliographical Note

On traditions of Abraham the proselyte, see Samuel Sandmel, *Philo's Place in Judaism: A Study of Conceptions of Abraham in Jewish Literature* (Cincinnati: Hebrew Union College Press, 1956); Edward Adams, "Abraham's Faith and Gentile Disobedience: Textual Links between Romans 1 and 4," *JSNT* 65 (1997), especially 55–62; also Martin Goodman, *Mission and Conversion: Proselytizing in the Religious History of the Roman Empire* (Oxford: Clarendon Press, 1994), 89, 130; N. L. Calvert, "Abraham and Idolatry: Paul's Comparison of Obedience to the Law to Idolatry in Galatians 4.1–10," in *Paul and the Scriptures of Israel*, ed. C. A. Evans and J. A. Sanders, JSNTSup. 83 (Sheffield: JSOT Press, 1992), 225–35.

Additional Note T. Problems in Translating Romans 4.1

> **What then shall we say that Abraham, our forefather according to the flesh, found?** (Romans 4.1).

This somewhat awkward English sentence (we might smooth it out a little by creating a passive: "What then shall we say was found by Abraham, our forefather according to the flesh?") seems to represent the most likely intention of the preferred text of Nestle 27 (so KJV, NAB, NRSV),[123] and for the purposes of my exposition I have treated it as a question posed by Paul's dialogue partner.[124]

But we need to bear in mind two facts. First, identifying the words of Paul's dialogue partner involves (as we have admitted) a certain amount of guesswork:[125] thus, perhaps, as Moo suggests, we are meant to hear Paul himself using "a rhetorical question to introduce the next stage of his argument."[126] Second, and more important, in this case the text, and textual variants, allow for other ways of understanding 4.1, such as:

1. "What did Abraham our forefather discover with respect to the flesh?"[127]—an interpretation that finds additional support in the considerable group of manuscripts that place *eurēkenai* between *propatora* and *kata sarka*;

2. "What, then, are we to say about Abraham, our forefather according to the flesh?"—an interpretation that finds support in the small group of manuscripts (including B) that omit *eurēkenai* altogether, and in the fact that the position of *eurēkenai* in other manuscripts varies (so RSV, NEB, BJ, REB, NRSV margin);[128]

3. "What then shall we say [*ti oun eroumen*]?" constituting a separate question, thus: "What then shall we say? That we have found Abraham to be our forefather according to the flesh?" (so BEP)—in which case the answer implied in what follows is evidently "No."[129]

Whichever solution to this little problem they choose, most scholars (and, by implication, most translations) seem to agree, nonetheless, with Cranfield's general statement that "the purpose of this verse is to raise the question of Abraham as the most obvious possible objection to the statement that glorying has been excluded (3.27)."[130] "The apostle offers to demonstrate by means of the history of Abraham that his justification before God is owed to faith and not to observance of the works of the Law."[131]

123. So Barrett, *Romans* 85; Cranfield, *Romans* 225; Fitzmyer, *Romans* 369; Käsemann, *Romans* 105; Lagrange, *Romains* 81–82; Rhys, *Romans* 45.

124. So Stowers, *Rereading Romans* 232.

125. See Robert L. Brawley, "Multivocality in Romans 4," in *Society of Biblical Literature 1997 Seminar Papers* (Atlanta, Georgia: Scholars Press, 1997), 295; also, footnote 68 on page 92.

126. Moo, *Romans* 259.

127. Dunn, *Romans* 1.198.

128. Sanday and Headlam, *Romans* 98–99.

129. Richard Hays, "Have We Found Abraham to Be Our Forefather According to the Flesh? A Reconsideration of Romans 4:1," *NovT* 27 (1985): 251–70; Stowers, *Rereading* 234.

130. Cranfield, *Romans* 1.226; similarly Fitzmyer, *Romans* 371, and Moo, *Romans* 259–60.

131. BEP, note on 4.1.

5

Demonstration and Defense (5.1–11.36)

Peace with God through Christ

Demonstration (5.1–21)

Reconciliation in Christ (5.1–11)

Some studies treat Romans 5.1–11 as the conclusion to the previous section of Paul's address rather than the opening to the next, and this is understandable, since rhetorically the verses function partially as a pivot, or hinge, between the two. They link what is about to be said to what has gone before, and they do so by means of various rhetorical hooks[1]—such as echoes of expressions already used—that reach back into the opening argument.[2]

So the purpose of 5.1–11 is to point backward and forward. Paul has presented a dissuasive, arguing *against* dependence on anything save God's justice and grace—God's justice and grace, manifested in the cross of Jesus Christ, and witnessed to in

---

1. For the metaphors of "hinges," "pivots," and "hooks," applied to verbal composition, see H. Van Dyke Paranuk, "Oral Typesetting: Some Uses of Biblical Structure," *Biblica* 62 (1981): 153–68; "Transitional Techniques in the Bible," *JBL* 102.4 (1983): 525–48.

2. The purpose of such echoes and resonance in a composition designed to be heard is, as Eric Havelock suggests, to "avoid sheer surprise and novel invention. . . . [T]he basic method of assisting the memory to retain a series of distinct meanings is to frame the first of them in a way which will suggest or forecast a later meaning which will recall the first without being identical with it. What is to be said and remembered later is cast in the form of an echo of something said already; the future is encoded in the present." (Eric A. Havelock, "Oral Composition in the *Oedipus Tyrannus* of Sophocles," *NLH* 16 [1984]: 183). The task of an effective speaker, according to Paul's contemporary Quintilian, was "not so much . . . to discover the question, the central argument, and the point for decision of the judge (an easy task), as that we should continually keep our attention on the subject, or, if we digress, keep looking back to it, lest in our desire to win applause we should let our weapons drop from our grasp" (*Institutio Oratoria* 3.11.26, trans. H. E. Butler); similarly, the author of *To C. Herennius* insisted on the need to be "dwelling on the same topic and yet seeming to say something ever new. . . . We shall not repeat the same thing precisely—for that, to be sure, would weary the hearer and not refine the idea—but with changes" (4.42.54, trans. Harry Caplan).

the Law. In particular, he has argued against dependence on the Law itself. Now he must argue *for* something. He must demonstrate what he calls "my gospel," and in so doing he must defend it against certain difficulties that have, indeed, already been raised—namely, the suggestion that his gospel militates against the moral life and that it implies God is no longer faithful to the promises. In the dissuasive, Paul merely noted that these were *not* positions he held, being at that point more concerned with undermining his opponents' views than defending his own. Now he must try to show why. Beginning, then, from the assertion of "peace with God" (5.1) and "reconciliation" (5.11), he will lead us to a series of comparisons between life in the community of Adam and life in the community of Christ (5.12–19), and so to the triumphant proposal that "grace" now exercises "dominion," leading to "eternal life through Jesus Christ our Lord" (5.20–21). This proposal will then be defended throughout 6.1 to the end of 11, and it is in these chapters that Paul's more detailed defense against the particular charges that I have just mentioned will find its place.

Therefore, he begins, **being justified by faith** (5.1a)—the word **therefore** and the reference to **being justified by faith** evidently refer to what has already been said, and offer the first and most obvious of the backward-reaching hooks—**we have peace [*eirēnē*] with God through our Lord Jesus Christ** (5.1b). This **peace** must, at the very least, be an end to *polemos* ("war")—the war upon God declared by humanity from the foundation of the world, and already described by Paul (1.18–3.20). "God has," as he wrote on another occasion, "through Christ reconciled us to himself" (2 Cor. 5.18). Yet perhaps the biblically alert would think particularly of the messianic "peace" promised by the prophet:

> His rule shall be great,
>   and of his peace [*eirēnē*] there shall be no limit,
> upon the throne of David,
>   and his kingdom,
> to set it right and to take its part
>   in justice and in judgment from now on and for ever.
>   (LXX Isa. 9.6)

and by the psalmist, who saw God offering his people the ancient salutation:

> for [the Lord God] will speak "Peace!" [*eirēnēn*] upon his people.
> Indeed, his salvation for those who fear him is near,
>   that glory may dwell in our land. (LXX. Ps. 84.9–10 [MT 85.9–10])

Through Christ, Paul says, **we also have access to this grace, in which we have taken our stand, and** so now **we** actually **boast** (*kauchōmetha*)[3]—not (in marked contrast to the "boasting" of which Paul spoke before [see 2.17, 3.27]) in something we might claim for ourselves, but **in hope of the glory of God** (5.2), hope for the "glory" that the psalmist promised, hope for that very same "glory" from which, as Paul earlier reminded us, we "all fall short" (3.23), a glory that will be, as it was in the begin

---

3. It is unfortunate that many of the major English translations obscure this rather obvious hook to what has gone before by using a word other than "boast" to translate *kauchōmetha* here and at 5.3 (e.g., KJV "rejoice . . . glory", RSV "rejoice . . . rejoice", NEB "exult . . . exult": contrast, however, NAB, NRSV).

ning, "a gift by God's grace" (3.24). As Paul wrote on another occasion to the Corinthians, "Let the one who boasts, boast in the Lord" (1 Cor. 1.31; apparently alluding to LXX Jer. 9.23–24).

And not only that, but we even boast [*kauchōmetha*] **in our sufferings** (5.3). The chain of associations by which Paul comes to this conclusion is that **suffering creates endurance** (*hupomonēn*), **and endurance creates a proven character** (*dokimēn*), **and a proven character creates hope**[4] (5.3–4). Common experience of suffering is that it can and often does lead to bitterness and despair, but the suffering of which Paul speaks, *endured in union with Jesus Christ* (compare 8.17), offers a new possibility. Such suffering, he says, can form in those who experience it qualities of **endurance** and **proven character** (*dokimēn*)—qualities that are the basis of that self-control which was the ideal of the ancient world, and which are also, of course, the complete opposite of that "reprobate [*a-dokimon*] mind," dominated by passions and leading to moral chaos, that he has earlier described (1.18–32). These qualities lead us to **hope,** and already that **hope does not put us to shame** (5.5a).

Naturally it does not! Since freedom from "shame" is a mark of the gospel (as Paul told us in 1.16), so it is also a mark of the life of "peace with God" lived by in the power of the gospel. All this is **because the love of God has been poured out** [*ekkechutai*] **into our hearts, through the Holy Spirit that has been given to us** (5.5b).

Again and again we find in Scripture the picture of God "pouring out" like water signs both negative and positive of the divine presence. So the psalmist begs that God will "pour out [*ekcheon*] wrath" on his enemies (LXX Ps. 68.25 [MT 69.25]; compare 78.6 [MT 79.6], Hos. 5.10), while Zechariah looks for "a spirit of grace and mercy" (12.10) and Sirach for "wisdom" and "mercy" (1.9, 18.11). Yet the most striking use of the word is surely in Joel, in a passage that was certainly associated in Christian understanding with that gift of the Spirit to the church of which Paul is speaking here:

> And it shall be after these things,
>   I will also pour out [*ekcheō*] from my Spirit upon all flesh,
> and your sons and your daughters will prophesy,
>   and your elders dream dreams and your youths see visions. (LXX Joel 3.1;
>   compare Acts 2.17)

God's Spirit is the mark of God's presence, the divine breath and power, at work in the human heart; and the presence of that Spirit in the Christian community is the surest sign that what "God promised beforehand" (1.2) is being fulfilled.

---

4. This rhetorical figure, which works by means of a thread of associated ideas leading to a climax, can be paralleled from sources as varied in time and concern as, on the one hand, the fifth century BC comedian Epicharmus—"From the sacrifice, a feast; from the feast, there was drinking . . . [;] from the drinking, carousing; from the carousing there was swinish behavior; from the swinish behavior, [judgment]!" (Kaibel 118, Fr. 148)—to a second century rabbi, Phineas ben Jair. Phineas, in a passage that is, in certain respects, oddly reminiscent of Paul, first presents us with a series of reflections on the grief that will be associated with the Messiah's coming, then speaks of the qualities that spring from devotion to "our Father in Heaven": "Zeal leads to cleanliness, and cleanliness leads to purity, and purity leads to self-restraint (*prýšwt*), and self-restraint leads to sanctity, and sanctity leads to humility, and humility leads to the fear of sin, and the fear of sin leads to piety, and piety leads to the Holy Spirit, and the Holy Spirit leads to the Resurrection of the dead, and the resurrection of the dead comes through Elijah of blessed memory" (*m. Soṭa*, 9.15, trans. Philip Blackman).

As regards the **love of God** (*hē agapē tou theou*), certainly it is God's love for us (subjective genitive) that **has been poured out** upon us like life-giving water, and so constitutes the basis and guarantee of our hope (compare 8.39; 2 Cor. 13.13). Yet in this particular context the phrase does carry an element of ambiguity, and (once again) there is no need to pretend otherwise. Still less is there reason to claim that those who recognize that Augustine's objective interpretation (*non qua nos ipse diligit, sed qua nos facit dilectores suos*—"not as he loves us himself, but as he makes us his lovers")—is possible (*De spiritu et littera* 32.56) are guilty of some dark theological agenda, such as supposing that faith is formed by love. Did Augustine suppose that? C. H. Dodd seems to have struck the right balance: "The meaning of this very fundamental statement is not simply that we become aware that God loves us, but that in the same experience in which we receive a deep and undeniable assurance of His love for us, that love becomes the central motive of our own moral being (cf. I John iv. 19: We love because he loved us first)."[5]

For while we were still weak, at the right time, Christ died for the ungodly (5.6). Certainly Paul's hearers would not have been unfamiliar with the idea that the truly noble would be willing to die for another, or for something they cared about. This was an idea at home in Jewish tradition. In the time of the Maccabees was it not true that "many in Israel . . . chose to die rather than be defiled by food or to profane the holy covenant"? (1 Macc. 1.62–63) It was also at home outside Judaism. We have already had occasion to quote Horace, uttering sentiments of whose correctness he would have expected no one to be in any doubt: "It is sweet and fitting to die for one's country [*dulce et decorum est pro patria mori*]" (*Odes* 3.2.13).[6] Such an idea went naturally with the notion of self-control,[7] and was also often associated with friendship: "What is my purpose in making a friend? So as to have someone for whom I may die, someone I can follow into exile, someone for whose life I may stake myself as security, and pay the price" (Seneca, *Letters* 9.10). Needless to say, mere human experience forces us to admit that in practice such generosity is not common—**indeed, rarely will anyone die for a just person**—but at least Paul grants the possibility: **for a good person, one might even dare to die** (5.7).

So much is implied if Paul is using the phrases **for a just person** and **for a good person** more or less synonymously. Cranfield, however, regards the **good person** as meaning one's benefactor, to whom one would have a particular obligation, and this

---

5. Dodd, *Romans* 74.

6. So Aristotle had written: "It is true of the good man too that he does many acts for the sake of his friends and his country, and if necessary dies for them" (*Nicomachean Ethics* 9.8.9, trans. Sir David Ross).

7. A connection clearly understood in the following, from Epictetus: "Helvidius Priscus saw this too, and acted accordingly: for when Vespasian had sent word to him not to attend the Senate, he answered, 'It is in your power not to allow me to be a senator; but as long as I am one, I must attend.' 'Well then, if you do attend, at least be silent.'—'Do not ask for my opinion, and I will be silent.'—'But I must ask it.'—'And I must say what seems right to me.'—'But if you do I will put you to death.'—'Did I ever tell you that I was immortal? You will do your part, and I mine: it is yours to kill, and mine to die without trembling; yours to banish me, mine to depart without grieving" (*Discourses* 1.2.19–21, trans. Elizabeth Carter, rev. Robin Hard). In the same spirit are St. Perpetua's comments as she prepared for martyrdom, cited above in additional note L.

may indeed be how Paul's original audience would have understood him.[8] In that case, the point that Paul is about to make is even stronger. Such is the incredible generosity of the gospel, that whereas normally the client ought to be willing to die for the benefactor, in this case the benefactor dies for the client:

> **God demonstrates his own love toward us in that while we were still sinners, Christ died for us. Much more then, being now justified by his blood, we shall be saved from wrath through him. (5.8–9)**

This generosity of the gospel is the basis of our hope: **for**, as Paul notes in a simple a fortiori argument, **if, when we were enemies, we were reconciled to God by the death of his Son, much more, being reconciled, we shall be saved by his life; and not only that, but we are also boasting [*kauchōmenoi*] in God** (5.10).

This is the third time in this brief section that Paul has claimed for Christians what was earlier the forbidden attitude, but the "boasting" of which he now speaks is, as in the two previous occurrences, based on nothing of our own. It is "boasting" **through our Lord Jesus Christ** (the solemn presentation of the title suggests a conclusion and is almost liturgical) **through whom we have now received the reconciliation** (5.10–11).

Life in Adam and Life in Christ (5:12–21)

Following this claim to experience "peace with God," Paul begins the main part of his demonstration and defense of the gospel with a *synkrisis* ("comparison") contrasting the grief brought to human life by Adam with the hope and joy that have come through Jesus Christ (5.12, 15–21).

> **Therefore, as sin entered the world through one man and through sin death, and thus death passed to all, so that [*eph' hō[i]*][9] all sinned ... as through one man's disobedience many were made sinners, so through one man's obedience many were made righteous. (5.12, 18b)**

This is the essence and heart of Paul's claim throughout this section. Despite later Christian concerns, it is evident that Paul is here interested neither in Adam for his own sake, nor in the precise way in which Adam's legacy of sin was passed on to those who came after. Paul wishes to say something about life in the community of Christ, and he says it by contrasting it with life in the community of Adam. To understand Paul's rhetoric, we need therefore to forget all the questions that were later raised by Augustine, and be aware rather of the ancient world's understanding of community.

Our forebears before the Enlightenment had in general a deep sense of human solidarity. It was not that they were unaware of people as individuals, or that they did not care for them as such—one has only to read Euripides or Shakespeare to see that *that* was not the case—but in general they saw human existence as having little

---

8. Cranfield, *Romans* 1. 264–65; see further Bruce M. Winter, *Seek the Welfare of the City: Christians as Benefactors and Citizens* (Carlisle, England: Paternoster Press; Grand Rapids, Michigan: Eerdmans, 1994) 35; A. D. Clarke, "The Good and the Just in Romans 5:7," *TynBul* 41 (1990): 128–42.

9. On the interpretation of *eph'hō[i]*, see additional note U.

meaning except in relationship to others. There is a modern Western (and particularly North American) ideal of the "man alone," who needs no one, who stands on his own two feet against the world, and who, at the end of every adventure, rides off alone into the sunset rather than be tied down to community or place. To our forebears, such an "ideal" would have sounded like a description of damnation.[10] For the ancients, to be in hell, to be damned, was precisely to be "forgotten," to be a "wanderer" over the face of the earth, belonging nowhere: such, before his salvation by the goddess, was the fate of Lucius in Apuleius's *Metamorphoses*; such the plight of the sad old warrior in the Old English poem *The Wanderer*, remembering the joys of the table shared with fellow warriors, remembering the joys of knowing his liege lord, and grieving because all are gone.

The Hebrews shared this attitude. So Cain's penalty in Genesis 4.12 is to be "a fugitive and a wanderer on the earth," and his reaction to it is that it is the worst thing that could be imagined, "more than I can bear." In Jewish understanding as in pagan, communities of human beings naturally belong together, and stand or fall together, for better or worse. So an unknown Palestinian Jew, living only a few decades after Paul, wrote, "O Adam, what have you done? For though it was you who sinned, the fall was not yours alone, but ours also who are your descendants" (2 (4) Ezra 7.118; compare 2 Sam. 24, Josh. 7, m. *Sanh.* 4.5). As Johannes Pedersen said of biblical Israel in a now classic statement,

> When we look at the soul, we always see a community rising behind it. What it is, it is by virtue of others. It has sprung up from a family which has filled it with its contents, and from which it can never grow away. The family forms the narrowest community in which it lives. But wherever it works, it must live in community, because it is its nature to communicate itself to others, to share blessing with them. Loneliness, the lack of community, the Old Testament only knows as something unnatural, an expression that life is failing.[11]

Hence neither Jew nor Greek understood either "peace" or "justice" (which naturally involved "faithfulness" and "loyalty") to be things that one could have *by oneself*. "Peace" is being in harmonious relationship with those to whom one is bound; "justice" is proper behavior toward them; both are essentially communal concepts.

Equally, of course, it is impossible to have "honor" alone, for how can there be honor where there is no one to honor you and none for you to honor? Plutarch, in his *Reply to Colotes*, takes for granted (and summarizes perfectly) the entire complex of ideas: "[T]o live well is to live in fellowship, in friendship, temperately, and justly" (*Reply to Celotes* 2 [*Moralia* 1108c]). There is therefore no contradiction between the ideal of *egkrateia* ("self-control") and what we have called "solidarity." On the contrary, the proper basis for self-control was precisely to be in right relationship with others, and, in particular, to be in right relationship to the right master. For

---

10. On ancient notions of "solidarity," see also Luther H. Martin, "The Anti-Individualistic Ideology of Hellenistic Culture," *NUMEN* 41.2 (1994): 118–40, and literature there cited; there is a useful summary with bibliography in Bruce J. Malina, "Understanding New Testament Persons," in *The Social Sciences and New Testament Interpretation*, ed. Richard L. Rohrbaugh (Peabody, Massachusetts: Hendrickson, 1996), 41–46; see further additional note V.

11. Johannes Pedersen, *Israel: Its Life and Culture* (London: Oxford University Press, 1926), 2.263.

Epictetus, that involved the quest of philosophy (*Discourses* 4.1.177); for a Jew such as Eleazar, it meant subjection to God and God's Law (4 Macc. 5.33–35).

This is the background to what Paul is saying in Romans 5.12–21—and, indeed, in the whole of chapters 5 to 11. The community of Adam is bound to Adam; and in this respect **Adam was a type** (a pattern, or model) **of the one who was to come** (5.14c), for the community of the Messiah is likewise bound to the Messiah. For Christians, therefore, union with Adam is subsumed in union with Christ. This is God's gift.

But the free gift is not like the trespass (5.15a).

Why not? The old community began with loss, for Adam disobeyed; there is, however, an overflowing generosity in God's gift to the new community that does far more than merely recover what was lost. **For if many died through the trespass of one, much more have the grace of God and the free gift in the grace of the one man Jesus Christ abounded for many** (5.15b).

Again, unlike Adam, Christ did not merely have to take upon himself the disobedience of Adam: Christ had to take upon himself the whole tally of human disobedience that *began* with Adam—that entire tally of disobedience of which Paul has already spoken (1.18–3.20). In this respect also, therefore, **the free gift is not like the effect of the sin of the one: for the judgment following one trespass led to condemnation, but the free gift following many trespasses leads to** fulfillment of God's **just requirement** [*dikaiōma*] (5.16).[12]

The contrast is, moreover, between life and death. **For if, through the trespass of one, death reigned through that one, much more assuredly will those who receive the abundance of grace and the free gift of justice reign in life through the one Jesus Christ** (5.17). "For as in Adam all died, so also in Christ shall all be made alive" (1 Cor. 15.22).

Therefore, just as one man's trespass led to condemnation for all, so one man's act of justice [*dikaiōmatos*] **leads to justification** [*dikaiōsin*] **and life for all. For just as by the one man's disobedience the many were made sinners, so by the one man's obedience the many will be made just** (5.18–19).

Christ's **act of justice**—his right behavior toward God—was manifested in his **obedience** whereby (as Paul observed on another occasion) he "did not regard equality with God as something to be exploited, but emptied himself, taking the form of a

---

12. I thus take *dikaiōma* at 5.16 in its normal Pauline and LXX sense (BAGD, δικαίωμα 1). Paul's expression then appears to be somewhat elliptical but is nonetheless perfectly clear. *How* God's action in Christ "leads to the just requirement" will be spelled out at greater length in 8, beginning from 8.3, where Paul will speak of God "sending his own son in the likeness of sinful flesh, that the just requirement of the Law might be fulfilled in us": on which see pages 146–55. Commentators and translators from Jerome onward have, however, generally translated *dikaiōma* here as if it were *dikaiōsis* (that is, "justification")—the grounds normally offered being that Paul has used *dikaiōma* rather than *dikaiōsis* for rhetorical reasons, in parallel with *katakrima*. LS and LEH offer, however, no parallels for such a sense for *dikaiōma*; and BAGD offers only very uncertain parallels, namely, from a Greek fragment of 1 Enoch 104.9 (where there is no possible way to be sure that the Greek text does not intend *dikaiōma* in its normal LXX sense) and from v.l. Ezek. 18.21 (where, in any case, *dikaiōsis* appears to have replaced not *dikaiōma* but *dikaiosunē*, and is evidently used in its normal sense). Of course Paul *does* believe that Jesus' *dikaiōma* leads to our *dikaiōsis*, and he will say so at 5.18; but it does not follow that that is what he is saying at 5.16.

slave, being born in human likeness; and being found in human form he humbled himself, and became obedient to the point of death—even death on a cross" (Phil. 2.6–7). Adam's **disobedience** places Adam's community in alienation from and opposition to God. Christ's **obedience** places Christ's community in a proper relationship to God. Thereby, as Paul noted on yet another occasion, whereas "the first Adam became a living being, the last Adam [became] a life-giving spirit" (1 Cor. 15.45).

In Jewish writings of the New Testament period, as N. T. Wright has pointed out, it is consistently the case that "what God intended for Adam will be given to Israel. They will inherit the second Eden, the restored primeval glory." "For God has chosen them for an everlasting Covenant, and all the glory of Adam shall be theirs" (*Rule of the Community* 1QS 4.24, trans. Geza Vermes). If, then, there is to be a "last Adam," "he is not an individual, whether messianic or otherwise. He is the whole eschatological people of God."[13] Paul, however, is clear that in the first place this eschatological role belongs to Jesus, and to him alone (as in 1 Corinthians 15, Romans 6, and [probably] Philippians 2); it is only through its union with Jesus that the privileges pertaining to this role belong also to God's people—a change that, in view of the ancients' communal understanding of personality, perhaps appeared less dramatic to them than to us.

This is the overall thrust of Paul's argument in 5.12–19. At verses 13–14, however, he seems to have sensed a problem, namely, the absence of Law between Adam and Moses. Such an absence inevitably meant that the sins of those who lived between Adam and the giving of the Law were not the same as either Adam's sin or Israel's sin, since they were sins committed in ignorance[14]—**sin indeed was in the world before the Law was given, but sin is not counted where there is no Law** (5.13). Clearly there is a difference between breaking a commandment when we know we are breaking it and when we don't; for the former, as Paul has already observed, leaves us "without excuse" (1.18–21; compare 3.20, 4.15). Nevertheless, as he has also pointed out, action that departs from the will of God, whether in ignorance or not, remains action that departs from the will of God and has its consequences: "[A]ll who have sinned without the Law will also perish without the Law" (2.12). Therefore **death** [personified] **reigned from Adam to Moses, even over those whose sins were not like the transgression of Adam** (5:14a).[15]

Formally, verses 13–14 may be something of a digression. As regards content, however, their reference to the **Law** prepares the ground for Paul's concluding proposition, which is also his final triumphant comparison and contrast between life in the community of Adam and life in the community of the Messiah. Linking "life in Adam" specifically to the history of Israel, Paul asserts that **Law slipped in to increase the trespass** (5.20). This, in Paul's understanding, is the *effect* of the Law (which is in itself good and holy—see 7.12) on sinners (see further 7.7–25). His statement is not without that irony which the ancients seem to have found easier to ap-

13. N. T. Wright, *The Climax of the Covenant: Christ and the Law in Pauline Theology* (Edinburgh: Clark, 191), 21.

14. Adam did not, of course, possess the complete Law; nevertheless, he had received a command from God, which placed him in a "Law" position, and he disobeyed it.

15. On sin committed in ignorance, see additional note M (b).

preciate than we do. The irony is heightened by Paul's personification of "Law" and by his choice of the verb **slipped in** (*parerchomai*—almost "slipped in unnoticed")— a word that carries evident (and, in the context, even ludicrous) associations with action undertaken surreptitiously.[16]

But, Paul concludes, **where sin increased** [*epleonasen*], **grace abounded all the more, so that as sin reigned in death, grace also might reign through justice**—the gracious justice of God—**to eternal life through Christ Jesus our Lord** (5.20–21). The sins of Adam and the sins of Israel alike have been overwhelmed by the faithfulness of God in Jesus Christ.

Additional Note U. The Meaning of *Eph'hō[i]* at Romans 5.12

The interpretation of *eph'hō[i]* at Romans 5.12 constitutes a problem that has been recognized from antiquity. Granted a number of minor variations, at least three main possibilities should be mentioned:

1. Augustine, using the old Latin, *in quo omnes peccaverunt*, came to the conclusion (after some hesitation) that *in quo* referred to Adam, and interpreted the passage to mean "through one man death came into the word . . . in whom [*in quo*] all sinned" (see *Contra duas epistolas Pelagianorum* 4.4.7). Such an idea would certainly not have been impossible for Paul, and recent interpreters defending this interpretation have understandably appealed to 1 Corinthians 15.22, as well as invoking ancient ideas of "solidarity."[17] Two objections are, however, generally raised against this view of the present passage. First, and most important, the meaning thus required for Greek *epi* plus the dative is difficult—indeed, apparently without any clear parallel (see Smyth, 1689.2, BD § 235). Second, and perhaps less important, the antecedent thus claimed for *eph'ō*—that is, *di'henos anthrōpou*—is very early.

2. The overwhelming majority of modern commentators prefer to understand *eph'hō[i]* at Romans 5.12 as equivalent to *epi touto hoti*, or the causal conjunction *dioti*, and translate it by something like "since," "because," or "inasmuch as": a possibility recognized by BAGD (ἐπί, 2.1.b.g); BD (§235.2 [with caution]); Moule, *Idiom* (132); and Zerwick, *Biblical Greek* (§127). This view is also represented by a majority of the translations (KJV, RSV, NEB, NAB, NRSV, BEP). Yet this interpretation, too, is controversial—and particularly so since an important essay published in 1955 by S. Lyonnet made evident the difficulty in supposing that *eph'hō[i]* at Romans 5.12 could possibly be an equivalent for *hoti*: "[T]he current alleged use of the one in place of the other has by no means been proved."[18] The parallels to this usage alleged by

---

16. BAGD, ταρέρχομαι, 1.b.d; LS, ταρέρχομαι, V; compare Paul's own use of the verb at Gal. 2.4. Paul's observation is, of course, no more intended as an attack on the Law itself, or on study of the Law, than is the often-quoted *baraita* of R. Judah, which also states (in essence) that the presence of the Law increases the trespass: "R. Judah son of R. Ilai expounded: What is the meaning of, *Shew my people their transgression, and the house of Jacob their sins* (Isa. 58.1)? '*Shew my people their transgression*' refers to scholars, whose unwitting errors are accounted as intentional faults; '*and the house of Israel their sins*'—to the ignorant, whose intentional sins are accounted to them as unwitting errors" (*b. B. Meṣ* 33b, trans. H. Freedman)

17. On solidarity, see further, additional note V.

18. S. Lyonnet, "Le sens de ἐφ ' ᾧ en Rom 5,12 et l'exégèse des Pères grecs," *Biblica* 36 (1955): 455.

BAGD and BD from Paul and other ancient authors generally prove, on investigation, to be uncertain or invalid.

3. Once, when Plutarch was lecturing in Rome, a soldier delivered a letter from the emperor to a man called Rusticus, who was in the audience. "There was a silence," Plutarch writes, "and I paused, so as to let him read the letter, but he declined to do so, nor did he open it until I had finished and the session had broken up, so that [*eph'hō*[*i*]] everyone admired his gravity" (*Curiosity* 15 [*Moralia* 522e], trans. Donald Russell, altered). This consecutive or consequential meaning of *eph'hō*[*i*] is, as Joseph Fitzmyer has recently demonstrated, actually quite well attested in texts of the period (compare Plutarch, *Cimon* [*Parallel Lives*] 8.6.4; *Aratus* [*Parallel Lives*] 44.4.1; Cassius Dio, *Roman History* 59.19.1–2, 59.20.3; Diogenes Laertius, *Lives of Eminent Philosophers* 7.173.1–5, and other examples cited by Fitzmyer).[19] It seems, therefore, the most natural way to understand Paul's use here. Byrne's objection that it "makes little sense in the context"[20] is nothing to the point since, as I have said before, it is axiomatic that we interpret our authors on the basis of what they appear to say, not on the basis of what we think they ought to say. Actually, the consecutive interpretation of *eph'hō*[*i*] at Romans 5.12 makes perfectly good sense. Paul is simply saying that, as a result of what happened in the history of Adam—the entry of sin into the world, the entry of death through sin, and the spreading of death to all—as a result of that, *all* have sinned, including, of course, Israel as well as the gentiles. This is a point that Paul has already made (3.23) and will make again (5.18–19).

Bibliographical Note

There is an excellent summary of earlier discussions of this problem in Cranfield, *Romans* 1.274–79. See further S. Lyonnet, "Le sens de ἐφ ' ᾧ en Rom 5.12 et l'exégèse des pères grecs," in *Biblica* 36 (1955): 436–56; Joseph Fitzmyer, "The Consecutive Meaning of ΕΦ'Ω in Romans 5.12," *NTS* 39.3 (1993): 321–39.

Additional Note V. Solidarity

Louis Dumont makes a useful distinction between "the *empirical* subject of speech, thought, and will, the individual sample of mankind as found in all societies," and

> the independent, autonomous, and thus essentially non-social moral being, who carries our paramount values and is found primarily in our modern ideology of man and society. From that point of view, there emerge two kinds of societies. Where the individual is a paramount value I speak of individualism. In the opposite case, where the paramount value lies in society as a whole, I speak of holism."[21]

Such holism, often referred to by the (not very satisfactory) phrase "corporate personality" or, as I prefer to refer to it, "solidarity," has been fairly commonly posited of ancient Israel—notably since H. Wheeler Robinson's influential essay "The He-

19. Joseph A. Fitzmyer, "The Consecutive Meaning of *eph'hō*[*i*] in Romans 5.12," in *NTS* 39.3 (1993): 323–39.

20. Byrne, *Romans* 183.

21. Louis Dumont, *Essays on Individualism: Modern Ideology in Anthropological Perspective* (Chicago: University of Chicago Press, 1986), 25.

brew Conception of Corporate Personality."[22] Thus John Reumann wrote of "that important Semitic complex of thought in which there is a constant oscillation between the individual and the group—family, tribe, or nation—to which he belongs, so that the king or some other representative figure may be said to embody the group, or the group may be said to sum up the host of individuals."[23] What is less commonly conceded is that in this matter ancient Israel was broadly at one with her neighbors.

In speaking of "individualism" in contrast with "holism," Dumont is not speaking of individuals who *withdraw* from the world to pursue a life of asceticism and denial and even, as some would say, through constant intercession to become *closer* to the rest of the world. All these were concepts with which our forebears were entirely familiar. Dumont is speaking of those who, thinking they are normal and full members of their societies, yet consider themselves in relationship to those societies to be independent, autonomous, and essentially unobligated. *That* is the concept that the ancients, the medievals, and virtually everyone else before the Enlightenment would have found surprising.

Alexis de Tocqueville, in 1835, writing his by no means unsympathetic account *Democracy in America*, felt that he had to explain himself even for using the word *individualisme*—as well as seeing no reason to disguise his sharply critical reaction to the phenomenon for which it stood:

> *Individualism* is a novel expression, to which a novel idea has given birth. Our fathers were only acquainted with *égoïsme* (selfishness). Selfishness is a passionate and exaggerated love of self, which leads a man to connect everything with himself and to prefer himself to everything in the world. Individualism is a mature and calm feeling, which disposes each member of the community to sever himself from the mass of his fellow-creatures, and to draw apart with his family and friends, so that after he has formed a little circle of his own, he willingly leaves society at large to itself. Selfishness originates in blind instinct; individualism proceeds from erroneous judgment more than depraved feelings; it originates as much in deficiencies of mind as in perversity of heart. Selfishness blights the germ of all virtue; individualism, at first, only saps the virtues of public life; but in the long run it attacks and destroys all others and is at length absorbed in downright selfishness.[24]

22. H. Wheeler Robinson, "Corporate Personality in Ancient Israel," first published in *Werden und Wesen des Alten Testaments: Vorträge gehalten auf der Internationalen Tagung Alttestamentlicher Forscher zu Göttingen vom 4.–10. September 1935*, ed. P. Volz, F. Stummer, and J. Hempel. Beihefte zur Zeitschrift für die Alttestamentliche Wissenschaft, 66. Berlin: Töpelmann, 1936.

23. Introduction to H. Wheeler Robinson, *Corporate Personality in Ancient Israel*, Facet Books, Biblical Series 2, ed. John Reumann (Philadelphia: Fortress Press, 1964), v. This small volume was a reprint of Robinson's 1936 paper, together with a related paper, "The Group and the Individual in Israel." Compare also Johannes Pedersen, *Israel: Its Life and Culture*, 4 vols in 2 (London: Oxford University Press, 1926–40 [1920–34]), 263–310, and passim.

24. Alexis de Tocqueville, *Democracy in America*, trans. Henry Reeve, rev. Francis Bowen (New York: Vintage Books, 1954 [1835]), 104). It is interesting to reflect that the collapse, under postmodernist critique, of one of the main Enlightenment assumptions upon which "Individualism" was built—namely, the autonomy of the self (*Cogito, ergo sum*)—seems to have done nothing to inhibit the phenomenon of Individualism itself; and this may be because the postmodernist critique has also caused another Enlightenment assumption to collapse—namely, the knowability of certain kinds of truth. By collapsing knowledge into the self, postmodernism has made the admission that we do not

We admire so splendid a statement of human interdependence as that in John Donne's *Meditation*, composed early in the seventeenth century:

> No man is an island, entire of itself; every man is a piece of the continent, a part of the main; if a clod be washed away by the sea, Europe is the less, as well as if a promontory were, as well as if a manor of thy friends or of thine own were; any man's death diminishes me, because I am involved in Mankind; And therefore never send to know for whom the bell tolls; it tolls for thee.[25]

Yet we need to recall that for all the magnificence of Donne's rhetoric (which his hearers will certainly have appreciated) the passage expressed, nonetheless, what they would have regarded as a commonplace, as something unarguable. So Richard Hooker, though less splendidly, says exactly the same thing:

> God hath created nothing simply for itself: but each thing in all things, and of everything each part in other hath such interest that in the whole world nothing is found whereunto any thing created can say, *I need thee not.*[26]

One instance of antiquity's sense of solidarity is provided by one of its most common images of society—the body. Classically, the image had been used in Plato's *Republic*:

> "The best ordered state is one in which as many people as possible use the words, 'mine' and 'not mine' in the same sense of the same things." "Much the best." "What is more, such a state most nearly resembles an individual. For example, when one of us hurts his finger, the whole partnership of body and soul, constituting a single organism under a ruling principle perceives it and is aware as a whole of the pain suffered by the part, and so we say that the man in question has pain in *his* finger. And the same holds good of any other part in which a man suffers pain or enjoys pleasure." "Yes," he agreed, "and, as you said, the same thing is true of the best-run communities." "That is because such a community will regard the individual who experiences gain or loss as part of itself, and be glad or sorry as a whole accordingly" (462c–d, trans. Desmond Lee).

Among the best-known examples was the parable by which, in the early years of the Roman Republic, Menenius Agrippa persuaded plebeian soldiers to return to the service of Rome after they had withdrawn to the Mons Sacer and were threatening to found their own republic (Livy, *From the Founding of the City* 2.32; Dionysius of Halicarnassus, *Roman Antiquities* 6.83.3–88.4, especially 6.86.1–5; Plutarch, *Coriolanus* [*Parallel Lives*] 6.1–4; Plutarch's version was to be dramatized by Shakespeare: see *Coriolanus* 1.1.93–151).[27]

---

know what the self is far less significant than it might otherwise have been. The personalized transistor, "virtual reality," and the concept of a "cyberspace" where one can and even *ought* to "create one's own reality" all represent the flourishing of an Individualism still well able to nurture the illusion that it is dependent upon nothing but itself.

25. John Donne, *Meditations upon Emergent Occasions* 17.

26. *Sermon on Pride* 2.

27. Shakespeare has, however, some interesting changes of emphasis and makes use of other sources, perhaps because in some respects the "body" metaphor had become overly familiar by the year 1608: see *Coriolanus* 1.1.86–89; see further R. B. Parker's comments in *The Tragedy of Coriolanus*, R. B. Parker, ed., *The Oxford Shakespeare* (Oxford: Clarendon Press, 1994), 18–19.

For examples more nearly contemporary with Paul, we might cite Seneca: "All that you behold, that which comprises both God and man, is one—we are the parts of one great body" (*Letters* 95.52, trans. Richard M. Gummere) or Epictetus,

> What then is the calling of a citizen? To consider nothing in terms of personal advantage, never to deliberate on anything as though detached from the whole, but be like our hand or foot, which, if they had reason, and understood the constitution of nature, would never exercise any impulse or desire, except by reference to the whole. (*Discourses* 2.10.4, trans. Elizabeth Carter, rev. Robin Hard)

This attitude of the ancients to society is perhaps, in contemporary thinking, more clearly reflected in (and more easily expressed through) certain African approaches to social relationships than much Western (and particularly, as de Tocqueville observed, North American)[28] thinking since the Enlightenment. Specifically, I am thinking of the African concept of *Ubuntu*, derived from the not easily translatable Xhosa concept, *Umuntu ngumuntu ngabanye bantu*—a proverbial expression meaning, as Michael Battle says, "that each individual humanity is ideally expressed in relationship with others and, in turn, individuality is truly expressed. Or 'a person depends on other persons to be a person.'"[29] Most of Paul's contemporaries—Jew and pagan alike—would have understood that perfectly. To the stoic Epictetus, for example, it seemed axiomatic:

> How is it, then, that some external things are said to be in accordance with nature, and others contrary to it? Because we consider ourselves in detachment from everything else. I will say that it is natural for the foot, for instance, to be clean. But if you take it as a foot, and not as a detached object, it will be fitting for it to walk in the dirt, and tread upon thorns, and sometimes even to be cut off for the sake of the body as a whole; otherwise it is no longer a foot. We should reason in some such manner concerning ourselves also. What are you? A man. If then, indeed, you consider yourself as a detached being, it is natural for you to live to old age, and be rich and healthy; but if you consider yourself as a man, and as a part of the whole, it will be fitting, on account of that whole, that you should at one time be sick; at another, take a voyage, and be exposed to danger; sometimes be in want; and possibly it may happen, die before your time. Why, then, are you displeased? Do you not know that, just as the foot in detachment is no longer a foot, so you in detachment are no longer a man? For what is a man? A part of a city, first, of that made up by gods and men; and next, of that to which you immediately belong, which is a miniature of the universal city. (*Discourses* 2.5.24–26, trans. Elizabeth Carter, rev. Robin Hard)

In this context I am reminded of a story (I cannot recall its source) of an African Christian who expressed surprise that Westerners ever took to Christianity or the New Testament, since both seemed to him, in their understanding of society, alien to Western attitudes as he experienced them, and much closer to African attitudes. The answer to his implied question was, of course, that it was *pre-Enlightenment* Europeans who took to Christianity—and that they would doubtless have found much in modern Western attitudes just as alien as he did.

---

28. de Tocqueville, *Democracy in America* 104.

29. Michael Battle, "The Ubuntu Theology of Desmond Tutu," in *Archbishop Tutu: Prophetic Witness in South Africa*, ed. Leonard Hulley, Louise Kretzschmar, and Luke Lungile Pato (Cape Town: Human and Rousseau, 1996), 99–100.

Of course we must not romanticize ancient (or African) societies, which, for all their notions of solidarity, were (and are) no more perfect than our own. Desmond Tutu himself points to one of the dangers of "solidarity," or *ubuntu*, and the concomitant advantage of a measure of "individualism":

> We have a strong sense of community. Because Westerners have a strong sense of the value of the individual, they are able to take personal initiatives. It's not so easy, when you are a community-minded person, to go against the stream.[30]

It is also only too easy for societies in which one is deeply conscious of the link between one personality and the rest of the group (the nation, the tribe, the family) to dehumanize all who are *not* members of the group—a weakness from which in antiquity neither Jew nor pagan, neither Greek, Roman, nor barbarian could claim exemption. This makes, indeed, Paul's own breadth of vision the more remarkable, as we shall see when we come to consider Romans 12.14–21, with its apparent assertion of concern for the essentially *human* hopes and problems even of those who are outside the believing community—rejoicing "with those who rejoice," and weeping "with those who weep."[31]

Defense 1. Does the Gospel Undermine the Commandment? (6.1–8.39)

The Gospel and Obeying God's Commands (6:1–23)

The triumphant proposition of 5.20–21 also, however, sets the stage for the first of Paul's "students" to raise an objection to the gospel as Paul has described it. **"What shall we say then? Shall we *continue* in sin, so that grace may increase?"**(6.1). That might indeed seem to follow from what Paul has said. So the underlying question throughout this and the next two subsections of the letter will be, as we might express it, "What does it mean to live in dependence on the faithfulness of God?"

The immediate question, **"Shall we continue in sin . . . ?"** suggests that one result of proclaiming the gospel might be exactly what W. H. Auden's Herod said it would be: "Every crook will argue: 'I like committing crimes. God likes forgiving them. Really the world is admirably arranged.'"[32]

Moreover, the form of the question, even down to its vocabulary, evidently arises from what Paul has just said (5.20–21). Yet that same form also betrays the questioner's misunderstanding. The same verb **increase** (*ploenazō*), used by Paul at 5.20 of sin, is used by the questioner at 6.1 of grace—and that is the clue. The "increase" of sin is not parallel to an "increase" of grace, because sin and grace are not two parallel "things" that proceed or recede together, or even in the same way. Sin

---

30. Desmond Tutu, "Where Is Now Thy God?" cited in Michael Battle, *Reconciliation: The Ubuntu Theology of Desmond Tutu* (Cleveland, Ohio: Pilgrim Press, 1997), v.

31. See pages 201–204.

32. W. H. Auden, *For the Time Being: A Christmas Oratorio* (London: Faber and Faber, 1946). It is interesting to note that Auden set on the title page to the poem an extract from the section of Romans that we are considering: "*What shall we say then? Shall we continue in sin, that grace may abound? God forbid. Romans VI.*" I owe this reference to my late, and sadly missed, colleague, Gilbert F. Gilchrist, professor of political science at the University of the South.

is *distortion*, departure from God's will, the destruction of relationships for which we were created; grace is *graciousness*, *favor*, or *goodwill*: and God's graciousness toward us in Christ is, in particular, that favor whereby we are received into a new relationship with God, by means of union with Christ.

Therefore the answer to Paul's imaginary questioner is clear: **By no means! How can we who died to sin go on living in it? Do you not know that all of us who have been baptized into Christ Jesus have been baptized into his death?** (6.2–3).[33]

The very fact of solidarity—of being now in the community of Christ—places a demand upon us. To have been baptized into Christ Jesus is to have accepted a new identity—an identity that involves the cross, and therefore also the resurrection. **Therefore we have been buried with Christ by baptism into death**—we *have* been so buried, the past tense of the verb indicating that this is not something for which we should be hoping, or which we should be looking to experience, but that it is something that *has* happened to us, once for all, and irrevocably—**so that, just as Christ was raised from the dead by the glory of the Father, so also we might walk** [*peripatēsōmen*: aorist subjunctive] **in newness of life** (6.4).

So that . . . so also: there is an unbreakable connection between what is past—the raising of Christ—and what is now to follow—**that we *might* walk**, the change of tense and mood indicating that Paul now speaks of something that is not simply past, but rather a new beginning: our walking **in newness of life**.

In what follows Paul does not so much explain what he has said as reiterate and confirm it. **For if we have become grown together** with him **in the likeness of his death, certainly we shall also be in** the likeness **of his resurrection.**[34] **We know that our old self** [*palaios anthrōpos*—literally, "our old human being," our humanity as bound to the community of Adam] **was crucified together** [*sunestaurōthē*—literally, "was con-crucified"] with Christ, **in order that the body of sin**—our whole person, insofar as we are oriented away from God—**might be rendered powerless, and we might be no longer enslaved to sin, for whoever has died** in this way—that is, in fellowship with Christ—**has been justified from sin** (6.5–7).[35] Sin (personified) is a power that enslaves the community of Adam; but those who are in the community of Christ are freed from that enslavement. Certainly they do not yet enjoy the full experience of perfect communion with Christ, but that communion is their destiny: **if we have died with Christ, we believe that we shall also live with him. We know that Christ, being raised from the dead, will never die again; death has**

33. However much we might wish it otherwise, Paul here offers no information whatever about the history of baptism or its relationship to other religious practices, Jewish or pagan: in fact he "offers" no information about baptism at all. Answering the charge that "my gospel" might logically lead to a life of moral indifference, he simply appeals to what he evidently supposes both he and his hearers already know about baptism: namely, that to have been baptized into Christ is to have been united with the person and destiny of Jesus Christ.

34. On the problems of translating 6.5, see further additional note W.

35. It seems better to take 6.7 this way, associated closely with what precedes (as is implied by "for" [*gar*]), and using the words in their common Pauline sense, rather than appealing to Paul's possible use of a much later rabbinic maxim—"Once a man dies, he is free from [all] obligations, and thus R. Johanan interpreted: *Among the dead I am free* [MT Ps. 88.6]: once a man is dead he is free from religious duties" (*b. Šabb.* 151a, trans. H. Freedman)—whose relevance is at best doubtful. See Fitzmyer, *Romans* 436–7.

no more dominion over him. The death that he died, he died to sin, once for all;
but the life he lives, he lives to God. **Thus**, far from "continuing in sin," those who
are in Christ's community **must reckon** [*logizesthe*] themselves **dead to sin, and alive
to God in Christ Jesus** (6.8–11). "The resurrection," as Guy Fitch Lytle puts it, "has
broken down the barriers between this world and the next, and that has changed
everything."[36]

Inevitably, therefore, those who are in the community of Christ cannot possibly be content to **let** the tyrant **sin exercise dominion** in their **mortal bodies, so as
to be obedient to its desires; nor will** they **offer** their **members**—the specific parts
of their existence in the world—**to sin as instruments for injustice; instead** they
are to offer themselves **to God, as those who have been brought living from the
dead, and** their **members as instruments of God's justice. Sin shall not reign over**
them, **for** they **are not under Law**—they are not, that is, living in that dependence
upon the Law and their own knowledge of the Law that is, as we have already seen,
in Paul's view deeply unfaithful to the Law—**but under grace** (6.12–14)—they are,
that is, living in that proper dependence on God's graciousness to which, in fact,
the Law points (cf. 3.21, 31).

Paul is not, of course, saying that those who are in the community of Christ will
or can remain sinless: the exhortatory sections in every Pauline letter are testimony
to Paul's realism on that score. But he is saying that for those who offer themselves
(sinners though they are) to God as God's "instruments," for those who live in dependence on God's grace, the essential power of sin to alienate them from God and
destroy their lives is broken. Therefore, evidently, the suggestion that they might at
the same time choose to ignore the breaking of that power by "living in sin"—that
is, *accepting* sin's dominion over them—is absurd.

But Paul's questioner has not finished: indeed, Paul's words lead directly to the
next challenge. **"What then? Shall we sin because we are not under Law, but under
grace?"** Paul replies bluntly: **By no means!** (6.15). Yet this is a more dangerous question than the former, precisely because, in making no foolish claims (such as that
our sin causes God's grace to increase) it is closer to the reality.

Surely Paul is saying that for those who are "under grace," as opposed to being
"under the Law," sin does not really matter?

In a sense the answer is, "Yes, he is saying that"—just as the priest who says "The
Lord has put away all your sins" after giving absolution is saying that the penitent's
sins no longer really matter—but only in a sense. Our sin "does not really matter" in
that we are not excluded from God's people because of it, in that God remains gracious toward us in spite of it: but wrong actions are still wrong actions, and sin is still
sin, and both still have consequences.

**Don't you know that if you present yourselves as obedient slaves to anyone,
then you are slaves to the one whom you obey, whether it be to sin for death, or
to obedience for justice?** (6.16).

Again the biblically alert might recall the opening sections of Wisdom, which
spoke of those "mortgaged to sin," in whom Wisdom would not dwell, and who had

---

36. Guy Fitch Lytle III, "Elegies in the Resurrection," *STR* 40.3 (1997): 293.

made a covenant with death (Wisd. of Sol. 1.4,16).[37] Being baptized into Christ means that we now have our true master, justice, rather than the wrong master, sin: **Thanks be to God!—because you were once slaves to sin, but you have given obedience from the heart to the pattern of teaching to which you were handed over and, set free from sin, you have become slaves to** God's **justice** (6.17–18).

This is a somewhat strange observation and has caused commentators considerable difficulty, some even regarding it as a non-Pauline gloss. Slaves were obliged to obey their masters, whatever their personal feelings; **obedience from the heart** appears to be contrasted with that. The passive **handed over** seems to imply the action of God, who has put believers in a situation where the risen Lord can stamp the **pattern** of his own obedience upon their lives. "They are not given a 'law'—a set of moral instructions—which they ought now to attempt to fulfill. Rather, they are 'given up' to a new ethical 'force' (the obedience of the risen Lord welling up within them; cf. v. 11; Phil. 2.5)" (Byrne).[38]

Of course, slavery is a very limited metaphor by which to describe our relationship with the God of Israel, and Paul apologizes for it. **I am speaking in human terms because of your natural limitations** (6.19a). Nonetheless, the slave metaphor does have one great strength, namely, that it speaks of our belonging to another,[39] and that is Paul's point here. Therefore, **just as you once presented your members as slaves to uncleanness** [*akarthasia*] **and lawlessness** [*anomia*] **leading to** still more **lawlessness, so now present your members as slaves to** God's **justice, leading to sanctification** [*hagiasmon*] (6.19b).

The vocabulary of "uncleanness" and "lawlessness" as opposed to "sanctification" (or "holiness") is the vocabulary the Septuagint used not only to speak of Israel's calling to be a holy nation separate from other peoples (LXX Exod. 19.6; compare, for example, Lev. 11.44–45, 19.2, 20.25–26, 22.32–33) and the defilements that might be incurred by those who were seeking to live within the Law (LXX Lev. 15.31, 16.21), but also of flagrant violation of God's commandments, whether by Jews (LXX Exod. 34.7, Ezek. 22.15, 36.25, 1 Macc. 1.49, 1 Esdras 1.47) or gentiles (LXX Gen. 19.15, 1 Macc. 2.44, 2 Esdras 9.11). It is surely not an accidental irony that Paul echoes this vocabulary now in speaking to those who would regard sin as unimportant because of God's grace. That, he says, is how they all lived once: but now they must live as those who are, in fact, already receiving the blessing promised long ago through Ezekiel to a one-day-to-be-purified Israel—"For I will take you from the nations, and gather you from all the lands, and I will bring you into your land. I will sprinkle clean [*katharon*] water upon you, and you shall be clean [*katharisthēsesthe*] from all your uncleannesses [*akatharsiōn*] and from all your idols, and I shall cleanse [*kathariō*] you" (LXX Ezek. 36.24–25); which is to say that Paul's hearers are to live

---

37. Those philosophically educated might think of Epictetus: "For the value you place on an external object, whatever it may be, makes you subservient to another" (*Discourses* 4.4.1, trans. Elizabeth Carter, rev. Robin Hard; compare 4.1 *On Freedom*, in its entirety). It is hardly surprising then that the particular idea—that if we serve sin, we belong to it—was obviously quite commonplace, being used also by the Fourth Evangelist and 2 Peter (John 8.34; 2 Pet. 2.19).

38. Byrne, *Romans* 202.

39. See pages 57–58.

as those who know that Eden is already being restored, humanity is being given its original glory, and Adam's disobedience is being put right.

As he contemplated this restoration, perhaps Paul was tempted to launch into the song of praise that he would eventually utter at 8.31–39; if so, he resisted that impulse. He had been speaking of slavery and freedom, and there was more to be said: **When you were slaves of sin, you were "free" in regard to justice. But then what return did you get from the things of which you are now ashamed? The end of those things is death. But now that you have been set free from sin and have become slaves of God, the return you get is sanctification and its end, eternal life** (6.20–22).

It was quite common for slaves at the time to be given a *peculium*—money or property that they might manage more or less as their own, even though they were incapable of legal ownership:[40] so too, Paul observes grimly, sin pays **wages** (*opsōnia*)— payments for services rendered[41]—and they are **death, but the free gift of God is eternal life in the Christ Jesus our Lord** (6.23).

Additional Note W. On Translating Romans 6.5

For if we have become grown together [*sumphutoi*] with him in the likeness of his death, certainly we shall also be in the likeness of his resurrection. (6.5)

The sentence is elliptical, and difficult.

1. As regards *sumphutoi*, some commentators see the obvious horticultural metaphor as dead, and interpret as little more than "'united' or 'assimilated.'"[42] That was not, however, how Cyril of Jerusalem read the passage, and (particularly in view of Romans 11.17–24) the possibility remains that his interpretation may have been broadly what Paul intended:

> Paul cried with all exactness of truth, "For if we have become grown together in the likeness of his death, we shall be also in the likeness of his resurrection." Well has he said "grown together [*sumphutoi*]"! For since the true Vine was planted in this place, we also, by partaking of the Baptism of death, have become "grown together" with Him. And fix your mind with much attention on the words of the Apostle. He has not said, "For if we have become grown together in his death," but "in the likeness of his death." For upon Christ death came in reality . . . but in your case only the likeness of death and sufferings, whereas of salvation not the likeness, but the reality. (*Catecheses* 2.7, trans. R. W. Church, altered)

2. The other major questions are in regard to the relationship of the phrase "in the likeness of his death" to the rest.

A. Is the dative "likeness" (*homoiōmati*) here to be understood as directly dependent on *sumphutoi* (that is, "we have become grown together with the likeness of his death")? Or is there an implied pronoun ("with him"), which the listener is to

---

40. *OLD*, peculium 1.a.

41. Most commonly of a soldier's pay; see BAGD, ὀψώνιον; LS, ὀψώνιον 2: the Latin equivalent is *stipendium* (compare Vg. Rom. 8.23). Note also, however, LS, ὀψώνιον 3.

42. Cranfield, *Romans* 1.307.

supply, in which case *homoiōmati* is instrumental ("we have become grown together with him by means of the likeness of his death")?

B. What, in any case, is meant by *homoiōma*, which (like English "likeness") is capable of bearing either a positive sense ("a *real* likeness"—making plain that while there is difference, there is also similarity) or a negative sense ("a *mere* likeness"—making plain that while there is similarity, there is also difference), depending on the context?

In regard to both cases, Cyril seems to have understood Paul in the latter of the two possible senses ("we also, by partaking in the Baptism of death, have become 'grown together' with him . . . 'in the likeness of his death.' For upon Christ death came in reality . . . but in your case only the likeness of death"), and I elect, cautiously, to follow him.

The Gospel and the Law (7:1–8:39)

Having discussed and dismissed suggestions that accepting the gospel means that disobeying God does not matter, Paul now turns to the much broader question that underlies such suggestions. Granted that we are not under Law but under grace, how are we to understand our relationship to the Law? The form in which Paul raises this question—**Or don't you know, brothers** and sisters—at once makes it clear that he regards it as closely connected with what he has already said: **don't you know—for I am speaking to those who know the Law—that the Law has dominion over a person for so long as they live?** (7.1). In our baptism, as Paul has reminded us, our former *anthrōpos* died, crucified with Christ (6.6), leaving us in the position of a woman under the Law whose husband has died, now free to give ourselves **to another man**, that is, to Christ (7.1–3). **Likewise, my brothers** and sisters, **you**—the old, Adamic "you," the "you" of the **old self**, the *palaios anthrōpos*—**have died as far as the Law is concerned through the body of Christ.** You have, as Paul put it of himself on another occasion, "been crucified with Christ" (Gal. 2.20a)—**so that you may belong to another, to him that was raised from the dead in order that we may bear fruit for God** (7.4). To put it another way, "[I]t is no longer I who live, but Christ who lives in me; and the life I now live in the flesh I live by faith in the Son of God who loved me and gave himself for me" (Gal. 2.20b).

What else can be the conclusion of everything that has been said? Adam's sin has been put right (5.12–21), God through the Messiah has brought us life out of death (6.1–14), Israel has been cleansed (15–23)—in a word, the new age is here, and the promises are beginning to find their fulfillment. How then can we possibly choose to live as if we still belonged to the former age and the powers of the former age?

Yet there is more to be said about that former age and its constraints: **While we were** living **in the flesh** [*en tē(i)sarki*]—while, that is, we were living in the realm of merely human fellowship, human understanding, human hope[43]—**the sinful pas-**

---

43. On "flesh," see additional note X.

sions,[44] aroused by the Law, were at work in our members to bear fruit for death; but now we are discharged from the Law, dead to that which held us captive, so that we serve not under the old written code but in the newness of the Spirit [*en kainotēti pnuematos*] (7.5–6). (It is possible that by *en kainotēti pnuemati*—literally, "in newness of spirit"—Paul here intended to speak of nothing more than our renewed inner life. So we might translate, "with a renewed spirit." On the other hand, the implied contrast with being **in the flesh** [7.5] makes it more likely that he was intending to speak of the work of God's Spirit.)

The sinful passions, Paul has said, were **aroused by the Law** (7.5a). That is hardly the first time he has used language connecting the Law with sin (compare 3.20, 4.15, 5.20, 6.14), but this seems to go further. Now he seems to be saying that the Law, far from being, as some claimed,[45] the only effective tool whereby a person may achieve true "self-control" (*egkrateia*), had actually undermined it, rousing those **sinful passions** that are self-control's enemy. This assertion sets the stage for the next part of the argument.

Again the imaginary student raises a hand: **"What then shall we say? That the Law is sin?"** (7.7a). Is Paul saying that the entire conception of Torah, the whole Sinai covenant, was in fact a mistake, a deviation from the will of God?

By no means!

Yet, if it had not been for the Law, I should not have known sin (7.7b).

Who is the "I" in this statement? Is it Paul himself? Not, it appears, according to some who studied the text in antiquity, notably Origen. It seems likely that in Origen's view Paul was here using the rhetorical technique commonly referred to in Greek as *prosōpopoiia*, or "speech in the character of another."[46] This was a technique whereby

44. Though its general intention is clear enough, this is a difficult phrase: literally, "the passions of the sins" (*ta pathēmata tōn hamartiōn*). The word *pathēmata* in Paul (always plural) frequently means "sufferings," in a good sense (e.g., Romans 8.18); here, evidently, it has a negative sense. The genitive *hamartiōn* ("of sins") is presumably either subjective (qualifying) (that is, "the passions that belong to sins" or "the sinful passions") or objective (that is, "the passions that lead to sins" or "the sin-producing passions"): but in either case, it seems to be individual acts of sin that are in mind. Again, however, the word *hamartia* is normally used by Paul in the singular and expresses, as we have seen (additional note M) Paul's sense of sin personified as a "power" at work in humanity. For *particular* sins, Paul seems to prefer words such as *parabasis* ("transgression" or "trespass" [literally, "overstepping"]) (as at Romans 2.23, 5.14) or *paraptōma* ("error" [literally, "false step"]) (as at Romans 4.25, 5.15–16, 20, 11.11–12). On the occasions when Paul does use *hamartia* in the plural, it seems often to be in quotations from Scripture (e.g., Romans 4.7, 11.27) or in what appear to be allusions to formularies (e.g., Galatians 1.4). So perhaps here, too, he is using a standard formula from early Christian preaching.

45. Thus, for the author of 4 Maccabees, piety (*eusebia*) means adherence to the Law of Moses, and through that adherence comes "pious reason" (*ho eusebēs logismos*), which alone enabled the martyrs of Israel to remain masters of themselves throughout their ordeals: "O offspring of the seed of Abraham, children of Israel, obey this Law and be altogether true to your religion, knowing that pious reason is master over the passions, and not only over pains from within but also from outside ourselves" (4 Macc. 18.1–2, trans. H. Anderson, altered); in the same spirit, among the reasons given by Philo for circumcision is that it represents the excision of desires (*Special Laws* 3.8–9).

46. It is clear that Origen saw Paul's use of *prosōpopoiia* as the obvious way to explain the apparent contradiction between 7.14 and other Pauline statements such as 1 Corinthians 6.20, Galatians 3.13, and Galatians 2.20 (*Commentary on Romans*, fragment 41[Ramsbotham 3.15–16]). Unfortunately, the extant fragments of Origen's commentary do not allow complete certainty as to how he understood the rhetoric of the earlier part of the section (that is, 7.7a–13); still, as Kenneth Stowers points

the speaker represented the *ethos* either of a type: "for example, what words would a husband say to his wife as he was about to go on a journey or what words would a general say to his soldiers in the face of mortal dangers?" or else of a specified character: "for example, what words would Cyrus say as he pushes on to the Massagetae or what words would Datis say as he converses with the King after the battle of Marathon?" (Theon, *Progymnasmata* 8, trans. James R. Butts)[47]

Sometimes, as Quintilian pointed out, the character to be presented was identified; sometimes the character was introduced without identification by a phrase such as "At this point someone will interpose"; and sometimes, as in Romans 7.7b–25, the speech was simply inserted "without mentioning the speaker at all" (*sine persona sermo*)" (*Institutio Oratoria* 9.2.37).[48] In any case, the element of dramatization involved was brought out by a change of tone in delivery—a technique so common, incidentally, that Quintilian, in his advice about reading, warned against excess of it: "I do not," he said, "like some teachers, wish speeches in the character of another [*prosopopoeias*] to be indicated in the manner of a comic actor, though there should be some modulation of the voice to distinguish such passages from those where the poet is speaking in his own person" (1.8.3, trans. H. E. Butler, altered).

Who, then, in Romans 7.7, is the "I"? Some (notably, Ernst Käsemann) have said, "Adam." Since, however, the entire subject of this section is the Law given at Sinai, and since, moreover, Paul is about to quote explicitly from the Sinai covenant, the rhetoric in every way demands that the "I" must represent someone living under *that* dispensation, and therefore cannot be Adam. At the very least, therefore, the "I" has to be "a Jew," or "one living under the Law"—which, incidentally, will include something of Paul's own history.[49] Since, however, it is the *entire* history of Israel, and the giving of the Law within that history, that is called into question by

---

out, "the principles that [Origen] lays out in his discussion of 7.14–25 seem to apply to 7.7–13", and that he understood it along the same lines appears at least probable (*A Rereading of Romans: Justice, Jews, and Gentiles* [New Haven: Yale University Press, 1994], 266). Stowers's discussion of this entire question (16–21, 260–84) is invaluable, although I do believe him to be mistaken in his view of Paul's intended audience.

47. It was also used to represent known individuals. Cicero's use of *prosopoeia loquentis pro reo* ("a speech in the character of one speaking on behalf of the accused"), while defending Scaurus seems to have hovered somewhere between the two (see Quintilian, *Institutio Oratoria*, 4.1.69): the speech itself is lost. According to Quintilian it was part of a speech defending Scaurus on a charge of bribery [4.1.69]. For further distinctions and views of the ancient theoreticians, see Heinrich Lausberg, *Handbook of Literary Rhetoric: A Foundation for Literary Study*, Matthew T. Bliss, Annemiek Jansen, and David E. Orton, trans. (Leiden: Brill, 1998), especially §826–29, 369–72.

48. "This involves a mixture of figures, since to *prosōpopoiia* we add the figure known as omission (*detractio*), which in this case consists in the omission of any indication as to who is speaking" (Quintilian, *Institutio Oratoria* 9.2.37; compare 9.3.18).

49. It is important to note that this view is based not only on concerns of theological coherence but also on the demands of the rhetoric: so (correctly, in my view) Jean-Noël Aletti: "The *partitio* [7.5–6], in fact, indicates clearly that in 7.7–25 Paul does not consider the *present* situation of the baptized, as though he were *simul justus et peccator*, but rather that of the person remaining within the framework of the (Mosaic) law and which, according to Paul, belongs to the past ('when we were . . .')" ("The Rhetoric of Romans 5–8," in *The Rhetorical Analysis of Scripture: Essays from the 1995 London Conference*, ed. Stanley E. Porter and Thomas H. Olbricht, JSNTSS 146 (Sheffield, England: Sheffield Academic Press, 1997), 300. That there will inevitably be something of Paul's own history in his presen-

the last question ("Is the Law sin?"), it is perhaps best if we take even "a Jew" in its fullest possible sense: it is as if it were "Israel" itself, God's own possession, that stands before us in the "I." Paul is thinking, as Frank Theilman has put it, "not simply of himself but of his people and of the biblical story of their disobedience."[50]

> **Yet, if it had not been for the Law, I should not have known sin. I should not have known what it is to covet if the Law had not said, "You shall not desire** [*epithumēseis*]" [see LXX Exod. 20.17, Deut. 5.21; compare Rom. 13.9]. **But sin, seizing its opportunity in the commandment worked in me every desire** [*epithumia*]. . . . (7.7b–8a)

As I have already noted, enslavement to "desire" (*epithumia*) was precisely, in Jewish eyes, what went with idolatry—in other words, what characterized gentiles; and according to apologists such as Josephus, Philo, and the author of 4 Maccabees (possibly Paul's exact contemporary), the Jews' possession of the Law was precisely what made them superior in this respect—that is to say, better able to control their desires, and so better able to achieve self-control.[51] There is therefore deep irony in Paul's choice of "You shall not desire . . ." as representative of that Law, and even more in his claim that, far from enabling Israel to achieve *egkrateia*, her possession of the Law had actually worked against it. In the presence of Law, moreover, the nature of sin itself is changed.

> **Apart from the Law, sin lies dead. I was once alive, apart from the Law**—from Adam to Moses, sin was not reckoned—**but when the commandment came, sin revived and I died; and the commandment that was meant for life turned out, for me, to be for death.** (7.8b–10)

Undoubtedly the Law given to Israel promised life: "And the Lord commanded us to do all these statutes, to fear the Lord our God, for our good always, that he might preserve us alive, as at this day" (LXX Deut. 6.24; compare 30.16, Lev. 18.5; Sir. 17.11–14 ["the law of life"]; Ps. Sol. 14.2–4); and undoubtedly, just as Moses had known it would, it had proven to be death: "For I know that after my death you will surely act corruptly, and turn aside from the way which I have commanded you; and in the days to come evil will befall you, because you will do what is evil in the sight of the Lord, provoking him to anger through the work of your hands" (LXX Deut. 31.29; compare 16–21, Bar. 2.30).

> **For sin, finding opportunity in the commandment, deceived** [*exēpatēsen*] **me, and by it killed me** (7.11).

Here, for those who would see the "I" as Adam, is the strongest part of their case: certainly the phraseology of "deception" reminds us of Eve's encounter with the ser-

---

tation of "one living under the Law" is the element of truth in Gerd Theissen, *Psychological Aspects of Pauline Theology*, trans. John P. Galvin (Philadelphia: Fortress Press, 1987), 241–43, who understands the section 7.7b–25 as autobiographical; similarly Michael Winger, *By What Law: The Meaning of Νόμος in the Letters of Paul* (Atlanta, Georgia: Scholars Press), 171–72.

50. Frank Thielman, "The Story of Israel and the Theology of Romans 5–8," in *Pauline Theology*, vol. 3, *Romans*, ed. David M. Hay and E. Elizabeth Johnson (Minneapolis: Fortress Press, 1995), 194.

51. Cited on page 139, footnote 45.

pent (compare LXX Gen.3.13, where Eve claims that the serpent "deceived [*ēpatēsen*]" her; also 2 Cor. 11.3) and is probably intended to. Just as, I suspect, Paul earlier used with deliberate irony language that recalled Israel's disobedience at Sinai in order to describe the apostasy of the gentiles (1.23; compare LXX Ps. 105.20),[52] so now, I suspect, he uses language that recalls humankind's primeval disobedience in order to speak of Israel's disobedience following Sinai. It is all part of his underlying claim that Israel, too, is "in Adam," and needs the same grace of God as is needed by the gentiles (3.23–24).

> *So the Law, on the one hand is holy, and the commandment is holy and just and good—*
> "Did then that which is good work death in me?"[53]
> *By no means! But it was sin, in order that it might be shown to be sin, working death in me through what is good, in order that through the commandment sin might be shown to be sinful beyond measure.* (7.12–13)

As Paul has already said, "Law slipped in to increase the trespass" (5.20). Israel's sin before Sinai might be described as unwitting; after Sinai, Israel *knew*, and henceforth sin was essentially rebellion, "sin with a high hand," for which the Law could offer no atonement (Num. 15.30).[54]

Paul's use here of the language of external power creating psychological and moral states is, as Kenneth Stowers points out, typical of the soliloquies of *prosōpopoiía* and of the tragic monologue.[55] Doubtless, as Stowers also observes, Greek polytheism facilitated such a way of expressing the human dilemma of conflicting goods and obligations; nonetheless, in thus speaking of sin as a "power" governing our actions and inspiring conduct, Paul is also incorporating a tendency that may be observed elsewhere in post-biblical Judaism, notably in the Dead Sea Scrolls (for example, in the treatment of the "Spirit of Falsehood" in the *Rule of the Community* [1 QS] 4).[56] Paul's point, in any case, is to stress that in this case it is sin, not the Law, that causes the problem. *For the Law, as we know, is spiritual. But I am fleshly, sold* into slavery *under sin* (7.14).[57] Our reaction to the Law is like that of sick people who are made more sick by good food: there is nothing wrong with the food, and the fact that they are made worse by it merely indicates the seriousness of their condition.

---

52. On 1.22–23, see page 79.

53. Precisely who is envisaged by Paul making this interruption is unclear, but identification is not important. Certainly the dialogue at this point falls well within boundaries for *prosōpopiía* envisaged by Quintilian: "By this means we display the inner thoughts of our adversaries as though they were talking with themselves . . . or without sacrifice of credibility we may introduce conversations between ourselves and others, or of others among themselves, and put words of advice, reproach, complaint, praise, or pity into the mouths of appropriate persons. Nay, we are even allowed in this form of speech to bring down the gods from heaven and raise the dead, while cities also and peoples may find a voice" (*Institutio Oratoria* 9.2.30–31).

54. On "sin with a high hand," see also additional note M.

55. Stowers, *Rereading of Romans* 272. So Seneca's Phaedra, already driven by her illicit passion for Hippolytus, declares, "This comes from Venus! . . . and now through us she takes revenge" (Seneca, *Phaedra* 124–25, trans. E. F. Watling).

56. On this tendency, see additional note M (a).

57. On Origen's interpretation of this verse as *prosōpopoiía*, see pages 139–40, footnote 46.

Nevertheless, good food in itself cannot be their road to health; so, according to Paul, the Law in itself can provide no road to *egkrateia*—self-control. On the contrary,

> **I do not understand my own actions. For I do not do what I want, but I do the very thing I hate. Now if I do what I do not want, I agree that the Law is noble** [*kalos*]—that is, that it reflects the divine beauty, order, and serenity.[58] **So then it is no longer I that do** the thing I hate, **but sin that dwells within me. For I know that nothing good dwells within me, that is, in my flesh. I can will what is noble** [*to kalon*], **but I cannot do it.** (7.15–18)

This section will immediately have resonated with any among Paul's audience, Jew or gentile, who had the slightest acquaintance with the Hellenistic educational tradition and, in particular, its attitude to *akrasia* (lack of self-mastery: the opposite of *egkrateia*).

Locus classicus for countless presentations and discussions of the problem of *akrasia* was the story of Medea, daughter of Aeetes, king of Colchis, whose husband Jason deserted her. Euripides, in perhaps his most powerful tragedy, portrays her inner conflict. Motivated by rage and desire for revenge, she has decided upon a terrible course of action that involves killing her own children. Twice she hesitates, moved by smiles of her babies (*Medea* 1040–48) and by her love for them (1056–58), but in the end she decides to do it, even though fully recognizing the wickedness of her proposed action. "I am overcome of evil," she says.

> Now, now, I learn what horrors I intend,
> But passion overmastereth sober thought. (1077, 1078–79, trans.
> Arthur S. Way)[59]

As Ovid put it in his own reflection on her story,

> *Video meliora, proboque;*
> *Deteriora sequor.*
> I see the better and I approve;
> I follow the worse. (*Metamorphoses* 7.20–21)[60]

---

58. Greek *kalos* ("beautiful") had come in Hellenistic thinking to be used of that which was in a state of harmony, health, wholeness, and order, internal and external, and hence to carry the moral sense of "honorable," "noble" (see, e.g., Diogenes Laertius, *Lives of Eminent Philosophers* 7.101). The occasional use of *kalos* in the LXX to translate Hebrew *ṭôb* ("good") (notably, e.g., in the priestly creation narrative: see LXX Gen. 1.4, 10, 12, 18, 21, 25, 31) served to bring this range of semantic possibility within the sphere of Jewish thinking, wherein *erga kala* ("beautiful works") became particularly associated with works of mercy (so, e.g., Mark 14.6 // Matt. 26.10–12; see Grundmann, "καλός," in *TDNT* 3.536–50; see further Pietro Rossano, "L'Ideale del bello (καλός) nell'etica di S. Paolo," in *SPCIC* 2.373–82).

59. Medea was, of course, a non-Helene (i.e., a barbarian). Phaedra (see page 142, footnote 55) was another example of a non-Helene unable to control her passions: "Unreason drives me into evil. I walk upon the brink with open eyes; / Wise counsel calls, but I cannot turn back / To hear it; when a sailor tries to drive / His laden vessel counter to the tides, / His toil is all in vain. His helpless ship / Swims at the mercy of the current. Reason? What good can reason do?" (Seneca, *Phaedra*, 178–84, trans. E. F. Watling).

60. The classic discussion of the problem is that in Aristotle, *Nichomachaen Ethics* 7.1.1–10.5 (1145a–1154b) (cited in additional note L).

Debate in the philosophical schools often focused on whether Medea's choice of wrong action resulted, in the last analysis, from misunderstanding. She was, after all, a non-Helene, a barbarian, which meant that she was not properly educated. If she had been better informed and better educated, would she have acted with more self-control? (this, for example, was the opinion of Epictetus, *Discourses* 1.28.7–9; compare 2.26.1–7, 3.7.18; 4.1.1–5). Alternatively, did her wrong actions result from the defeat of reason in a battle that is waged in human souls between *distinct* powers of reason, appetite, and emotion? (the Platonic and popular view: thus, for example, Plutarch, *On Moral Virtue* [*Moralia* 441–52]).

That Paul's hearers would have heard a resonance between Paul's expressions—**I do not do what I want, but I do the very thing I hate**—and this debate seems virtually certain, and it seems hard to suppose that they were not intended to hear it.

Certainly the substance of Paul's discourse remains rooted in the entirely Jewish question that he is considering—the relation of those under grace to the Law. On the other hand, the Greek's caricature of non-Greeks—their problem is that they lack *egkrateia* because they do not have the proper education—is exactly parallel to one Jewish attitude to gentiles: "Great are thy judgments and hard to describe; therefore uninstructed souls have gone astray" (Wisd. of Sol. 17.1). In other words, if gentiles had studied the Law, they would be able to live properly: and it is at this attitude that Paul is aiming. On the contrary, he says, it is **sin**, *not* lack of instruction, that turns the **holy and just and good** Law into its opposite, a **Law of sin**; and it is **sin** that takes even those who would follow the Law **captive**.

> *For I do not do the good I want, but the evil I do not want is what I do. Now if I do what I do not want, it is no longer I that do it, but sin that dwells within me. So I find it to be the Law that when I want to do what is noble [*to kalon*], evil lies close at hand. For I delight in the Law of God in my inmost self, but I see another "Law" in my members, at war with the Law of my mind, and making me captive to the Law of sin that dwells in my members. Wretched one that I am [*talaipōros egō anthrōpos*]! Who shall deliver me from this body of death?* (7.19–24a)

The final declaration—**Wretched one that I am!**—sounds, as Stowers points out, "almost like a parody of the tragic outcry."[61] Epictetus comments on just such cries from the tragedies ("Wretch that I am! [*talas egō*]!"), asking, "What are tragedies but the portrayal in tragic verse of the sufferings of those who have admired things external?" (*Discourses* 1.4.23, 26, trans. W. A. Oldfather, altered). Epictetus, indeed, hears just such a cry uttered by *any* who tie themselves to the things of the flesh, rather than the life of reason and intelligence, "For what am I? A wretched, semi-person [*talaipōron anthrōparion*]!" (1.3.5).

---

61. Stowers, *Rereading of Romans* 271. In the *Metamorphoses*, shortly before uttering the well-known lines cited above, Medea describes herself as "wretched" (*infelix*) ("Drive from your maiden breast the flames you have conceived—if you can, wretched one! [*excute virgineo conceptas pectore flammas, si potes, infelix!*]") (7.17–18); as it happens, *infelix* is the precise word chosen in the Vg. to translate *talpairos* at Romans 7.24. In spirit, of course, personified Israel's outcry is very close to that of the seer in 2 (4) Ezra: "For what good is it to us, if an immortal time has been promised to us, but we have done deeds that bring death?" (7.119; compare 7.62–69, 116–126).

Perhaps Paul saw in those cries a profounder concern, and certainly he offered to those who identified with them more hope. Until this point, the soliloquy uttered by personified Israel has been entirely, so to speak, "pre-Christian," lacking, as has often been pointed out, mention of Christ or the Holy Spirit. The rhetorical strategy is, in fact, parallel to that which Paul used in 1.18–3.20.[62] Now, however, Paul steps outside his tragic model, and Israel herself declares the solution to her dilemma. It is not the facile "do-it-yourself" solution offered by Phaedra's nurse in Seneca's drama—a solution that was, as Seneca himself, as a dramatist, clearly recognized, no solution at all[63]—but God's solution.

> *Who shall deliver me from this body of death? Thanks be to God, through Jesus Christ our Lord!* (7.24b-25a)

"Jesus Christ is the new human being, standing beyond all piety, beyond all human possibility . . . He is the one who has passed from death to life. . . . Thanks be to God: through Jesus Christ our Lord I am not the wretch that I am" (Barth, *Romans* 269).

With this climax, Israel's soliloquy ends, and Paul takes up the theme again in his own voice—a change that could easily be indicated by the reader's change of tone.[64] Two conclusions follow from what "Israel" has said. They apply to Paul (and also to his readers, though rhetorically he will apply them simply to himself), and he presents them in parallel:

> So then [*ara oun*], left to myself, I am slave to God's Law in my mind, but in the flesh, I am a slave to sin (7.25b)

and,

> So then [*ara oun*], there is no condemnation for those that are in Christ Jesus (8.1).

Here are the keys with which we may answer the question, "Granted that we are not under Law but under grace, how are we to understand our relationship to the Law?" **For the Law of the Spirit of life in Jesus Christ has set you**[65] **free from the Law of sin and death** (8.2).

---

62. See page 92.

63. In response to Phaedra's earlier outcry (cited page 142, footnote 55), the nurse says, "Cleanse your pure heart at once of such vile thoughts; / Smother the flame and give no countenance / To evil hopes. Stand up to Love and rout him / At the first assault, that is the surest way / To win without a fall" (Seneca, *Phaedra*, 130–33 trans. E. F. Watling).

64. See Quintilian, *Institutio Oratoria* 1.8.3, cited on page 140.

65. It is not easy to choose here between the various readings attested to by the ancient witnesses: "you" (singular), "me," "us," and no expressed object at all. All are possible, but each could also be explained as possibly a copyist's error or improvement. Certainly the two former are much better attested, so that it is probably between them that we should choose. I prefer "you" because it is, in the context, the most surprising of the possibilities, being obviously linked neither to the "I" that has preceded (7.25b) nor to the "us" that is to come (8.4). It is indeed possible, as Cranfield suggests, that at this point Paul wanted to make sure that each of his listeners realized that the point being made applied to them personally and individually (*Romans* 1.377). In any case, as Fitzmyer points out, it is evident that Paul is referring to *anyone* who has faith in Jesus and so is justified (*Romans* 483), so the meaning of the passage is not greatly affected, whichever reading we choose.

Again, just as with Paul's earlier contrast between "the Law of faith" and the "Law of works" (3.27), I think that it is not two different "Laws" of which Paul speaks here, but the same Law—the Mosaic Law—understood rightly or wrongly.[66] Understood as if it were in itself a way to salvation, the Law simply shows me my sin (3.20) and condemns me to death: it becomes, in other words, a Law of sin and death. Understood properly, in dependence upon God's Spirit of life in Christ Jesus, the Law itself shows me the truth (3.21): for—**what was impossible for the Law, in that it was weak through the flesh—God, sending his own Son in the likeness**[67] **of sinful flesh and as a sin-offering,**[68] **condemned sin in the flesh,**[69] **in order that the just requirement [*dikaiōma*] of the Law might be fulfilled in us** (8.3–4a).

What is the **just requirement** of the Law? It is, above all and beyond all, exactly what it was from the beginning: "to glorify [God] as God" and to "give thanks to him" (1.21); therefore it is **fulfilled in us, who walk not according to the flesh,** that is, not in dependence on the merely human and creaturely, **but according to the Spirit,** in conscious dependence on the living and dynamic power of God alone, at work in us (8.4b).[70]

66. See the very full and careful discussion in Wright, *Climax of the Covenant* 193–216, especially 200–214. For the view that Paul does not speak in 8.2a of the Mosaic Law, see Cranfield, *Romans* 1.375–76; Räisänen, *Paul and the Law*, WUNT 29 (Tübingen: Mohr [Siebeck], 1983; Philadelphia: Fortress Press, 1986), 52; Winger, *By What Law* 194–96.

67. God did not send his son "in the flesh of such sin [*en sarki hamartias toiautēs*] as one enslaved to the Law of Sin is slave to, but 'in the likeness [*en homoiōmati*] of' such 'flesh'" (Origen, *Commentary on Romans*, fragment 45 [Ramsbotham 3.17]). It is entirely proper to see here the beginnings of tension between the need to speak of Jesus' closeness to God and the need to speak of him as truly human, even though the full articulation of this problem, and the debate surrounding it, was still to come. Thus, "the term ὁμοίωμα denotes a limit . . . Jesus came in the likeness of sinful flesh. He was passively exposed to sin, but in distinction from us he did not actively open himself to it" (Käsemann, *Romans* 217). The same insight (and the same underlying question) is articulated in a different way at 2 Corinthians 5.21; compare Hebrews 4.15. See J. Schneider "ὁμοίωμα"in TDNT 5.191–98: for a different view, Vincent P. Branick, "The Sinful Flesh of the Son of God (Rom. 8:3): A Key Image of Pauline Theology," CBQ 47 (1985): 246–62; also Florence Morgan Gillman, "Another Look at Romans 8.3: 'In the Likeness of Sinful Flesh,'" CBQ 49 (1987): 597–604.

68. The phrase (*to*) *peri* (*tēs*) *hamartias* occurs so regularly in the LXX in connection with the sin-offering (e.g., LXX Lev. 4.3, 18, 35) as to amount almost to a technical term; it is also used, metaphorically, in LXX Isaiah 53.10—a passage that was, of course, early appealed to in Christian attempts to understand Jesus' death. "The technical usage seems to be so widely prevalent in the LXX as to make the sacrificial allusion self-explanatory" (Byrne, *Romans* 243); see further Wright, *Climax of the Covenant* 193–223, especially 220–23.

69. The Greek of the entire first part of the sentence (8.3) is elliptical (most translations supply additional verbs) and the movement from the opening clauses to the main verb evidently involves an anacoluthon. Yet like the KJV translation, which I have broadly followed, the passage is easier to grasp when read aloud than when stared at and perfectly illustrates the fact that Romans is a text designed, in the first instance, to be heard. In any case, Paul's somewhat awkward expressions may have arisen from his again making use of a liturgical or credal formula that he might have expected his hearers to know. Comparison with similar "sending" expressions at Galatians 4.4, John 3.16–17, and 1 John 4.9 suggests this possibility, the purpose of such formulae being always, as Reginald H. Fuller notes, "not to speculate about the Redeemer's pre-existence, but to assert that the historical mission of Jesus rests on the divine initiative" (*The Foundations of New Testament Christology* [New York: Scribner's, 1965], 195.

70. On "Spirit," see additional note Y.

Good things—even the very best things, even the Law—if treated as gods, become demons: and to treat good created things as gods is to live "in the flesh" (7.7–24, and 25a). By contrast, the section 8.2–4 speaks of the new life of the believer in Christ—a life based upon God's act of salvation in Christ, and lived therefore in the realm of God's Spirit. **For those who live according to the flesh mind about the things of the flesh** (or, **are on the flesh's side:** *ta tēs sarkos phronousin*),[71] **but those who live according to the Spirit** mind about the things **of the Spirit** (or, are **on the Spirit's side**) (8.5). Those, as Cranfield says, "who allow the direction of their lives to be determined by the flesh are actually taking the flesh's side in the conflict between the Spirit of God and the flesh, while those who allow the Spirit to determine the direction of their lives are taking the Spirit's side."[72]

For the mind of the flesh is death, but the mind of the Spirit is life and peace. For the mind that is set on the flesh is hostile to God. It does not submit to God's Law; indeed it cannot, and those who really live in the flesh cannot be pleasing to God (8.6–8)—so is confirmed what "Israel" already, in essence, has said (7.14): that problems in our relationship to the Law do not arise because there is something wrong with the Law, but because we are "fleshly."

Now, however, is the moment when Paul can reassure his hearers: **but you are not in the flesh, but in the Spirit, if indeed** [*eiper*][73] **God's Spirit dwells in you!** (8.9a) You therefore are already living in fulfillment of the "just requirement" of the Law. **If anyone does not have Christ's Spirit, that person does not belong to him. But if Christ's Spirit is dwelling in you then, although the body** [*sōma*][74] **is mortal because of sin**—certainly Christians continue to sin and will continue to need, along with praising God, that constant round of contrition that must also mark any life that is in the process of sanctification—nevertheless, **although the body is mortal because of sin, the Spirit**[75] **is life, because of justice**—because of God's justice, which is God's covenant loyalty to us (8.9b–10). **If the Spirit of the One who raised Jesus from the dead dwells in you, the One who raised Jesus from the dead will also** at the final resurrection[76] **make alive your mortal bodies** [*sōmata*] **through his Spirit dwelling in you** (8.11).

71. *Ta tinos phronein* seems quite often to carry the sense of being "of someone's party" or "on someone's side" (compare Mark 8.33, Josephus, *Antiquities* 14.450; see LS, φρονέω 2.2.c; Lagrange, *Romains* 196; Cranfield, *The Gospel According to Saint Mark* [Cambridge: Cambridge University Press, 1972], 280–81), and this may be the sense intended here.

72. Cranfield, *Romans* 1.386.

73. Doubtless Käsemann is correct in saying that Greek *eiper* ("if indeed," "if after all") here "does not have a conditional and limiting sense but an affirmative sense" (*Romans* 223; compare LS, εἴπερ 2, BAGD, εἰ 6.11). So Chrysostom: "He often uses this 'if indeed (*eiper*),' not to express a doubt, but even when he is quite sure of something, and as equivalent to 'since indeed'" (*Homilies on Romans* 16.8); also the OL, which translates *si quidem*. Paul's expression is, nonetheless, not without an element of ambiguity, as is indicated by the Vg. rendering *si tamen*.

74. On "body," see additional note Z.

75. Various commentators and translations (e.g., RSV, NEB; contrast, however, KJV, BEP) take it that Paul is at this point referring to the human spirit. C. K. Barrett's objection to this suggestion remains, in my view, decisive—that if Paul had here meant to speak of the human spirit, "he would have said, 'The spirit is alive', not 'the spirit is life'" (*Romans* 159).

76. Calvin saw here a reference to continual sanctification of the faithful through the work of the Holy Spirit "by which he gradually mortifies in us the remains of the flesh and renews in us the

So then, my brothers and sisters—Paul's choice of expression implies that, after his elaborate comparison (*synkrisis*) of life "in the flesh" with "life in the Spirit," he is coming to a conclusion—**so then**, the relationship of those under grace to the Law is not one of dependence, as if the Law, or our human knowledge of the Law, or our human keeping of the Law, were in some way a path to life—all of which, for all their "spiritual" pretensions, are merely ways of living "in the flesh"; nor is our relationship to the Law one of counterdependence—"Let us do evil that good may come"—which is merely a mirror image of what it claims to reject and is still a form of living "in the flesh." **So then, my brothers** and sisters, **we are under an obligation: not to the flesh, to live according to the flesh, for if you live according to the flesh you are going to die; but if in the Spirit you put to death the deeds of the body [*tou sōmatos*],**[77] **you will live** (8.12–13). The choice is, as it has always been, the choice of two ways, of life and of death (Deuteronomy 30.15); but those, Jews and gentiles alike, who have put their trust in Christ have already chosen life.

For all who are led by the Spirit of God are children of God (8.14). Notions of Israel as God's "child" and of Israelites as God's "children" are rooted in Jewish Scripture and scriptural tradition (for example, LXX Exod. 4.22–23, Deut. 14.1, Wisd. of Sol. 12.7, 21; 16.10, 21, 26; 18.13; 19.6; *Bib. Ant.* 32.10; 3 Macc. 6.28), and had come to be a way of expressing the Jewish eschatological hope:

> And the Lord said to Moses, "I know their contrariness and their thoughts and their stubbornness. And they will not obey until they acknowledge their sin and the sin of their fathers. But after this day they will return to me in all justice and with all their heart and soul; and I shall cut off the foreskin of their heart and the foreskin of the heart of their descendants. And I shall create for them a holy spirit, and I shall purify them so that they will not turn away from following me from that day and for ever. . . . And I shall be a father to them, and they will be children to me. And they will all be called 'children of the living God,' and every angel and every spirit will know and acknowledge that they are my children and I am their father in uprightness and justice. And I shall love them." (*Jub.* 1.22–25, trans. O. S. Wintermute, altered; compare *1 Enoch* 62.11; *Pss. Sol.* 17.26–27; *Test. Mos.* 10.1–3; *Sib. Or.* 3.702–4)

But just as Paul had earlier declared that Abraham was the father of *all* who put their trust in Christ, Jew and gentile alike (4.16), so now he declares that *all* who put their trust in Christ, Jew and gentile alike, are part of God's family. **For you did not receive the spirit of slavery to fall back into fear, but you have received the Spirit**

---

heavenly life" (*Romans* 166). It is, however, probably better to follow Chrysostom (*Homilies on Romans* 13.8) and Augustine (*Propositions from the Epistle to the Romans* 51.1–3), both of whom saw here a reference to the work of the Spirit in the final resurrection.

77. We might have expected Paul to say here "deeds of the flesh [*tēs sarkos*]" rather than "deeds of the body," and some witnesses (e.g., D, F, and G) actually make that change. It remains evident, nonetheless, that *sōma* was Paul's choice of word. Käsemann points out that the body "is not yet identical with the σάρξ as subjection to the world, but is threatened by it, since the power of the flesh has a point of attack in our body, which is still dominated by the earthly" (*Romans* 226), and doubtless that is true. On the other hand, perhaps we should simply bear in mind that Paul (like other ancient writers) sometimes moves between the different possible senses of *sōma* without troubling to explain himself and expects us to follow: see additional note Z.

of adoption [*huiothesias*][78] (8.15a). How are they to know that? It is a part of their experience, for it is by the power of that Spirit that **we cry "Abba! Father!"** (8.15b). Their impulse to participate in the characteristic prayer of the Christian community—that peculiar form of address to God that was evidently hallowed by association with Christ himself (Mark 14.36) and that survived in Aramaic when virtually the entire tradition had been translated into Greek[79]—that alone served to show that they had received the **Spirit of adoption**. As Paul himself wrote at greater length on another occasion,

> in Christ Jesus you are all children of God, through faith. For as many of you as were baptized into Christ have put on Christ. There is neither Jew nor Greek, there is neither slave nor free, male nor female; for you are all one in Christ Jesus. . . . When we were children, we were slaves to the elemental spirits of the universe. But when the time had fully come, God sent forth his Son, born of woman, born under the Law, to redeem those who were under the Law, so that we might receive adoption [*huiothesian*]. And because you are children, God has sent the Spirit of his Son into our hearts, crying, "Abba! Father!" (Gal.3.26–28, 4.3b-6)

The same Spirit bears witness in support of our spirit that we are children of God— the Spirit of God concurring with us as we claim in praise, penitence, or intercession our special relation to God[80]—**and if children, then also heirs, heirs of God and co-heirs with Christ, given that we suffer with him, in order that we may be glorified with him** (8.16–17).

Here is the final answer to the question of the commandment, and the believer's relation to it, which has occupied Paul since 6.1, and, in particular, to the question of obedience with which he began ("Shall we continue in sin . . . ?"), for to live in dependence upon the faithfulness of God is to live in a filial relationship, as the beloved child of God, and so in union with God's Messiah. "It is," as Howard Rhys observes, "a relationship dominated not by fear but by love . . . made effective by the indwelling of God's Spirit."[81]

Here, moreover, as Karl Barth saw, is in a nutshell the ground of all ethics.[82] Our character must follow from our hope. Those who live by love will suffer with love in a universe that persecutes love—a universe of which they are, for all their hope, still part (compare 7.25–8.1, 8.10–11; compare Mark 8.34–35), but always with

---

78. Although formal adoption was not normal among Jews (the word *huiothesia* does not even occur in the LXX), it was a widespread Greco-Roman practice, and the image is one that Paul could therefore expect his non-Jewish hearers in particular to understand. See F. Lyall, "Roman Law in the Writings of Paul—Adoption," *JBL* 88 (1969): 458–66; M. W. Schoenberg, "*Huiothesia*: The Word and the Institution," *Scripture* 15 (1963): 115–23.

79. See James Barr, "'Abba, Father' and the Familiarity of Jesus' Speech," *Theology* 91 (1988): 173–79; Joseph A. Fitzmyer, "Abba and Jesus' Relation to God," in *À cause de l'Évangile: Études sur les Synoptiques et les Actes offertes au P. Jacques Dupont, O.S.B. à la occasion de son 70e anniversaire,* ed. R. Gantoy. LD 123 (Paris: Les Éditions du Cerf, 1985), 15–38.

80. The normal sense of the compound verb *summartureō* appears to be "bear witness (or testify) along with or in support of" someone else (see LS, συμμαρτυρέω; BAGD, συμμαρτυρέω, and examples cited).

81. *Romans* 103.

82. See Barth, *Church Dogmatics,* 2.2.§37, 592–93.

the assurance of a share in love's glory—**that** they **may be glorified with him**! So, by an irony, that very thing which humankind as a whole has refused to give to God (1.21; compare 3.23) is now promised to humankind as God's gift.

This talk of the Spirit's presence, of suffering, and of glory, in turn brings Paul back full circle to the themes of "affliction," "endurance," and "hope of the glory of God" from which his "demonstration" began (5.1–5). **For I consider that the sufferings of this present time are not worth comparing with the glory that is to be revealed to us**. Why? First, because of the place where we stand in the story—the story Paul told at the opening of his dissuasive, of the gracious creation that revealed the invisible God, and humanity's refusal to acknowledge that God (1.18–32), the story Paul took up again at the opening of his demonstration, telling us how, though sin indeed "entered the world through one man and death through sin death, and so death passed to all" (5.12), yet that curse was absorbed in grace (5.15–21), and the story to which he now returns, taking it to a new stage. **For the creation** (*ktisis*)(that is, "the things that have been made" (1.18), the created order distinct from humanity[83]—**waits with eager longing [***apokaradokia***][84] for the revealing of the sons and daughters of God** (8.19). No one has written more powerfully about this verse— nor, I think, with a truer insight into its intention—than Karl Barth:

> Whither can humankind turn its eyes—humankind, disconsolate in what it is and longing restlessly to be what it is not—without encountering the eyes of others equally disconsolate and filled with a longing equally restless? Nay more, these eyes are bent on humankind, directing to it their earnest questioning. . . .
>
> "In every creature St. Paul, with his sharp, discerning, apostolic eye perceived the holy and beloved Cross" (Luther). What is it that humanity perceives and discovers, finds and apprehends, in its research and in its experience? We know the COSMOS to be ours: we seek to find our rest in nature and in history. But instead, with fatal necessity, we discover everywhere—our own unquiet.[85]

---

83. While it need not be doubted that here (in contrast to the ambiguity of 1.20 [see page 78, footnote 27]) the word *ktisis* refers to "the creation" (i.e., "what has been created") rather than "the act of creation," precisely *what* in creation is being identified has been discussed at least since Augustine, and continues to cause debate. Does Paul mean "humanity," or does he mean "the created order in general"? In view of what Paul has already said about human rebellion in 1.18–32, it seems hard to see how he could now be describing *humanity's* subjection to vanity as "not of its own will," and the most likely inference is surely therefore that he here means by *ktisis* more or less what he meant by "the things that have been made" at 1.20—namely, as suggested above, "the created order, apart from humanity." For an account of the debate, see Olle Cristoffersson, *The Earnest Expectation of the Creature: The Flood Tradition as a Matrix of Romans 8:18–17*, Coniectanea biblica, New Testament Series 23 (Stockholm: Almqvist and Wiksell, 1990); also, for fascinating illustrations of the attitudes of post-apostolic Christianity, see François Bovon, "The Child and the Beast: Fighting Violence in Ancient Christianity," *HDB* 27.4 (1998): 16–21. For a recent full-length restatement of the argument for *ktisis* as "humanity," see A. Giglioli, *L'oumo o il creato? Κτίσις in s. Paolo. Studi biblici* 21 (Bologna: EDB, 1994); but note also the (in my view, devastating) critique in Settimio Cipriani, "ΚΤΙΣΙΣ: creazione o genere umano?" *RB* 44.3 (1996): 337–40.

84. So most commentators; but perhaps we should translate, "with desperate longing," as Theodore of Mospuestia ("*Karadokein* means 'to hope [*to elpizein*],' but *apokaradokein* 'to despair [*to apelpizein*]'" [fragment of the *Commentary on Paul's Epistle to the Romans* in Migne, *Patrologiæ* 824]), in which case Paul has in mind the creation's enduring frustration that springs from the "sufferings of the present time," which it, too, must endure, in union with humanity, because of humanity's disobedience.

85. *Romans* 306, 307.

For the creation was subjected to futility (not of its own will, but because of the one who subjected it, namely Adam)[86] **in hope—because the creation itself will be set free from the bondage of corruption and obtain the liberty of the glory**[87] **of the children of God** (8.20–21). The presence of sin and death in the world means that Paul, like Qohelet before him, sees **futility** (*mataiotēs*, that is, vanity, purposelessness) haunting all things (compare LXX Eccles. 1.2, 14). This is the effect of Adam's disobedience, as God had said: "[C]ursed is the earth by your deeds" (LXX Gen. 3.17).

That the effects of that disobedience would finally be reversed and paradise restored was, as we have noted, the beginning and end of all Jewish hope. In that day the rest of creation would also participate in joy:

> For the mountains and the hills before you
> shall leap forth, receiving you with joy,
> and all the trees of the field shall clap with their branches.
> Instead of the thorn shall come up the cypress,
> instead of the fleabane shall come up the myrtle. (LXX Isa. 55.12b–13a; compare
>   11.6–9, 43.19–21, 1 *Enoch* 45.4–5, 51.4–5, 71.1; 2 [4] Ezra 8.51–54, 2 *Apoc.*
>   *Bar.* 29.5–8)

Just as the creation, through the disgrace of humanity, its human head, has had to participate in the **bondage** that **corruption** imposes, so the creation **will** participate in that particular **liberty** which is proper to it when humanity has its proper **glory**—the "glory," that is, from which humanity fell short when it worshiped and served the creature rather than the creator (3.23, 1.25). And this will be the true end of the story—or perhaps, after a false start, its true beginning.

But in Christ, according to Paul, this reversal has already begun (5.15), and so the creation, and the church, are like women in childbirth, whose labor has started: **We know that the whole creation groans together** [*sustenazei*][88] **and travails to-**

---

86. So Chrysostom: "[The creation] became corruptible. For whose sake and because of what? Because of you, oh humankind [*dia se ton anthrōpon*]!" (*Homilies on the Epistle to the Romans* 14.5). The alternative, preferred by most recent commentators, is to understand the "one who subjected it" to be God; but this involves understanding *dia* with the accusative as implying *agency*, when its normal usage is implying *cause or grounds* for something—in this case the cause being Adam, whose disobedience caused the creation to be subjected to vanity.

87. Cranfield is surely correct in insisting that "the liberty of the glory [*tēn eleutherian tēs doxēs*]" not be treated as if "of the glory" were merely adjectival (as in, e.g., the NAB, which translates the phrase as "glorious freedom"). Not only does this obscure the evident rhetorical parallel with "the bondage of corruption," it also obscures Paul's sense, which is plainly not that the rest of the creation will obtain *humanity's* "glorious liberty" (a contradiction in terms) but that the rest of creation will enjoy *its own* "liberty"—that liberty which is proper to it when its human head is no longer in disgrace (*Romans* 1.415–16).

88. The image might be borrowed from some Hellenistic philosophers, who compared the earth in spring to a woman in childbirth: "when the groaning earth gives birth in travail to what has been formed within her" (Heraclitus Stoicus, *Quaestiones Homericae* 39 [58.9]). On the other hand, suggestions of a connection between Romans 8.22–23 and Jewish ideas of the "birth pangs of the Messianic age" are unlikely to be correct. It is not even certain that rabbinic ideas about the "birth pangs of the Messiah" (*cheblô shel mashîach*) were current in the first century. In any case, as Cranfield points out, "the metaphor is a very natural one to express the thought of severe distress from which a happy and worthwhile issue is to be looked for" (*Romans* 1.416, note 2).

gether until now; and not only the creation but we ourselves, who have the first fruit [*tēn haparchēn*][89] of the Spirit, groan (*stenazomen*) inwardly as we wait for our adoption [*huiothesian*],[90] the redemption of our bodies (8.22–23). Already we have received "the Spirit of adoption" and "are children of God" (8.15a), but as yet our status as God's children is hidden, and our bodies are still subject to death. The future **redemption of our bodies** means, however, that (as Paul wrote on other occasions) what is at present "sown in weakness" will be "raised in power"; and then "the Lord Jesus Christ will change our lowly body to be like his glorious body, by the power that enables him to subject all things to himself" (2 Cor. 15.43, Phil. 3.21). The life of grace is to wait in this hope and to live as those who are actively preparing for it.

For in hope we have been saved [*esōthēmen*] (8.24a)—the aorist passive form of the verb **saved** makes clear that the salvation of which Paul speaks is something already achieved, essentially and definitively, on the cross (compare 3.25), while the dative **in hope** [*tē[i]* . . . *elpidi*]) however we choose to classify it grammatically (instrumental, modal, advantage, or whatever), indicates equally clearly that the full realization of that salvation remains in the future. **Now hope that is seen is not really "hope"—for who "hopes" for what they already see? But if we hope for what we do not see, then we wait for it with endurance** (8.24b–25)—that "endurance" which is alone the basis of the proper self-control that marks a healthy humanity (compare 5.3–4).

That is the first of Paul's reasons for refusing to compare present suffering with future glory—and it is to do with the story, and with telling the story right, as Paul sees it. It is not, however, his only reason. His second reason is based on present Christian experience. Just as the story, properly told, gives assurance for the future, so **likewise the Spirit** even now **helps us in our infirmities: for** in our present weakness **we do not** even **know what** [*ti*][91] **we should pray for that is right** (8.26a). Here, too, an aspect of the story finds its fulfillment, for had not David in his consciousness of his own utter sinfulness prayed for just such a presence?—

> Create in me a clean heart, O God,
>   and renew a right spirit within my inner parts;

---

89. "First fruit" (*haparchē*) is properly used in secular Greek of the first part of a sacrifice, such as hairs cut from the offerer's forelock (Euripides, *Orestes* 96), and of a part of something being consecrated for the whole (Herodotus, *Histories* 4.71). In the LXX also it is normally used of the cultus (e.g., LXX Exod. 22.28 [MT 22.29], 23.19; Num. 18.12; Deut 18.4; 2 [4] Esdras 20.38), but also occasionally noncultically (e.g., LXX Deut. 33.21, Ps. 77.51 [MT 78.51], 104.36 [MT 105.36]; Sirach 24.9). In the latter connection it seems simply to mean "first part" (hence the "first-born" of Egypt in the passages from the psalms) and it is clearly in this latter sense that Paul uses it at Rom. 8.23: the Spirit is the first part of the promised inheritance of the faithful. Commentators have aptly compared Paul's reference to the Spirit as God's *arrabōn* ("down-payment") to us, at 2 Corinthians 5.5.

90. A number of ancient authorities (notably P46, D, and G) omit "adoption" (*huiothesia*), and in view of 8.15–16 it is tempting to follow them; but for precisely that reason the longer (and generally better attested) text, with its apparent contradiction begging to be "corrected," is more likely to be what Paul said.

91. It is unclear whether *ti* means *what* to pray, or what to pray *for*; but in any case, as Cranfield points out, *ti* should not be treated simply as an equivalent of *pōs* (as, e.g., do NEB, RSV, and NRSV; but contrast KJV, NEB margin, BEP) (Cranfield, *Romans* 1.422).

Cast me not away from your countenance,
  and take not your Holy Spirit from me.
Restore to me the joy of your salvation,
  and uphold me by your guiding Spirit. (LXX Ps. 50.12–14 [MT Ps.
  51.12–14])

There is, moreover, a request that is according to God's will, and that request is made as **the Spirit himself intercedes for us with groans too deep for utterance** (8.26b).

Doubtless the **groans** of the Spirit are in some sense parallel to the groaning of creation and the church (8.22, 23), yet they are also different, for we groan in our own pain, whereas the Spirit's **groans** are an element of that same divine identification with the grief of the world whereby God "made him to be sin who knew no sin, that we might become the justice of God in him" (2 Cor. 5.21).

Those commentators are surely quite wrong who see in the words **we do not know** a reference to misunderstanding or misuse of any particular *type* of prayer, such as glossolalia.[92] Paul's point is at once simpler and more profound than that. Paul's point is that *all* our prayer is offered under the burden of weakness and ignorance, which are the fruits of our disobedience. I am no more justified by prayer and piety than I am justified by works of the Law. Even at prayer, I stand only by the justice and grace of God. **And the one who searches hearts knows what is the intention of the Spirit: that he intercedes for the saints according to** the will of God (8.27).

We know that all things work together for good (or, he [God] **works all things together for good,** or he [the Spirit] **works all things together for good),**[93] **for those that love God,** that is, those **who are called according to** God's **purpose** (8.28)[94]— for preceding our love for God is always God's love for us. The life of grace rests upon a single security: and that security is not a life of prayer, nor an attitude to the Law, nor anything else in creation: that security is God.

The distinction between the possible ways of understanding 8.28a is not really so important as has sometimes been implied. Whatever, grammatically, is the subject of the verb **works together,** it is clear that Paul speaks of his confidence in God's overarching providential care; and in no case does he claim that bad things do not happen to believers. Paul's own life—let alone the life of his Lord—could scarcely have led him to such a view as that (compare 2 Corinthians 11.23–29). What is affirmed here is simply a conviction that even in "bad" things, God still works for our final good—a conviction that will form an important part of the argument of the next section of the letter (9.1–11.36).

92. Käsemann, *Romans* 239–42.

93. All three translations of the Greek are possible, and the second is supported by a textual variant, the addition of *ho theos* after *synergei* in P46, A, and B. Such a variant, however, probably represents an effort to remove the problem, and is therefore unlikely to be original. Of the three possibilities, the first (so KJV, BEP; contrast RSV, NEB, BJ) appears to be the simplest and most natural way of translating the text; it avoids the somewhat awkward adverbial treatment of "all things" (*ta panta*) that is required by both the other possibilities; and it is how Jerome understood the passage (Vg. *omnia cooperantur in bonum* is quite unambiguous).

94. Origen (according to Rufinus) admitted that this way of understanding the passage was possible: against that, one is bound to take seriously the fact that, along with virtually all the Greek commentators, he seems to have preferred to understand the reference to be to the *human* purpose—that is, the human choice to serve God (Migne, *Patrologiæ* 14.1125–26).

The life of grace is, then, lived on no other basis than that of God's goodwill. **For those whom God foreknew he has also predestined to be conformed to the image of his Son, in order that he might be the firstborn among many brothers and sisters** (8.29). Here again, if we are to listen to Paul, we must forget later dogmatic disputes. Paul is still telling the biblical story. "Foreknowing" speaks of God's decision and election—even as God "knew" Abraham beforehand:

> Shall I hide from Abraham my child what I am doing? Abraham shall become a great and mighty nation, and all the nations of the earth shall be blessed in him. For I have known that he will charge his offspring and his house with him, and they will keep the ways of the Lord, to do justice and judgment. (LXX Gen. 18.17–19; compare Amos 3.2)

and likewise Jeremiah,

> Before I formed you in the womb I knew you,
> and before you were born I consecrated you,
> I appointed you prophet for the nations. (LXX Jer. 1.5)

and, of course, Paul himself—for God, who

> had set me apart before I was born and called me through his grace, was pleased to reveal his Son in me, so that I might proclaim him among the Gentiles. (Gal. 1.15–16)[95]

Paul knows, from the biblical story and from his own experience, that before any human act or choice, there is an eternal love that has already sought and cared for us, a love that set us apart before we were born, that called us through grace, and that has **predestined** us **to be conformed to the image of his Son, so that he might be the firstborn among many brothers** and sisters (8.29b).

Yet again, we are speaking of the recovery of Adam's glory. Humanity, created in the "image" of God (LXX Gen. 1.26–27), failed to manifest that image faithfully. Now that image is manifested in Christ, who, in Paul's view, is "the image of God" (2 Cor. 4.4), and into whose "image" we are being transformed in our turn (2 Cor. 3.18). This, Paul says, is the love that **has called, . . . has justified**, and has also already **glorified** believers (8.30)—so giving to humanity what humanity in the beginning refused to give to God (1.21).

What then shall we say to all this? (8.31a) Paul sweeps together all that he has been saying into an affirmation of the certainty of God's grace. **If God is for us, who is against us?** (8.31b) "My enemies turn back, in the day when I call upon you: lo, I know that you are my God!" (LXX Ps. 56.10 [MT 56.10b–11a]) **He who did not spare** [*ouk epheisato*] **his own son**, even as Abraham "did not spare [*ouk epheisō*]" Isaac (LXX Gen 22.12, 16), **but gave him up for us all** (for Isaac there was, of course, a divine intervention, but for the son of God there was no such intervention), **how shall he not with him freely bestow upon us all things?** (8.32) **Who shall lay anything to the charge of God's elect?** (8.33a) Again we are to picture a courtroom

---

95. Jeremiah 1.5, together with Isaiah 49.1–6 (which, without using a word for "know," clearly implies God's "foreknowing"), evidently influenced Paul: certainly the language in which he here speaks of his call is reminiscent of them.

(compare 3.24a). **It is God that justifies. Who will condemn?** (8.33b–34a) **Christ who died,** who **was raised**, and who is exalted, himself **intercedes for us** (8.34). In all this, Paul and his fellow believers are like Isaiah:

> Also the Lord has become my helper.
>> Therefore I have not been ashamed . . .
> because the one who justifies me is drawing near.
>> Who is condemning me?
> Let him stand up together with me.
>> And who is condemning me?
> Let him draw near to me.
>> Behold, the Lord God is helping me.
> Who will harm me? (LXX Isa. 50.7a, 8–9a)

Nothing, then, in heaven or earth, whether natural (8.35–37) or supernatural (8.38–39a), **will be able to separate us from the love of God in Christ Jesus our Lord** (8.39b). That is the promise of life lived in dependence solely upon the justice and grace of God.

Additional Note X. Flesh

Sarx ("flesh") and its cognates (*sarkikos* [rare] and *sarkinos*, both meaning something like "of the flesh" or "fleshly") were basically used in literary Greek to speak of the flesh of the body, and of animal flesh. *Sarx* is therefore naturally contrasted with *psychē* ("soul") (so Plutarch, *Reply to Colotes* 20 [*Moralia* 1118d]), with *nous* ("mind" or "intelligence"), *epistēmē* ("knowledge"), and *logos orthos* ("right reason") (so Epictetus 2.8.2–3). *Sarx* is what distinguishes humankind from the gods, and being so considered, can be referred to contemptuously as "my miserable bits of flesh [*ta dustēna mou sarkidia*]" (Epictetus 1.3.5). Its pleasures, and even its needs, are naturally to be contrasted (disadvantageously) to those of the *psychē* (Plutarch, *Table Talk* 5 [*Moralia* 672d–673b]) and the wise will be wary of them, for to indulge them is to abandon self-control. Its pains and its pleasures are alike transitory and therefore less significant (so Diogenes Laertius's summary of the views of Epicurus in *Lives of Eminent Philosophers* 10.137).

There were evidently Jews whose literary usage was broadly at one with this. "For when that which is superior, namely Mind [*nous*], becomes one with that which is inferior, namely Sense-perception, it resolves itself into the order of flesh [*to sarkos genos*], into sense perception, the moving cause of the passions [*tēn pathōn aitian*]. But if Sense the inferior follow Mind the superior, there will be flesh [*sarx*] no more, but both of them will be Mind" (Philo, *Allegorical Interpretation* 2.50); "Compare, friend, the good of the flesh [*to sarkos agathon*] to the good of the soul [*tēs psychēs*] and of the All. The good of the flesh is irrational [*alogos*] pleasure, that of the soul is the mind of the universe, even God" [*Giants* 40]. Similarly, the author of 4 Maccabees (writing at some time between 63 BC and AD 70): "If therefore because of piety an old man despised tortures even to death, most certainly devout reason is governor over the passions. But some might say, 'Not all have full command of the passions, because not all have prudent reason.' But as many as attend to religion with a whole heart, these alone are able to control the passions of the flesh, since they believe that they, like our patriarchs Abraham, Isaac, and Jacob do not die to God, but live to God" (4 Macc. 7.16–19).

In the LXX *sarx* had been used to translate Hebrew *bāśār*, which can also mean simply the flesh of the body (see, for example, Job 19.20). By extension, however, *bāśār*—and hence *sarx*, when translating it—was further used to speak of humanity in its entirety: hence, "all flesh [*bāśār* /*sarx*] shall see the salvation of our God" (MT/ LXX Isa. 40.5; compare MT Joel 2.28/ LXX Joel 3.1), and it could be used to refer to all creaturely life of any kind: as in the instruction to Noah to bring into the ark creatures "from all flesh [*mikkol-bāśār* / *apo pasēs sarkos*]" (MT/LXX Gen. 6.19).

Paul's usage of *sarx* seems to combine elements of normal Greek literary usage with the particular emphases of the LXX. Thus, for Paul, as for the LXX, it is evident that *sarx* involves a good deal more than merely the tissue of the physical body: so, for example, he says that "the fruits of the *sarx* are plain . . . idolatry, sorcery, enmity, strife, jealousy, anger, selfishness, dissension" (Gal. 5.19–20)—all characteristics that could perfectly well be possessed by an entity that did not have a *physical* body at all. On the other hand, for Paul as for the Greek literary tradition generally, *sarx* represents a sphere that is viewed with suspicion, if not entirely negatively. *Sarx* is at best weak. At worst, with its "passions and desires" it is directly opposed to "self-control" (Gal. 5.23, 24). For Paul, in general, we may say *sarx* represents the *merely* human, the *merely* creaturely, including not just the physical, but the mental, the intellectual, and even the ostensibly religious, *apart from its sanctification through the Holy Spirit.*

Hence the Galatians' very "religious" desire to be circumcised is, in Paul's eyes—since it does not come from the gospel—a plain example of turning to "the flesh" (Gal. 3.2: compare Phil. 3.3). As John Calvin said, "Under the term flesh Paul always includes all the endowments of human nature, and everything that is in humankind, except the sanctification of the Spirit."[96] Needless to say, those who insist on living on this purely human and creaturely level "cannot please God" (Rom. 8.8).

Additional Note Y. Spirit

Greek *pneuma* ("spirit") and its cognates (*pneumatikos*, "spiritual"; *pneumatikōs*, "spiritually") are basically associated with "breath" or "wind," and are thus, in the LXX, an excellent translation for Hebrew *ruach*, which has exactly the same associations (thus, for example, compare MT and LXX Genesis 1.2, 8.1, Jonah 4.8 ["wind"] and Genesis 6.17, Ezekiel 37.5 ["breath"]).

Since breathing involves movement and indicates life, *pneuma* naturally becomes associated in general usage with life itself (for example, Polybius uses *pneuma echein*, meaning, more or less, "to be alive" [*Histories* 31.10.4; compare Plutarch, *Pericles* [*Parallel Lives*] 13]), with the inner life (in which sense it can become virtually synonymous with *psychē* ["soul"]) (thus Epictetus, "the little body [*to sōmation*] must be separated from the little spirit [*tou pneumatiou*], either now or later, just as it was separated before" [2.1.17]), and so finally with the divine—in particular, with di-

96. Calvin, *Romans* 151.

vine inspiration ("in-breathing") (so Plutarch, *On Exile* [*Moralia* 605a]; compare *Numa* [*Parallel Lives*] 4.6). In all these settings the original (concrete) associations with "wind" and "breath" seem never entirely to be forgotten, so that the word always conveys a sense of something essentially dynamic, moving, and creative; it is perhaps this, above all, that distinguishes the associations of *pneuma* from those of *nous* ("mind"), which is also associated with the inner life, but more in reference to the faculty of intelligence, thought, and contemplation.

While biblical writers generally do not share the interest in the body/soul dichotomy that characterizes the Greeks, still these further associations of *pneuma* make it an excellent translation for *rûaḥ* in many passages of the Bible that speak of the inner life (such as Ps. 51.12, 19 [LXX 50.12, 19]). The human "spirit" is from God, who gives it to all "flesh" (Num. 16.22) so as to bring life even out of death (Ezekiel 37.1–14) or withdraws it so as to bring death (Gen. 6.3). Finally, the Spirit can denote the action and presence of God—in creation (Gen. 1.2, Psalm 32.6 [MT 33.6]), in the inspiration of kings and prophets (Isa. 11.2, 61.1–2), and in sanctification and as a sign of God's presence with the people of God—in which connection it becomes associated with eschatological hope (Ezekiel 11.19, 36.27).

Pauline usage, while evidently not unrelated to Greek usage in general, is most obviously influenced by the LXX. *Pneuma* for Paul can speak of the inner life of the world (1 Cor. 2.12a), or of particular persons (1 Cor. 2.11a), but most often and most importantly speaks of the personal presence and power of God (1 Cor. 2.11b–13). Naturally, which of these is in mind at any particular point must be decided from the context. As in the LXX, so for Paul, the presence of God's Spirit marks the people of God and is associated with eschatological hope—hope that, for Paul, is now already being realized in the fellowship of Jesus Christ (see Rom. 8.3–27). Like the LXX, only rarely does Paul seem to reflect the Greek propensity to see body and soul as different parts of the human whole (possibly 1 Thess. 5.23); rather, to walk "according to the spirit" (*kata to pneuma*) means for Paul that the whole person is in the sphere of the divine activity, power, and dynamic, which is also the sphere of sanctification, as opposed, most evidently, to walking "according to the flesh" (*kata sarka*), which means that the whole person is in the sphere of the *merely* creaturely.[97] The close relationship of Jesus Christ to God leads in this context to an extension of usage, whereby Paul speaks of God sending "the Spirit of his Son" into the hearts of believers (Gal. 4.6; compare Rom. 8.14–16), and at other times uses expressions like "Spirit of Christ," "Spirit of Jesus," and (somewhat ambiguously) "Spirit of the Lord."

Additional Note Z. Body

Sōma, like English "body" by which it is usually translated, has a range of meaning from

1. "dead body" (as always in Homer; for example, *Iliad* 3.23), through
2. "living body" in contrast to *psuchē* or *pneuma* (for example, of Octavian's commander Cornifucius, first "shattered in body and mind" [*to te sōma*

97. On "the flesh," see additional note X.

kai tēn psuchēn]" [Appianus, *The Civil Wars* 5.112]; or Plutarch, one "should rule . . . not as a master rules a slave, but as the soul rules the body [*all'hōs psuchēn sōmatos*]" [*Advice on Marriage* (*Moralia* 142e), trans. Donald Russell]; for this sense in the New Testament we may compare Mark 5.29, 14.8), to

3. virtually "the total person" (as with Cornifucius, a little later in the same narrative, "after attending to his own person (*therapeusas de to sōma*) and taking a little rest" [Appianus, ibid.]), to

4. in a transferred sense, "body" as community or group, in which sense it offers a topos familiar to many ancient authors. No doubt this image came more naturally to the ancients than to us, since they had a different attitude to society.[98]

At Romans 8.10, as at 6.6 ("body of sin"), 7.24 ("body of death"), 8.11, and 12.1, Paul's meaning seems closest to sense 3; compare also Phil. 1.20. At Romans 8.13, by contrast, he seems closer to 2 (compare footnote 59 in this chapter; so also at 2 Cor. 5.6 and 2 Cor.12.2. At Romans 12.1–5 he moves naturally from 2 to the transferred sense, 4, the "body" as community—a sense that clearly appealed to him, since he also used it elsewhere: by implication at 1 Cor. 6.15, and in an extended fashion at 1 Corinthians 12.12–27.

As indicated in the course of my discussion of Paul's text at 12.1–5 there are, of course, ways in which Paul's use of the "body" metaphor must be distinguished from the examples cited under sense 4 above, not least because for him the church is not merely *a* body, but the body of Christ. Therefore, it is marked by a particular characteristic: "[A]ccept one another, as Christ has accepted you, for the glory of God" (15.7). This means, as Helmut Koester points out, that Christian conduct will

> be documented in the renunciation of one's privileges and in the acceptance of the weak conscience of other members of the church (1 Cor. 8.9–13)—even the conscience of a pagan observer (1 Cor. 10.28f)—as the criterion for one's own conduct . . . The Lord's Supper is not a mystery meal nor a sacred dinner for the perfect, but an eschatological meal for the whole community, which should give evidence that one understands what "the body of Christ" means. The "body of Christ" is the community of all Christians who have respect and patience for each other (11.17–34).[99]

The passages that Koester cites from 1 Corinthians might well be compared with passages reflecting similar concerns in Romans: notably, as regards accepting the weak consciences of other members of the church, 14.1–15.13, and as regards the pagan conscience, 12.17b.

This granted, there is no good reason to set Paul completely apart from his literary context, or to deny that that context both conditioned his language and made it, at least in some respects, immediately comprehensible. In some respects, even at

---

98. For examples of the image of society as "body," see on solidarity, additional note V.

99. Helmut Koester, *Introduction to the New Testament*, vol. 2, *History and Literature of Early Christianity* (Berlin: de Gruyter, 1982), 124–25.

times in its details, his vision of "the body of Christ" is a vision of the ideal Hellenistic community.[100]

Defense 2: Does the Gospel Call in Question God's Faithfulness to the Promises? (9.1–11.36)

The Problem of Israel's Unbelief (9:1–10.10)

There remained a problem, a problem that undoubtedly caused Paul some of the "sufferings" of which he had just spoken (8.18)—his own words are **great sorrow and unceasing anguish** (9.2)—a problem about which he had prayed; and perhaps he had come to see that he did not know "what to pray for" (8.26):

> **I am speaking the truth in Christ, I am not lying; my conscience bears me witness in the Holy Spirit, that I have great sorrow and unceasing anguish in my heart. For I could pray** [*ēuchomēn gar*][101] as did Moses **to be myself accursed, and cut off from Christ, for the sake of my brothers** and sisters, **my kin by race!** (9.1–3)

To the uninitiated, Paul's outburst may seem surprising, or irrelevant—but only to the uninitiated. For here, in fact, Paul touches on the single outstanding issue that threatens to bring down everything he has so far constructed. If the gospel is God's power to save (1.16), how is it that many in Israel are not being converted to Christ? Is God, after all, unreliable—since God has (apparently) failed the Jews? Is God unfaithful to the promise? (If so, how can we trust God? Perhaps God will be unfaithful to the church, too?) Again, if the Law actually focused sin in Israel, which seems to be the upshot of what Paul has said on several occasions (3.20, 5.20, 7.7–11, 8.7–8) what does that mean? Was Israel actually *disadvantaged* by possessing the Law (compare 3.9)? Could it be that Jeremiah had in fact spoken the truth in his desperate cry—"O master, Lord, you have then utterly deceived this people and Jerusalem, saying, 'Peace shall be yours!'—and lo, the sword has taken hold of their life" (LXX Jer. 4.10)? And these are Paul's **brothers** and sisters—a title he does not give lightly, nor as a matter of courtesy. These are members of God's household, and the problem is therefore a problem within that household. **They are Israelites, and to them belong the adoption** [*huiothesia*!—the extension of that privilege to gentiles does not mean that it is no longer Israel's privilege], **the glory, the covenants, the legislation, the worship, and the promises; to them belong the fathers, and**

---

100. See Eduard Schweizer and Friedrich Baumgärtel, "σῶμα, σωματικῶς, κτλ.," in *TDNT* 7.1024–85; see further Robert H. Gundry, *Sōma in Biblical Theology: With Emphasis on Pauline Anthropology*, SNTSMS 29 (Cambridge: Cambridge University Press, 1976), especially 135–244.

101. Despite Vg, KJV, RSV, and BEP (but contrast NEB), the usual sense "pray" for *euchesthai* (LS, εὔχομαι; BAGD, εὔχομαι 1) is surely to be preferred here to the weaker "wish" (compare 2 Cor. 13.7, 9)—particularly since the phrasing of the passage suggests strongly, as Cranfield points out, that Paul had in mind Moses' prayer at LXX Exodus 32.32: "And now, if you will forgive their sin, forgive; and if not, blot me out of your book which you have written" (*Romans* 2.454).

from them, according to the flesh, comes the Christ[102] **who is over all, God blessed for ever!**[103] **Amen.** (9.4–5)

What then? In what follows (9.6–11.36) Paul will argue that, far from being a sign that God has rejected Israel or canceled the promises, the failure of some in Israel to believe is only a temporary phenomenon and is part of God's overall plan. The section is in some ways the most rhetorically striking of the entire letter, and makes extensive use of virtually the entire range of techniques of the podium and the classroom. There will be rhetorical questions (9.14, 21, 10.8, 14–15, 18, 19, 11.1, 7, 11); there will be dramatic intervention by and argument with imaginary opponents (9.14–21); there will be protestations of the author's own passion and sincerity (9.1–4, 10.1, 11.1); there will be direct appeal to the hearers (11.13, 25); there will be antithesis and parallelism (11.15–16); there will be illustrative parable (11.16–21); and there will be extensive citation of authority—naturally, in view of the subject, scriptural authority (9.9, 12–13, 15, 17, 25–29, 33, 10.5–8, 11, 15, 16, 19–21, 11.2–4, 8–10, 26–27).

Paul at once grasps the bull by the horns. **It is not as though the word of God had failed** (9.6a). It has never been the case that mere physical descent marked the true Israel. **For not all who are descended from Israel belong to Israel, and not all are children of Abraham because they are his seed, but** as it is written, *Through Isaac shall your seed be called* (9.6b–7, alluding to LXX Gen. 21.12). What matters is not physical descent, but God's promise: **that is to say, it is not the children of the flesh who are the children of God, but the children of the promise who are reckoned as** Abraham's *seed.* (Of course, as Paul obviously knew, Isaac *was* Abraham's child "according to the flesh." The expression **it is not the children of the flesh** is hyperbole. The point is that it is not the "flesh" alone that matters: what matters is God's promise.) **For promise is what this word is about:**[104] **At** *around this time I shall return, and Sarah will have a son* (see LXX Gen. 18.10). **And not only this, but also when Rebecca had conceived at one time by one man [**ex henos koitēn hechousa],[105] **our father Isaac**[106]—**though they were not yet born and had done nothing either good or bad, in order that God's purpose of election might continue, not because of works but because of God's call, it was said to her,** *The elder will serve the younger* (see LXX Gen. 25.23) (9.10–12). In the case of Isaac, it might have been argued that since he was the son of Sarah, he *did* have an advantage "according to the flesh" over his brother Ishmael, who was only the son of her handmaid Hagar (LXX Gen. 16.1–6); no such advantage could be claimed for Jacob over Esau—

---

102. On the eight privileges of Israel listed by Paul, see additional note AA.

103. On the translation of 9.5b, see additional note BB.

104. Literally, "for of promise is this word." As Sanday and Headlam noted, the positioning of the predicate is evidently "in order to give emphasis and to show where the point of the argument lies" (*Romans* 242).

105. The Greek *koitē* literally means "bed," "bedstead," but by natural extension comes to mean "act of sexual intercourse" and even "seminal emission" (LS, κοίτη 4.4, BAGD, κοίτη a, b).

106. There is, strictly, a grammatical problem here: the Greek seems to be lacking a finite verb, although its general sense is clear enough.

indeed, the advantages "according to the flesh" were all the other way. Throughout it all, however, it is God's *promise* that is the important thing, and that means that some, even of Abraham's seed, even Jacob's elder brother, are left in unbelief, **as it written, *Jacob I loved, but Esau I hated***[107] (see LXX Mal. 1.2–3) (9.13).

That may make it clear that the failure of some in Israel to believe is consistent with the story of Israel as told in Scripture, but it hardly answers the question about God's own faithfulness. **What shall we say then?** If God treats some of Abraham's seed in this way even before they are born, is God really faithful to the promise to Abraham? Or—**Is there injustice on God's part? (9.14a) By no means!** God is not unjust—disloyal to the covenant—for God has always made clear that gifts of the promise were dependent simply on God's sovereign will to be gracious and nothing else at all. **For he says to Moses,** following the incident of the golden calf, when Moses had prayed that God would relent and not punish Israel, ***I will have mercy on whom I have mercy, and I will have compassion on whom I have compassion*** (see LXX Exod. 33.19; compare Exod. 32.30–33.16). **So it depends not upon human will or exertion, but upon God's mercy (9.14b-16). Mercy** (*eleos*), not human effort or desire, is the key to God's dealing with Israel.[108] Even in God's dealing with rebellious gentiles, human will is not the key, **for the Scripture says to Pharaoh, "I have raised you up for the very purpose of showing my power in you, so that my name may be proclaimed in all the earth"** (9.17, alluding to LXX Exod. 9.16). Even Pharaoh in his obduracy remained "an object of God's design and choice, chosen as an instrument for the execution of the salvific plan for the Hebrews, just as Moses himself was" (Fitzmyer).[109] **So then, God has mercy on whomever he wills, and hardens [*sklērunei*] the heart of whomever he wills (9.18)**—seed of Abraham and gentile alike. Paul's language about God "hardening the hearts" of unbelievers is itself, of course, taken from Scripture, where it is used not only of rebellious Pharaoh (see LXX Exod. 4.21), but also of rebellious Israel: "O Lord, why did you make us err from your way, and hardened our hearts [*esklērunas ēmōn tas kardias*], so that we did not fear you?" (LXX Isa. 63.17).

God's actions are, then, perfectly consistent with God's promises, as Scripture records them—which may, on one level, save God's reputation for faithfulness to the promises, but still leaves grounds for an objection: If it is God who hardens our hearts,

---

107. Here, again, we have hyperbole: "hated" is virtually equivalent with "loved less" (compare, "So Jacob . . . loved Rachel more than Leah . . . . When the Lord saw that Leah was hated, he opened her womb" [LXX Gen. 29.30–31]). From the viewpoint of the one who is "loved less" it is, of course, an understandable hyperbole.

108. "Mercy" (*eleos*) is a key concept in this section of Paul's demonstration. *Eleos* and its cognates occur nine times in Romans 9–11, as opposed to twice in the rest of the letter. This is not, of course, to suggest that there is any inconsistency between Romans 9–11 and the rest. On the contrary, while the word *eleos* may not be frequent elsewhere, *charis* ("grace") and its cognates abound (see additional note D). However it may be expressed, the *fact* that God is merciful is surely never absent for very long from Paul's thinking.

109. Fitzmyer, *Romans* 567.

"Why does he still find fault? Who is able to resist his will?" You, sir[110]—on the contrary![111]—who are you to answer back to God? *Will what is molded say to its molder, "Why have you made me thus?"* [citing LXX Isa. 29.16; compare 45.9–13] Has the potter no right over the clay, to make out of the same lump one vessel for honorable use and one for menial? (9.19–21)

"But man is *not* a pot!" protested one twentieth-century commentator, and thereby showed, perhaps, that he was not hearing Paul's language as Paul intended it. Isaiah himself used the image of the potter more than once, not merely as warning (LXX Isa. 29.16), but also as a way of speaking of God's faithfulness to the promise (LXX Isa. 45.9–13) and God's continuing love for Israel, a love such that not even Israel's repeated disobedience could cause to end: "And now, O Lord, you are our Father, and we, clay, are all the work of your hands" (LXX Isa. 64.7).[112]

Besides that, the point of the similitude, as Cranfield points out, "lies in the fact that the potter—as potter—must, in order to fulfill the rational purposes of his craft, be free to make, from the same mass of clay, some vessels for noble, some vessels for menial use . . . . It cannot be emphasized too strongly that there is naturally not the slightest suggestion that the potter's freedom is the freedom of caprice . . . . [I]t is, therefore, perverse to suppose that what Paul wanted to assert was a freedom of the Creator to deal with His creatures according to some indeterminate, capricious, absolute will."[113] In fact, God's purpose is always, in Paul's view, gracious.

110. See, on 2.1, page 91.

111. The phrase *menoun* in a response can introduce either an affirmation of what has just been said ("so then"), or a correction ("nay rather") (see LS, μέν B.2; BAGD, μενοῦν, μενοῦνγε; compare BD §450.4). Combined with the enclitic particle *ge*, Paul appears to use it here in correction and at 10.18 in affirmation.

112. As a scriptural image for God "the potter" is not, of course, confined to Isaiah: see also LXX Job 10.8–9, where it is presented as grounds for God's continuing loving kindness; also LXX Jer. 18.1–12, Sir. 33.13, and, in view of Rom. 9.20b–21, perhaps most striking of all, Wisd. of Sol. 15.7. In extrabiblical Judaism the image continues to be present in, for example, the conclusion to the *Community Rule*—"What shall one born of woman / be accounted before thee? / Kneaded from the dust, / his abode is the nourishment of worms. / He is but a shape, but moulded clay, / and inclines towards dust. / What shall hand-moulded clay reply? / What counsel shall it understand?" (1QS 11.22, trans. Geza Vermes)—and several points in the *Thanksgiving Hymns* (1QH 1.21, 3.23, 4.29). Perhaps we do not understand this metaphor properly because we lack sufficient experience of potters who throw by hand. I have more than once watched such a potter, and been struck not only by what I can only describe as her *gentleness* and *involvement* with the material on which she was working but also by the degree to which, it seemed, she was *pouring herself* into it. In this connection, one might profitably reflect on the following comments of the sculptor, Barbara Hughes:

> I have a love affair with clay. I found out some twenty-five years ago that something happens between the clay and me, and that together we can create more than is inside either of us individually.
>
> Sometimes I come to the clay with a very concrete image in mind (often one that is born of months of dreams, reading, drawing and "living-with"). Other times, I just bring to the clay a willingness to be surprised. Sometimes, out of those meetings comes sculpture.
>
> Art, for me, is about receiving and giving. When I am being most open and most willing to enter life, the images that come to me seem most like gifts. I then want to share them. A friend once said he thought I was making "sculpture that heals." I would like that to be true of my work. When I sit down with the clay, of course, I can only make what is there to be made. But it is the possibility that some images will be shared, and something received, that keeps me doing it.

113. Cranfield, *Romans* 2.492.

> But what if God, desiring[114] to show his wrath and make known his power, has endured with much patience [that divine **patience** (*makrothumia*) which, as Paul has already observed, is "meant to lead to repentance" (2.4)] **vessels of wrath that are ripe for destruction?** (9.22)

Strictly, Paul's Greek at 9.22 is grammatically incomplete—he presents us with the protasis of a conditional sentence, but does not provide the apodosis. There is, however, no need to make very much of this. Ellipsis of the apodosis is actually no more unusual in ancient Greek than in modern English ("If only I could!" "And if I did?") and is paralleled more than once in the New Testament (Mark 9.23, Luke 19.42, John 6.62, Acts 23.9). Paul's sense remains perfectly clear: he challenges his hearers to consider as a possibility what he actually believes to be the case.

The expression **vessels of wrath** (*skeuē orgēs*) implies that *at this point in the story* those referred to are the objects of God's anger. There is, of course, no implication that they need to remain so. Indeed, the divine **patience** that **has endured** them is by its nature a constant sign they need *not* remain as they are, and an invitation to repent (compare 2.4). As for what will then happen, Cranfield aptly compares Ephesians, where the writer speaks of himself and those to whom he writes as having been "*by nature* [!] children of wrath [*tekna phusei orgēs*]" but now "made alive together with Christ" (Eph.2.3–4).[115]

Similarly with **ripe for destruction**—it is significant that Paul does not say *prokatērtismena* ("prepared in advance")—a word he certainly knows, for he uses it at 2 Corinthians 9.5—but merely *katērtismena* ("prepared," "ready," or, as I suggest, **ripe**): the whole point being, again, that those of whom Paul speaks are in a state where they seem to be begging for destruction *at this point in the story*. By whom, then, have they been thus made **ripe**? Even in *koinē* Greek written by a Jew, we should not simply assume that all passives are "divine." In this case Chrysostom was surely on the mark when he suggested that Paul's meaning is that the vessels have prepared *themselves*—that Pharaoh, for example, was "fully ripe indeed, but to be sure, from his own resources and by himself" (*Homilies on Romans* 16.8). What matters, in any case, is that the divine **patience** surrounds Pharaoh and all those others of whom Paul speaks. Thus the entire phraseology with which he describes their sin is really only a foil whereby he may make clear the miracle of that patience, and the grace that follows it.

> Suppose this divine patience, he says, **and** suppose also that it is **in order to make known the riches of his glory for the vessels of mercy, which he has prepared beforehand [*proētoimasen*][116] for glory, even us whom he has called, not from Jews only, but also from gentiles!** (9.23–24)

114. It is possible to understand the participle "desiring" (*thelōn*) concessively (that is, "although God desired"), but the causal understanding (as above: virtually, "because God desired") is probably correct. God's grace *is* for Paul the way in which God characteristically expresses Wrath—the divine "No!"—against human ungraciousness. "God's wrath is revealed from heaven against all the impiety and injustice [*adikian*] of humanity [*anthrōpōn*]," and the climax of that revelation is on Calvary (1.18, 3.23–26) (Cranfield, *Romans* 2.494–95).

115. Cranfield, *Romans* 2.495.

116. It will be noted that when, in contrast to 9.24 *katērtismena*, Paul *does* want to speak of divine "preparing beforehand," the word he chooses is absolutely unambiguous—and it is a preparation

Though the means may seem hard, the purpose has always been and is always **mercy**—the very **mercy**, again, that is promised by Scripture, that very **mercy** which now extends to Jews like Paul but also, wonder of wonders, to gentiles who have become believers!—**as indeed he says in Hosea,**

> Those who were not my people I will call "my people,"
> and her who was not beloved I will call "my beloved" (alluding to Hos. 2.23)

> And in the very place where it was said to them
> "You are not my people,"
> there they will be called "sons and daughters of the living God" (citing LXX Hos. 1.10) (9.25–26)

And what of the failure of so many in Israel?
But Isaiah cries out concerning Israel,

> *Though the number of the sons of Israel be as the sands of the sea, only a remnant of them will be saved; for the Lord will execute his sentence upon them completely and decisively* [literally, "for the Lord will accomplish a sentence (*logon*) upon the earth, completing and curtailing it"]. (9.27–28, alluding to LXX Isa. 10.22–23 and Hos. 2.1)[117]

The force of the Isaiah passage here is, it must be confessed, somewhat obscure: though evidently it is part promise, part warning. The verses seem to be chosen by Paul because they contain an allusion to the **remnant** (*hypoleimma*): meaning, for Isaiah, those Israelites who would survive Assyrian captivity, for the apostle, those who would accept Jesus the Messiah. The survival of such a **remnant** is, as Paul will make clear (see 11.1–6, especially 11.5) a sign that God has not forsaken Israel, but continues to fulfill the promises made to her and through her. This survival is also, as it has always been, something that comes about "by grace," not a matter of human decision, but of God's election.
And as Isaiah predicted,

> *If the Lord of hosts had not left* [egkatelipen] *us a seed, we should have fared like Sodom and been made like Gomorrah.* (9.29, citing LXX Isa. 1.9).

The idea of "the remnant" is present here too—the connection being particularly evident in Greek, since *egkatelipen* (from *egkataleipein*) is cognate with *hypoleimma*.

---

for glory. There is *no* such word used of, and evidently in Paul's thinking no conception of, "preparation" for destruction. To change the metaphor, God's "book," as spoken of elsewhere in Scripture (Exod. 32.32; Ps. 69.29; Rev. 3.5, 17.8, 20.12, 15) and by Paul himself (Phil. 4.3) is always "the book of life." As Barth observed, "One's name may not be in this book. It can be blotted out from it. And yet there are not two columns, but only one. Similarly, the concept of the divine πρόθεσις used in Romans 8.28 and 9.11 and Eph. 1.11 etc. relates to the divine election to salvation, but only to that election as such, and not to the accompanying non-election, or rejection. The problem began to be obscured when the "book of life" came to be spoken of as though it had in it a death column" (*Church Dogmatics* 2.2.§32.1, 16).

117. Paul has here largely departed from the LXX of Isaiah 10.23, which itself is a very free rendering of a difficult Hebrew original (with Paul's version, however, compare LXX Isa. 28.22). Paul's own version is not easy, but the translation above probably renders something like the intended sense—which is, incidentally, not far from the probable meaning of the Hebrew.

Clearly present also is the assertion of God's continuing grace. In other words, far from being a surprise, or a sign of arbitrariness, unfaithfulness, or injustice on God's part, the failure of many in Israel was also foretold in Scripture. It is, and always has been, a part of the story—and its result was **mercy.**

What shall we say then?—that gentiles who were not pursuing justice obtained justice, the justice that is *by faith* [*ek pisteōs*]? (9.30). It would, of course, have been nonsense to pretend that no pagans attempted to live virtuously, or even that they never succeeded (compare 2.14–16, 27), and in saying that the gentiles **were not pursuing justice,** Paul was not saying those things. It is, as invariably in Paul, the justice of God, witnessed in God's Law, that is here in question. Those who do not have the privilege of knowing God's Law can hardly, in the nature of things, have been concerned with *pursuit* of that justice, and yet—and this *is* Paul's point— some among the gentiles have stumbled upon it, *ek pisteōs*—**by faith.** Here Paul again echoes Habakkuk 2.4, and hence Romans 1.17, and so the whole argument 1.16– 4.25. Some among the gentiles have stumbled upon God's justice simply because God is faithful and has confronted them with that justice in the face of Jesus Christ, summoning them to faithfulness in return!

"But do we then also say that **Israel, which was pursuing a Law of justice did not attain to Law?"** (9.31). What does Paul mean by a "Law of justice"? A Law that teaches justice? A Law that promises justice? Justice that comes from the Law? A Law that is a means to justice? The connection implied here by the genitive is, as often, imprecise and ambiguous, but in broad terms the question at issue is clear enough: *Are we saying that, in a sphere where some pagans have succeeded, so to speak, by accident, the people of God have failed?* It is Paul's imaginary interlocutor who is speaking again—and this time finds the teacher in agreement. Paul's answer, implicitly, is "Yes."

Why? (9.32a).

Because, Paul says, they pursued the Law **not *by faith*** (*ek pisteōs*)—not, that is, on the basis of faithfulness, God's faithfulness calling us to be faithful, the basis on which alone Habakkuk had said that the "just" would "live"—**but as if** it were a matter **of works** (9.32b).[118]

What does Paul mean by that?[119] His following words are perhaps intended as explanation. **They stumbled over the *stone of stumbling,*** as it is written, *Behold I*

---

118. The text here presents us with two major problems.

First, how did Paul expect his hearers to understand the connections of his (unpunctuated) Greek? The translation above is based on the view that only "Because [it was pursued] not 'by faith' but as if [it were] of works [*hoti ouk ek pisteōs all'hōs ergōn*]" was intended as the answer to "Why? [*dia ti?*]" The alternative view is that there should not be a major punctuation point after "works [*ergōn*]"—in which case it appears that Paul was answering the question "Why did Israel fail?" by saying (in essence), "Because . . . they stumbled [i.e., failed]." While the apostle was, presumably, as capable of such an occasional lapse in logic as any one else, since we can on this occasion, and without altering his text, absolve him from it, there seems little reason not to do so.

Second, it is in any case necessary to assume an implicit verb after *hoti*—either in the indicative, or, if we do not punctuate after *ergōn*, a participle. What verb should it be? The only reasonable possibility seems to me to be a form of the verb that Paul has already used, that is, "pursue [*diōkein*]."

119. The phrase "not 'by faith,' but as if [it were] of works" has been interpreted as a reference to Jewish ideas of salvation by "works-righteousness" as opposed to the Christian salvation by "faith righ-

lay in Zion a stone of stumbling and a rock of offense [*skandalou*]*, and whoever puts their trust in him shall not be put to shame* [*kataischunthēsetai*] (9.32c–33). The passages from the LXX to which Paul here (somewhat vaguely) seems to allude— Isaiah 8.14 and 28.16 with which he follows it—may early have received an interpretation in Christian tradition (Mark 12.10, Acts 4.11, 1 Peter 2.4) whereby the *stone of stumbling* was Jesus, and those who put their trust in him are the ones who will *not be put to shame* (compare Romans 1.16!)[120] If that is how Paul understands the allusion, then the first part of his explanation is that many in Israel are not living *by faith* because they do not accept the faithfulness of God manifested to them in the crucified Jesus, who is God's Messiah. It is, however, not entirely certain that the "stone *testimonium*" existed before Paul, and perhaps we should simply associate the "rock" here with God, or, in E. Elizabeth Johnson's more nuanced fashion, with "the proclamation of God's righteousness in Christian preaching."[121] In either case, it does not seem that Paul's overall sense is greatly altered.

Paul continues, however,

> **Brothers** and sisters, **my heart's desire and my prayer to God for them is that they might be saved. I bear them witness that they have a zeal for God, but not according to knowledge. For not knowing God's justice, and seeking to establish their own** [*tēn idian*]**, they did not subject themselves to God's justice.** (10.1–3)

I bear them witness . . .—here, inevitably, we must suppose Paul to be criticizing the view that had earlier been his own. According to his own testimony, he had grown up a Pharisee (Phil. 3.5–6, Galatians 1.13–14). Precisely what *that* will have meant is not as clear as we should like, but it is possible to make some suggestions. Jacob Neusner observes,

> Among those sympathetic to the Pharisaic cause were some who entered into an urban religious communion, a mostly unorganized society known as the fellowship [*havurah*]. The basis of this society was meticulous observance of Laws of tithing other priestly offerings as well as the rules of ritual purity outside the temple where they were not mandatory. The members undertook to eat even profane foods (not sacred tithes or other offerings) in a state of rigorous levitical cleanness. At table, they compared themselves to Temple priests at the altar.[122]

If we see such a group as connected with the Mishnah tractate *Toharot* ("Purities"— the one tractate in the Mishnah that seems likely in its entirety to go back to the period before 70), we shall probably not be far wrong: for this, too, is the work of those who choose to conduct their day-to-day lives as if they were living in the

---

teousness" that Paul advocates. Such a view is, as E. P. Sanders (among others) has demonstrated exhaustively, "completely wrong": see *Paul and Palestinian Judaism: A Comparison of Patterns of Religion* (London: SCM Press; Philadelphia: Fortress Press, 1977), 233. Jews of all persuasions were perfectly well aware that Israel's election and salvation were not on the basis of her works, and "salvation by works righteousness" is not an idea that we find in Jewish traditions of the period.

120. E. Elizabeth Johnson, "Romans 9–11," in *Pauline Theology*, vol. 3, *Romans*, ed. David M. Hay and E. Elizabeth Johnson (Minneapolis: Fortress Press, 1995), 230.

121. See Cranfield 2.511–12; Fitzmyer, *Romans* 580.

122. Jacob Neusner, *Judaism in the Beginning of Christianity* (London: SPCK, 1984), 27.

Temple. The purpose of such a formulation is clear: "to preserve the cleanness of the people of Israel, of the produce of the land of Israel, of the sexual life of Israel, of the hearth and home of Israel."[123] All that would certainly be one possible way of understanding and pursuing "a Law of justice."

Also notable in Romans 10.1–3, however, is Paul's **witness** to the Jews' **zeal** in this cause—the more notable, in that "zeal" is the word that he also uses of himself in speaking of his earlier life. Before his call he had, he says, been "zealous for the traditions of [his] fathers" and "zeal" led him to be "a persecutor of the church" (Gal. 1.13–14, Phil. 3.5–6). It seems clear that in a number of circles in first-century Judaism (including some linked to Pharisaism), **zeal** was associated not merely with passionate adherence to the Law for oneself but also with the commitment of those who (looking to Phinehas as their example [Num. 25.1–18, Psalm 106.30–31; compare 149.5–9]), were willing to act violently against any who were seen as violating Israel's purity by compromise with paganism.[124] This is the **zeal** that would have led a Pharisee like Saul to persecute those who defiled Israel by proclaiming a humiliated Messiah—a "Messiah" who had been crucified by pagans and had signally failed to bring about the redemption of Israel that God's justice demanded (Phil. 3.6, 1 Cor. 15.9). This is the **zeal** that would, in 66, lead such Pharisees to cohere with other revolutionary groups in launching a war against pagans who were presuming to govern the holy land of Israel. This may have been seen by such Pharisees as the **zeal** that would alone be acceptable to God in that great day when God finally acted to vindicate Israel, sending his victorious Messiah to punish alike both gentiles and renegade Jews.

Granted, then, its polemic tone, **seeking to establish their own justice** could be said to reflect precisely the religion of the Pharisees as described by Neusner and *Toharot*, concerned, as it was, with Israel's own purity, while the mention of **zeal** would be especially appropriate to those who, in order to make plain their own faithfulness in the Day of the Lord, were prepared to act violently against those whom they regarded as corrupting Israel's purity; and all this, I imagine, was what Paul had in mind when he declared that some in Israel were pursuing **justice . . . as if** it were a matter **of works**.

But such **zeal**, Paul says, is **not according to knowledge**—the **knowledge** that came to him on the Damascus road, where he was overwhelmed by that same crucified Messiah whose followers he had been persecuting. There, he believed, he was encountered by the Son of God and learned that the crucified Jesus was, after all,

123. Neusner, *Method and Meaning in Ancient Judaism: Third Series* (Atlanta, Georgia: Scholars Press, 1981), 20–21.

124. Within Pharisaism, perhaps, as Martin Hengel has argued, such "zeal" should be particularly associated with the house of Shammai (*The Zealots: Investigations into the Jewish Freedom Movement in the Period from Herod I to 70 A.D.* [Edinburgh: Clark, 1989] 200–206, 334). Possibly we should even associate Saul of Tarsus, before his conversion, with that house, as N. T. Wright suggests: see *Christian Origins and the Question of God*, vol. 1, *The New Testament and the People of God* (London: SPCK, 1992), 184–203 especially 192; also Hans Hübner, *Law in Paul's Thought* (Edinburgh: Clark, 1984 [1978]). Given, however, our limited and fragmentary knowledge of Pharisaism at this period, such suggestions—particularly the latter—must remain in the realm of speculation. See the comments of Sanders on this point: *Paul and Palestinian Judaism*, 138, note 61.

the true and living Lord. And if that were so, then everything was changed. Then it became evident that the story as Saul in his **zeal** had been telling it was being told wrongly. **For** then it turned out that **the Messiah**—not the zealous and victorious Messiah who destroyed pagans (not, that is, the Messiah "according to the flesh" whom Paul had previously "known" [2 Cor. 5.16–17]), but the crucified Messiah, the humiliated Messiah, the apparently defeated Messiah, *that* Messiah—**is the end** [*telos*, that is, the goal, the fulfillment][125] **of the Law**, so as to lead **to** God's **justice for all who have faith** [*pisteuonti*] (10.2–4). It is Jesus, the "defeated" Jesus, who is, as N. T. Wright has strikingly expressed it, "the climax of the covenant."[126] **For Moses writes that** *the one who does* **the justice that is based on the Law** *shall live by it* (10.5, alluding to LXX Lev. 18.5). The word **for** (*gar*) makes it plain that this is tied to what has preceded it.[127] To whom then does it refer? Evidently it refers to the Messiah, **the end of the Law**, of whom Paul is already speaking. He has done **the justice that is based on the Law**, and he **shall live by it**. "The man of whom Moses says (10.5) that he shall live by the fulfilment of the Law, the man who wills and means the Law is Christ; he will fulfil the Law by his death, and raised from the dead he will live" (Barth).[128]

But (*de*) **justice that is** *based on faith* (*ek pisteōs*: that is to say, it is based on God's faithfulness calling to us and enabling us to be faithful in return), that justice personified now addresses us directly. Who is that "justice"? It is surely Christ himself of whom Paul speaks—Christ himself who is, as Paul says on another occasion, "justice, and sanctification, and redemption" (1 Cor. 1.30). Therefore the **but** (*de*) of 10.6 (which is a very weak way of expressing contrast and often hardly implies contrast at all)[129] is not to be understood as setting 10.6 *against* 10.5, as if protesting or refuting it. If there is a contrast, it is rather that whereas 10.5 pointed to Christ's achievement, 10.6–8 points to what that achievement now means for us. It speaks of "the righteous status that we have through faith in him"(Cranfield).[130]

But **justice that is based on faith says thus,**

Do not say in your heart, Who will ascend into heaven? **(that is, to bring Christ down)** *or Who will descend into the abyss?* **(that is, to bring Christ up from the dead).** *But what does it say? The word is already near you, on your lips and in your heart,* that is, the word of **God's faithfulness** that **we proclaim** (10.6–8, echoing LXX Deut. 30.11–14).

This citation from Deuteronomy originally referred to the necessity and simplicity of carrying out the Law's precepts: but interpreters earlier than and contem-

---

125. On "the end of the Law," see additional note CC.

126. "In the Messiah are fulfilled the creator's paradoxical purposes for Israel and hence for the world. He is the climax of the covenant" (Wright, *Climax of the Covenant* 241).

127. This would be made clearer in translations if the paragraph break were made after 10.5 rather than (as in, e.g., NRSV) before it.

128. Barth, *Shorter Romans* 127.

129. The particle *de* is often used as a simple connective, without implying contrast: see BAGD, δέ.

130. Cranfield, *Romans* 2.521–22; see Barth, *Shorter Romans* 127; *Church Dogmatics* 2.2.§34.3, 245–46.

porary with Paul had already seen in it references to the divine Wisdom.[131] A midrash in Baruch is particularly striking. Speaking of Wisdom, the writer asks,

> Who has gone up into heaven, and taken her?
>   and brought her down from the clouds?
> Who has gone over the sea and found her,
>   and will buy her for pure gold?
> No one knows the way to her,
>   or is concerned about the path to her.
> But the one who knows all things knows her,
>   he found her by his understanding. (Bar. 3.29–32)

It is evident that Paul stands in this general line of interpretation. Christ (who in Paul's view *is* "our Wisdom" [1 Cor. 1.30, again]) has already been brought **down** to us, because in God's moment he was "born of David's seed" (1.3), and already he has been brought up **from the dead**, for God has "raised him for our justification" (4.25). So *the word*—the only word that matters, God's word, the word that saves, **the word of faith that we proclaim**—is *already near* us.

The proper activity for believers is therefore not to be frantically considering, as Paul had once considered, what *we* must be doing to establish *our own* justice, nor even to be overly anxious about our failings in this regard, but rather to be acknowledging joyfully what *God* has done through the Messiah: **because if you confess with your lips that Jesus is Lord, and have faith** [*pisteusēs*] **in your heart that God raised him from the dead, you will be saved; for it is held in faith** [*pisteuetai*] **with the heart so that we may experience** God's **justice, and it is confessed with the lips so that we may experience** God's **salvation** (10.9–10).[132]

Additional Note AA. The Eight Privileges of Israel at Romans 9.4–5

The eight privileges of Israel listed at Romans 9.4–5 are all rooted in the biblical story of Israel.

1. "The adoption [*huiothesia*]" makes use of a Hellenistic term (see page 149, footnote 78) to speak of the biblical status of Israel, chosen by God as the "first-born son [*huios prōtotokos*]" (LXX Exod. 4.22).
2. "The glory [*hē doxa*]" is throughout Scripture the sign of God's presence with Israel (for example, LXX Exod. 16.7, 10); see additional note J.
3. "The covenants [*hai diathēkai*]" (compare, for example, Wisd. of Sol. 18.22; Ecclus 44.11–12, 18; 2 Macc. 8.15) presumably refers to the covenants with Abraham, Isaac, Jacob, and their descendants (LXX Gen. 15.1–20, 17.1–19; Exod. 2.24), with Israel at Sinai (LXX Exod.

---

131. See Dunn, *Romans* 2.604–5; see further M. Jack Suggs, "'The Word Is Near You': Romans 10:6–10 with the Purpose of the Letter," in *Christian History and Interpretatation: Studies Presented to John Knox*, ed. W. R. Farmer, C. F. D. Moule, and R. R. Niebuhr (Cambridge: Cambridge University Press, 1967) 289–312.

132. On other ways of interpreting 10.5–10, see additional note DD.

19.5, 24.1–8), and in the plains of Moab (LXX Deut. 29.1–31.13), and with David (LXX 2 Kingd. 23.5; Ps. 88.4–5, 29 [MT 89.4–5, 29], 131.11 [MT 132.11]). (The singular *hē diathēkē* [offered by P46, B,D,G, Vg (cl)] would refer simply to Sinai and is therefore the easier reading; for precisely that reason Nestle 26 is doubtless correct in preferring the plural.)

4. "The legislation [*nomothesia*]" could (like its English translation) refer either to the actual reception of the Law in Israel or to its content. Perhaps the latter is more likely here (as at 4 Macc. 5.35, 17.16; Philo, *On Abraham* 1.5, *On the Cherubim* 26.87).

5. "The worship [*hē latreia*]" occurs nine times in the Old Testament; where it translates Hebrew, it is used to render '*abodah* (service), and eight of the occurrences (not 3 Macc. 4.14) have to do with cultic practices: thus LXX Jos. 22.27 (of the worship of Israel's God), Exod. 12.25, 26, 13.5 (of the Passover), 1 Macc. 1.43 (of the false *latreia* imposed by Antiochus Epiphanes), and 2.19, 2.22 (of the true worship of Israel's God).

6. "The promises [*hai epaggeliai*]": in view of Romans 4.13, 16–22 (compare Gal. 3.16–29) Paul must mean at least the promises to Abraham; but the Scriptures are full of God's promises, and Paul might equally have been thinking of passages such as LXX 2 Kingdoms 7.12, 16 [MT 2 Sam. 7.12, 16] or Jeremiah 31.31–37.

7. "The fathers [*hoi pateres*]" presumably refers specifically to Abraham, Isaac, Jacob, and the twelve, although Paul, like others, can use the word to refer to the entire wilderness generation (1 Cor. 10.1; compare Acts 7.19).

8. Finally, "of their race, according to the flesh, is the Messiah" underscores the fact that the Messiah was (and is) a Jew.

Additional Note BB. On Translating Romans 9.5

I have rendered this verse, **to them belong the fathers, and from them, according to the flesh, comes the Christ who is over all, God blessed for ever! Amen**. So, in substance, KJV, BEP; contrast RSV (but not margin) and NEB (but not margin). Granted the ancient manuscripts had no punctuation, this remains the simplest and most natural way of understanding the best attested Greek text that we have and has the support of Rufinus's version of Origen (Migne, *Patrologiæ* 14.1140), Chrysostom (*Homilies on Romans* 16.1), Theodore of Mopsuestia (*In Epistolam Pauli ad Romanos Commentarii Fragmenta* 9), and Augustine (*Propositions from the Epistle to the Romans* (59.1–5). Virtually the only argument against it is an argument *e silentio*—that Paul nowhere else uses the word *theos* of Christ (but note [1] his willingness to approach Christ in prayer [2 Cor. 12.8–9] and [2] his application to Christ of LXX passages where *kurios* represents the Divine Name [for example, Romans 10.13; see page 175]). On the other hand, against the proposal of RSV and NEB to understand the doxology as separate from Paul's reference to the Messiah (thus, ". . . the Christ. God who is over all be blessed for ever!") is the stylistic consideration that in Jewish usage both biblical and extrabiblical, when *eulogētos* occurs in independent doxologies, it is invariably the first word of the sentence (for example, LXX Gen. 9.26)—

a consideration so significant that Cranfield regards it as in itself "almost conclusive."[133] (The one apparent exception to this of which I am aware—LXX Ps. 67.19 —is where *kurios ho theos eulogētos* has been inserted as a gloss *before* the normal *eulogētos* et cetera, and is evidently not intended as a doxology in the normal sense at all, but an indicative statement.)

Additional Note CC. "The End of the Law" at Romans 10.4

Greek *telos* (like Latin *finis* and English "end") commonly bears a range of meaning all the way from "fulfillment, completion, consummation" to simple "finish, termination" (as in *telos echein*, "to be finished") (LS τέλος, BAGD τέλος). The older Greek interpreters were generally clear that Paul intended the former of these senses at Romans 10.4—notably Origen (who in Rufinus's Latin paraphrase says of 10.4, "*Finis enim legis Christus: hoc est perfectio legis*" [Migne, *Patrologiæ* 14.1160]); John Chrysostom, who compares the phrase "Christ is the *telos* of the Law" with the notion that "health is the *telos* of medicine" (*Homilies on Romans* 17.2); and Theodoret of Cyrrhus, who notes that "the Law led us to our master, Christ [*ton Despotēn, Christon*]. Therefore, one who has faith in Christ is one who fulfills the goal [*ton . . . skopon*] of the Law" (Migne, *Patroligiæ* 82.164). No doubt this unanimity of interpretation was in part a result of the influence of Matt. 5.17 (so Eusebius, *Demonstratio Evangelica* 8.2.33), but it remains impressive.

Among modern commentators, however, the question has been debated, and a number have opted for understanding *telos* at Romans 10.4 as "termination," notably Sanday and Headlam—"Law as a method or principle of righteousness had been done away with in Christ";[134] so also, among modern translations, NEB ("Christ ends the law") and JB; contrast, however, RV and RSV (both using the ambiguous "end"), and BEP (*culmine*—also ambiguous). There is no need to repeat here arguments that have been extensively presented elsewhere—Käsemann understandably speaks of "the apparently endless debate [*dem wahrscheinlich nie endenden Streit*]."[135]

Suffice it to say that in my view the opinion of the ancient interpreters remains the more soundly based. Given Paul's virtually categorical statement in 3.31, taking into further consideration passages such as 7.7–14, 8.3–4, 13.8–10, and noting, finally, that Paul repeatedly cites Scripture to provide authoritative support for his positions, it appears to me that the argument of Romans simply allows no room for notions of the Law having been "abolished" in Christ. It cannot be too strongly urged that Paul was not a Protestant reformer and was not fighting the Reformation's battles—though Calvin and Luther too, as it happens, agreed with the Greek fathers about the meaning of *telos* here: "This is why he says: 'Christ is the end of the Law,' in other words, every word in the Bible points to Christ. That this is really so, he proves by showing that this word here, which seems to have nothing whatsoever to do with Christ, nevertheless signifies Christ."[136] "Indeed, every doctrine of the

---

133. Cranfield, *Romans* 2.467. See his entire discussion: 2.464–70.
134. Sanday and Headlam, *Romans* 284; similarly Dodd, *Romans* 165, and Käsemann, *Romans* 282–83.
135. Käsemann, *Romans* 282 [*An die Römer* 270].
136. Luther, *Lectures on Romans* 10.4 [Pauck 288].

law, every command, every promise, always points to Christ. We are, therefore, to apply all its parts to him."[137]

What Paul was saying at Romans 10.4 was that Christ is the *goal* of the Law and that he has become this for the express purpose of making God's justice available for all who believe in him. As the gar (**for**) at the beginning of the phrase indicates, this statement is an *explanation* of what has preceded it—it shows just *why* (in Paul's view) the Jews, though entirely right in seeking to "pursue the Law," had in fact not done so "according to knowledge," and hence, seeking to establish "their own" justice, had not truly subjected themselves to God's justice (10.3). Naturally, Paul goes on immediately to quote and interpret the Law (10.5–11), in order to illustrate the claim he has just made about it.[138]

Additional Note DD. On the Interpretation of Romans 10.5–10

Two problems in these verses should be noted:

1. There is a textual question. Should *hoti* follow "writes," as implied in the translation I have given (page 168) following the preference of Nestle-Aland 25? Or should it follow "law" (*nomos*) leading to a translation something like, "For Moses writes of the justice that is based on the Law that [*hoti*] 'the one who does it shall live by it'" as preferred by Nestle-Aland 26 (following P46, B)? The latter reading certainly makes it more apparent that Paul has exactly quoted LXX Leviticus 18.5, and for that reason seems the more likely to be secondary.

2. There is also the much more difficult question as to the relationship intended by Paul between the two texts of Scripture to which he alludes in 10.5–6. It would be idle to pretend that my view of the intention of these verses is held by most (or even many) commentators. Indeed, were it not for the presence of Karl Barth and C. E. B. Cranfield—admittedly, no mean supporters!—the ranks on my side of the question would look rather thin. Some commentators are mild in their objections to what I will call the "Barth-Cranfield" view, conceding, like Moo, that "Christ's satisfaction of the law's requirements as a basis for securing righteousness for those who are his is a Pauline concept," and merely seeing "no good basis in the text to introduce it here."[139] Others are quite forceful in their objection, Dunn going so far as to say that this interpretation "completely misses the point" and "would make Jesus

---

137. Calvin, *Romans* 221–22, 852–61.
138. See Cranfield, *Romans* 2.515–20, 852–61. Dunn (*Romans* 2.589–91) and Moo (*Romans* 638–43) attempt to nuance the position, but I am not sure that they add anything. Certainly, as Moo points out, it is true that the finish line in a race *is* "both the 'termination' of the race (the race is over when it reached) and the 'goal' of the race (the race is run for the sake of reaching the finish line)" (Moo, *Romans* 641). But that is precisely the point: it is the *race* that is over when the finish line is reached, not the finish line. Indeed, if the finish line had ceased to be authoritative, there would be no way of knowing the race was over. Certainly Ephesians 2.13–16 is relevant in this context: but here, quite clearly, what is at issue is that in Christ our relationship to the Law has *changed* (compare Romans 4.16). It is, according to the author of Ephesians, in its function as "the wall of partition, the enmity" (Eph. 2.14) that the Law has been "abolished," *not in its function as witness to Christ*: see Marcus Barth, *Ephesians* 1–3 (New York: Doubleday, 1974), 290–91. See further Barth, *Romans* 375–76!
139. Moo, *Romans* 647; similarly, as regards the related problem of Galatians 3.12, Bruce, *Galatians*, 163.

an exemplar of Israel's nationalist righteousness."[140] Fitzmyer observes that Barth-Cranfield's view is "an eisegetical solution," and that, I think, is correct, at least in the sense that it requires us to suppose something about Paul's thinking that he did not, at this precise point, spell out (but compare 3.31, 8.4). We ought then to take note of two other possible interpretations of Romans 10.5–6. Neither of them, as I shall point out, is without its problems.

Both interpretations focus on the element of contrast that is understood to be implied by the *de* at the beginning of 10.6 (but see page 168 and footnote 129). The question then becomes, What is being contrasted with what?

1. In Käsemann's view, what Paul means by 10.5–6 is that "the Lawgiver Moses stands over against the personified righteousness of faith. Where he demands action understood as achievement, she demands reception of the word. . . . Finally, the theme of the word that is near is brought into view insofar as the Spirit brings with him the new covenant and as in 2 Cor. 3:14ff. . . . removes the veil between creature and creator."[141] Hence the important distinction is between "Moses writes" (*graphei*) (10.5), referring to "Moses as the mediator of a law which Judaism misunderstood," and "justice says" (10.6), referring to "the promise related to Abraham as the recipient of God's direct address."[142] "Something is 'letter' not because it is fixed in writing but only when it raises a demand for achievement. On the other hand, what is set in writing can 'speak' when it is the promise of grace."[143]

This is a solution involving at least as much eisegesis as Barth-Cranfield. That Paul intended a theologically significant distinction between "writes" and "says," parallel to that between "letter" and "spirit" at 2 Cor. 3 is not impossible, but is hardly self-evident. This suggestion has, moreover, the further disadvantage that it has Paul making a point that appears to fly directly in the face of the biblical text, according to which it is the Leviticus passage, if anything, that is presented as "God's direct address," and the passage from Deuteronomy that is "related to Moses as mediator of a Law."

2. The majority of commentators take it that Leviticus 18.5 in 10.5 refers to the hopeless quest demanded by Moses whereby we must seek our own righteousness before God, as opposed to Deuteronomy 30.11–14 in 10.6, which speaks of the righteous status we have through faith in Christ. "Paul," says Fitzmyer, "understands the Leviticus passage to be speaking of the 'uprightness that comes from the Law' and the Deuteronomy passage as 'that which 'comes from faith.' He thus sets them in opposition."[144] That, more or less, is also the position of Sanday and Headlam, Byrne, Dunn, and Moo.[145]

Simply as rhetoric, this apears at first glance to work better than either the Käsemann's or the Barth-Cranfield view. That is its appeal. The objection to it lies,

---

140. Dunn, *Romans* 2.601.
141. Käsemann, *Romans* 284, 285.
142. Käsemann, *Romans* 286; see 283–92.
143. Käsemann, *Romans* 287.
144. Fitzmyer, *Romans* 588.
145. Sanday and Headlam, *Romans* 285–86; Byrne, *Romans* 317–18; Dunn, *Romans* 600–602; Moo, *Romans* 642–50.

however, in precisely what it claims: that Paul set two passages from Scripture "in opposition" to one another. That objection is fatal.

First, the idea that Paul posited such an opposition involves him in an understanding of Scripture quite contradictory to his normal view—which is, as we have seen, that the Law, properly understood *points to God's justice by faith* (3.21–22, 31, 4.1–25; compare Gal. 3.8). To put it another way, for Paul, the "justice that is by the Law"—that is, *truly* based on the Law—to which Leviticus refers must be related positively to "the justice that is by faith" which he hears speaking from Deuteronomy. Why? Simply because "justice by faith" is, in Paul's view, what the Law teaches. The text from Deuteronomy cannot therefore possibly have been offered to contradict or correct the text from Leviticus, but only to complement, qualify, or explain it.

Second, the idea that Paul would have set one text of Scripture against another goes against everything we know about the way in which (1) Jews in general at this period handled sacred Scripture, and (2) the ancients in general handled authoritative texts. Certainly it was understood that such texts were often cryptic and needed interpretation. That did not alter the fact that there could not possibly be any real inconsistency between one part of such a text and another. If there appeared to be such an inconsistency, it was because the interpreter had not looked deep enough.[146] To have claimed that he saw such an inconsistency in the Scriptures would have been for Paul to admit, in effect, that he had not thought through his position.

Two other considerations may be relevant:

1. The "Barth-Cranfield" view appears to make sense in connection with Paul's other reference to Leviticus 18.5 at that (admittedly elliptical and very difficult) section in Galatians 3:

> Now it is evident that no one is justified before God by the Law, for "the just shall live by faith." "The Law" is not "by faith," but "the One who does them shall live by them": Christ redeemed us from the curse of the Law, becoming a curse for us— as it is written, "cursed is everyone that hangs on a tree"—so that the blessing of Abraham might come on the gentiles through Jesus Christ, so that we might receive the promise of the Spirit through faith. (Gal. 3.11–14)

Perhaps here too, as Barth suggested, "The one who accomplishes the righteousness which is of the Law, i.e. the merciful will of God expressed in the Law, is . . . the *Messiah* of Israel."[147] Indeed, without some such implicit understanding as this, there is a step missing in Paul's argument, for he goes on immediately to say that Christ "redeemed us from the curse of the Law, becoming curse for us" (referring to the Cross). How could Christ's (accursed) death have redeemed us from the curse of the Law *unless* he was the one who had accomplished perfectly the Law's righteousness?[148]

---

146. See James L. Kugel, *Traditions of the Bible: A Guide to the Bible As It Was at the Start of the Common Era* (Cambridge, Massachusetts: Harvard University Press, 1998), 17–20; see further J. S. Vos, "Die Hermeneutische Antinomie bei Paulus (Galater 3.11–12: Römer 10.5–10)," in *NTS* 38 (1992): 254–270.

147. Barth, *Church Dogmatics* 2.2.§34.3, 245.

148. So Cranfield, *Romans* 2.522, footnote 2; compare also Vos, "Antinomie," 257–58. This is *not*, however, the view of this passage taken by most of the major commentators on Galatians: see for example Burton, *Galatians* 167–68; Bruce, *Galatians* 163; Matera, *Galatians* 124; Martyn, *Galatians* 330–34; also Wright, *Climax of the Covenant* 137–56.

2. Why did Paul insist on appealing to Leviticus 18.5 at all?—and particularly in the letter to the Galatians, where on the face of things it manifestly did not square easily with his thesis? Evidently, he appealed to it because it was quoted against his position by his opponents.[149] Therefore in his defense he was obliged to show that it would fit his position rather than theirs.[150] He did so by declaring that there had indeed been one who had performed the righteousness that the Law required, that Moses' words in Leviticus 18.5 were therefore validated and fulfilled in the Messiah (Christ being the *telos* of the Law, as Paul would later say), and that therefore, for those who were in union with Christ, a new situation had arisen.

This was the view, doubtless refined and developed by further reflection, that Paul then carried forward into his letter to the Romans.

The Final Salvation of All Israel (10.11–11.32)

This saving justice of God is available for *everyone* who has faith and confesses the name of the Lord—and this plainly does not mean just Jews, because **the Scripture says, Everyone *who trusts in him will not be put to shame*** (10.11, alluding to LXX Isa. 28.16). Paul has already cited this passage at 9.33; now he prefaces it with **Everyone** (*pas*) to stress the universality of its application. Again, we can hardly fail to see Paul's personal experience of the risen Messiah involved here, for a central part of that experience was, he believed, that God had been pleased "to reveal his Son in me, that I might proclaim him among the Gentiles" (Gal. 1.16).

For there is no distinction between Jew and Greek; the same Lord is Lord of all and bestows his riches upon all who call upon him. For, *everyone who calls on the name of the Lord will be saved* (10.12–13, citing LXX Joel 3.5 [MT 2.32]). If this were not the case, then either the same Lord would not be Lord of all, or else that Lord would not be faithful to his entire creation. It is, once again, as Paul now sees it, monotheism itself that is stake (compare 3.29–30). It is, moreover (as at 3.29–30), the one God who has acted through his Messiah of whom Paul speaks: in the LXX text of Joel it is clear that "the name of the Lord" (*to onoma kuriou*) refers to the Name of the LORD, the God of Israel; here, in view of the immediately preceding reference to confessing Jesus as Lord in 10.9, it seems that the phrase refers to Jesus.

---

149. There is in our sources, as it happens, some evidence of some Jews who in certain circumstances did not insist on physical circumcision for gentile coverts (Josephus, *Ant.* 20.34–48; Philo, *Special Laws* 1.1–11, 304–6; *Abraham* 92): without exception they are regarded negatively. Philo, for all his allegorizing, himself *insists* on the physical rite. Josephus clearly implies that proposed avoidance of circumcision for a royal convert was political time-serving and goes on to describe the convert's prosperity *after* circumcision as evidence "that those who fix their eyes on God and trust in Him alone do not lose the reward of their piety" (20.48). With all this, we may aptly compare Paul's own words at Galatians 1.10: "Am I trying to please people?" Doubtless "people-pleaser" was precisely what some opponents called him when he declared circumcision unnecessary for gentiles.

In connection with Leviticus 18.5 it may not, incidentally, be entirely irrelevant that later rabbinic tradition on more than one occasion specifically associated the verse with discussions about the possibility of *gentiles* being righteous, sometimes seeming to imply that gentiles must study the whole Torah (see *b. B. Qam.* 38a), and sometimes only "the seven Noachian commandments (see *b. Sanh.* 59a) (see also *Midr. Exod.* 30.22).

150. Vos, "Antinomie," 265–67.

Just how does this come about? **How then are they to call upon one in whom they have not had faith? How have faith in one of whom they have not heard? How hear without one who preaches? And how preach, if they are not sent?** The ability to call on God is itself a gift, mediated through the mission of God's people, which is also a gift: **as it is written, *How timely are the feet of those who publish good news of good things*** (10.14–15, alluding to LXX Isa. 52.7).

But not all have listened to the good news (10.16a).

Indeed, Scripture consistently shows that throughout history many have not accepted the gift of God's revelation:

> *for Isaiah says, Lord, who has had faith in what we have heard?* [10.16, citing LXX Isa.53.1]. **So then, faith is based on hearing, and hearing comes by means of the word of Christ. But I say, Have they not heard? Indeed they have** [*menoun ge*]![151] (10.16b–18a)

Throughout the entire passage 10.14–18a there has run a wordplay based on *pisteuein* ("have faith") and its cognates, and *akouein* ("hear") and its cognates. This is virtually impossible to reproduce in English. Simply marking each point where *pisteuein* or *akouein* or one of their cognates appears, the passage might be rendered as follows:

> How then are they to call upon one in whom they have not had faith [*pisteuein*]? How have faith (*pisteuein*) in one of whom they have not heard [*akouein*]? How hear [*akouein*] without one who preaches? And how preach, if they are not sent? As it is written, *How beautiful are the feet of those who publish good news of good things*.
> But not all have listened [*akouein*] to the good news. For Isaiah says, Lord, *who has had faith* [*pisteuein*] *in what we have heard* [*akouein*]? So then, faith [*pisteuein*] is based on hearing [*akoein*], and hearing [*akouein*] comes by means of the word of Christ. But I say, Have they not heard [*akouein*]? Indeed they have!

An awareness of this wordplay makes much less likely theories that 10.17 has been misplaced, or is illogical,[152] or even that it is a gloss. Granted that it involves repeating briefly what has already been said in 10.14–15, it works very well *rhetorically*. Paul, having made his preliminary point that there have always been those in the world who have failed to accept the divinely ordained messengers (10.16), briefly recapitulates what has been said about faith and hearing, before moving forward to his main point, which will be to include Israel among those who fail to accept the divine messengers:

> —for,
> *Their voice has gone out to all the earth,*
> *and their words to the ends of the world.* (10.18b, citing LXX Psalm 18.5 [MT 19.5]).

Paul begins the final part of his discussion in the most general terms, citing a psalm that speaks of the glorification of God in the natural order—and so calls to mind not only his indictment against the whole of humanity in 1.20–21 but also that sense

---

151. On *menoun ge*, see page 162, footnote 111.
152. So Barrett, *Romans* 205.

of the creation's longing for the restoration of the divine order that he expressed at
8.19. Then, however, he moves to the real thrust of his questioning:

> **But I say, Did Israel not know?** (10.19a)

This time Paul inserts no response of his own; he simply recites the Scriptures that,
in his view, record the indictment of Israel.

> First Moses says,
> > *I will make you jealous of those who are not a nation*
> > *with a foolish nation I will make you angry* (citing LXX Deut. 32.21).
> Then Isaiah says, amazingly,[153]
> > *I have been found by those who did not seek me;*
> > *I have shown myself to those who did not ask for me—*
> but of Israel he says,
> > *All day long I have held out my hands to a disobedient and contrary people.*
> (citing LXX Isa. 65.1–2) (10.19b–21)

Commentators have occasionally noted that Paul's implicit answer to the question
"Did Israel not know?" appears to contradict his earlier assertion that Jewish "zeal
for God" was limited by their "*not* knowing the justice of God" (10.2–3). The contradiction is, however, formal, not substantial. What I learn but do not act upon, I
cannot be said truly to know—with this difference from genuine ignorance, that my
lack of knowledge is now culpable. The ignorance of which Paul speaks in this respect is, of course, only an aspect of that universal ignorance of which he spoke earlier—the universal human ignorance of those who "even though they knew God,
did not glorify him as God or give thanks to him, but they became futile in their
thinking and their senseless heart was darkened. Claiming to be wise, they became
fools" (1.21–23). If we insist on pretending to be stupider than we are, we finish by
being as stupid as we pretend to be.

This brings Paul full circle, back to his original problem. Given that many in
Israel have rejected the gospel, what of Israel now? "**Are we then saying that God
has rejected** [*apōsato*] **his people** [*ton laon autou*]?" (11.1a) For the biblically alert,
however, the very wording of the question implies the answer, for it echoes familiar
passages of the LXX that make clear that this can never be the case: "because the
Lord will not reject [*apōsetai*] his people [*to laon autou*], for the sake of his great name"
(LXX 1 Kingd. 12.22 [MT 1 Sam. 12.22]; compare Psalm 93.14 [MT 94.14])—and
this time Paul does reply on his own account: **By no means!** (11.1b). Paul himself is
evidence that God has not rejected Israel. **For I also am an Israelite, from the seed
of Abraham, from the tribe of Benjamin** (11.1c).

It is probably not so much himself as a Jew who has accepted Jesus the Messiah
that Paul has in mind here (though that is surely relevant), nor even, as Luther suggested, that God has by grace called a follower from one who had opposed Christ
with such special fury that if anyone from Israel were to have been cast off, it would

---

153. Literally, "is so bold as to say." Cranfield is surely correct that Paul's use here of *apotolman*
is more probably intended "to underline the astonishing nature of what is said in Isaiah 65.1a than . . .
to indicate the psychological state of the prophet" (*Romans* 2.540).

surely have been he,[154] though that, too, is surely relevant. Rather, the point is the work that God has given Paul to do as "apostle to the gentiles" (compare 11.13). The very fact that God has called an Israelite for that task is surely the clearest possible evidence that Israel and her children continue to participate actively in the work of Christ and God's purposes for the world.[155] **God has not rejected** [*apōsato*] **his people** [*ton laon autou*] **whom he foreknew** (11.2). The suggestion is denied with the very words in which it was offered, with the addition of the grounds for its rejection, namely that this is the people whom God **foreknew**—to whom God chose to be joined in a pledge of love that God will not break. **Or do you not know what the Scripture says in** the story of Elijah,[156] **how he pleads with God against Israel, Lord, they have killed thy prophets, they have demolished thy altars, and I alone am left, and they seek my life. But what is God's reply to him? I have kept for myself seven thousand who have not bowed the knee to Baal.** (11.2–4, alluding to LXX 3 Kingd. [MT 1 Kings] 19.10, 14). The ancient story of Elijah, who lived in a time of national apostasy, is the clearest possible testimony to the fact that God always keeps some faithful among the people of God.

So, too, **at the present time there is a remnant** [*leimma*][157] **chosen by grace** (11.5)—and no doubt it includes not only Paul, but the good Jewish believers in the Roman congregation. **But** it was grace that brought them all there, not their own achievements, and **if it is by grace, it is no longer on the basis of works; otherwise grace would no longer be grace** (11.6).

What then of the others? What of those who have not been brought, by grace, to believe? **Israel** as a whole has **failed to obtain what it sought**—so much has already been said (9.31), but now that must be qualified—**election obtained it, but the rest were hardened, as it is written,**

God gave them a spirit of stupor,
eyes that should not see and ears that should not hear,
down to this very day. (11.7–8, echoing LXX Deuteronomy 29.4 [MT 29.3]
    and Isaiah 29.10.)

The use of the abstraction **election** (*hē eklogē*) rather than, as we might expect, the more concrete "the elect ones" (*hoi eklektoi*) serves further to emphasize that the existence of the redeemed community is God's action and God's grace, not a human

---

154. "For if God has cast away his people, then above all he would have cast away the apostle Paul who fought against him with all his strength" (Luther, *Romans* 305).

155. "But if [God] had been about to cast off Israel, [God] would hardly have chosen from them him to whom He entrusted all the preaching, and the affairs of the world, and all the mysteries, and the whole economy" (Chrysostom, *Homilies on Romans* 18.3; compare also Barth, *Shorter Commentary* 135).

156. Literally "in Elijah"—the usual way in antiquity of referring to a passage in a larger text by indicating the subject matter. Thus, Thucydides refers to what Homer says, "in the delivery of the sceptre [*en tou skēptrou hama tē*[*i*] *paradosei*]," that is, "in the part of the *Iliad* that describes how Agamemnon's sceptre came to him," namely, *Iliad* 2.101–109 (*Peleponnesian War* 1.9); Philo reminds his readers what Scripture says "in the curses [*en tais arois*]," that is, "in the section of Genesis describing how God cursed those involved in the primal disobedience," namely, Genesis 3.14–19 (Philo, *On Husbandry* 107); and Jesus refers to "the book of Moses, at the bush [*epi tou batou*]," that is, "in the section of Exodus containing the story of the burning bush" (Mark 12.26).

157. See page 164, on 9.27–28.

achievement. At the same time, Deuteronomy and Isaiah are not only echoed but also strengthened so as to bring out very clearly the thought of God's "hardening."

> **And David says,**
> **Let their feast become a snare and trap,**
> **a stumbling block [skandalon] and a retribution for them;**
> **let their eyes be darkened so that they cannot see,**
> **and bend their backs continually [dia pantos)**[158] **(11.9–10).**

Here Paul cites LXX Psalm 68.22–23 (MT 69.22–23), a psalm that in Christian tradition was already associated with the work, and in particular the suffering, of Christ. So understood, this passage, which curses those who have persecuted the righteous sufferer, becomes the most terrible of Paul's indictments against his own people—but precisely the fact that it is by the divine decree that their eyes are darkened is also the grounds for their hope, and the grounds for Paul's answer to his own next question. Just as "election obtained it" makes clear that those who stand do so only by divine grace, being potentially just as "hardened" as the rest, so "the rest were hardened" cannot be divorced from the fact that "hardening" and "stumbling" are not God's last word.

I say, therefore, have they stumbled [eptaisan] so as to fall?[159]

By no means! But through their trespass [paraptōmati] salvation has come to the gentiles, so as to make Israel jealous (11.11). Paul may here be playing on the relationship between *ptaien*, "stumble," and *paraptōma*, literally "false step." In any case, the passage from Deuteronomy that he earlier cited in a negative way—*I will make you jealous of those who are not a nation, with a foolish nation I will make you angry* (citing LXX Deut. 32.21) is now echoed positively. Knowledge of what God is doing among the gentiles will lead Israel to "jealousy" and hence to a softening of heart. The pattern of hardening for the sake of others, which is already a part of the Jewish story—the pattern that Paul discerned in the stories of Esau and Pharaoh— is now being repeated, in Paul's view, in the history of Israel herself. But Paul never said of Esau or Pharaoh or any others that their rejection was *final*, and now he says of the Jews—**Now if their trespass [paraptōma] means riches for the world, and their failure means riches for the gentiles, how much more will their fullness [plērōma] mean! (11.12).** The word *plērōma*, like English **fullness**, can carry a range of implications, from "full measure" in the sense of "that which makes something full or

---

158. Presumably with the implication that those who are bent over cannot see properly. Despite RSV ("for ever"), the correct rendering of *dia pantos* is certainly "continually" or "unceasingly" (so NEB; compare BEP, *costantemente*). It commonly has this meaning in extrabiblical Greek (see LS, διά, and BAGD, διά 2.1a, for citations), and this is its normal sense in the LXX, where it generally translates Hebrew *tamid* (as in the verse cited by Paul here, where it translates *tamid* at MT Ps. 69.23). Not only does "continually" square better than "for ever" with the general usage of *dia pantos*, it also makes better sense. "Continually" speaks of constant unbelief "down to this very day" (11.8) but does not necessarily imply that the unbelief will last for ever. "For ever," by contrast, would make nonsense of the next step in Paul's argument, which will be to state plainly that Israel has *not* in fact fallen irrevocably (Rom. 11.11). See further C. E. B. Cranfield, "The Significance of *Dia Pantos* in Romans 11.10," in SE 2.1 (1964), 546–50.

159. Literally, "they [the Jews in general] have not stumbled [eptaisan] so as to fall, have they?" The metaphorical use of *ptaien* to speak of a moral or spiritual rather than a physical fall follows naturally from the reference to a "stumbling block" in 11.9, and in any case occurs also in the Old Testament: see, for example, LXX Deut. 7.25.

complete"—in which case the "*plērōma* of Israel" here is roughly equivalent to "all Israel" at 11.26—to "full measure" in the sense of "fullness, fulfilment"—in which case the "*plērōma* of Israel" here means something like "Israel when Israel becomes what Israel is really supposed to be."[160] As so often, it is impossible to be certain precisely which of these possibilities Paul intended or even, given his choice of word, whether he wished to distinguish between them.[161]

But I say to you gentiles[162] who have believed—who perhaps think that Jews who have not believed are finally lost—**inasmuch as I am apostle to the gentiles,** this work is never carried out without the Jewish people also in mind, for I **magnify my ministry** (*tēn diakonian mou*)—that divine service to which I was appointed by Christ himself[163]—**in order to make my fellow Jews** [*mou tēn sarka:* literally, "my own flesh"] **jealous, and thus save some of them** (11.13–14). As his expression makes clear, Paul still thinks of himself in human terms as part of the Jewish people (compare 9.1–3), even hoping by his own work to provoke them to envy the gifts given to the gentiles—particularly, perhaps, he has in mind the outpouring of the Spirit, which gentile communities have received in generous measure (Gal. 3.2; 2 Cor.1.22), and which for Paul is a sign of the dawn of the new age. **For if their rejection** of the gospel **means the reconciliation of the world, what will their acceptance** of it **mean, but life from the dead? If the dough offered as first fruits is holy, so is the whole lump; and if the root is holy, so are the branches** (11.15–16).[164] God has from the beginning claimed Israel for his own—it is the consecrated "first fruit" (compare LXX Numbers 15.17–21, especially v.20); it is the foundation, the "root"—and so it remains.

What, then, of gentiles who have believed? **But if some of the branches were broken off, and you** [*su*],[165] **a wild olive shoot, were grafted in their places to share the richness of the olive tree, do not boast over the branches** (11.17–18a). Why ever should shoots from a wild olive be grafted onto a cultivated olive? We learn one reason from Columella, a contemporary of Paul who wrote on agriculture. Speaking of the cultivation of olive tress, he observed,

> It also happens frequently that, though the trees are thriving well, they fail to bear fruit. It is a good plan to bore them . . . and to put tightly into the hole a green slip taken from a wild olive-tree; the result is that the tree, being as it were impregnated with fruitful offspring, becomes more productive. (*On Agriculture* 5.9.16, trans. E. S. Forster and Edward H. Heffner)

160. LS, πλήρωμα; BAGD, πλήρωμα. Similarly at 11.25, "the fullness [*plērōma*] of the gentiles" could mean either "full number of the gentiles" or "the gentiles when they have become the people that God created them to be."

161. On Calvin's understanding of this passage, see additional note FF.

162. On the significance of this expression as evidence of the composition of the Roman church, see further, additional note OO.

163. On "ministry," see further, additional Note EE.

164. Although Paul's general intention at 11.15–16 is clear enough, there are several problems of detailed interpretation: on which see, additional note GG.

165. Paul had used the second person plural at 13a (*humin de . . . tois ethnesin*, "to you gentiles") and will return to it again at 11.25; here, strikingly, he uses the second person singular, perhaps because it makes the appeal more directly personal.

The purpose of the grafting was, then, *to rejuvenate the cultivated olive with the vigor and strength of the wild*. No wonder that gentiles so grafted might be inclined to **boast**! But Paul will have none of it—or, at least, will insist that it be kept firmly in proportion. **If you do boast, remember it is not you that supports the root, but the root that supports you! (11.18b)**

You may say, "Branches were broken off so that I might be grafted in." Very well (11.19–20a). Paul grants the element of truth in this. **But they were broken off because of want of faith** [*apistia*]—their removal certainly had nothing to do with any merit on your part!—**but you stand because of faith** (11.20bc)—which means, in effect, because of God's gift, for as Paul has just implied, no one believes in one of whom they have not heard, and no one hears without a messenger, and there are no messengers unless they are sent (10.14–15). **So do not be proud, but stand in awe.** The grounds of that awe are plain. **For if God did not spare the natural branches, perhaps he will not spare you. Note then the kindness and the severity**[166] **of God: severity toward those who have fallen, but God's kindness toward you, provided you continue in his kindness; otherwise, you too will be cut off** (11.21d–22). Evidently those who begin to talk and act as if they stood on the grounds *of their own justice* are acting exactly like those others who were caused by God to stumble, and will reap the same reward. **And even the others, if they do not persist in their want of faith, will be grafted in, for God has power to graft them in again** (11.23)—and this, rather than indulging feelings of superiority, should be the hope and even the expectation of the gentile church. **For if you have been cut from what is by nature** [*kata phusin*] **a wild olive tree, and grafted, contrary to nature** [*para phusin*], **into a cultivated olive tree, how much more will those natural** (*kata phusin*)[167] **branches be grafted back into their own tree!** (11.24)[168] Human disobedience "cannot confront God with an everlasting fact. God remains free as regards the disobedient, just as he remains free as regards the obedient" (Barth).[169]

For I do not want you to be unaware [*ou gar thelō de humas agnoein*])[170] **of this mystery** [*mustērion*, that is, this divine secret, now revealed to you]),[171] **brothers and sisters, lest you be wise in your own eyes** (echoing LXX Proverbs 3.7, where the

---

166. For God's "kindness [*chrēstotēs*]," compare 2.4 (page 93, fn. 69). "Severity [*apotomia*]" is not an uncommon word; it is found, for example, in a neutral sense, in Dionysius of Halicarnassus, who speaks of Marcius Coriolanus as possessed of "a severity [*apotomia*] that made no concession to reasonableness" (*Roman Antiquities* 8.61.2; compare *De Liberis Educandis* [attributed to Plutarch, *Moralia* 13d]), and in a negative sense, in Philo (*Special Laws* 2.94; *Flaccus* 95); in the New Testament it occurs only here. The cognate adverb *apotomōs* does, however, occur elsewhere in the New Testament. It is used by Paul himself at 2 Cor. 13.10 (see also Titus 1.13). The cognates *apotomos* and *apotomōs* occur several times in Wisd. of Sol. (e.g., 5.20, 22) (see LEHC ἀπότομος, -ος, -ον; also ἀποτόμως).

167. For Paul's use of the phrases *para phusin* and *kata phusin*, compare 1.26; see additional note K.

168. Certainly there is here an element of fantasy in Paul's use of his agricultural metaphor, but his meaning is perfectly clear, and there is nothing improper in such a fantasy, given the context. For a similar use of the same metaphor, we may compare Marcus Aurelius Antoninus, *Meditations* 11.8. As Origen, according to Rufinus's paraphrase, observed, Paul "fits things to his matter rather than his matter to things [*res magis causis quam causas rebus aptavit*]" (Migne, *Patrologiæ* 14.1195).

169. *Shorter Romans* 143.

170. Compare 1.13; see page 63.

171. On "mystery," see additional note HH.

sage speaks of those who rely on their own insights, and do not acknowledge God): **a hardening in part has come upon Israel, until the fullness of the gentiles**[172] **comes in, and so all Israel will be saved, as it is written, Out of *Zion the Deliverer will come, he will banish ungodliness from Jacob. And this will be my covenant with them** (citing LXX Isa. 59.20–21a) **when I take away their sins** (alluding to LXX Isa. 27.9) **(11.25–27).**

The positioning of the Greek phrase here translated **in part** (*apo merous*) is such that Paul's words could mean *either* "a partial hardening has come upon Israel" (so, roughly, KJV ["a blindness in part"], NEB ["a partial blindness"], BEP [*indurimento parziale*])—that is, the "hardening" is not complete because it may only be temporary, in accordance with what Paul has just said about the possibility of the "natural branches" being grafted back (11.23–24); *or* it could mean "a hardening has come upon part of Israel" (so RSV)—that is, *some* "natural branches" have been broken off, but not all, as is also implied by Paul's earlier contrast between the "remnant" and "the election," on the one hand, and "the rest," on the other [11.5–7]). Which Paul meant (or even if at this point he consciously distinguished) is, once again, impossible to say. In either case, he was clearly saying that Israel's **hardening** was limited in its implications and was no ground for gentile "boasting."

Who are **all Israel** who will be saved? In the Scriptures "all Israel" refers to Israel the nation (for example, LXX 3 Kingd. 12.1; Dan. 9.11). Similarly in postbiblical writings when, for example, the *Testament of Benjamin*, asserts that "all Israel will be gathered to the Lord" (*T. Benj.* 10.11), and the rabbis much later declare that "all Israel [*kol-Yisrael*] has a share in the world to come" (*m. Sanh.* 10.1). It is from within this field of discourse that we must hear Paul. He is not saying that every Jew will be saved, and neither, of course, were the rabbis who composed the passage I have just quoted from the Mishnah (nor does Paul's earlier expression "the fullness of the gentiles" say that of gentiles). He *is* speaking of Israel as a whole, of ethnic Israel, and claiming for her a full share in the final redemption.

How then will Israel **be saved**? Paul does not say[173]—any more than he says, on another occasion, how the dead will be raised, or with what body they will come (1 Cor. 15.35). His concern, here as there, is not to issue forecasts, but to speak of the faithfulness and justice of God, who never forgets a promise, even though the promise may not be fulfilled in quite the way we expected. "Israel's redemption follows the acceptance of the gentile world. This . . . characterizes the heart of the mystery disclosed by Paul and marks the specific element in the revelation received by him" (Käsemann).[174] Needless to say, such a promise not only reverses some Jewish expectations but also goes beyond the texts from Isaiah that Paul advances in support of it (11.26–27)—yet not unreasonably so. For when Isaiah spoke of "the deliverer"[175] in 59.20–21, he was evidently speaking of God's faithfulness—of a spirit

---

172. On "fullness [*plērōma*]" see pages 179–80, and footnote 160.

173. On problems that have arisen in connection with this question, see further additional note II.

174. *Romans* 314.

175. For Isaiah, in both MT and LXX, "the deliverer" is evidently God; for Paul, probably if not certainly, "the deliverer" is the Messiah. Cranfield (*Romans* 2.578) quotes a passage from the Babylonian Talmud as evidence that Isaiah 59.20–21 was interpreted of the Messiah by the rabbis (*b. Sanh.* 98a,

that would rest upon Israel and words put into her mouth that would not fail her "from now and for ever" (LXX Isa. 59.21); and Isaiah 27, in speaking of the taking away of sins, made clear that Israel's hope was not based on her own merit but on that same divine justice, which would indeed purge Jacob's iniquity, so that "those who are lost in the land of the Assyrians and those lost in Egypt will come in" (LXX Isa. 27.13).

Hence—**As regards** the proclamation of the **gospel they are** indeed **enemies of God, for your sake; but as regards election they are beloved, for the sake of the fathers** (11.28). Paul never wrote a sentence that he crafted more carefully, and it sums up all that has gone before. "Unbelief" in relation to the gospel has indeed led to the breaking off of branches, and in that sense to enmity with God; but God's faithfulness to God's promise does not allow such enmity to be the last word, and so the latter proposition radically qualifies and relativizes the former. Israel is beloved **for the sake of the fathers**[176]—which means, as Paul made clear in his account of Abraham, not that any of the patriarchs had on his own account "something to boast about" before God (4.2), but simply, again, that God made promises, and God is faithful. **For the gifts and the call of God are irrevocable** (*ametamelēta*, that is, "unregretted," "not to be repented"—the Greek word standing first in the sentence, for emphasis: "Unrepentable are the gifts and the call of God!") (11.29).

> This is the last word which in every present and in respect of every member of this people has to be taken into account in relation to Israel's history from its beginnings into every conceivable or inconceivable future. . . . But this is also the last word even in relation to the present state of the Jews. . . . [T]hey are beloved of God . . . who always loves *first*, who loves even where He is not loved in return. (Barth)[177]

For just as you once were disobedient to God, but now have received mercy through their disobedience, so also these have now been disobedient in respect to the mercy shown to you, so that they also may now [nun] receive mercy (11.30–31).[178]

Now? Paul's choice of word is at first sight surprising—so surprising that manuscripts as early as P46 were omitting it. And yet perhaps it is not so surprising, for already Christ is risen. "What this striking second νυν makes quite impossible for Christian anti-Semitism (he that has ears to hear, let him hear) is the relegation of the Jewish question into the realm of eschatology" (Barth).[179] **For God has consigned**

---

citing Rabbi Jonathan [mid-third century]). The passage is, of course, far too late to be of direct relevance to Paul, but *might* be the residue of earlier traditions known to him.

176. On "the fathers," see additional note AA. Paul's expression reminds us of later rabbinical notions of "the merits of the fathers," and it is possible that he is alluding to such ideas. Again, however, most of the material generally cited in this connection (e.g., commenting on Exod. 14.15, "R. Baanah says: 'Because of the merit of the deed which Abraham their father did, I will divide the sea for them'" (*Mek. Beshallah* 4, trans. Jacob Z. Lauterbach; compare *Exod. Rab.* 21.8) is far too late to be of direct relevance to Romans. See, however, A. Marmorstein, *The Doctrine of Merits in the Old Rabbinical Literature*, revised (New York: Ktav, 1968), 2–46 and passim; also Sanders, *Paul and Palestinian Judaism*, especially 183–98.

177. Barth, *Church Dogmatics* 2.2.303.
178. On problems of translating 11.30–31, see additional note II.
179. Barth, *Church Dogmatics* 2.2.305.

all to disobedience, that he may have mercy upon all (11.32). Once this is admitted, there is nothing left to be debated: there is only praise to be offered.

> *O the depth of the riches and wisdom and knowledge of God!*
> How unsearchable are his judgments,
>   and how inscrutable are his ways!
> For who has known the mind of the Lord,
> *or who has been his counselor?* (citing LXX Isa. 40.13–14)
> or who has given him a gift,
> that he might be repaid?
> For from him and through him and to him are all things.
> To him be glory for ever. Amen. (11.33–36)

Again Paul concludes where humankind, in his view, failed to begin, by giving glory to God.

Additional Note EE. Ministry

Diakonia ("ministry") and its cognates are comparatively rare words in non-Christian Greek, generally used to refer to service or function commissioned and performed on behalf of and for the sake of another—such as, for example, a boy prince waiting on his royal father at a banquet, a priest serving a god, or some other service of the state. As John N. Collins has shown by an extensive survey of the entire literature, ancient and Hellenistic,[180] the words tend to occur in more formal kinds of writing, such as poetry, oratory, and philosophy; especially they occur in passages about the gods, or prayer (for example, Plato, *Statesman* 289–290b; *Test. Abraham* 9.24; Lucian, *Icaromenippus* 20);[181] and sometimes they seem to be used to lend dignity to less formal types of writing, such as romance (for example, Chariton, *Callirhoe* 8.8.5).

The basic sense (despite still often-heard claims to the contrary) is not "waiting at table" but that of "going between," as a representative, agent, or attendant. (Even when the word is used of "waiting at table," this is only a particular example of "go-between"—the table attendant "goes between the diner and the kitchen.")[182] The task involved in itself may (or may not) be menial, but in any case gains nobility because of the one for whom and in whose name it is performed. Thus Hermann W. Beyer offered four examples from Josephus of *diakoneō* in the sense of "to wait at table" (*Antiquities* 6.52, 11.163, 11.166, 11.188): all (although Beyer did not note it) involve "waiting" on a king.[183] Essentially, then, the words speak of "a mode of activity rather than of the status of the person performing the activity. Thus they are not expressing notions of servitude."[184]

Christian usage developed its own particular nuances, but is not therefore essentially different from non-Christian. Collins, near the conclusion of his study, summarizes the position as follows:

---

180. J. N. Collins, *Diakonia: Re-interpreting the Ancient Sources* (New York: Oxford University Press, 1990).
  181. Collins, *Diakonia* 84–85, 98–100.
  182. Collins, *Diakonia* 335.
  183. Hermann W. Beyer, "διακονέω, διακονία, διάκονος," in *TDNT* 2.81–93: see 2.83.
  184. Collins, *Diakonia* 335.

In Christian writings . . . the verb always signifies carrying out a task established either by God, by the terms of an ecclesiastical office, or by the authority of an apostle or by an authority within the community, in all cases with that special connotation of the sacred that characterizes so much of its use in all senses and that of its cognates in non-Christian sources, and which leads Paul to designate both his own apostolic task and the spiritual functions of all Christians as "ministries" or διακονίαι.[185]

In no way, therefore, can the term *diakonia* be confined to philanthropic work, although, of course, philanthropic work may be included in it. So in Mark 10.45 the work of Christ himself, his self-offering as a "ransom for many," is appropriately spoken of as his *diakonia* for God, in distinction from that *diakonia* which, as royal Son of Man, he might have been expected to require of others.

At Romans 11.13 it is then of a commissioned sacred ministry that Paul speaks— specifically, in this instance, "the sacred mission with which he has been charged to venture with the word of the gospel to lands that are not Israel" (1.6–8; compare Gal. 1.12, 1 Cor. 3.5, 2 Cor. 3.6, 6.4, 11.15, 23; also Col. 1.24–27, Eph. 3.8–9, Acts 9.15).[186]

Elsewhere in Romans, immediately following a reference to the "gift" of prophecy, Paul speaks of the "gift" of *diakonia* possessed (presumably) by some in the Roman congregation—possibly speaking of their appointment to leadership (12.7; see pages 198–99); at 13.4 he speaks of the Roman civil administration (though pagan) as, nonetheless, involving sacred appointment, since the administrator (whether he knows it or not) is "God's *diakonos*" toward believers "for good" (see page 206); at 15.7 Christ himself is spoken of as *diakonos*, in a usage that exactly corresponds to that in Mark 10.45 (see page 215); and at 15.25 Paul will speak of taking the gentile collection to Jerusalem as "ministering [*diakonōn*] to the saints"—this, too, being evidently regarded by him as a *diakonia* (15.31) for which he, in fellowship with the gentile churches, has a sacred commission (compare 15.27; 2 Cor. 9.11–14).

Finally, at 16.1, Paul speaks of Phoebe as *diakonos* of the church at Cenchreae, a title whose precise content cannot be asserted with certainty, but which surely spoke of a commissioning for leadership in the congregation (compare Phil. 1.1). In Bengt Holmberg's view, while being a *diakonos* in the early church certainly implies functions of "serving," this "does not exclude the fact that the persons performing them are at the same time leaders of the congregations (and become increasingly so)."[187] In view of Paul's own frequent use of the title in reference to those who proclaimed the gospel, including himself, it seems extraordinarily unlikely that in Phoebe's case alone it should be limited (as seems to be implied by Cranfield) to "practical service of the needy" or "the practical expression of Christian compassion and helpfulness"[188]—although, of course, as with any Christian "ministry" worth the name, that is not to say that such works of philanthropy are excluded.

185. Collins, *Diakonia* 251.

186. Collins, *Diakonia* 211.

187. Bengt Holmberg, *Paul and Power: The Structure of Authority in the Primitive Church as Reflected in the Pauline Epistles*, Coniectanea Biblica, New Testament Series 11 (Lund: CWK Gleerup LiberLäromedal), 1978), 102.

188. Cranfield, *Romans* 2.781.

Additional Note FF. Calvin's Understanding of Romans 9–11

Calvin's view of Romans 9–11 has been, and in some quarters still is, influential. Calvin regarded Pharaoh's "hardening" (9.17) as both "to proclaim the name of God" and also as a mark of "predestination to destruction." He observed that

> Paul's purpose is to make us accept the fact that it has seemed good to God to enlighten some in order that they may be saved, and blind others in order that they may be destroyed.[189]

In line with this, Calvin took the Greek *katērtismena* at 9.22 to mean "appointed and destined for destruction."[190]

Why would God do this? There is no explanation that we could understand, Calvin says, for God's will is incomprehensible to us.

> It is clear that Paul advances no higher cause than the will of God. . . . Conceited men are resentful, because, in admitting that men are chosen or rejected by the secret counsel of God, Paul offers no explanation, as though the Spirit of God were silent for want of reason, and does not rather warn us by his silence—a mystery which our minds do not comprehend, but which we ought to adore with reverence. . . . Let us know, therefore, that God refrains from speaking to us for no other reason than that he sees that his boundless wisdom cannot be comprehended within our small measure.[191]

In Calvin's view, a similar predestination for destruction was being spoken of for the Jews at 11.7–10. Thus, of verse 7, he wrote, "Paul's meaning in regard to the reprobate is that their ruin and condemnation stem from the fact of their having been forsaken by God."[192] But this involved Calvin in a problem when he came to 11.11: "I say, therefore, have they stumbled so as to fall? By no means! But through their trespass salvation has come to the gentiles, so as to make Israel jealous." Calvin himself saw the problem: "Whereas previously he [Paul] connected certain ruin with the blindness of the Jews, he now gives them a hope of rising again. These two ideas are quite contradictory."[193] Calvin's solution was this:

> The apostle is speaking at one time of the whole of the Jewish nation and at another time of individuals. This explains the fact that at times he says that the Jews have been banished from the kingdom of God, cut off from the tree, and cast into headlong destruction by the judgment of God, while on other occasions he denies that they have fallen from grace.[194]

It must be said plainly that Paul's text gives no warrant at all for the distinction that Calvin here makes. The notion—required by Calvin's view—that a "they" is being referred to in Romans 11.8–9 who is different from the "they" in 11.11 is rhetorically quite impossible—indeed, absurd. Once that is admitted, however, it must

189. Calvin, *Romans* 206, 207.
190. Calvin, *Romans* 211.
191. Calvin, *Romans* 208–9.
192. Calvin, *Romans* 243.
193. Calvin, *Romans* 246.
194. Calvin, *Romans* 245–46.

also be admitted that Paul evidently did *not*, then, think that what he had spoken of in verses 8–9 was the Jews' "certain ruin," and once *that* is admitted, Calvin's entire understanding of the section unravels.

As Karl Barth (himself a sympathetic critic of Calvin, but still a critic) wrote of Romans 11,

> The question answered in v.11, like that of v.1, had perhaps actually been raised by Gentile Christians in the Pauline Churches: "Have they stumbled that they should fall?" Is it according to God's design and intention that they have been hardened and thus made to fall—so that they should finally be excluded from that "obtaining" (v.7) . . . ? If Paul's answer is again: μὴ γένοιτο, this means that a conceptual possibility is repudiated by him as not merely inadmissible in substance and in logic, but absolutely absurd and even blasphemous. A positive answer to this question is something not even remotely intended by him in the preceding passage.[195]

Additional Note GG. Problems of Interpretation in Romans 11.15–16

> **For if their rejection** of the gospel **means the reconciliation of the world, what will their acceptance of it mean, but life from the dead? If the dough offered as first fruits is holy, so is the whole lump; and if the root is holy, so are the branches.** (11.15–16)

Although the general intention of these verses is, in context, probably clear enough, a number of detailed problems of interpretation continue to trouble critics. Of these the most commonly identified are as follows:

1. Some commentators understand **their rejection** (and consequently **their acceptance**) objectively, and take it to refer to God's (temporary) rejection (and future acceptance) of Israel.[196] Paul's entire argument seems, however, to suggest that he intended the **their** subjectively. It is not "God's rejection of Israel" that has led to the reconciliation of the world but, as Paul has been at pains to point out, Israel's (for the present) rejection of the gospel, which has been providentially used by God as a means of extending the knowledge of God to the gentiles.[197]

2. Exactly what Paul intended to signify by **life from the dead** (*zōe ek nekrōn*) has been, and remains, disputed. For Origen, according to Rufinus (Migne, *Patrologiæ* 14.1190–91), and for many later commentators, it is a reference to the general resurrection at the end of history, which will be preceded by the conversion of the Jews. "Thus the conversion of Israel is for the apostle the last act of salvation history. . . . Gentile-Christians, too, must take into account the eschatological significance of Israel" (Käsemann).[198] On the other hand, when Paul speaks of the general resurrection, his usual phrase is *anastasis nekrōn*, "resurrection of the dead" (6.5; compare 1 Cor. 15.12, 13, 21, 42). So Calvin regarded Paul's expression as figurative: "We understand resurrection here to mean the act by which we are transferred from the

195. Barth, *Church Dogmatics*, 2. 2. §34.4, 278.
196. So Cranfield, *Romans* 2.562; Moo, *Romans* 693–94.
197. So Fitzmyer, *Romans* 612.
198. Käsemann, *Romans* 307.

kingdom of death to the kingdom of life."[199] Still others, notably Leenhardt, refer the image to the Jewish people, whose acceptance of the gospel will mean for them a movement from death to life, "the reawakening of the people of the promise, and its spiritual resurrection by the inspiration of the Holy Spirit."[200] There is no way to certainty on the question.

3. In view of the context, the association of the two metaphors in 11.16 (**the dough as first fruit** (*hē aparchē*) . . . **the root** and **the branches**) with the foundation of Israel appears the most likely intention: God claimed Israel through the patriarchs (compare 11.28) and at Sinai, and will not relax that claim. That is how I have taken them in my interpretation (see page 180).

Many among the Church fathers, however, associated the **first fruit** with Jesus Christ (for example, Theodore of Mopsuetstia *In Epistolam Pauli ad Romanos* [Migne, *Patrologiae* 66.857/8]), and that remains a possibility. In support of it is the fact that Paul actually calls Christ *haparchē* at 1 Corinthians 15.20. Still others have referred the double metaphor to the Jews who had become followers of Jesus. This is supported by the fact that Paul elsewhere calls the first converts of a particular area *haparchē* (for example, Rom. 16.5; 1 Cor.16.15). Barth suggested that the double metaphor might even have been intended to apply to all three.[201] All these suggestions remain possibilities.

On the other hand, the parallelism between the two parts of the verse seems to make very unlikely Cranfield's suggestion that the two metaphors refer to different things ("the first fruits" to Jewish Christians, "the root" to the Patriarchs).[202] That parallelism would be slightly, but not fatally, weakened if one accepted P46's and others' omission of *ei*, "if" before *hē riza*, "the root," but it is generally conceded that that omission is not likely to be original.[203]

Additional Note HH. The Mystery

The word *mustērion* in Hellenistic religion characteristically speaks of a divine secret that is revealed to the initiate. The concept is described in the Homeric *Hymn to Demeter* (which, however, uses the synonym *orgia* rather than *mustēria*): the goddess Demeter went

> to kings who administer law, . . . and revealed the conduct of her rites and taught her secret worship [*orgia*] not to be transgressed, nor pried into, nor divulged. For great awe of the gods stops the voice. Blessed is the mortal on earth who has seen these rites, but the uninitiate who has no share in them never has the same lot once dead in the dreary darkness. (*Hymn to Demeter* 474–82, trans. Helene P. Foley, altered)

For the word itself, and a writer closer in time to Paul, we turn to Lucian, whose hero Demonax, in

---

199. Calvin, *Romans* 248.
200. Leenhardt, *Romans* 284–85.
201. Barth, *CD* 2.2.285.
202. Cranfield, *Romans* 2.564.
203. See, e.g., Nestle-Aland 27.

the matter of the mysteries [*to tōn mustēriōn*], . . . said that he had never joined them because if the mysteries [*ta mustēria*] were bad, he would not hold his tongue before the uninitiate but would turn them away from the cult, while if they were good, he would reveal them to everybody out of his love for humanity. (*Demonax* 11)

In the LXX of Daniel, *mustērion* translates Aramaic *raz*, and here, too, refers to the hidden purpose of the God of Israel, revealed to God's faithful servant (so, evidently, LXX Dan. 2.18–23, 27–30, 47). With this we may well compare the use of *raz* in the Dead Sea Scrolls, where it, too, denotes God's secret, once hidden, now revealed to the faithful: see *Habbakuk Pesher* (*Commentary on Habbakuk*) 1 QpHab 7.5–6, 13–14.

In the Pauline corpus *mustērion* is almost a technical term (Rom. 11.25, 16.25; 1 Cor. 2.1 [probably], 7, 4.1, 13.2, 14.2, 15.51; compare Eph. 1.9, 3.3, 4.9, 5.32, 6.19; Col. 1.26, 27, 2.2, 4.3; 2 Thess. 2.7; 1 Tim. 3.9, 16). For Paul, too, the *mustērion* is a divine secret that has been hidden and is now revealed to God's servants.

Additional Note II. The Salvation of All Israel

And so all Israel will be saved . . . (Romans 11.26).

How will all Israel be saved? Paul does not say. The absence of explicit reference to Jesus Christ in this section (he was last mentioned at 10.9) has led some commentators to argue that Paul envisages Israel's "salvation" being brought about through the power of God by a "special path" (*Sonderweg*),[204] apart from prior conversion to Jesus the Messiah. According to this view, the covenant referred to by Paul at 11.27 is the Mosaic covenant between God and Israel (2 Sam. 23.5), on the basis of which God will save Israel, to be distinguished from the "new covenant" of Jeremiah 31.33, which comes to fruition in Jesus, and on the basis of which God will save the gentiles. "As Paul says," Krister Stendahl writes, "the Jews have the *huiothesia*—the status of children. They do not need to come to Christ in order to be children of God. Because they have the *huiothesia*, they live in the world as a light."[205] According to John Gager, when Paul said, "God is one, and he will justify the circumcised by faith, and the uncircumcised through faith" (3.30), he "uses faith here

---

204. In this connection, the word is usually associated with, and is certainly used by, Franz Mussner: "The *parousia* Christ saves all Israel without a preceding conversion of Jews to the gospel. God saves Israel by a 'special path' which likewise rests upon the principle of grace (*sola gratia*) and thereby maintains the divinity of God, his 'choice,' his 'call,'. . . . God saves all Israel through Christ (*solus Christus*) and, indeed, 'through grace alone' and through 'faith alone' without the works of the Law, since Israel's *emunah* turns now totally toward the Christ who comes again. Thus in the 'special path' of the saving of all Israel, the Pauline doctrine of justification remains completely effective." (*Tractate on the Jews: The Significance of Judaism for Christian Faith*, trans. Leonard Swidler [London: SPCK; Philadelphia: Fortress Press, 1984], 34).

205. Krister Stendahl, *Final Account: Paul's Letter to the Romans* (Minneapolis: Fortress Press, 1995), 42; he pursues the same line of thought in "Qumran and Supersessionism—and the Road Not Taken," *PSB* 19.2 (1998): 134–42. Compare, with changes of emphasis, John G. Gager, *The Origins of Anti-Semitism: Attitudes Toward Judaism in Pagan and Christian Antiquity* (Oxford: Oxford University Press, 1983), 260–64; Lloyd Gaston, *Paul and the Torah* (Vancouver: University of British Columbia Press, 1987), 92–99, 147–50.

not as the equivalent of faith in Christ but as a designation of the proper response to God's righteousness, whether for Israel in the Torah or for Gentiles in Christ."[206]

Other commentators totally reject such a view of Paul's intentions. These ideas are, they say, doubtless well intentioned as regards Jewish-Christian dialogue; as exegesis of Paul, they are utterly improbable. Paul has just said that it is Jewish *unbelief* (*apistia*) that has led to some of Israel's branches being cut out from the basic stock, and he has further said that their abandoning this unbelief will lead to their being grafted back (11.20, 23). This accords with his earlier observation that "God is one, and he will justify the circumcised by faith, and the uncircumcised through faith" (3.30). To suggest, however, that Paul has two notions of what constitutes this saving faith, one brought about by God apart from Christ for Jews, and one through Christ for Gentiles and believing Jews, hardly accords with the earlier and fundamental claim with which he preceded all this, namely, that "the gospel" (that is, "the gospel of his Son" [1.9]) "is the power of God for salvation to *everyone* who has faith, to the Jew first, and also to the Greek" (1.16).[207]

How should we respond to this debate? As a first move, I think we have to say that those who reject the "two covenant" position are basically correct: that position does make nonsense of much of Paul's earlier argument.

As a second move, however, I think we need to admit that the "two covenanters" do make some points. Paul *does* say "all Israel will be saved" and does not, actually, speak of their coming to faith in Christ—at least, he does not do so very clearly, and in the relevant passage (see Romans 11.25–36) does not mention Jesus at all, which is unusual for him. Of course, we can always claim that the Jews' coming to faith in Christ is what Paul actually *meant* at 11.25–36, for certainly that is a perfectly possible way of understanding the passage, and, in view of the rest of Paul's theology, one may reasonably argue, it is the *necessary* way. I have myself presented an exegesis of these particular verses, earlier, that allows for something like this general understanding. I did that, because it seemed necessary to do so if I were to be faithful to Paul's text. At the same time, however, in exegeting those particular verses, I *did not spell out this understanding explicitly*. Why? Because Paul himself does not do so, and therefore it also seemed necessary not to be explicit, if I were to be faithful to what he wrote.

So the question remains: If Paul *did* mean by 11.25–26 that (as Moo puts it) "the end-time conversion of a large number of Jews will therefore come about only through their faith in the gospel of Jesus the Messiah,"[208] why did he not say so? This was not, after all, a subject on which he was usually reticent!

One way out of this dilemma—which several critics have taken recently—is to bite the bullet and say Paul had involved himself in a contradiction. "Paul's solution," E. P. Sanders writes,

> to the problem posed by Israel is a somewhat desperate expedient. Does he really think that jealousy will succeed where Peter failed? How can the promise be irre-

---

206. Gager, *Origins of Anti-Semitism* 262.
207. So, for example, Fitzmyer, *Romans* 620; Moo, *Romans* 725–26.
208. Moo, *Romans* 726.

vocable if it is conditional on a requirement which most Jews reject? . . . What is interesting is how far Paul was from denying anything that he held deeply, even when he could not maintain all his convictions at once without both anguish and finally a lack of logic . . . [as at] Romans 9–11, where his Jewish and his Christian convictions come into conflict in his own mind. Once we see past the exegetical difficulties to the troubles of the man who wrote them, a moving picture arises, one that is partly poignant and partly stirring. We see Paul the Jew and Paul the apostle of Christ, convinced that God's will is that he be both at once, and therefore never questioning their compatibility, but sometimes having more than a little difficulty reconciling his native convictions with those which he had received by revelation. . . . He knew that righteousness is only by faith in Christ, but still he tried repeatedly to find a place for the Law in God's plan . . . [and] desperately sought a formula that would keep God's promises to Israel intact, while insisting on faith in Jesus Christ.[209]

That is a moving picture—but is it true? Sanders's portrait is of a Paul profoundly concerned with the problem of Judaism, "desperately seeking a formula that would keep God's promises to Israel intact"—and that, I think, is precisely the problem with it. *Of course* Paul was deeply concerned for his people—he says so (Romans 9.1–3), in language (as we noted above) that echoes the pentateuchal narratives of Moses, who was also concerned for his people. But because he was a faithful Jew (and one like Moses—see Exodus 32.11–12), the heart of that concern was for the *honor of Israel's God*. Paul gives the issue away as soon as he starts to discuss it: **It is not**, he asserts, **as though the word of God has failed** (9.6).

God's honor involves God's people because they are the people to whom God had made promises. Like Moses (Exodus 32.13), Paul knows that, **for the sake of the fathers**, God cannot finally reject Israel—not because the patriarchs were such marvelous people but because God made promises to them (11.28; compare Exodus 32.13). How, then, does Paul defend God's honor? Like any good witness, he tells the story. There were, he points out, elections and rejections in the past, and times when God hardened hearts, as in the case of the gentile Pharaoh—and always it was for the sake of Israel (chapter 9, especially 9.17, 22–26). Now Israel in her turn has been disobedient (9.27—10.21). But what of it? Israel is still beloved (11.1–24), and her **hardening in part** (11.25) is merely for the sake of the gentiles, until their **fullness** has come in, and then, of course, **all Israel will be saved**, as God promised (11.25–32). Here there are no contradictions, there is simply a story and the promise of a happy ending.

I confess I find it very hard indeed to believe that Paul could or would have imagined the end of that particular story as having, for anyone or anything in creation, absolutely nothing to do with Jesus Christ—but even granted that, the question would still remain, just *how* would it all come about? Here, pace "two covenanters" and "one covenanters" alike, Paul offers no forecasts, and no explanations. In particular, we may note, he offers no forecasts of the Christians finally "winning."

---

209. E. P. Sanders, *Paul, the Law, and the Jewish People* (Philadelphia: Fortress Press, 1983), 199. Similarly, Heiki Räisänen: Paul "contradicts himself when discussing . . . the problem of Israel's reluctance to accept the gospel" (*Paul and the Law* 264).

According to Paul, only God will win, and the rest of us will be the better for it. **For God has consigned all to disobedience, that he may have mercy upon all** (11.32).

Why are there no explanations? How could there be? Perhaps we can (and need) say no more than that one does not, if one has any sense, "explain" love stories—one tells them. Perhaps above all one cannot explain the story of a divine love so prejudiced in humanity's favor that it will reconcile us to itself even at the cost of the cross. Therefore, as with the cross itself, so in the matter of all Israel's salvation, Paul offered no explanations. He only told what he knew of the story—namely, that, as Charles Wesley was to put it centuries later,

> 'Tis mercy all, immense and free,
> For O, my God, it found out me.

"Two covenant" and "one covenant" positions appear to have one striking feature in common: both imagine a Paul who presumed to mount God's throne and hear the divine counsels, whereas the evidence—and particularly Romans 11.26–36—suggests that the real Paul was content to fix his eyes on what he saw as the astonishing mercy of the cross, to remember the promises and the faithfulness of God, and to declare God's unfathomable and inexhaustible generosity.

"There is," wrote Lady Julian of Norwich,

> a deed which the Blessed Trinity will perform on the last day, as I see it, and what the deed will be and how it will be performed is unknown to every creature who is inferior to Christ, and it will be until the deed is done. . . . This is the great deed ordained by our Lord God from without beginning, treasured and hidden in his blessed breast, known only to himself, through which deed he will make all things well. For just as the Blessed Trinity created all things from nothing, just so will the same Blessed Trinity make everything well which is not well.

Then, for a moment, as Julian thought again of the evils of the world, and even of the teachings of the church—what she had been taught, for example, about those who died outside the faith of the church—it seemed to her

> impossible that every kind of thing could be well, as our Lord revealed at this time. And to this I had no other answer as a revelation from our Lord except this, What is impossible to you is not impossible to me. I shall preserve my word in everything, and I shall make everything well. (*Showings* [long text] 32, trans. Edmund Colledge, O.S.A, and James Walsh, S.J.)[210]

So, I believe, with Paul.

It is ironic that in order to express my understanding of Paul I have felt constrained at this point to quote not biblical critics, but saints. Ironic, but not, perhaps, surprising. Certainly Lady Julian and Charles Wesley were both closer in spirit and understanding than most of us to the one who concluded,

> **O the depth of the riches and wisdom and knowledge of God!**
> **How unsearchable are his judgments,**
> **and how inscrutable are his ways!**

---

210. Edmund Colledge, O.S.A., and James Walsh, S.J. (eds. and trans.), *Julian of Norwich: Showings* (New York: Paulist Press, 1978), 232–33.

For who has known the mind of the Lord,
or who has been his counselor?
or who has given him a gift,
that he might be repaid?
For from him and through him and to him are all things.
To him be glory for ever. Amen. (Rom. 11.33–36)

Additional Note JJ. On Problems of Translating 11.30–31

I have presented in my exegesis what I think is the most obvious way to understand
11.30–31, which might, literally, be rendered as,

> For just as you once were disobedient to God,
> but now you have received mercy in [*dative*] their disobedience,
> so also these now have been disobedient in [*dative*] your mercy,
> so that they also may now receive mercy.

The two parallel datives (both rendered by "in" in the literal translation) are evidently
to be understood in different senses, the first (*tē[i] toutōn apeitheia[i]*) as causal, and the
second (*tō[i] humeterō[i] eleei*) as a dative of advantage—a shift, however, that Greek
speakers would have made quite easily, experiencing simply a natural play on two
possible senses of the construction. There is also, incidentally, a shift in sense between
the two parallel possessives—"their disobedience" and "your mercy"—the former
being evidently subjective ("the disobedience that they indulged in") and the latter
objective ("the mercy that you have received"). It is, however, much easier for us to
feel comfortable with this particular shift, since our own English possessives are capable of the same ambiguity. The alternative way of translating 11.30–31, frequently
suggested, is to regard the second dative as part of the purpose clause, translating "so
that, by the mercy shown to you, they also now may receive mercy" (so RSV). This,
while grammatically just possible (see LS *hina*; BDF §477.1), is manifestly somewhat
strained (Lagrange called it "*construction bizarre*"!)[211]—not least because, while it now
understands the two datives as identical in sense, it does so at the expense of ignoring
the evident overall parallel construction of the entire sentence. To judge by the arguments advanced for it, and as is often the case when commentators attempt to persuade us to accept strained translations, this suggestion is really only an attempt to
make what seems to the commentators to be better sense—in this particular case, to
make 11.30–31 consistent with other parts of 11. Once, however, the force of the second dative is correctly understood, 11.30–31 appears in any case to be perfectly consistent with the rest of 11—notably 11.11–26.

---

211. Lagrange, *Romains* 287.

6

Exhortation (12.1–15.13):

An Invitation to the Christian Life

Grounds for the Exhortation: The Proper Response
to God's Mercies (12.1–2)

Paul has presented a dissuasive, arguing *against* dependence on anything save God's grace and God's justice, manifested in the cross of Jesus Christ, and witnessed to in the Law. In particular, he has argued against dependence on the Law itself. He has then presented a demonstration, arguing *for* what he has called "my gospel," and in so doing he has defended it at length against two suggestions that have been raised— first, that his gospel militated against the moral life, and second, that it implied God was no longer faithful to the promises.

Now Paul must move to the climax and purpose of his protreptic: the exhortation, or *parainesis*. The good news of God's grace and justice require a response. If Paul's addressees accept the gospel he proclaims, then it is required that they affirm not only in word but also in deed the communal values that flow from it.

> **I appeal to you therefore, brothers** and sisters, **by the compassion of God, to present your bodies as a sacrifice, living, holy, and acceptable to God, which is your reasonable worship.** (12.1)

I appeal to you (*parakalō . . . humas*) is the normal expression with which to introduce *parainesis*, and signals what is to come. **Therefore** (*oun*) links the *parainesis* to what has gone before. **By the compassion of God** (*dia tōn oiktirmōn theou*) indicates the grounds on which it is so linked. This is the only occasion in Romans where Paul uses the word *oiktirmos*.[1] The form is plural and, in one less soaked than he in the rhetoric of the LXX, it would be natural to render it into English by a translation in the plural, such as the KJV's and RSV's "by the mercies of God." The plural of *oiktirmos* is, however, the normal way in which the LXX renders Hebrew *raḥămîm*, which though plural in form, is *singular* in implication,[2] and so Paul's intention here,

---

1. Elsewhere Paul uses it twice, at 2 Corinthians 1.3, and Philippians 2.1.

2. BDB, רַחֲמִים; GKC §145h. See further H. J. Stoebe, "רחם, *rḥm*, pi. to have mercy," in *TLOT* 3.1225–30, especially 1226–27.

too, is probably better rendered by the singular. It is not various manifestations of the divine compassion but the divine **compassion** itself—all that has earlier been referred to by his talk of God's grace (*charis*) and God's mercy (*eleos*)—of which Paul now speaks: it is the divine compassion toward humankind, revealed and effected in the person of Jesus Christ.[3]

Paul's exhortation is **to present your bodies**—that is, your total persons, your-selves[4]—**as a sacrifice**—which is to say, as no longer your own, but God's. Such a sacrifice is **alive**, since it is the offering of one who now walks in "newness of life" in union with Jesus Christ (6.4), **holy**, since it is the offering of one who belongs to God, **and acceptable to God**, since it is what God desires. This is **your rational[5] worship**[6]—that is, not only the worship of God that is appropriate to a rational, reasonable being but also the only form of worship that is rational as a response to God's **compassion**.

No doubt, as Cranfield observes, such an offering does find an appropriate focus in the cult,[7] and that Paul took seriously the cult and its place in the church's life is evident from what he said about it on other occasions (for example, 1 Cor. 11.2–34, 14.26–40); that, nevertheless, is not the force of the present passage. What is at issue here is that, just as for the Hebrew prophets no worship was real apart from obedience of life (Isa. 1.11–17; Hos. 6.6; Amos 5.21–24), so for Paul, the mark of **rational worship** will be life in its every aspect lived as by one who belongs to God, and is, like Paul himself, "the slave of Jesus Christ" (1.1).

> **And do not be conformed** [*mē syschēmatizesthe*] **to this age, but be transformed** [*metamorphousthe*] **by the renewing of the mind** (12.2a).

Chrysostom here saw a real distinction between the two verbs. "Paul does not say, 'change the fashion [*metaschēmatizou*]' but 'be transformed [*metamorphou*]' to show that the world's ways are a fashion [*schēma*], but virtue's not a fashion, but a kind of real form [*morphē*], with a natural nobility of its own" (*Homilies on Romans* 20.2). Chrysostom's opinion may have been right, and the older commentators tended to follow him. So Sanday and Headlam: "Do not adopt the external and fleeting fash-ion of the world, but be ye transformed in your inmost nature."[8] More recent com-mentators have, however, tended to doubt it. Thus Cranfield follows J. Behm, who

---

3. So the Vg at 12.1 correctly rendered dia *tōn oiktirmōn theou* by the Latin *per misericordiam dei*; similarly BEP, *della misericordia*. (At 2 Cor. 1.3 and Phil 2.1 Paul's plural usage seems also to be influ-enced by the LXX, and there, too, singular "compassion" is probably the better translation.)

4. On "body," see additional note Z.

5. *Logikos* ("rational") had long been a term common in philosophical discourse. Stoics gener-ally emphasized that a human being was a *zōn logikon* ("a rational being") (thus Epictetus, *Discourses* 2.9.2); and Epictetus directly connected this with worship: "For what else can a lame old man as I am do but sing the praise of God? If, indeed, I were a nightingale, I would act the part of a nightingale: if a swan, the part of a swan. But, since I am a rational [*logikos*] creature, it is my duty to praise God" (*Discourses* 1.16.20, trans. Elizabeth Carter, rev. Robin Hard). The word *logikos* does not occur in the LXX, but of course the notion of a worship that is inseparable from inward disposition is familiar enough: see, e.g., LXX Ps. 50.18–29 (MT Ps. 51.18b–19).

6. On worship (*latreia*), see additional note AA.

7. Cranfield, *Romans* 2.601–5.

8. Sanday and Headlam, *Romans* 353.

concluded after comparing *morphē* with its synonyms, including *schēma*, that "in view of the interchangeable use, the nuances . . . are not enough to establish firm boundaries between the terms."[9]

Be that as it may, what is, perhaps, more important is that the present tense of both verbs indicates an ongoing process, which in the one case must be stopped, and in the other must be allowed to continue. Moreover, the passive mood of both verbs indicates, on the one hand, that those who do not seek to close themselves to the influence of **this age** are, in fact, taken over—losing thereby that self-control (*egkrateia*) which is the mark of the properly human—and, on the other, that those who seek the path indicated by Paul, though not presuming to achieve perfection on their own account, are nevertheless thereby **transformed by the renewing of the mind** [*tou noos*]. They are, in other words, cleansed and restored from that "reprobate mind [*adokimos nous*]" (1.28), at the mercy of the "desires of their hearts" (1.24), which was their lot when they did not see fit to acknowledge God (1.28). The end of this will be **so that** now they may **make trial** [*dokimazein*] **of the will of God— what is good, and acceptable, and perfect** (12.2). The verb *dokimazein* means both "to assay, test, make trial of" and (hence) "to approve."[10] Here the former sense is probably uppermost.

The sum of Paul's opening instruction is, then, something that, for all it has been transformed in Christ, he had perhaps in some sense already learned when he was still a Pharisee: that God's call was so to live in the ordinary events of this world as if thereby offering worship to God. Thereby believers would work out in the world what had already taken place in them through Christ.[11] As Paul said to the Philippians: "[W]ork out your own salvation with fear and trembling, for God is at work in you, both to will and to work for his good pleasure" (Phil. 2.12b–13).

Some Basic Principles for Life in the Church (12.3–13)

For by the grace given to me I say to each one among you . . .

Paul begins the substance of his exhortation solemnly, **I say to you**, and again cites the grounds upon which he gives it, but this time in such a way—**by the grace given to me**—as to stress that he himself is one who depends upon the compassionate goodwill of his sovereign: "[F]or I am the least of the apostles, who am not worthy to be called 'apostle,' because I persecuted the church of God" (1 Cor. 15.9). At the same time, his use of the expression **each one** (*hekastos*) makes the address personal, though addressed to all.

What Paul advises in the first instance is *sōphrosunē*, "moderation," "reasonableness"—the classic Hellenistic virtue.[12] **I say to you**, he says, playing on words,[13] **not**

---

9. J. Behm, "μορφή, μορφόω, μόρφωσις, μεταμορφόω," in TDNT 4.744; Cranfield, *Romans* 2.605–7.

10. LS, δοκιμάζω, BAGD, δοκιμάζω 1,2a,b.

11. See further H. D. Betz, "The Foundation of Christian Ethics According to Romans 12:1–2," in *Witness and Existence: Essays in Honour of Schubert M. Ogden*, ed. P. E. Devenish and G. L. Goodwin (Chicago: University of Chicago Press, 1989), 55–72.

12. On "moderation," see additional note KK.

13. See further BDF §488.1b.

to think of yourself more highly [*huperphronein*] than you ought to think [*phronein*], but to think [*phronein*] with moderate thinking [*eis to sōphronein*], as God has as-signed to each the measure of faith (12.3).

The adverbial clause here translated **as God has assigned to each the measure of faith** is understandably described by Byrne as "cryptic,"[14] and it is perhaps impos-sible to be sure exactly what Paul intended by it. The most obvious problems are (1) that it is evidently elliptical, the dative **to each** (*hekastō[i]*) standing for something like *hekastos hōs autō[i] ho theos* ("each [of you] as God has assigned to him or her"); (2) that **measure** (*metron*), in Greek as in English, can mean *either* "standard" or "criterion" (by which something is measured), or "amount" or "proportion" (the result of measurement); (3) that **faith** (*pistis*) has, as we have seen, a range of meaning (see page 62, and footnotes 16 and 17); and (4) that it is not clear whether the genitive phrase **measure of faith** (*metron pisteōs*) is intended subjectively (that is, perhaps something like "faith's criterion") or objectively (that is, perhaps something like "the amount of faith"). Rudolf Bultmann made a connection between 12.3 and 12.6, and saw the intended reference in 12.3 as "not merely to stages or grades of πίστις, but to differences conditioned by individual gifts and situations."[15] This is possible; but I think it more likely that by *pistis* here Paul is loosely referring to what he has asserted from the beginning to be of the essence of the gospel—that it is bound up with God's faithfulness toward us setting us free for faithfulness in response. To take *that* seriously as one's "standard" or **measure**—considering the level of God's faith-fulness in Christ toward each of us, and the level of faithfulness to which each of us is thereby invited (so 12.1)—is surely among the best antidotes anyone could have against the temptation to think of oneself **more highly** than one **ought to think**.

Paul continues with an image that he apparently liked, for he uses it elsewhere (see 1 Cor. 6.15, 12.12–27), and that would certainly have been familiar to the more literate among his audience, since it was something of a topos among other Greco-Roman writers—that is, the metaphor of the community as a body.[16] For Paul, of course, the community of faith is something more than simply *a* body, for it is "the body of Christ" (1 Cor. 12.27).

> **For as in one body we have many members, and all the members do not have the same function, so we, though many, are one body in Christ, and individually, members one of another, having then[17] gifts that differ according to the grace given us.** (12.4–6a)

Paul has moved in a straight line from his declaration of the divine compassion to the community that acknowledges its dependence on that compassion—the church. The believers are **members one of another** (12.5): as they are united with each other "in Christ," so their being cannot properly be understood save in terms

14. Byrne, *Romans* 371.

15. Rudolf Bultmann, "πιστεύω, πίστις, πιστος, κτλ.," in *TDNT* 6.219.

16. On this sense of "body," see additional note Z.

17. The participle phrase "having then [*echontes de*]" (12.6) is treated as dependent upon "we are [*esmen*]" in 12.5: so KJV, BEP. The alternative (suggested perhaps by the presence of the particle *de*) is to punctuate after 12.5 and assume that Paul expects us to supply a verb, such as RV, RSV "let us use them."

of their relationship to the whole body.[18] All their particular **gifts** (charismata) are rooted in the one gift that finally matters, God's **grace** (*charis*) **given to** them in Jesus Christ (12.6).[19] Paul regards all such gifts (1) as mediated by the Holy Spirit (so much so that on another occasion he can use simply the adjective *pneumatikos* ("spiritual") to speak of them (1 Cor. 14.1), (2) as particular ways in which individual Christians share in God's grace (*charis*)—which grace is, of course, finally and essentially the same for all, and (3) *as given by God to individual members for the benefit of all*. There are, as Paul observed on another occasion, "varieties of gifts," but it is always "the same Spirit" who gives them, and they are always "for the common good" (1 Cor. 14.4, 7).

It was perhaps with a certain twinkle in the eye that Helmut Koester recently declared that "early Christian ethics is not at all interested in the moral individual"[20] (there is, after all, *some* connection between individual and communal morality), but twinkle in the eye or not, such a declaration is evidently a good deal nearer the truth than those still-too-commonly heard descriptions of a Paul who teaches justification by faith in such a way that it leads simply to a personal sense of forgiveness, a personal ethics, and a personal piety. For Paul, proper response to the gospel is always ecclesial. He never asks whether a particular behavior or the exercise of a particular gift will assist one's *own* growth or spirituality. His question is invariably, "Will it build up the community?" (see 1 Corinthians, throughout)

> Of what **gifts**, then, does he speak here?
> **if prophecy, according to the analogy of faith;** (12.6b)

Here, the intended sense of the adverbial clause **according to the analogy of faith** is a problem. Chrysostom understood Paul to be saying that the ability to prophesy was proportionate to the capacity of the prophet's own faith: "For since he has sufficiently comforted them, [Paul] wishes also to make them eager to contend, and the more diligent to work, showing that they themselves give the grounds whereby they receive more, or less" (*Homilies in Romans* 21.1). Bultmann, as I have noted, believed that the reference was to differences conditioned by individual gifts and situations, and connected 12.6 with 12.3.[21] Accepting the connection with 12.3, I would suggest that the intention here is related to that which I proposed for the adverbial clause there: prophets are to prophesy in accordance with the standard set by the gospel—the faithfulness of God in Jesus Christ, and the faithfulness to which they are summoned in response.

> **if ministry, in ministry;** (12.7a)

Ministry (*diakonia*)[22] here possibly refers to commissioning as *diakonoi* by and in the name of the Roman congregations. The specific tasks that would have been involved

---

18. The phrase "members one of another" (*to de kath'heis allēlōn melē*) is not easy: but see BDF §305.

19. On "grace," see additional note D.

20. Helmut Koester, "The Community of the New Age: Paul's Letters as a New Political Theology for Christian Community," *HDB* 27.4 (1998): 26.

21. See page 197, and footnote 15.

22. On "ministry," see additional note EE.

in such *diakonia* are not clear to us, but that they would have involved exercising a degree of leadership seems likely. An alternative interpretation of *diakonia* at 12.7a is sometimes offered—that it refers specifically to the practical service of the needy in the congregation (compare Matt. 25.44–45, Acts 6.1, Rom. 15.25)—and this is certainly not impossible but is rendered less likely by the fact that such service seems to be covered in the final three of five other "charisms" that Paul is about to name:

> those who teach, in their teaching; those who exhort, in their exhortation; those who contribute, in liberality; those who give aid, with zeal; those who do acts of mercy, with cheerfulness. (12.7b–8)

There follows a series of counsels, all related to the life of the church. The basis of all is the first: **Let love** [*agapē*] **be genuine** (12.9a). Genuine **love** is the only possible appropriate response to the gift of God in Christ: "For in Christ Jesus neither circumcision nor uncircumcision is of any avail, but faith working through love" (Gal. 5.6). But what, in concrete terms, does this mean? It means all of you,

[A]   **Abhorring what is evil,**
     holding fast what is good.

[B]   **Caring for one another with brotherly** and sisterly **affection,**
     outdoing one another in showing honour,
     never flagging in zeal;

[C]   **being on fire with the Spirit,**
        serving the Lord;

[B']   **rejoicing in hope,**
     enduring in tribulation,
     being constant in prayer;

[A'] **contributing to the needs of the saints,**
     practising hospitality. (12.9b–13)

As indicated by the layout above, I incline to accept C. H. Talbert's suggestion that "there is an inherent unity in *vv.* 9b–13."[23] In particular, Talbert notes the participles as imperatives that mark the passage ("abhorring," "holding fast," and so on) and are not found in other Pauline exhortatory sections.[24] I also incline to accept David Alan Black's identification of a chiastic structure here, with the central portions marked particularly clearly in Paul's Greek by the arrangement of the definite articles: [B] *tē*[*i*] . . . *tē*[*i*] . . . *tē*[*i*] . . . [A] *tō*[*i*] . . . *tō*[*i*] . . . [B'] *tē*[*i*] . . . *tē*[*i*] . . . *tē*[*i*]. . . .[25] Much more difficult to answer is the question as to the source of the material. Did Paul create it himself? Does it, as Barrett suggested, go back "to a Semitic source originating in very primitive Christian circles"?[26] Do we have here fragments of

---

23. C. H. Talbert, "Tradition and Redaction in Romans xii.9–21," *NTS* 16 (1969–70): 84.

24. Talbert, "Tradition and Redaction," 86. See further Moulton, *Grammar* 1.180–83, and H. G. Meecham, "The Use of the Participle for the Imperative in the New Testament," *ExpTim* 58 (1946–47): 207–8.

25. David Alan Black, "The Pauline Love Command: Structure, Style, and Ethics in Romans 12.9–21," *FilNeot* 2 (1989): 5.

26. Barrett, *Romans* 240.

Jesus tradition? Perhaps materials that were already a part of the early catechesis? It seems, for the present, virtually impossible to choose with confidence between these possibilities.

The translation **outdoing one another in showing honor** is how Chrysostom understood Paul at 12.10b (*Homilies in Romans*, col. 605); but the expression is not entirely clear and might mean "anticipate one another in showing honor" (so Theophylact [col. 508], and Vg, *honore invicem praevenientes*). On the other hand, the general sense is clear: as members of the same family, believers will properly compete only in their concern for each other's honor. Similarly, the expression translated **being on fire with the Spirit** (*tō[i] pneumati zeontes*) (12.11b) could simply mean "being fervent in [your] spirit" (compare Acts 18.25); but the proposed structure of the passage makes a reference to the Holy Spirit (parallel to "serving the Lord") much more likely. Naturally, **the needs of the saints** will be a concern (12.13), because that is of the very essence of the church: when the poor were shamed in the eucharistic celebration at Corinth, it was evident that those who participated in the Eucharist had failed to discern the nature of the Lord's body (1 Cor. 11.20–29).

The picture presented is then of a community of grace, whose members, being graced and living in hope, are therefore graceful to each other. "Ethical conduct is not designed to further one's own moral perfection, but to promote the welfare of the neighbour and to build up the congregation" (Helmut Koester).[27] To this extent the community Paul envisages is marked by the Christian ideal. Yet that ideal, as we have noted, was by no means alien to pagan notions either of honor or of communal solidarity.[28] We need not deny that, just as Paul's picture of life in the community of Christ began with the classic Hellenistic virtue of *sōphrosunē*, so in other respects—its concern with familial affection, mutual **honor**, and that ability to **endure** which is the mark of true self-control—that community would also be an ideal Hellenistic community.

Additional Note KK. Moderation

I have rendered *eis to sōphronein* at 12.3 as **with moderate thinking,** but the fact is, for all they are common and constant words throughout the whole range of Greek literature, representing a quality admired and sought after in all periods of Hellenism, still *sōphrosunē* and its cognates have such a range of associations—"moderation," "temperance," "sobriety," "reasonableness" among them—that it is virtually impossible to settle on a single English concept that will do them justice.[29]

Sōphrosunē is closely bound up with *egkrateia* (self-control),[30] and sometimes a synonym for it:[31] thus, classically, for Plato, "moderation [*sōphrosunē*] is self-control [*egkrateia*] over pleasures and desires [*epithumiōn*]" (*Republic* 4.430e; compare *Phaedo* 68c, Aristotle, *Rhetoric* 1.9.9). *Sōphrosunē* is also therefore closely linked with *aidōs*

27. Helmut Koester, *Introduction to the New Testament*, vol. 2, *History and Literature of Early Christianity* (New York: de Gruyter, 1982), 141.

28. See additional note E, on "honor" and "shame," especially page 74.

29. Ulrich Luck, "σώφρων, σωφρονέω, σωφρονίζω, σωφρονισμός, σωφροσύνη," in *TDNT* 7.1097.

30. On "self-control," see additional note L.

31. LS, σωφροσύνη 2; BAGD, σωφροσύνη 2.

(modesty)—which speaks of proper respect (including self-respect) and a sense of honor: indeed, it can be claimed that "*aidōs* is the greatest part of *sōphrosunē*" (Thucydides, *History* 1.84.3). Since *sōphrosunē* naturally involves good judgment and rationality, it is obviously opposed to *mania* (madness, frenzy, or delirium) (for example, Xenophon, *Memorabilia* 1.1.16).[32]

Jewish and Christian writers in the first century of the Christian era were certainly moving in the same field of discourse. For Josephus, it is a mark of Moses' greatness that "he did not make religion a department of virtue, but the various virtues— I mean justice, moderation [*sōphrosunēn*], fortitude, and mutual harmony in all things between the members of the community—departments of religion" (*Against Apion* 2.170; compare 4 Macc. 1.1–6, 30–32). According to Acts, when Festus shouts "at the top of his voice" at Paul, "Paul, you are raving [*mainē*]! Much learning is driving you mad [*eis manian*]!" Paul's response is exactly as we should expect of one possessing the Hellenistic virtues: "I am not mad [*ou mainomai*], your Excellency, but I utter words of truth and reasonableness [*sōphrosunēs*]" (Acts 26.24–25). The writer to Timothy invites the women members of the Christian congregation to the behavior that every good Hellene admired in men *or* women: they are to be adorned "with proper self-respect [*aidous*] and sobriety [*sōphrosunēs*]" (1 Tim. 2.9). At Romans 12.3, then, it is entirely to be expected that Paul would oppose thinking *eis to sōphrosunein*, that is, **with moderate** [or sober] **thinking**, to the temptation **to think of yourself more highly** [*huperphronein*] **than you ought to think** [*phronein*]—which latter would, of course, be a form of *mania*, madness, and the very opposite of that *aidōs*, modesty, proper self-respect, which should mark the people of God.

Relations with the World at Large (12.14–13.14)

The form of the grammatical construction changes from the participle used as an imperative to the simple imperative (**Bless** [*eulogeite*] . . .), which will then have two infinitives **rejoice** [*chairein*] . . . **weep** [*klaiein*] . . .) and a further series of participles dependent upon it. With that change comes a change of Paul's subject, for he now moves from the exhortation regarding hospitality—still, however, related to behavior within the church—to exhortation regarding "hospitality" of another sort—that is, relationships with those who are beyond the boundaries of the believing fellowship.

He begins—perhaps because it is where he began himself (1 Cor. 15.9; Gal. 1.13), perhaps because he knows the Roman church has suffered from it, and may suffer from it again—with what seems to be the extreme case: **Bless those who persecute [you]—bless, and do not curse them!** (12.14) The inclusion of **you** (*humas*) by P46 and some other authorities hardly limits the sense of this expression, since it is scarcely credible that Paul did *not* have in mind at least those who persecuted the church.[33] Apropos of which, Cranfield[34] aptly quotes John Calvin,

---

32. BAGD, σωφροσύνη 1.

33. See, however, page 203, footnote 39. Mark D. Jordan suggests that "concrete urgency" is "appropriate to protreptic" (see "Ancient Philosophical Protreptic and the Problem of Persuasive Genres," in *Rhetorica* 4 [1986]: 322).

34. Cranfield, *Romans* 2.641.

> Although there is hardly any one who has made such an advance in the law of the Lord as to fulfill this precept, yet no one can boast of being a child of God, or glory in the name of Christian, who has not partially undertaken this course, and does not struggle daily to resist the will to do the opposite.[35]

On the other hand, the omission of *humas* by the greater weight among the ancient authorities (together with the fact that its inclusion can probably be explained as an accommodation to Matthew 5.44) leaves open the still more generous possibility that Paul regarded *all* who persecuted others, for whatever cause, as in need of the church's prayer. He continues,

Rejoice with those who rejoice, weep with those who weep, thinking in harmony with each other, not being haughty, but associating with the lowly. (12.16a)

The expression translated **thinking in harmony with each other** (*to auto eis allēlous phronountes*) means either (as understood by Chrysostom [*Homilies on Romans* 22.2] and, according to Rufinus, Origen [Migne, *Patrologiæ* 14.1222]) something like "having the same concern and esteem for each other as for yourselves" (so NEB, BEP), or else it means "having a common mind" (so RSV). In neither case need we assume that Paul's concern has ceased to be the church's relationship with those outside the church. Paul was doubtless perfectly capable of understanding that the manner in which believers treated each other was a factor in the attitude of the world to the gospel and the community that professed the gospel (compare John 17.20–23, 1 Pet. 2.12).

> **Do not become wise in your own estimate, repaying no one evil for evil, but taking thought for what is *noble in the sight of all*** [alluding to LXX Proverbs 3.4], **if possible, so far as it depends upon you, living peaceably with all, never avenging yourselves, beloved, but leave it to the wrath of God, for it is written, *Vengeance is mine, I will repay, says the Lord*** [citing LXX Deut. 32.35, but close to MT, and closer still to the Targum]. (12.16b–19)[36]

Despite the reluctance of some commentators to allow it, it seems hard to see what could be intended by the obvious allusion in this section to LXX Proverbs 3.4 ("Take thought for things noble [*kala*] before the Lord and before humankind") other than an appeal to the *sensus communis* of humanity as to what is proper in human behavior (so RSV, NEB, BEP; compare Phil. 4.8–9). Here we have, as Pietro Rossano has expressed it, Paul's "willingness to present the Christian life as perfection, and beauty, and therefore as a response to the noblest aspirations of his hearers."[37] Such an appeal does not—again, despite some commentators—involve Paul in contradicting what he has earlier said about the universality of human sinfulness. Certainly Paul has asserted that all (including Israel), in "professing themselves to be wise"

---

35. Calvin, *Romans* 274.

36. For example, Neophyti 1: "Vengeance is mine and I am he who will repay" (trans. Martin McNamara and Michael Maher), in Alejandro Díez Macho, *Neophyiti 1: Targum Palestinense ms de la Biblioteca Vaticana*, vol. 5, *Deuteronomio* (Madrid: Consejo Superior de Investigaciones Cientificas, 1978), 564 (txt. 269).

37. Pietro Rossano, "L'Ideale del Bello (καλός) nell'etica di S. Paolo," *SPCIC* 2.382; the entire paper repays study (*SPCIC* 373–82).

have become "fools" (1.22), but it by no means follows that all human understanding of what constitutes good and evil is therefore to be rejected. On the contrary, in Paul's view (as noted earlier) humankind as a whole has since the creation of the world (1.20) possessed knowledge of God, and *therefore* humankind as a whole is subject to God's wrath—God's passionate "No!"—for its rejection of that knowledge. In particular, as regards the evil deeds of humanity, they are, according to Paul, above all to be condemned because "*knowing the judgment of God that those who do such things are worthy of death*, [they] not only do them, but applaud those who do them" (1.32). If human judgments of good and evil were actually worthless, then Paul's criticism—not to mention his argument—would entirely lose its point.

Living **peaceably with all** means, of course, foregoing personal vengeance, **for it is written, Vengeance is mine, I will repay, says the Lord**. As it happens, neither in the LXX nor in the MT is this statement of God's prerogative applied to the question of personal vendetta. The interpretation that finds in it grounds for forbidding such a vendetta is a later development, witnessed in the Qumran writings (for example, *The Manual of Discipline* [1 QS 10.17–18]) in the pseudepigrapha (for example, 2 Enoch 50.3–4), and, of course, in this passage in Paul.[38] Far from pursuing a vendetta,

> **if your enemy is hungry, feed him; if he is thirsty, give him drink; for by so doing you will heap burning coals upon his head** [citing LXX Proverbs 25.21–22a]. **Do not be overcome by the evil, but overcome the evil with the good.** (12.20–21)

For all the looseness of its construction, this short section (12.14–21) is quite remarkable. That there are such things as universal human rights and obligations is in the late twentieth century a fairly widespread assumption, at least in Western Europe and North America. Western Europeans and North Americans tend therefore to forget how unusual—and in some respects even novel—that assumption is in the history of human thought. In Paul's day both Jews and pagans tended in general to regard those who were outside their particular communities as being, by that very fact, somewhat less than fully human. Certainly Paul was not the only Jew to see in the Deuteronomic declaration of God's prerogative in taking vengeance grounds for forbidding the personal vendetta: but generally, as Kent L.Yinger has shown, such prohibition is applied *within the community of faith*.[39]

How unusual, therefore, is the present passage, with its assertion of concern for the essentially *human* hopes and problems even of those who are outside the believ-

---

38. See Kent L. Yinger, "Romans 12:14–21 and Nonretaliation in Second Temple Judaism: Addressing Persecution within the Community," *CBQ* 60.1 (1998): 74–96, especially 76–87.

39. Yinger, "Romans 12:14–21 and Nonretaliation," 76–87. But I am not convinced by Yinger's attempt to show that Paul, too, speaks only of relationships within the household of faith. His argument falls in particular, I think, over Paul's use of the word "persecute" (*diōkein*)—"Bless those who persecute" (12.14). Albrecht Oepke noted that when used negatively in the New Testament, this verb is "always in the sense of religious persecution" ("διώκω," in *TDNT* 2.230). It refers to harassment of the "insider" (from the household of faith's point of view) by the "outsider," and that, pace Yinger (90), is not in the least altered by the fact that such persecution may involve Jews persecuting other Jews, or even persecution by members of one's own family. Certainly that is how Paul regularly uses the word in a negative sense: see Gal. 1.13, 23, 4.29, 5.11, 6.12; 1 Cor. 15.9; Phil. 3.6.

ing community—rejoicing **with those who rejoice,** and weeping **with those who weep.** We have only to read a study of ancient attitudes such as Paul Veyne's essay "Humanity" in Andrea Giardina's *The Romans* to be made aware what a remarkable step forward such a conception represents, while reflection on Thomas Jefferson's wrestling with the problem of slavery goes some way to indicating how difficult was the notion of "human equality" or "human rights" for a basically enlightened person as late as the beginning of the nineteenth century.[40] Perhaps needless to say, the briefest reflection on twentieth-century history (for example, on the Holocaust, or racial tensions in the United States, or religious and nationalist conflicts in the Balkans, in Ireland, and in the Holy Land) provides salutary evidence of the degree to which the notion is still imperfectly grasped or realized.

There is, of course, a theological connection between what Paul is now asserting as proper behavior for the believing community toward its enemies and the argument that has preceded it. The entire thrust of Romans 9–11 has been that those whose hearts are presently "hardened" can yet be recipients of God's "mercy." What, then, can the church see, even in **those who persecute,** but those who are destined in God's purposes to be "co-heirs" (8.17)? Had not Paul himself been a persecutor? In seeking to **bless** her persecutors the church is therefore, in the last analysis, simply seeking a blessing for herself, looking for the completion of her own life, in God, and in union with "the whole creation" that "groans together in travail until now" (8.22).[41] In this practice, moreover, her members find a further way to that self-control which was their ideal: for only by so praying can they avoid being **overcome by the evil** and instead **overcome the evil with the good.**

In connection with the attitude of believers to those outside the church, Paul now moves to a more specific question. **Let every person be subject to the governing authorities** [*exousiais*] (13.1a).[42] By the **authorities** (*exousiai*) it seems likely that Paul here meant primarily the civil authorities, in other words, what we now tend to speak of as "the State."[43] In common with the broad consensus of pagan and Jewish thinking in the Greco-Roman world he regards all such institutions as related to divine authority: **for there is no authority except from God, and** therefore **the au-**

---

40. Paul Veyne, "Humanity," in *The Romans*, ed. Andrea Giardina, trans. Lydia G. Cochrane (Chicago: University of Chicago Press, 1993), 342–69; on Thomas Jefferson, see e.g., Dumas Malone, *The Sage of Monticello* (Boston: Little, Brown, 1981), especially 316–32, and literature there cited.

41. Doubtless there is also a psychological connection. Those who discipline themselves not to hate their enemies are unlikely quickly to give way to the self-indulgence of hating each other.

42. I thus perceive a natural progression between 12 and 13.1–7, and see the passage as particularly appropriate to the Roman situation: compare Guerra, *Romans and the Apostolic Tradition*, 160–64. At the same time it should be noted that many commentators have found the relationship of 13.1–7 to the rest of Romans constituting, to say the least, an oddity: "Our section is an independent block. In view of its singular scope it can be pointedly called an alien body in Paul's exhortation, although the catchword of subordination connects it to the other admonitions" (Käsemann, *Romans* 352). See further Käsemann, "Principles of Interpretation of Romans 13," in *New Testament Questions of Today* (Philadelphia: Fortress Press, 1969), 196–216; Luke Timothy Johnson, *Reading through Romans* (New York: Crossroad, 1997), 185–91. For an approach that sets the discussion in a wider context, see Douglas R. Edwards, *Religion and Power: Pagans, Jews, and Christians in the Greek East* (New York: Oxford University Press, 1996), especially 42–45, 65–71.

43. For other views of "the authorities" see further, additional note LL (1).

thorities with which you must deal—that is, the Roman emperor and his servants and officials—**have been instituted by God** (13.1b).[44] The second part of this statement is in the present context just as important as the first. Concrete as always in his hortatory concerns, Paul is speaking to the present situation of those in Rome whom he addresses, although he is (as I have noted) also arguing from a generally held principle with which he would have expected his auditors to agree. He speaks of the situation with which believers are faced in society at large, and of the Roman *imperium* as he perceives it at present in relation to the church.

Such a view of the present Roman *imperium* as **instituted by God** in fact pointed in two directions. On the one hand, and on one level, it did serve to call in question any form of disobedience to the *imperium* so long as the *imperium* limited itself to functions proper to its scope; on the other hand (as the prophetic tradition made clear), it left the *imperium* in principle open to challenge wherever and whenever it claimed too much for itself or betrayed the purposes of its institution (see 2 Samuel 12.1–13!) What, then, of the situation in which Paul found himself? What most people in the ancient world hoped for from the empire, along with a measure of justice, was a reasonable degree of peace and stability. Successful emperors, such as Augustus, Vespasian, and Hadrian, seem to have grasped this. During the first five years of his reign (54–59 AD), while he was still under the influence of Burrus and Seneca, Nero seemed to have grasped it, too. At this period the new emperor was regarded with high hopes, and, disappointing though it may be for those who wish to extract from Paul's every word lasting principles, there seems not the slightest reason to suppose that Romans, probably written about 56 AD, does not reflect that situation.[45]

So, then, Paul notes,

> **whoever resists the authorities is resisting what God has instituted, and those who resist will incur judgment. For the** present **rulers are not a terror to the good work, but to the bad. Would you [sing.] have no fear of the authorities? Then do what is good, and you [sing.] will have praise [*epainon*] of them, for they are God's minister [*theou . . . diakonos*] to you [*soi*: sing.] for what is good. But if you [sing.] do wrong, be afraid; for he does not bear the sword in vain; he is God's minister [*diakonos*] to execute his wrath upon the evildoer.** (13.2–4)

44. On "the authorities" as "instituted by God," see further, additional note LL (2).

45. See Tacitus, *Annals* 13.51; Suetonius, *Life of Nero* 10–18 (the admission is the more striking in that both sources are, of course, hostile to Nero); see further Colin Wells, *The Roman Empire*, second edition (Cambridge, Massachusetts: Harvard University Press, 1992), 117; William L. Lane, "Roman Christianity during the Formative Years from Nero to Nerva," in *Judaism and Christianity in First Century Rome*, ed. Karl P. Donfried and Peter Richardson (Grand Rapids, Michigan: Eerdmans, 1998), 202–3.

The dangers of treating this particular Pauline text as a statement of "lasting principles" has been, alas, made only too evident in the history of the church. Although Leo Baeck was, I think, mistaken in his own understanding of Paul, one can hardly not sympathize with or not acknowledge the justice of his observation that it has been too easy for Christians to get "from the Pauline exhortation . . . to the point of first tolerating every despotism and of then soon consecrating it" ("Romantic Religion" in *Judaism and Christianity: Essays by Leo Baeck*, ed. and trans. Walter Kaufmann [New York: Atheneum, 1970], 214.)

Diakonos is here used in its basic sense to speak of one appointed to an office performed on behalf of the one who appoints.[46] Specifically, Paul is again saying that those who have civil authority have it from God for the good of the individual citizen—which includes, of course, the execution of **wrath** against evildoers, for which reason they **bear the sword**.

Various commentators have connected **bear the sword** (*machairan phorei*) with the Roman *ius gladii*. In Paul's day, however, *ius gladii* referred only to the right of provincial governors to condemn to death a Roman citizen serving in the armed forces under their command, and so, as an allusion, was hardly likely to be relevant to those whom Paul addressed. His words are probably better understood as a loose reference to the general life-and-death power of the Roman *imperium*.[47]

In other words, as the author of 1 Peter has it, we are to submit ourselves to "every human ordinance for the Lord's sake, whether to the emperor, as supreme, or to governors, as appointed by him for the punishment of evildoers and the praise of those who do good (2.13–14)."[48] In saying this, Paul and the author of 1 Peter were simply affirming again their basic view that human administrations are commissioned by God for the sake of those administered (as opposed, for instance, to the aggrandizement of the administrators)—and if there is a single universal principle to be extracted from what either of them says, it is that. **Therefore one must be subject, not only in consideration of** God's **wrath, but also for the sake of conscience** (13.5).

On the other hand, we should note again, such an attitude toward civil authority must also serve to make that authority entirely limited and *relative*. If it is instituted by God, and *diakonos* of God, then it is subject to God and may not claim for itself the honor that is God's alone. Hence Paul's advocacy of submission **for the sake of conscience** did not imply blind submission to *any* rule, however tyrannous or unjust.[49]

But the issue in Romans 13.1–7 involved, perhaps, something more specific than a general attitude toward the *imperium*, and in two respects.

First, it is possible that Paul's exhortation to **do what is good** [*to agathon poiein*], so as to receive **praise** (*epainon*) from the civil authority, would have been heard by his audience—and intended by him—as a reference to their duties as citizens to act, according to their means, not merely in accordance with the laws but also as *patrons*

---

46. On *diakonos* see further, additional note EE.

47. See A. N. Sherwin-White, *Roman Society and Roman Law in the New Testament* (Oxford: Clarendon Press, 1963), 8–11; also the useful note by Eastland Stuart Staveley, "*Provocatio*," in *OCD* 892–93.

48. On the duty of the authorities to minister justice, see, again, additional note LL (3).

49. For all the well-nigh unbridgeable difference of *attitude* and *emotion* between Paul and the Apocalypse, it does not seem to me that there is here an essential *theological* difference; or, to put it another way, here is the point at which an intellectual bridge can be built between them. Paul is counseling respect for the state perceived *as God's agent*. The Apocalypse opposes the state perceived as *claiming for itself divine honors* (Rev. 13.1–18). "From John's prophetic standpoint Rome's evil lay primarily in absolutizing her own power and prosperity . . . . The special contribution of Christian martyrdom is that it makes the issue clear. Those who bear witness to the one true God, the only true absolute, to whom all political power is subject, expose Rome's idolatrous self-deification for what it is" (Richard Bauckham, *The Theology of the Book of Revelation*. New Testament Theology [Cambridge: Cambridge University Press, 1993], 38–39.

and *benefactors* to the community at large, actively seeking "the welfare of the city" (Jer. 29.7)—whereby, of course, they would gain "honor" not simply for themselves, but for the church and for the gospel. In this connection the use of the second person singular in 13.3 (**Would you** [sing.] **have no fear of the authorities?** and so on) may be particularly significant, making clear that this injunction is addressed to individuals rather than to the church as a whole: for it would be evident that only persons of considerable means could undertake the kind of benefactions that would expect, and receive, public praise.[50]

Second, according to Tacitus, there were at this period growing complaints in society at large about taxation—so much so that in 58, Nero responded by proposing to abolish all indirect taxation (*Annals* 13.50–51). Was Paul anxious lest believers, living, as they knew themselves to be, in the new age, would have strong feelings about this—and an immediate temptation to resist payment? Did he fear that they might bring themselves into dispute with the **authorities** over an issue that did not have any direct bearing on the gospel? If so, his next words were appropriate to address such concerns. **For the same reason you also pay taxes, for the authorities are God's public servants** [*leitourgoi*],[51] **attending to this very thing. Pay to all of them what they are owed** [*opheilas*], **tribute to whom tribute** is owed, **tax to whom tax** (13.6–7a). Such subjection to the **authorities** is not, moreover, merely a matter of the proper settlement in cash or goods; it is also a matter of **respect** and **honor.** As believers are concerned with the proper honor of God and of those within the believing community, so they are concerned with the honor of those beyond it, paying **respect to whom respect** is due, and **honor to whom honor** (13.7b)—for all, potentially, are members if God's people.[52]

Having exhorted proper behavior toward those inside and those outside the church, Paul plays on the notion of **what** is **owed** (*opheilas*) to bring him full circle back to the point from which he began. It is all—even paying the proper taxes, and certainly the giving of proper honor—a part of love (*agapē*). **Owe** [*opheilate*] **no one anything, save to love** [*agapan*] **one another;**[53] **for whoever loves the neighbor has fulfilled the Law. For** *Thou shalt not commit adultery, Thou shalt not kill, Thou shalt not steal, Thou shalt not covet,* **and whatever other commandment there is, is summed up in this one word,** *Thou shalt love thy neighbor as thyself* (citing LXX Leviticus 19.18). **Love does not work evil against the neighbor. Therefore love is the fulfillment** [*plērōma*] **of the Law** (13.8–10). In speaking thus of love (*agapē*), Paul followed one tendency in approaching the Law that, according to the later rabbinic traditions, had been evident since the time of Hillel (*b.Šhabb.* 31a). This need not surprise us, nor does it represent a lapse from Paul's earlier comments about our inability to "fulfill" the Law. Paul has from the beginning made clear that accepting "my gospel" involves taking God's commandments just as seriously as does

---

50. On "patronage," see additional note A.

51. On "public servant," see additional note MM.

52. There may well be in 13.7 an echo, and even, perhaps, an exegesis, of words that Paul had heard attributed to Jesus: "Pay [*apodote*] to Caesar the things that are Caesar's, and to God the things that are God's" (Mark 12.17 // Matt. 22.21, Luke 20.25).

53. On "owe no one anything," and its possible connection with patronage, see additional note A.

any other position (2.12–16); in the light of that gospel, and *in Christ*, he can now, without reservation, exhort to the most humanly impossible aspect of those commandments—and understood, at that, more broadly than at its source. For in the passage from Leviticus that Paul cites, it is evident that the "neighbor" in question can only be a fellow member of God's people (LXX Leviticus 19.18); in Paul's context, it is naturally extended to any human contact—since all, potentially, are members of God's people.[54]

And this, knowing the time, that it is high time for you to awake out of sleep. For salvation is nearer to us now than when we first believed (13.11). The new age is already beginning for believers. Already they are like those who stretch and blink and prepare to begin a new day: **the night is far gone, the day is at hand. Let us therefore cast off the works of darkness and put on us the armor of light; let us conduct ourselves becomingly** [*euschēmonōs*—that is, with grace and dignity], **as in the day, not in reveling and drunkenness, not in debauchery and licentiousness, not in quarreling and jealousy**—not, in other words, in the wild behavior that characterizes those who lack self-control and are the slaves of *akrasia*—**but put on the Lord Jesus Christ, and make no provision for the flesh, to gratify its desires** (13.12–14).

Additional Note LL. Further Thoughts on "the Authorities"

"The Authorities" as Angelic Powers?

A number of scholars in the earlier part of this century, most notably Oscar Cullmann in *The State in the New Testament*,[55] suggested that by "authorities [*exousiai*]" Paul intended to refer to supernatural and angelic powers that he understood to stand behind empirical states, or else that he intended a reference both to the empirical state and the supernatural powers.[56] Among the most important arguments presented in favor of this were that

1. elsewhere in the Pauline epistles *exousia* in the plural refers to supernatural angelic powers (e.g., 1 Cor. 15.24),
2. the question of the subjection of angelic powers to Christ was important for Paul and for the early church (e.g., 1 Cor. 15.24; compare Col. 1.15–18, 2.9–10, Eph. 1.20–23, 3.10, 6.12, 1 Pet. 3.22), and
3. passages such as 1 Cor. 2.8. and 6.3 seem to assume just such a relationship between the angelic and human authorities.

Despite this, the majority of recent exegetes have argued that the sense of *exousiai* must be determined by its context and that at Romans 13.1 the word is most naturally understood as referring simply to those human civil authorities to whom believers

---

54. On the command to love, see further C. Spicq, O.P., *Agapè dans le Nouveau Testament: Analyse des textes*, vol. 1 (Paris: J. Gabalda, 1958), 259–66; Victor Paul Furnish, *The Love Command in the New Testament* (London: SCM Press; Nashville, Tennessee: Abingdon, 1972), especially 108–11; E. P. Sanders, *Paul, the Law, and the Jewish People* (Philadelphia: Fortress Press, 1983), 93–122.

55. Oscar Cullmann, *The State in the New Testament* (New York: Scribner's, 1956), 53–70, 95–114.

56. Cullmann, *State in the New Testament*, 65, 66, 113–14.

must, in the world, be subject (compare 1 Pet. 2.13). In my opinion, this remains the view most likely to be correct. In particular, the exhortation to believers to "subject themselves" to the *exousiai* would, on the "angelic" understanding, imply that having first been "subjected" to Christ the angelic powers are now in some way "recommissioned" in Christ and given authority over believers—a development in mythology for which the New Testament gives not the slightest encouragement.

"The Authorities" as "Instituted by God"

This "plain" interpretation of *exousiai* does not, of course, alter the fact that Paul did regard human civil powers as ordered and ordained by God for the sake of the governed (13.3–4). Such a view—that it is God who sets up (and, incidentally, overthrows) rulers—is plainly Jewish (LXX 2 Sam. 12.7–8; Isa. 45.1–3; Jer. 27.4–7, 2.21, 37–38 and passim; Sir. 10.4; Wisd. of Sol. 6.1–11); and it was evidently followed, not only by Paul but by later Christian tradition. So Polycarp will later tell the proconsul of Asia that Christians "have been taught to give honour to rulers and authorities [*exousiais*] instituted by God, as is fitting" (*Martyrdom of Polycarp* 10.2; compare 1 *Clem.* 60.4–61.2). That said, it should not be implied that pagans were not capable of similar insights. Cicero, asking why Rome dominated the world, considering "we have excelled neither Spain in population, nor Gaul in vigour, nor Carthage in versatility, not Greece in the arts," put it down to *pietas, religio* (that is, respect or awe for the divine), and "a unique wisdom by which we perceive all things to be ruled and governed by the power of the gods [*sed pietate ac religione atque hac una sapientia quod deorum numine omnia regi gubernarique perspeximus*]" (*Haruspicum responsis* 9.29).

The notion of duly constituted authorities as "instituted by God" had, incidentally, plenty of mileage in it: it was still to be alive and well as late as the end of the sixteenth century. Thus the speech provided by Shakespeare for Sir Thomas More (and preserved for us, remarkably, in what appears to be Shakespeare's own handwriting) in that curious compilation *Sir Thomas More*[57] (written sometime between 1594 and 1603) is still making exactly the point that Paul was making more than fifteen hundred years earlier. Obedience to authority is necessary, More says to the rioters,

> For to the king God hath his office lent
> Of dread, of justice, power and command,
> Hath bid him rule, and willed you to obey;
> And, to add ample majesty to this,
> He hath not only lent the king His figure,
> His throne and sword, but given him His own name,
> Calls him a god on earth. What do you then,
> Rising 'gainst him that God Himself instals,
> But rise 'gainst God? (*Sir Thomas More* 2.3.106–14)

57. Anthony Munday and others; revised by Henry Chettle, Thomas Dekker, Thomas Heywood, and William Shakespeare, *Sir Thomas More*, ed. Vittorio Gabrieli and Giorgio Melchiori, The Revels Plays (Manchester, England: Manchester University Press, 1990).

The speech and the entire scene as Shakespeare has arranged it (the quelling of a riot) have features that have reminded critics of the riot-quelling scene with Menenius Agrippa in *Coriolanus* (1.1.101–69, see additional note Z).[58] The connections between the two sets of ideas (the authorities as instituted by God, and the state as a body) would not, needless to say, have been regarded as superficial, either by Paul's contemporaries or Shakespeare's. Nevertheless, the direct line of descent for More's argument is made clear by Shakespeare himself, in More's previous speech to the rioters:

> First, 'tis a sin
> Which oft th'apostle did forewarn us of,
> Urging obedience to authority,
> And 'twere no error if I told you all
> You were in arms 'gainst God. (*Sir Thomas More*, 2.3.99–103)

The Duty of the Authorities to Minister Justice

Paul's view that it was the purpose and duty of the civil authority to administer justice (Rom. 13.4) likewise had plenty of mileage in it—as is witnessed by the *Book of Common Prayer* (1662), still observing that those in authority are "truly and indifferently [i.e., impartially] [to] minister justice, to the punishment of wickedness and vice, and to the maintenance of [God's] true religion, and virtue"[59]—although, for all the magnificence of Cranmerian language, one must grant Paul the advantage over Cranmer and the author of 1 Peter in that he states the positive function before the negative.

Additional Note MM. Public Servant

Strictly, *leitourgos* refers to a "public servant" (that is, one who performs a *leitourgia*, or public service), such as the lictors (officers attending the consuls or other magistrates, and responsible for carrying out sentences on offenders) (for example, Plutarch, *Romulus* [*Parallel Lives*] 26.3). The word and its cognates occur in this sense in the LXX—of those, for example, who attend upon the king, or members of his family (LXX 2 Kingd. 13.18; 3 Kingd. 10.5). Paul uses *leitourgos* metaphorically of one who has been acting on behalf of the Philippian church in relation to himself (Phil. 2.25).

In view of ancient conceptions of society, such public service is never strictly separable from divine service (Aristotle, *Politics* 7.10 [1330a 8f.]). Nevertheless, there are strands connecting it with specifically "divine service," and the word is sometimes so used in the LXX. Occasionally this is in connection with priests (for example, LXX Isa. 61.6: "you shall be called priests [*hiereis*] of the Lord, servants [*leitourgoi*] of God"; compare 2 Esdras 20.40 [MT Neh. 10.40], Sirach 7.29–30 [ac-

---

58. See *More*, ed. Gabrieli and Melchiori, 102, note 112–13.

59. From the prayer "for the whole state of Christ's Church," in "The Order of the Administration of the Lord's Supper or Holy Communion," in *The Book of Common Prayer and Administration of the Sacraments and Other Rites and Ceremonies of the Church According to the Use of the Church of England* [1662].

cording to Rahlfs's preferred reading]), but most commonly in connection with Levites (see LXX Exod. 37.19 [MT 38.21], as well as extensively throughout Numbers and 1 and 2 Chronicles). It is so used in Romans by Paul himself at 15.16.

Further Notes on Life in the Church: The Problem of the "Strong" and the "Weak" (14.1–15.13)

Paul returns to the subject of life in the church. Until this point his remarks—even those regarding taxation—have all been somewhat general in their application. Now he turns to what he evidently regards as a specific problem in the Roman community, although (as in his discussion with "the Jew" at 2.1–14) it is initially presented in terms that are quite oblique. He begins,

> Receive one who is "weak" in faith, but not with a view to settling matters over which there is dispute.[60] One has the faith to eat anything, but one who is "weak" eats only vegetables. (14.1–2)

Who, or what, are the **"weak"**? Various suggestions have been made. My own belief is essentially that of the Greek fathers.[61] Those Paul had in mind were a group—most, but not necessarily all, of Jewish descent[62]—who, while not imagining that their *fulfillment* of the *halakah* gave them grounds for any kind of claim against God, nonetheless still found in it the most appropriate way—perhaps even the only way—by which to express their faith. Of course, observance of the Jewish dietary Laws did not normally involve vegetarianism (although Scripture itself would have provided at least one precedent for Jews living in a pagan environment to choose a vegetarian diet and drink only water as a means of maintaining *kashrut* [see Dan. 1.3–16]), but, as Harry Gamble observes, we must be careful not to mistake "an obliqueness of approach for a generality of content."[63] By first stating the issue in a very general way, Paul's rhetoric allows anyone to think that, in certain circumstances, the **"weak"** might be they themselves. As James C. Walters observes, "The strategy lets readers move from common understanding to self-application" and "it avoids a direct attack upon any group whose ultimate integration into the community might thus be

---

60. The Greek phrase is susceptible of a variety of interpretations. In particular, *dialogismoi* ("matters over which there is dispute") could be taken in the negative sense of "scruples," so as to give the meaning "not to pass judgment on scruples" suggested by Cranfield (*Romans* 2.701). The more neutral sense "doubtful matters" or "matters over which there is disagreement" is perhaps preferable—if only because it permits us to understand Paul as less dismissive of a position that he is, after all, apparently about to say is allowable, and should even in some measure be supported, within the believing community.

61. So Origen (according to Rufinus) (*Commentary of Romans* 9.35 [PG 14.1234–5]), Chrysostom (*Homilies on Romans* 25.1 [PG 60.627]), and Theoderet (*Interpretatio* 140 [PG 82.200]). Among modern discussions see Cranfield, Romans 2.690–98; Fitzmyer, *Romans* 687–88; Dunn, *Romans* 799–800; also Guerra, *Romans and the Apologetic Tradition* 32–39, and Robert A. J. Gagnon, "The Meaning of 'ΥΜΩΝ ΤΟ 'ΑΓΑΘΟΝ in Romans 14:16," *JBL* 117.4 (1998): 675–89. For views of the identity of the "strong" and the "weak" different from that taken here, see additional note NN.

62. On the ethnic composition of the groups identified by Paul as "weak" and "strong," see further, additional note OO.

63. Harry Gamble, *The Textual History of the Letter to the Romans*. Studies and Documents 42 (Grand Rapids, Michigan: Eerdmans, 1977), 136.

hampered."[64] In any case, whether they thought of themselves as **"weak"** or **"strong,"** Paul's auditors would have heard him asking of them essentially the same thing: tolerance. **Let not the one who eats despise the one who abstains, and let not the one who abstains pass judgment on the one who eats, for God has welcomed him** (14.3). If the gospel by which both groups stand is *God's*, and if those who are Christ's *belong* to Christ, then **Who are you to pass judgment on someone else's household slave? It is before their own master that they stand or fall; and they will be upheld, for the master is able to make them stand** (14.4).[65]

One esteems one day as better than another, while another esteems all days alike (14.5a). The question Paul had in mind here was, presumably, over the continuing significance (if any) of the Jewish Sabbath and the festivals. Again, however, the matter is presented obliquely, and Paul's answer is also, in principle, the same as before—a request for tolerance. **Let everyone be fully convinced in their own mind. Those who observe the day, observe it in honor of the Lord. Those who eat, eat in honor of the Lord, since they give thanks to God** (14.5b–6). That, finally, is the response to God's grace that sets believers apart from rebellious humanity: they give God the honor that is God's due (contrast 1.21). **None of us lives to himself, and none of us dies to himself. If we live, we live to the Lord, and if we die, we die to the Lord; so then, whether we live or die, we are the Lord's** (14.7–8).

For to this end Christ died and lived again, that he might be Lord both of the dead and of the living. But you, why are you passing judgment on your brother and sister? Or you on the other side, why do you despise your brother and your sister? (14.9–10a). The lot of those who so scorn God's will and try God's patience will be just the same for those who claim to be believers as it will be for those unbelievers of whom Paul spoke earlier: judgment (2.1–16). **For we shall all of us stand before the judgment seat of God. For it is written, *As I live, says the Lord, to me every knee shall bend, and every tongue shall acclaim God*** (alluding to LXX Isa. 45.23 and 49.18).[66] **So, then, each of us will give an account of ourselves to God** (14.10b–12).

Therefore (*oun*)—the passage moves now to its conclusion: it is to this that everything said since 14.1 has pointed—**let us no longer pass judgment on one another, but rather decide this: not to put a stumbling block or an occasion of falling in your brother's or** your sister's **way. I know and am persuaded in the Lord**

---

64. James C. Walters, *Ethnic Issues in Paul's Letter to the Romans: Changing Self-Definitions in Earliest Roman Christianity* (Valley Forge, Pennsylvania: Trinity Press, 1993), 87; see the whole section, 84–92.

65. Paul makes here essentially the same logical move as at Galatians 6.17: "Henceforth let no one trouble me, for I bear on my body the marks of the Jesus." On slavery as a metaphor for salvation, see pages 57–58, on Romans 1.1.

66. In Philippians 2.10–11 Paul also echoes LXX Isa. 45.23, the context making clear, however, that the "Lord [*kurios*]" is Christ. In the present passage, a number of manuscripts have "the judgment seat of Christ" rather than "the judgment seat of God" at 14.10 (e.g., Aleph [c], C2, Ψ, 0209, 33, 1881) and a number of *other* manuscripts (e.g., B, F, G, 6, 630, 1739, 1881) omit "to God" at 14.12. If these represented Paul's original (and in both cases it is possible to see that the greater weight of manuscript tradition *might* have resulted from "improvements"), then Paul also used Isa. 45.23 here in reference to Christ.

Jesus that nothing is of itself ritually **unclean** [*koinon*]; **but if someone reckons some-thing to be unclean, for that person it is unclean** (14.13–14). Here, finally, Paul speaks plainly as to the real subject of his concerns in the present instance—and his conviction about them. **"Clean"** (*katharos*—see 14.20) and **"unclean"** are the lan-guage of *kashrut*, the dietary laws. The situation over observance of the Jewish Law that divides traditionalist and nontraditionalist at Rome *is* an example of that ri-valry between the **"weak"** and the **"strong"** of which Paul has been speaking, and his strictures apply to it, not because the question itself is important, but because not to care for another's concerns is to deny the spirit of the gospel, wherein "one died for all." **For if your brother** or your sister **is grieved on account of your food, you are no longer walking in accordance with love. Do not by your food destroy the one for whom Christ died. Do not therefore let your good thing be reviled** (14.15–16). Certainly Paul accepts that the limits of God's grace are not marked by such things as special foods or days on a calendar: **For the Kingdom of God is not food and drink but justice and peace and joy in the Holy Spirit. For one who thus serves Christ is pleasing to God and approved by humankind** (14.17–18). Yet pre-cisely because the Kingdom of God is about these greater things—**justice and peace**—one who is **"strong"** in faith will be led to be careful about lesser things, for the sake of others. **Do not destroy God's work for the sake of food. All things are indeed "clean," but for the one who so eats as to cause a stumbling block** for a brother or sister, **it**—that is, eating—**is evil. It is a noble thing to abstain from eating meat, or from drinking wine, or from anything else, by which your brother** or your sister **stumbles** (14.20–21). The issue for Paul is, as always, the church. Does what you are doing serve to build up the community, or to break it down? Does it help strengthen your brothers and sisters, or make them weaker?

As for **the faith which you have, keep it to yourself before God. Happy are those who do not bring condemnation on themselves over what they approve** (14.22). Fortunate indeed is the one who has no problems of conscience over prac-tical questions such as these! (Paul is, of course, referring to the issue under discus-sion. He is hardly saying that in *any* matter, if we think we are right, then we are.) **But those who do doubt are condemned if they eat, because** they do **not act by faith. Everything that is not** *by faith* **is sin** (14.23). These expressions are not easy, and have caused commentators' headaches for centuries. The key, perhaps, is to note that *ek pisteōs* has by this point in Romans become virtually a technical term for Paul and his hearers, and it is in the light of the entire previous argument, therefore, that we must understand it here. What Paul is claiming is that *only those actions are truly grace filled that proceed on the basis of our trust in God's own faithfulness, inviting our faithfulness in return.* "Hold thee to God! But who can maintain their hold, if they be not themselves held?" (Barth).[67] As for the word **everything** (*pan*) (14.23), Chrysostom was surely correct in understanding it, too, as referring in this context

---

67. Barth, *Romans* 522. Augustine evidently took *ek pisteōs* to mean "on the basis of Christian faith," and claimed that "even the good works of unbelievers are no good works of theirs, but are the good works of the One who makes good use of the works of evil people. But their sins are their own, by which they do good things in an evil way, for they do them, not with a believing but with an unbeliev-ing will, that is, with a foolish and a harmful will," and went on to cite Rom. 8.23 as authority for his

to the matters about which Paul was speaking (*Homilies on Romans* 26.3)—that is, the relationships of believers toward each other within the community of believers. Paul is, in other words, talking to those who are already *in Christ* and who have "given obedience from the heart to the pattern of teaching to which [they] were handed over and, set free from sin, have become slaves to God's justice" (Rom 6.17). It is *they* who are to see themselves and **everything** they do in the light of the *ek pisteōs* standard. Therefore Paul is not saying anything about the deeds of pagans, or about God's attitude to the deeds of pagans, and still less is he saying anything about how believers should "judge" the deeds of pagans—an action that he has, in any case, already in principle ruled out (2.1).

We, the "strong," ought to bear with the "weaknesses" of those who are not "strong," and not to please ourselves; let us each please the neighbor with a view to what is good and builds up the community (15.1–2). Cranfield's observation here is to the point:

> That it would be perverse to read into Paul's *mē heautois areskein* any notion that everything which is delightful to one ought to be avoided simply because it is delightful (a notion which the ill-informed not infrequently ascribe to the Puritans and their heirs) should be obvious. What is meant here by not pleasing oneself is not pleasing oneself regardless of the effects which one's pleasing oneself would have on others. What Paul is forbidding in particular is that strong Christians should please themselves by insisting on exercising outwardly and to the full that inner freedom which they have been given, when to do so would be to hurt a weak person's faith. [68]

Why should those who follow Christ exercise this restraint? Because that is the nature of the one who is their Lord and to whom they belong, **For Christ himself did not please himself; but, as it is written, *The reproaches of those who reproached you fell on me*** (citing LXX Ps. 68.10) (15.3)—and by that endurance he fulfilled the deepest implications of the Law itself. The reproaches with which rebellious humankind has reproached God since the creation of the world have now fallen upon the Messiah. **For whatever was written in former days was written for our instruction, that by steadfastness and by the encouragement of the Scriptures we might have hope** (15.4). On the basis of that hope, which is the same for them all, Paul can pray for them all: **May the God of steadfastness and encouragement**—God, in other words, who is the fountain of that patient endurance and that bracing exhortation from which alone we can acquire true *egkrateia*—**grant you to live in such harmony with one another, in accordance with Christ Jesus, that together you may with one mouth glorify the God and Father of our Lord Jesus Christ** (15.5–6).

Therefore accept one another, as Christ has accepted you, for the glory of God. For I declare [*legō gar*]—the phrase evidently introduces a solemn affirmation—

---

opinion (*Against Julian* 4.32, trans. Matthew A. Schumacher, altered)—surely going far beyond Paul's intention, and perhaps contrary to it (compare 2.15). A number of modern commentators take *pistis* in the sense of "one's confidence that one's *faith* . . . allows one to do a particular thing" (Cranfield, *Romans* 2.729), which likewise seems to ignore the general significance that the phrase *ek pisteōs* has acquired by this point in Romans.

68. Cranfield, *Romans* 2.731.

that Christ became a minister to the circumcised to show God's truthfulness, in order to confirm the promises given to the patriarchs, and in order that the gentiles might glorify God for his mercy (15.7–9a). That Paul again makes clear, at this point, his conviction that Christ has come *both* in fulfilment of God's promises to Israel *and* to redeem the gentiles plainly confirms that (as we have supposed) the issue between "weak" and "strong" was fundamentally an issue involving Jewish-versus-gentile traditions and ways of life. In this, as in all other issues, the key to a right understanding was to tell the story of Israel right. In Paul's view, God's abiding compassion for *both* communities—Jew and gentile—was what mattered in the story, and it was that divine compassion which was even now leading to the fulfillment of the Scriptures, **as it is written,**

> *Therefore I will confess thee among the gentiles,*
> *and sing to thy name* [citing LXX Ps. 17.50 [MT 18.50]],
> and again it is said,
> *Rejoice, O gentiles, with his people* [citing LXX Deut. 32.43],
> and again,
> *Praise the Lord, all gentiles,*
> and,
> *let all the peoples praise him* [citing LXX Ps. 116.1 [MT 117.1]],
> and further Isaiah says,
> *The root of Jesse shall come,*
> *he who rises to rule the gentiles;*
> *in him shall the gentiles hope.* (alluding to LXX Isa.11.1) (15.9b-12)

Paul's four quotations represent all three divisions of the Scripture (one from the Law, one from the Prophets, two from the Writings), although, since he himself draws attention to the particular source of only one of them, that he intended this general representation is not clear. What is clear is that for Paul, the mutual acceptance *now* of Jewish and gentile believers at Rome, together with the gentiles' praise of God for sending the Messiah, already makes present that final, universal, and eternal praise of God of which the Scriptures spoke and to which, properly told, the story pointed (see 3.21). So Paul ends his exhortation with a blessing—

> **May the God of peace fill you with all joy and peace in believing, so that by the power of the Holy Spirit you may abound in hope.** (15.13)

Additional Note NN. Other Opinions about the "Strong" and the "Weak"

Among suggestions that have been made, other than that which I have followed in my own exegesis, we should perhaps note the following:

1. The "weak" were legalists who sought to earn their righteousness before God, so demonstrating "a failure to grasp the fundamental principle . . . that [we] are justified and reconciled to God . . . by faith alone—or, better, by God's free electing grace, faith being [our] recognition that all is dependent not upon [ourselves] but God."[69] It seems, however, quite impossible to suppose that Paul would have re-

---

69. Barrett, *Romans* 256.

garded such a difference of opinion as merely involving *dialogismoi*—in either sense (see page 211, footnote 60). Had this been the case, he would surely have regarded the views of "the weak" as a fundamental denial of the gospel.

2. The "weak" were gentiles who continued practices (such as abstention from eating flesh and, on occasion, from drinking wine) associated with the Pythagoreans, as well as with devotees of the Dionysic and Orphic mysteries. What then are we to make of the fact that the "weak" regard "one day as more important than another"? We should still have to seek an explanation for that in Judaism, since it is hardly possible that Paul would have regarded an acceptance of pagan notions about "lucky" and "unlucky" days as to be tolerated.

3. The "weak" were adherents of "a type of Judaism which was under syncretistic influence [and] had gained entry into the community and apparently become a danger through the adherents it had won there."[70] This involves a speculation for which there is little evidence, and is, in addition, probably still open to the objections raised against 1.

4. The "weak" were those who are concerned about "things sacrificed to idols," knowing that meat purchased from pagan butchers in a pagan city would normally have been involved in sacrifice to a pagan deity, and similarly that libations will have been offered from the first fruits of the wine. In this case, the dispute between the "weak" and the "strong" is essentially the same as that which occupies Paul in 1 Corinthians 8 and 10. This suggestion is impressive not only in its parallels to the material we have in Romans 14.1—15.13 but also in the similarities of Paul's decision about it—that is, his appeal for mutual tolerance and sensitivity. But there are difficulties. One is bound to note that (1) if *eidōlothuta* ("things sacrificed to idols") were the problem in 14.1–15.13, it is odd that Paul never once, in the entire section, actually *uses* the word (contrast 1 Corinthians—at 8.1, 4, 7, 10, 10.19, as well as other expressions indicating what the problem is, such as 10.21–22); (2) in 1 Corinthians Paul clearly sees some danger involved in *eidōlothuta*, even for the allegedly *phronimoi* ("wise") (see 10.15–22); in Romans 14.1–15.13 he seems to see no danger at all in the practices of the "strong," except insofar as they harm the "weak"; (3) we are still left with the problem of explaining why some of the "weak" also esteem "one day as better than another" (14.5).

5. That in fact the "weak" and the "strong" do not correspond to any real groups in the Roman church at all. In Paul Karris's view, Paul has no firsthand knowledge of the Roman situation, and his exhortation in 14.1–15.13 is simply a generalized restatement of positions he had earlier taken with regard to the actual situation that had faced him in Corinth. "Paul's imperatives and arguments to the entire community indicate that he is not trying to create a community out of the disarray of 'the weak' and 'the strong' communities, but is concerned to show how an established community can maintain its unity despite differences of opinion."[71]

---

70. Käsemann, *Romans* 368.

71. Paul Karris, "Romans 14.1–15.13 and the Occasion of Romans," in Karl P. Donfried, ed., *The Romans Debate: Revised and Expanded Edition* (Peabody, Massachusetts: Hendrickson, 1991), 79; similarly, Victor Paul Furnish, *The Love Command in the New Testament* (Nashville, Tennessee: Abingdon, 1972), 115.

Certainly (as we have noted) Paul's expressions are restrained and "oblique," certainly there are points of principle in common between the issues raised here and in 1 Corinthians, and certainly Paul so designs his exhortation that sensitive listeners *might* initially identify themselves with the parties of which Paul speaks. Therefore I do concede that the section, and especially the opening part of it (14.1–12), *can* be heard as Karris takes it—and perhaps was intentionally written so. Nevertheless, Gamble's point (also already noted) stands: we must not mistake "an obliqueness of approach for a generality of content."[72] It remains that there *is* an underlying urgency about 14.1–15.13, there *is* a degree of specificity in the references to food and drink, to the esteeming of days, to what is "clean" and "unclean," and to Jew and gentile, such as to make it extremely unlikely, if not impossible, that the whole thing was intended *simply* as "general parainesis."

Why did Paul afterward feel a need—even as a matter of convention—to apologize for speaking **rather boldly** (15.15) to the Romans? Was it because he, a stranger and an outsider (in some senses) who had never met them, had written to them authoritatively at all? In part, possibly. My suspicion, however, is that he felt such a need above all because he had dared speak specifically (however "obliquely") to their situation and the problems within it. *He* knew that he was speaking specifically as he dictated, and *they* would know when they heard what he said. He might have added, in the language of his master, "Those who have ears to hear, let them hear!"— knowing well enough that there were some in his audience who would "hear" very clearly. As George La Piana said, even "if the allusions are obscure for us, certainly they were not for the Christians of Rome to whom the epistle was directed."[73]

Additional Note OO. The Ethnic Composition of the Roman Church

As a number of critics have pointed out, the actual situation of the Roman church and Paul's beliefs about it may not have been the same. Equally, of course, there is no compelling reason for supposing either that Paul had been totally misinformed or that he had misunderstood his information. In particular, if (as I do) one accepts 16.1–23 as an authentic part of the letter, it seems extraordinarily hard to believe that not one of those whom Paul addressed would have been willing or able to furnish him with reasonably accurate information on the subject or that he would not have been interested enough to pay attention to it.[74]

Be that as it may, it must be confessed that even Paul's own view of the composition of his addressees is not clear—as is evidenced by the number of critics who have come to totally opposite views of the question, some declaring the audience envisaged by Romans to have been predominantly Jewish,[75] others that it was pre-

---

72. Harry Gamble, *Textual History of the Letter to the Romans* 136.

73. George La Piana, "La Primitiva Comunità Cristiana di Roma e L'Epistola ai Romani," *Ricerche Religiose* 1 (1925): 213.

74. See Gamble, *Textual History* 92; Lane, "Roman Christianity during the Formative Years" 199–200.

75. E.g., Francis Watson, *Paul, Judaism, and the Gentiles: A Sociological Approach*. SNTSMS 56 (Cambridge: Cambridge University Press, 1986), 103–7.

dominantly or exclusively gentile,[76] and others taking an intermediate position.[77] The question has been well rehearsed and there is no purpose in attempting here to repeat the arguments in detail. Briefly, that Paul understood the Roman church to contain some who were of gentile background appears to me to be evident from 11.13–32 and 15.7–12; that he understood that it contained some who were of Jewish descent seems equally evident from 15.7–12 and 16.3, 11. Beyond that it is difficult to say anything with certainty about the proportions involved, and the passages in Romans sometimes pointed to as sources of further information turn out on investigation to be nothing of the kind.

Thus, at 1.5–6 Paul's mention of his apostolic commission to bring about **the obedience of faith for the sake of** Jesus' **name among all the nations, among whom are also you** states no more than the obvious fact—that the Roman church is in the midst of the gentile world, and therefore, even though not founded by him, falls within the terms of Paul's commission (11.13; compare Gal. 1.16, 2.7–9).[78] It says nothing whatever about his understanding of the composition of the Roman church and certainly is not grounds for assuming that he thought he was addressing an *exclusively* gentile community.

It is the same at 1.13, where he speaks of his hope for **some harvest** at Rome as **in the rest of the gentile world**—*en tois loipois ethnesin*, meaning literally, "among the other nations." That Rome was a gentile city was hardly to be denied. On the other hand, Paul's expression, though not precise—indeed, *because* it is not precise—affords us no grounds whatever for assuming that he thought of the Roman church itself as *exclusively* gentile. It is simply, once more, a reference to locality: here, at Rome, the capital of the gentile world, is where Paul, as apostle to the gentiles, wishes still to have "some harvest."

Later Paul addresses gentiles directly: **But I say to you gentiles, inasmuch a I am apostle to the gentiles, I magnify my ministry in order to make my fellow Jews jealous, and thus save some of them** (11.13–14). Once again, there is no particular reason to conclude from Paul's expression even that he regarded the Roman congregation as predominantly gentile. It is just as conceivable he would have spoken in this way if he had understood the gentile believers to be a small, but significant and vociferous, minority. Still less are his words reason to suppose he must have regarded his audience as *exclusively* gentile. On the contrary, the expression will have made perfectly good sense if it simply directed what followed at a particular section of the audience. The fact is, yet again, that nothing whatever can be deduced from this expression about Paul's understanding of the relative strengths or sizes of the groups in the Roman congregation, save what is self-evident: that he thought gentiles were present in sufficient numbers to be worth addressing specifically.

---

76. E.g., Johannes Munck, *Paul and the Salvation of Mankind* (London: SCM Press, 1959), 200–209; Stowers, *Rereading of Romans* 30–41.

77. E.g., Cranfield, *Romans* 21; Fitzmyer, *Romans* 33.

78. In view of Paul's own description of his work in 1 Cor. 9.19–25, not to mention the testimony of Acts (e.g., 13.14–51, 14.1–7, 17.7–15), it seems likely that the division envisaged in Galatians 2.9 is along geographic, rather than strictly ethnic grounds: see Burton, *Galatians* 98; Matera, *Galatians* 77–80; but contrast Martyn, Galatians 213–16; E. P. Sanders, *Law* 181.

As for the composition of the particular groups that Paul identifies in his exhortatory section as "weak" and "strong" (14.1–15.13): if we grant, as I do, that the division, and the resultant tensions that Paul endeavours to address, were largely caused by different attitudes to kashrut—the Jewish dietary laws[79]—we do well to note that while no doubt the majority of those who took a stricter view will have been of Jewish origin and a majority of those who wished to relax them will have been gentile, still, a *strictly* ethnic division does not follow. Paul himself was Jewish, yet evidently identified with the "strong" (15.1); so, we may suspect, did his "fellow workers" Prisca and Aquila (16.3). By contrast—as anyone who knows anything of the psychology of converts will be well aware—at least some among those who had previously been gentile proselytes to the Jewish synagogue and had *then* turned to Jesus might well have been more vigorous in defense of their (comparatively) newly acquired devotion to kashrut than those who had been born Jews.

What of Romans 16? Here at last we have something that at first sight looks like "hard" data. Out of twenty-six individuals known to Paul, five are certainly Jewish (Prisca, Aquila, Adronicus and Junia, and Herodion), and possibly two more (Maria and Apelles)—about 20 percent. Does that represent the proportions in the Roman church as a whole? But then—perhaps because he was Jewish, should we expect Paul to have a higher than average proportion of Jews among his personal acquaintance? On the other hand, because he was suspect among some Jews, would his personal acquaintance perhaps *not* have included those Jews in the Roman congregation (or congregations) whom some characterized as "the weak"? And what about those of the household of Aristobulus? Were they Jews? Unfortunately, here too our data turns out, on investigation, to be as "soft" as everywhere else.

At the end, we can only conclude where we began, that Paul, who was probably in a position to know, evidently thought that both Jews and gentiles were present in the Roman congregation in sufficient proportions for (1) their divisions to represent a serious threat to the church, and (2) it to be important for him to be heard by both groups, and, if possible, to carry both groups along with him. If I have the further impression that the gentiles *were* in fact the larger group, then that is perhaps only because I also have the impression (especially from 9–11) that the gentiles seem to have felt they were, in some sense, "winning." Perhaps the 20-percent-Jewish group that we surmised from Romans 16 might not be so far off target—but then, 20 percent would represent a sizable minority!

For what it is worth, these tentative observations about what may be surmised (or not surmised) of the ethnic composition of the Roman church from the Letter to the Romans appear to be consistent with our external evidence, such as it is. The origins of the Roman church are something of a mystery,[80] but an anonymous fourth-century Christian known to us as "Ambrosiaster" gives us an account that may not be far from the truth:

---

79. See pages 211–15; for other possible views of the "weak" and the "strong," see further, additional note NN.

80. George La Piana cited Duchesne, "Laissons le mystère planer sur cette première origine," and in terms of hard evidence it is difficult to see that we have made much progress beyond that: see "La Primitiva Comunità Cristiana di Roma e L'Epistola ai Romani," *Ricerche Religiose* 1 (1925): 209, footnote 1.

> It is known that Jews lived at Rome in apostolic times, because they were subjects of the Roman Empire. Those of them who believed [that is, in Jesus Christ] taught the Romans that, professing Christ, they should keep the Law . . . . Moreover one ought not to be angry with the Romans, but even to praise their faith; since, though seeing no displays of great deeds, nor any of the apostles, they accepted the faith of Christ, though with Jewish rites. (*Ad Romanos* 16.2)

Granted the social and physical mobility that marked the empire at this period, it is entirely possible that Christianity first came to Rome by way of Jewish travelers—merchants and others—engaged in commerce or other exchanges with the Jewish colony there.[81]

If the Roman church was founded by Jewish believers, it soon had to learn to do without them. In 49, the Emperor Claudius banished the Jews from Rome (Acts 18.2–3). According to Suetonius, the reason for this expulsion was that "the Jews constantly made disturbances at the instigation of Chrestus" (*Life of Claudius* 25.4). The words "at the instigation of Chrestus [*impulsore Chresto*]," perhaps taken by Suetonius from a police report, may well refer to the results of Messianist Jews spreading their views in the synagogues—particularly, views about the observance of the Law and the inclusion of gentiles. Along with Jews who believed in Jesus and Jews who did not, doubtless gentiles who were perceived to affect their customs were also expelled, since the Romans seem to have regarded those who lived like Jews as being Jews (Cassius Dio, *Roman History* 37.17.1). On the other hand, gentile (and Jewish) followers of Jesus who did *not* affect Jewish customs will probably have been left alone.

Hence, as James C. Walters has pointed out, the Claudian edict will have had a considerable effect on both the Jews' and the church's self-definition at Rome. It will have communicated to the former that they would be wise to emphasize to the authorities their difference from the church, so as to avoid being censored for disturbances caused by Christians; and at the same time it will have communicated to gentile believers that it was to *their* advantage not to be associated with Judaism.[82]

With the accession of Nero in 54, the banishment seems to have lapsed, and many Jews returned to Rome, among them (presumably) those who believed in Jesus as Messiah. By that time, however, the Roman church will have been run for five years by those who were least shaped by Jewish tradition. Inevitably, then, those who returned will have encountered fellow believers whose socialization was very different from their own—persons who did not keep Jewish Sabbath and dietary laws, and had no particular wish to do so. It is not difficult to imagine tensions arising between the two groups—tensions that may well have been exacerbated if the Roman community consisted (even in part) of house churches, some perhaps following Jewish customs, and some not (see Rom. 16.3–5, possibly also 16.10, 11), with the mem-

---

81. On the Jewish colony itself, George La Piana, "Foreign Groups at Rome during the First Centuries of the Empire," *HTR* 20 (1927): 183–403, contains much that is still valuable: especially 341–93.

82. James C. Walters, *Ethnic Issues in Paul's Letter to the Romans: Changing Self-Definitions in Earliest Roman Christianity* (Valley Forge, Pennsylvania: Trinity Press), 56–66.

bers of each doubtless motivated in part by a sense of loyalty and *obligatio* to their particular *patronus* or *patrona*.[83]

Such appears to me to be precisely the kind of situation envisaged by the Letter to the Romans as a whole, by Paul's constant proclamation of the impartiality of God's grace, and, in particular, by his exhortations at 14.1–15.13 and 16.17–20.

Finally, the reader may care to note that here, and throughout this study, I try to avoid the phrase "Jewish-Christian," which in discussion of Paul is an anachronism, and a confusing one at that. If there is one thing that scholars as different from each other as Daniel Boyarin, W. D. Davies, and N. T. Wright are agreed upon (and I agree with them), it is that Paul thought of himself as a faithful Jew, and regarded his commitment to Jesus as a way—in his view, the true way—of living out his Judaism.[84] The questions at issue for Paul were not about relationships between Jews and Christians, but about how God was fulfilling the promises through Jesus the Messiah, and about how Jews and gentiles who believed in that fulfillment should live in faithful response to it. As for "Christians," the earliest known occurrences of the word are all in documents written after 70 (Acts 11.26; Suetonius, *Nero* 16.2; Tacitus, *Annals* 15.44). Paul, so far as we know, did not even know the word.[85]

83. Clearly the house church was an element, and a significant one, in the rise and shaping of Christianity: see Peter Lampe, "The Roman Christians of Romans 16," in *The Romans Debate: Revised and Expanded Edition*, Karl P. Donfried, ed. (Peabody, Massachusetts: Hendrickson, 1991), 229–30, who sees this as a factor leading directly to Roman divisions; see also Lane, "Roman Christianity during the Formative Years," 208–13. A note of caution is sounded by Chrys C. Caragounis, "From Obscurity to Prominence: The Development of the Roman Church between Romans and 1 *Clement*," in *Judaism and Christianity in First-Century Rome*, Karl P. Donfried and Peter Richardson, eds. (Grand Rapids, Michigan: Eerdmans, 1998), 245–79.

84. "On my reading of the Pauline corpus, Paul lived and died convinced that he was a Jew living out Judaism" (Daniel Boyarin, *A Radical Jew: Paul and the Politics of Identity* [Berkeley: University of California Press, 1994], 2); compare W. D. Davies, *Paul and Rabbinic Judaism: Some Rabbinic Elements in Pauline Theology* (London: SPCK, 1948), 324; N. T. Wright, *What Saint Paul Really Said: Was Paul of Tarsus the Real Founder of Christianity?* (Oxford: Lion; Grand Rapids, Michigan: Eerdmans, 1997), 39–40.

85. See Rudolf Brändle and Ekkehard W. Stegemann, "The Formation of the First 'Christian Congregations' in Rome in the Context of the Jewish Congregations," in *Judaism and Christianity in First-Century Rome*, Karl P. Donfried and Peter Richardson, eds. (Grand Rapids, Michigan: Eerdmans, 1998), 117–18.

7

Epistolary Conclusion (15.14–16.23)

Paul's Plans (15.14–33)

Paul has insisted that while "his gospel" affirms the dignity and hope prepared for gentiles by their eventual inclusion in the eschatological people of God, that by no means implies that God has forgotten the promises to Israel, nor does it mean that the bulk of Israel will not eventually find their place in that people, even though for the present some may appear to be excluded (chapters 1–11). On the basis of this hope Paul has exhorted all in the church at Rome, Jew and gentile alike, to live in harmony, together acknowledging their dependence on the justice and mercy of God revealed in Jesus Christ (12–15.13). With that exhortation he has completed his protreptic. It remains for him to speak again of his own place in this, of his hopes, and of his plans.

He begins courteously, and exactly as the ancient theoreticians would have advised him to begin, with an expression of confidence in his hearers: **I myself am fully confident, my brothers** and sisters **that you yourselves are full of goodness, filled with all knowledge, and so quite capable of correcting one another. If on some points I have written to you rather boldly**—does he have in mind the exhortation to harmony that he has just given? Or is he thinking of the entire enterprise of writing thus authoritatively to a church he has not founded? Perhaps both.—although in this case, as I have indicated,[1] I do incline to suspect that the former represented the area of peculiar delicacy wherein he had chosen to tread and was therefore perhaps uppermost in his mind as he dictated. At any rate, the Romans may be sure that it is all only **by way of reminder**. In a somewhat similar vein the younger Pliny wrote on one occasion to his friend Maximus: "I know you need no telling, but my love for you prompts me to remind you to keep in mind and put into practice what you know already . . . . Please believe, as I said at the start, that this letter was intended not to tell, but to remind you of your duties" (*Letters* 8.24).

---

1. See additional note NN.

Nevertheless, for Paul's boldness there is a particular reason: **it is because of the grace given to me by God, to be a public servant** [*leitourgon*] **of Christ Jesus to the gentiles, ministering as sacred rite** [*hierourgounta*] **the gospel of God, in order that the offering of the gentiles may be acceptable, sanctified by the Holy Spirit** (15.14–16). Paul's description of his position is, as Byrne points out, among "the most solemn to be found in his writings. It amounts to a forceful claim to a unique status in the entire Christian movement."[2] *Leitourgos* is, as we have seen, commonly used for public service of any kind, but in view of the LXX's extensive connection of the word with Levitical service,[3] Karl Barth may well have been right in his suggestion that that, and not merely public service in general, was what Paul had in mind here;[4] and the verb *hierourgein* in both Jewish and gentile usage means "to perform sacred rites."[5] The entire sentence may therefore be intended as a single metaphor based on the liturgy of the Temple: Paul, like a Levite, assists Christ the true priest by performing as a sacred rite the proclamation of the gospel. Thus the apostle plays his own appointed part in the completion of Christ's sacrifice, which is the offering to God of the gentiles, who are united with Christ through baptism, in union with his sacrifice upon the cross. This, granted the omission of the temple metaphor, is precisely how Paul's role is understood in Colossians:

> in my flesh I complete what is lacking in Christ's afflictions for the sake of his body, that is, the church, of which I became a minister in accordance with God's work entrusted to me for your sake, to fulfill God's word, the mystery hidden for ages and generations, but now made manifest to his saints. To them God has chosen to make known what is the wealth of the glory of this mystery among the gentiles, which is Christ in you, the hope of glory. (Col. 1.24–27)

This boasting [*kauchēsin*] **then I have in Christ Jesus with regard to what pertains to God** (15.17). Such "boasting" is legitimate, since it is not a matter of glorifying Paul, but of glorifying God and God's Messiah:

> **for I shall not dare to say anything except what Christ has wrought through me to win obedience from the gentiles, by word and deed, by the power of signs and wonders, by the power of the Holy Spirit, so that from Jerusalem and as far round as Illyricum I have fulfilled the gospel of Christ, thus making it my ambition to preach the gospel, not where Christ has already been named, lest I build on another's foundation, but as it is written,**
>
> *They shall see who have never been told of him,*
> *and they shall understand who have never heard of him.* (citing LXX
>   Isaiah 52.15b) (15.18–21)

Paul's Greek is not here particularly graceful—perhaps he suffers from a certain embarrassment in speaking even in this qualified way of himself—but his general

---

2. Byrne, *Romans* 435.

3. On *leitourgos* see additional note MM.

4. Karl Barth, *Shorter Romans* 177. See also Cranfield, who aptly quotes J. A. Bengel: "*Christos est sacerdos: Paulus, sacerdotis minister*" (*Gnomen* 564; cited in Cranfield, *Romans* 2.755, footnote 4.).

5. With or without an expressed object; so, for example, Philo (*De Cherub* 28.§96) and Josephus (*Ant.* 14.4.3 §65; 17.6.4 §166)); and among pagan writers, Plutarch, *Alexander* [*Parallel Lives*] 31.

sense is clear. He sees himself as called in his work to be a pioneer, starting from Jerusalem (for "from Zion shall go forth the Law" [Isa. 2.3, Micah 4.2]) and setting up new communities of believers: thus he contributes to the fulfillment of God's promise through the prophets.

All this, however, leads Paul directly to his present plans, and to the Roman church's part in them. **This is the reason that I have so often been hindered from coming to you. But now, since I no longer have any room for work in these regions, and since I have longed for many years to come to you, I hope to see you in passing as I go to Spain, and to be sped on my journey** [*propemphthēnai*] **by you, once I have enjoyed your company for a little** (compare 1.11–12)[6] (15.22–24). Elsewhere Paul uses the word *propempein* when he speaks of being sent by a community with its support and as its representative (compare 1 Corinthians 16.6, 2 Corinthians 1.16).[7] It seems natural, therefore, to understand here that he was hoping the Roman church might accredit and support him in his Spanish mission[8]—in itself a solid enough reason for his endeavoring to make his own theological position understandable to them and for pleading for unity among them.

At present, however, Paul has another concern: **I am going to Jerusalem, ministering** (*diakonōn*)[9] **to the saints. For Macedonia and Achaia were pleased to make some contribution for the poor among the saints at Jerusalem** (15.25–26). This collection by the gentile churches for the believers at Jerusalem is in itself, we note, an act of *diakonia*—of sacred ministry (2 Cor. 8.4, 9.1). The gentiles **were pleased to do it, and indeed they are in debt to** the Jews, **for if the gentiles have come to share in their spiritual blessings, they ought also to be of public service to them in material blessings** (15.27). The gentiles' gift to Jerusalem is one sign that the Messianic age is here (compare, for example, Isa. 60.1–11, 66.10–14; Tob. 13.8–11; 1QM 12); above all, however, it is the sign of a fellowship in which Jews and gentiles are included with mutual respect—the gentiles, as Paul has said, being obligated to the Jews for things spiritual, the Jews to the gentiles for things material, each honoring and honored in the single household of God. As Paul, speaking of this very collection, wrote at another time to the Corinthians, "I do not mean that others should be eased and you burdened, but that as a matter of equality your abundance at the present time should supply their want, so that their abundance may supply your want" (2 Cor. 8.13–14).

What the collection did *not* mean, of course, was submission, or the humiliation of the gentiles: that, in Paul's view, was to tell the story wrongly. Of course such a view was (and is) a *possible* way to understand the tradition. Was it not said of the true king of Israel that "his enemies will lick the soil" (LXX Ps. 71.9 [MT 72.9])? As Origen said, commenting on Romans 3.21b, God's justice was witnessed to "by prophetic words that, through the Holy Spirit, spoke obscurely" (*Commentary on Romans* 5.4 [Scherer 150–51]). Indeed, as Dunn points out, "the collection itself may have been a bone of contention for this very reason, with Paul determined

6. Literally, "if first I am fulfilled in part by your company."

7. Luke also uses the word when he speaks of Paul and Barnabas being sent to Jerusalem as delegates of the church at Antioch (Acts 15.3).

8. On the proposed Spanish mission see, further, page 226, and footnote 13.

9. On "ministering [*diakonōn*]" see additional note EE.

that it should be understood as an act of mutual concern between Christian equals (hence the repeated 'were pleased' in verses 26 and 27), rather than as an act of submission."[10]

Having therefore finished [*epitelesas*] this and sealed [*sphragisamenos*] this fruit for them (15.28a)—Paul's expression here has long caused difficulty. Perhaps he intends a metaphor from farming to speak of his delivery of the collection ("this fruit") to Jerusalem: when the tenant delivers the produce to the owner, "sealing" implies delivery. On the other hand, perhaps by "having sealed" Paul means "having [by the delivery of the collection] set the seal of completion upon my work among the gentile churches"—in which case "the fruit" is what has accrued to *them* (the gentile churches) as a result of that work. It is impossible to be sure. Be that as it may—**I shall go on by way of you to Spain; and I know that when I come to you I shall come in the fullness of the blessing of Christ** (15.28b–29; compare 1.11–12).

Now, at last, comes the one request that Paul makes to the Romans for himself: **I appeal to you, brothers** and sisters, **by our Lord Jesus Christ and by the love of the Spirit, to strive together with me in your prayers to God on my behalf** (15.30). Paul has two reasons for asking for these prayers. First, **that I may be delivered from the unbelievers in Judea** (15.31a). Evidently Paul views the journey as dangerous: yet for him it is unavoidable. Why? Because it is an act of ministry (*diakonia*), of sacred service. Which brings him to the second reason he asks for the Romans' prayers: **And that my ministry [*diakonia*] for Jerusalem may be acceptable to the saints** (15.31b).

No doubt Jewish believers at Jerusalem could be as easily affected as any other Jews by the xenophobia that was to lead to the war of 66: and it is striking, in this context, to reflect that for Josephus the defining moment in the outbreak of the Jewish revolt was the decision that the Temple should not henceforth accept gifts or sacrifices from non-Jews (*War* 2.409–10). Therefore Paul asks those at Rome for their prayers, **so that by God's will I may come to you with joy and be refreshed in your company—may the God of peace be with you all! Amen** (15.33).

Commendation of Phoebe (16.1–2)

> I commend to you our sister Phoebe, deacon of the church at Cenchreae, that you may receive her in the Lord as befits the saints, and help her in any matter in which she may need your help, for she has been a patron to many, and to myself as well (16.1–2).

I have already noted some of the literary parallels with and context for Paul's commendation of Phoebe, and I have spoken in general terms of the significance of that commendation, observing that Phoebe was evidently a person of substance and social standing, that she was a leading member of the church at Cenchreae, that she was Paul's patron, and that she was almost certainly the bearer of his letter.[11] The

---

10. Dunn, *Romans* 2.874. See also G. W. Peterman, "Romans 15.26: Make a Contribution or Establish Fellowship?" *NTS* 40 (1994): 457–63.

11. See page 34. On the question as to whether Romans 16.1–23 is a part of the original letter, see page 21, footnote 26.

precise nature of her office as **deacon** (*diakonos*) at Cenchreae is no longer recoverable; that it was a title implying appointment to leadership seems virtually certain.[12] Did her journey to Rome, as Paul's patron, have a more direct concern with Paul's purposes in writing the Roman letter? Possibly. Perhaps it was indeed the case, as Robert Jewett has suggested, that the **matter** on which she was engaged was that she came on Paul's behalf to Rome to begin making logistical and tactical arrangements for the Spanish mission—a mission that, in view of the lack of earlier Jewish presence in Spain, and the linguistic situation, may well have faced Paul with peculiar difficulties and a need to revise his strategy.[13] Obviously, that is something we cannot know. In any case Paul asks that the Romans **receive** [*prosdexēsthe*] **her in the Lord**. *Prosdechomai* is a word that Paul elsewhere uses in connection with the Philippians' reception of their beloved Epaphroditas (Phil. 2.29) and is aptly connected by Jewett with our own expression "rolling out the red carpet."[14] That this is to be in a manner that **befits the saints** does not, as Cranfield notes, add anything in actual content to **in the Lord**, but does "call into play a special motive for the required Christian behavior, namely, the motive of Christian self-respect, of respect for one's own dignity as that of someone who belongs to Christ."[15]

Greetings to God's Household (16.3–16)

Having commended his patron Phoebe, Paul goes on to offer greetings by name to a number of the members of the Roman church. We have, again, already spoken in general terms of some of the literary parallels to these greetings, characteristic of what modern critics have identified as "the family letter." It remains to consider their specific place here and their relationship to the rest of Paul's letter.

The details at once indicate that some of those whom Paul salutes are personally known to him. Such are **Prisca and Aquila, my fellow workers in Christ Jesus, who risked their necks for my life, to whom not only I but all the churches of the gentiles give thanks; . . . also the church in their house** (16.3–5a). Prisca and Aquila are identified in Acts as Christians of Jewish descent who had been obliged to leave Rome with other Jews as result of the Emperor Claudius's expulsion decree (see Acts 18.1–3, 18, 26 [which uses the diminutive form "Priscilla"]). It is entirely congruent with this that in 1 Corinthians Paul sends greetings to the Corinthians from Prisca's

---

12. On Phoebe as "deacon," see also additional note EE.

13. Robert Jewett, "Paul, Phoebe, and the Spanish Mission" in *The Social World of Formative Judaism*, ed. Jacob Neusner, Ernest S. Frerichs, Peter Borgen, and Richard Horsley (Philadelphia: Fortress Press, 1988), 142–47. See also W. P. Bowers, "Jewish Communities in Spain in the Time of Paul the Apostle," *JTS* 26 (1975): 395–402—an effective demonstration that "there is . . . a lack on all sides of evidence that there were such communities in Spain" (402). I am sure that Paul regarded the mission to Spain as an important next step and that he felt that it was "according to the Scriptures" for him to take it. Abraham was, after all, to inherit the *world* (4.13). On the other hand, I see little evidence for R. D. Aus's suggestion that Paul thought bringing representative Christians from Spain to Jerusalem as a part of the collection enterprise would be directly linked to the "coming in" of the "full number" of the gentiles (11.25) ("Paul's Travel Plans to Spain and the 'Full Number of the Gentiles' of Rom. xi 25," *NovT* 21 [1979]: 232–62).

14. Jewett, "Paul, Phoebe" 150. Compare BAGD, προσδέχομαι 1.

15. Cranfield, *Romans* 2.782.

and Aquila's house church at Ephesus (1 Cor. 16.19). The salutation here, however, implies that they have now returned to Rome.

Others who appear to be personally known to Paul are **my beloved Epaenetus, who was the first convert in Asia for Christ . . . Mary, who has worked hard among you, . . . Adronicus and Junia, my kin** [*tous suggeneis mou*] **and my fellow prisoners, who are of note among the apostles, and were in Christ before me . . . Ampliatus, my beloved in the Lord . . . Urbanus, our fellow worker in Christ, and my beloved Stachys . . . Appelles, who is approved in Christ . . . my kinsman** [*ton suggenē mou*] **Herodion . . . Tryphaena and Tryphosa, the toilers in the Lord . . . the beloved Persis, she who has worked hard in the Lord . . . and Rufus, eminent in the Lord, also his mother and mine** (16.5–13).

Still others, to whom Paul refers without personal details, will presumably have been known to him by reputation, so that his greeting to them is an act of diplomatic courtesy. Such are **those who belong to the household of Aristobulus . . . the household of Narcissus . . . Asyncritus, Phlegon, Hermes, Patrobus, Hermas, . . . Philologus, Julia, Nereus and his sister, and Olympas** (16.10, 14–15).

A number among these are evidently of Jewish descent—**Prisca and Aquila, Andronicus and Junia**, and **Herodion**—the three last all claimed by Paul as "kin" (*suggeneis, suggenē* [16.7, 11]), an expression that in this context means at least "compatriots." That, as Sanday and Headlam observed, is probably what it *does* mean, rather than "relatives," since it is "most improbable that there should be so many relations of Paul amongst the members of a distant church," whereas that he should single out for mention members of the Roman church who were Jews would be "in accordance with the whole drift of the Epistle."[16] Others *may* have been Jewish, although it is not possible to be sure. Possibly **Mary** (16.6) was Jewish—and certainly she was, if we read her name in the form *Mariam*, along with P46 and Aleph.[17] Possibly also **Apelles** (16.10), bearing a Greek name that belonged to a Jew apparently known to the poet Horace:

> *credat Iudaeus Appella,*
> *non ego . . .*
> Appella the Jew may believe it,
> I don't . . . (Horace, *Satires* 1.5.100–101)

Aristobulus (16.10) (who is not addressed directly, and is presumably not a member of the church) could have been the quite recently deceased Aristobulos who was the grandson of Herod the Great and brother of Agrippa—in which case there were not only Jewish connections among those whom Paul greeted but also links to the imperial household. Aristobulos appears to have lived in Rome as a private citizen

16. Sanday and Headlam, *Romans* 423.

17. If, however, we read *Marian* along with A, B, C, and P (preferred by Nestle 26), then we could have the feminine form of Marius, which is a Roman name. Peter Lampe thinks it likely that Mary was not Jewish because Paul does not call her "kins[wo]man (*suyyenēs*)" ("The Roman Christians of Romans 16," in Karl P. Donfried, ed., *The Romans Debate: Revised and Expanded Edition* [Peabody, Massachusetts: Hendrickson, 1991], 225); but in view of his failure to refer to Prisca and Aquila in this way, and in view of possible further Jewish connections with Apelles and the household of Aristobulos, we are not really in a position to be sure that Paul in Romans 16 consistently referred to anyone he knew to be Jewish as *suyyenēs*.

and to have been a friend of the Emperor Claudius (see Josephus, *War* 2.§221–22; *Ant.* 20. §13). He had died at some time between 45 and 48, and after his death his household will likely have become part of the imperial household; but his former dependents will have continued to bear his name, *Aristobuliani*, and so would properly be addressed by Paul **those who belong to the household of Aristobulus** [*tous ek tōn Aristoboulou*] (16.10).[18] Support is lent to this possibility by the fact that the very next name that occurs to Paul is that of **my kinsman Herodion** (16.11)—a name that obviously suggests a relationship, perhaps as slave or freedman, to the Herod family.

Further imperial links are suggested by the names **Urbanus** and **Stachys** (16.9), both Roman slave names found among members of the imperial household (*CIL* 6.8607). **Narcissus** (16.11) (who, like Aristobulos, is not addressed directly and therefore is presumably not a member of the church) may have been a well-known—not to say notorious—freedman of the Emperor Claudius.[19] After Claudius was murdered in 54, Narcissus was arrested and compelled to commit suicide (Tacitus, *Annals* 13.1). Members of his household, like those of Aristobulus's household, though probably passing into the possession of the new emperor, will still have borne the name of their former master—*Narcissiani*—and so would appropriately be addressed by Paul as **those who belong to the household of Narcissus** [*tous ek tōn Narkissou*] (16.11). **Asyncritus** (16.14) (meaning "incomparable") was a name that belonged to one of Augustus's freedmen (*CIL* 6.12565).[20] **Julia** (16.15) could be the name of a free woman of the Julian *gens*, but was also a common name for slaves, and, again, particularly in the imperial household.

It is striking how prominently women figure among those to whom Paul refers. Apart from **Phoebe** herself (16.1), we have **Prisca**, who is named before her husband (16.3). Adolf von Harnack long ago noted that Prisca/Priscilla's name precedes that of her husband in both Paul's letters and in Acts, and plausibly deduced thereby that she was, of the two, the more significant figure in the early church.[21] There is **Mary, who has worked hard among you** (16.6), and **Junia** (*Iounian*)[22] (16.7), who is described, along with her husband (or brother) **Adronicus**, as **of note among the apostles** (*episēmoi en tois apostolois*). It is possible, grammatically, for this last phrase to have meant "notable in the eyes of the apostles," but it is much more likely that

18. This suggestion appears to have been first made by J. B. Lightfoot; see Lightfoot, *Saint Paul's Epistle to the Philippians* (London: Macmillan, 1898; reprint of fourth edition with additions and slight alterations) 174–75.

19. Also first suggested, so far as as I know, by Lightfoot, in *Philippians* 175.

20. See further *NDIEC* 2.85.

21. Adolf von Harnack, "Über die beiden Recensionem der Geschichte der Prisca und des Aquila in Act. Apost. 18,1–27," *SPAW* (1900), 2–13.

22. Despite RSV, NEB, it is evident that Paul should here be understood as using the accusative form of the female name *Iounia*, that is, Junia: so, correctly, NEB margin, NRSV, BEP, and probably KJV (whose translators will not have understood "kinsmen" as exclusively male [see *OED2*, "man" n.1. 1.1]). That Junia was a woman was certainly the opinion of Chrysostom (*Homilies on Romans* 31.2, cited above). Junia was, as it happens, a quite common Roman female name, whereas there is *no* other evidence (so far as I know) for a masculine name "Junias." See further Lampe, "Roman Christians" 223; Richard S. Cervin, "A Note Regarding the Name 'Junia(s)' in Romans 16.7," *NTS* 40.3 (1994): 464–70.

Paul intended us to understand by it "of note among those who are *designated* 'apostles'"—as he was understood by Chrysostom and the majority of the early commentators: "How great was the wisdom of this woman, that she was deemed worthy of the apostles' title" (Chrysostom, *Homilies on Romans* 31.2)—and that the word "apostles" is here to be taken in the sense in which it was used generally in the early church, of those who were commissioned by the church as evangelists.[23]

Then there are **Tryphaena and Tryphosa** (16.12a). Tryphaena and Tryphosa are women's names that occur in both Greek and Latin sources (see *CIG* 2.3092, 2819, 2839, 3348; *CIL* 6.15622–26, 4866, 15241), and both are connected with the noun *truphē* meaning "softness," "delicacy," or "daintiness." As Sanday and Headlam noted, Paul was, perhaps, not unconscious of the irony involved in the contrast between the significance of these names and the toughness of character manifested by those whom he described as **the toilers in the Lord**.[24]

There is **the beloved Persis**, another woman **who has toiled in the Lord** (16.12b). Persis was a name frequently used for female slaves, meaning "Persian" (*IGRom* 7.2074; *CIL* 5.4455]). There is the mother of Rufus, who is, indeed, **his mother and mine** (16.13).[25] There is **Julia**, and there is Nereus's **sister** (16.15).

It is also striking how many of these women are among those for whom, as we noted earlier, Paul's greeting apparently springs from personal acquaintance—a characteristic that at the very least, as Cranfield pointed out, is "highly significant evidence of the falsity of the widespread and stubbornly persistent notion that Paul had a low view of women, and something to which the church as a whole has not yet paid sufficient attention."[26] The fact is, in general terms, if there were not some grammatical or similar element in Paul's references to the women in this letter that makes it clear that they are feminine, there is absolutely nothing in his observations about their characters or work that would distinguish them from the men to whom he refers.[27]

What, then, of the relationship of these salutations to Romans as a whole? The entire collection of salutations, with its implied cross section of addressees, Jew and gentile, male and female, slave and free, assumes precisely that unity of *all* in Christ which is Paul's vision for the church and to which he has exhorted throughout.

> For as many of you as were baptized into Christ have put on Christ. There is neither Jew nor Greek, there is neither slave nor free, there is neither male nor female; for you are all one in Christ Jesus. And if you are Christ's, then you are Abraham's offspring, heirs according to promise. (Gal. 3.27–29)

23. On "apostle," see additional note B.

24. Sanday and Headlam, *Romans* 426: see further BAGD, s.v.s Τρύφαινα, Τρυφῶσα.

25. J. B. Lightfoot speculated that (1) since, of the four evangelists, only Mark (traditionally associated with Rome) describes Simon of Cyrene as "the father of Alexander and Rufus" (15.21), there must have been a prominent Christian at Rome called Rufus; and (2) possibly this was the Rufus mentioned in Romans 16.13 (*Philippians* 176).

26. Cranfield, *Romans* 2.789.

27. See further Bernadette Brooten, *Women Leaders in Ancient Synagogues*, Brown Judaic Studies 36 (Chico, California: Scholars Press, 1982), especially 38–39, 149–51; also, "'Junia . . . Outstanding among the Apostles' (Romans 16.7)" in *Women Priests: A Catholic Commentary on the Vatican Declaration*, ed. L. Swidler and A. Swidler (New York: Paulist Press, 1977), 141–44.

We should note, too, that the hint of imperial "name-dropping" would be an implicit discouragement for any who wanted to encourage confrontation between the church and the imperial system.

Paul's salutations, therefore, carry on indirectly the work of the rest of his text, and so does his conclusion to them. **Salute one another with a holy kiss** (16.16a). The public kiss was not something that had been common in Roman culture, but at this period of the empire seems to have been in the process of becoming more widely accepted. According to Suetonius, Tiberius felt constrained to legislate *against* public kissing (*Tiberius* 34.2). Paul's younger contemporary Martial evidently did not like the growing custom at all, and his remarks on the subject vary from the acid to the obscene (*Epigrams* 7.95, 11.98, 12.59). By contrast, according to Pliny the Younger, there was general delight when the Emperor Hadrian, on entering Rome in the summer of 99, greeted the members of the Senate "with a kiss, as they had kissed you at your departure [*senatum osculo exciperes, ut dimissus osculo fueras*]" (*Panegyricus* 23.1). Be that as it may, where it is accepted as appropriate, the public kiss generally signifies communion, affection, and respect. It can be a mark of reception into a community (Apuleius, *Metamorphoses* 7.9), or of reconciliation to a divinity, as when Apuleius kisses the priest Mithras on his initiation into the mysteries of Isis (*Metamorphoses* 11.25). Perhaps the **holy kiss** was among believers already a mark of celebrations of the Eucharist, as it certainly would be by the time of Justin,[28] and Paul was expecting his letter to be read out in such an assembly. In any case, such a kiss, shared among the believers at Rome, will be the sign of their unity in Christ (compare 1 Cor. 16.20, 2 Cor. 13.12, 1 Thess. 5.26; also 1 Pet. 5.14).[29]

All the churches of Christ salute you (16.16b). This "global greeting" as Fitzmyer calls it[30] is appropriately addressed to the church of the imperial capital on behalf of churches Paul has founded in Galatia, Asia, Macedonia, and Achaia. The expression itself is unusual—Paul speaks normally of "the churches [or "the church"] of God"—but in any case, as Calvin observed, here too, by sending such greeting, Paul was evidently "doing all that he could to bind together all the members of Christ by the bond of love."[31]

Paul in His Own Hand (16.17–20)

Yet, as Paul well knows, there remain those who create tensions and divisions within the community. Indeed, the very reference with which he has just concluded—to "all the churches of Christ"—may have served to remind him of those various causes of scandal and division with which he had constantly to struggle, and of which the sources of division within the Roman community were merely one example. Therefore (we may plausibly suppose) Paul takes the stylus from Tertius, his amanuensis,

---

28. "Having completed the prayers, we salute one another with a kiss. Then there is brought to the president . . . bread and a cup of wine mixed with water" (Justin, *Apologia Maior* 65.2–3).

29. See further Gustav Stählin, "φιλέω, καταφιλέω, φίλημα," in *TDNT* 9.118–46; W. Klassen, "Kiss (NT)," in *ABD* 4.89–92.

30. Fitzmyer, *Romans* 742.

31. Calvin, *Romans* 323.

and writes a final *subscriptio* in his own hand, beginning with the repetition of his authoritative *parakalō* (compare 12.1):

I appeal to you [*parakalō***], brothers** and sisters, **be on the lookout for those who create dissension and difficulties, in opposition to the teaching that you have learned** (15.17a). **Avoid them!** Here, in contrast to 14.1–15.13, he no longer speaks of particular groups—"the strong," "the weak," or whatever[32]—for he has passed beyond that stage of his argument. He speaks now not of a particular group or opinion at all, but of the principle that guided his argument even when he *was* speaking of such things—he speaks of an attitude to the community.

There are, Paul says, those who **create dissension and difficulties,** and it is that above all (that is, the creation of dissension, rather than the views of the dissenters) which is **in opposition to the teaching that you have learned.** What **teaching** is this? Not, of course, something specific to Paul's teaching, for the Romans were not members of a church founded by Paul. Rather, what is at stake is the fundamental "pattern of teaching" that sets believers free from sin and enables them to be slaves to God's justice—the "pattern of teaching" on which Paul has already congratulated them (6.17–18). It is the confession of faith itself that is called in question by the spirit of dissension and self-assertion, however and on whatever grounds (ultra "liberal" or ultra "orthodox") it may choose to articulate itself.

People like that are not serving our Lord Jesus Christ, but their own belly, and by fair speech and flattering words they deceive the hearts of fools! (16.18) So blunt is this language that some critics have found in its peremptoriness evidence that it cannot have been an original part of the Roman letter—in my view, again, mistakenly. Paul's rhetoric remains, as it has been throughout, epideictic. His expression about those who **serve . . . their own belly** is in the language of Jewish religious polemic and is a part of the general rhetoric of blame. In Paul's use (compare Phil. 3.19) and in that of his contemporaries (compare Philo, *On the Virtues* 182; 3 Macc. 7.11; *T. Mos.* 7.4) it is always used to speak of those who are perceived as abandoning God, regardless of the particular *way* in which they are doing this. Thus, in 3 Maccabees 7.11, it is used of Jews who have given up their religion altogether in order to avoid persecution (compare 3 Macc. 2.31). By contrast, in the *Testament of Moses* 7.4 (*deuoratores, gulae*: "gluttons, guzzlers") it is evident (compare 7.10) that those so described are still practicing Judaism, and in certain respects rather strictly, but not in a way of which the author approves. In other words, the only *content* to be derived from the expression is the author's disapproval. Beyond that, no precise meaning can be attached to it. Hence the error of looking at it for information about those referred to or for identifiable "party" features. As Dunn ob-

---

32. Nor, I think, is he speaking of hitherto unmentioned and possibly not yet present "false teachers"; but contrast, e.g., Käsemann, *Romans* 417–18 (who also admits that there is a case for regarding 16.17–20 as originally not a part of Romans at all [419]), and Moo, *Romans* 928–30 (who, in essence, doesn't [928]). On this latter question, see also (against authenticity) Robert Jewett, "Ecumenical Theology for the Sake of Mission: Romans 1:1–17+15:14–16:24," in *Pauline Theology*, vol. 3, *Romans*, ed. David M. Hay and E. Elizabeth Johnson (Minneapolis: Fortress Press, 1995), 89–108, especially 105–7 and literature there cited, and (in favor) J. Paul Sampley, "Romans in a Different Light: A Response to Robert Jewett," in *Pauline Theology*, vol. 3, ed. Hay and Johnson, 127–28, and literature there cited.

serves, "Who such people were is not made explicit, for Paul does not have any particular people in mind. He is dealing in the types of wisdom exhortation—the types
of evil to be avoided."[33]

This type of rhetoric is not, of course, unfamiliar to us—merely this form of it.
If I tell you that some people are "real losers," if you are wise you will be aware that
you know nothing about the objects of my abuse except that I have a low opinion of
them. The word "loser" in contemporary English is a part of the rhetoric of blame. If
you then hear me advising someone for whom I feel responsible to "steer clear of
losers. People like that kill everything they touch"—you will appreciate that I am
not talking about any particular individual at all, but an attitude of mind that I think
dangerous. That is exactly the kind of rhetoric in which Paul is engaging at Romans
16.17–20.

In the present context then, it is an attitude wherein the apostasy consists, and
it is an attitude—ostensibly, in others, but no doubt potentially in themselves
(1 Cor. 15.33)—against which Paul is warning the Romans. As for *them*—all of
them—even as he presumes to exhort them, he bases his exhortation on a generous,
even lavish, compliment: **for . . . *your* obedience is known to all** (compare 1.8) **so
that I rejoice over you** (16.19a)—no doubt, like all wise pastors, in that compliment affirming them for the very virtue that he hopes they will cultivate. Therefore
I would have you wise as to what is good and guileless as to what is evil (16.19b).
"Where the 'yes' of the Epistle to the Romans has once been spoken, there is obviously no need for much questioning to arrive at the 'no' to the reverse" (Barth).[34]
Then the God of peace will soon crush Satan under your feet! (16.20a). It is not,
we should note, "opponents" who are to be crushed, and still less is it members of
the church—not even those who might identify themselves as Paul's supporters—
who are to do the crushing. It is **Satan**, the adversary, the divider, who is to be crushed,
and it is God who will do it. "Then," as Paul wrote on another occasion, "comes the
end, when [Christ] delivers the kingdom to God the father after destroying every
rule and every authority and power" (1 Cor. 15.24). So Paul offers his final prayer
for the Roman church—and it is what he wished it from the beginning (compare
1.7b): **may the grace of our Lord Jesus Christ be with you!** (16.20b).

Greetings from Paul's Colleagues (16.21–23)

Paul's story is told, and his message complete. There remain final greetings from his
amanuensis and his colleagues. Yet they, too, in their way, illustrate what Paul has
been saying:

> **Timothy, my fellow worker, salutes you. So do Lucius and Jason and Sosipater,
> my kinsmen.**
> I **Tertius, the writer of this letter, greet you in the Lord.**
> **Gaius, who is host to me and to the whole church, salutes you. Erastus, the city
> treasurer, and our brother Quartus, salute you.** (16.21–3)

33. Dunn, *Romans* 2.906.
34. Barth, *Shorter Romans* 184.

The matter cannot, of course, be demonstrated, but it is possible, and even perhaps likely, that the Erastus here mentioned as **city treasurer** (*oikonomos tēs poleōs*) is the Erastus identified on a first-century marble paving stone at Corinth as having held the office of aedile: ERASTVS PRO: AEDILITATE: S: P: STRAVIT ("Erastus, in return for his aedileship, laid the pavement at his own expense").[35] The offices of aedile (Greek, *agoronomos*) and of **city treasurer** (Greek, *oikonomos tēs poleōs*, literally "steward of the city") are perhaps not the same,[36] but there is in any case not the slightest reason that the same person might not have held different public positions in the same city at different times. If so, then Erastus is, by implication, such a benefactor as Paul has perhaps suggested the wealthy among those he addresses should be (see 13.3). Against this suggestion it is sometimes objected that Erastus, as a Christian, could not have taken the oath of office; but we know from Philo that certain Jews held office at this period, and apparently they did so without compromising their monotheism. Philo is, as it happens, highly critical of the individuals in question on other grounds, so it is hardly likely that he would have omitted to mention their apostasy, if he had considered that to be the case. So it seems evident that Jewish, and therefore presumably Christian, exceptions were possible (see Philo, *Legum Allegoria* 3.167).

Be that as it may, it is certainly the case that at 16.21–23 the Jews Lucius, Jason, and Sosipater, and the gentiles Gaius, Erastus, and Quartus send their greetings together, in Christ. Those who receive them are thereby, implicitly, challenged to maintain the same spirit of unity, being themselves one fellowship in Christ. That unity is precisely what Paul has argued for, in every part of his discourse.

---

35. Rhys Carpenter, Charles H. Morgan, Oscar Broneer, and Robert L. Scranton, *Ancient Corinth: A Guide to the Excavations*, sixth edition (Athens: American School of Classical Studies at Athens, 1954), 74; compare Jerome Murphy-O'Connor, *St. Paul's Corinth: Texts and Archaeology* (Wilmington, Delaware: Michael Glazier, 1983), 37. See, in favor of the connection with Romans 16.23, Bruce M. Winter, *Seek the Welfare of the City: Christians as Benefactors and Citizens* (Carlisle, England: Paternoster Press; Grand Rapids, Michigan: Eerdmans, 1994), 180–97; contrast Gerhard Theissen, *The Social Setting of Pauline Christianity* (Edinburgh: Clark, 1882), 77–78.

36. Carpenter *et al.* suggest, however, that they might be the same (*Ancient Corinth* 74); see also Mason, *GTRI*, who lists *oikonomos* among three words used to translate Latin *aedilis*: see οἰκονόμος 4 (citing Rom. 16.23) (71), and *aediliis* (*municipii*, etc.) (175).

Epilogue

Unscientific Postscripts

Outsiders?

There is, Paul declared, no human standing before God save on the basis of God's justice and mercy—the same justice and mercy that was definitively, uniquely, and essentially revealed and made present for us in the person and work of Jesus Christ.[1]

Paganism—the deification of powers or forces within creation[2]—undermines Hebrew monotheism from one side. But a claim to status before God that is based on something other than God's justice and mercy undermines it from the other. It makes no difference whether the claim be (as among some Paul addressed at Rome) a claim based on knowledge of God's Law, or (as among some he addressed at Corinth) a claim based on knowledge of another kind, or on wisdom, or on gifts—any such claim undermines Hebrew monotheism, for any such claim asserts, by implication, that God is in some sense and in some measure *not* God of a part of the created order, or that there is something inherently wrong with a part of that order—such a claim asserts, in short, a dualism (Rom. 3.27–31, 10.12; compare 1 Cor. 8.4–6).

Paganism must be confronted by the Hebrew monotheist's unyielding claim that there is *One* Creator who has made all things well.

Dualism must be confronted by the Hebrew monotheist's unyielding claim that there is One Creator who has made *all* things well (Gen. 1.1–2.25).

Both claims, which are the same claim, require the confession that none stand before the One Creator, save on the basis of the Creator's justice and mercy.

---

1. Some of the material in what follows is also to be found in my editorial "Who is Heard?" in *STR* 42.1 (1998): 3–5.

2. In which category we must include pantheism, that is, the notion that God is *identical* with the created order. Pantheism is not, of course, to be confused with *panentheism*, that is, the notion that the totality of creation exists within God, although God is not absorbed into the world. Panentheism is only hostile to Hebrew monotheism if it denies that God created the world, and so denies that the world is in some sense distinct from God. See Rahner and Vorgrimler, *CTD* 333–34.

On such a basis as this Paul declared (among other things) that "all Israel will be saved" (11.26)—not (as we have noted) thereby claiming that every single Jew will go to heaven, but certainly affirming his conviction that Israel as a whole, ethnic Israel, will find there is a place for her in the final salvation.

Indeed, Paul went further, for he claimed finally, and on the same basis, that "God has consigned all to disobedience, that he may have mercy upon all" (11.32). *All.* How? As we have seen, Paul never said. Presumably because he did not think that he knew. Like Lady Julian, his confidence was simply in the thing itself, God's promise: "[T]his is the great deed ordained by our Lord God from without beginning, treasured and hidden in his blessed breast, known only to himself, through which deed he will make all things well."[3]

If we believe that, then what of mission? Do we need to do mission?

Of course we do. Will you know that my true love, whom I thought was dead and lost to me, is alive and in the house, and not bother to tell me because sooner or later I shall bump into her anyway? But that does not mean you must sneer at every thought or hope I ever had about her before your news, every intimation I had that she might be alive. Certainly we must aver that Jesus is Lord and Messiah. We cannot back away from that and remain faithful. I have no time at all for that notion of "interfaith dialogue" which involves all religions abandoning their claims to uniqueness and universality. As Robert Davis Hughes has said, such an approach "results not in interfaith dialogue at all but in a roundtable of liberals at which none of the actual religious cards is ever laid on the table, especially not the Christian ones. Far from respecting our dialogue partners, this position assumes they are not capable of taking our best shot, so we pull our punches. This kind of tolerance is both patronizing and unfaithful."[4]

But is there not a way of announcing our Lord that is not a put-down of all other hopes and all others who have hoped? "All human activity," Karl Barth said, "is a cry for forgiveness; and it is precisely this that is proclaimed by Jesus and that appears concretely in Him."[5] Why, then, should we jeer at that cry in any one, or claim that it does not appeal to the reality to which we appeal?

We must continue to witness to Christ by all means possible, even (as Saint Francis apparently said to his disciples on one occasion) if everything else fails, by using words. But we cannot assume that in the course of this witness we shall have nothing to learn or that we know what the other great monotheistic faiths' acceptance of our witness might look like.

Peter was sent by God to Cornelius the Roman, and he proclaimed to Cornelius God's gracious act in Christ (Acts 10.36–48). But first he listened to Cornelius's story, and from it he learned something about the very God whom he had been sent to proclaim (Acts 10.30–33). And he had the good manners to admit it (Acts 11.34–

---

3. Edmund Colledge, O.S.A., and James Walsh, S. J. (eds. and trans.), *Julian of Norwich: Showings* (New York: Paulist Press, 1978), 232–33.

4. Robert Davis Hughes III, "Christian Theology of Interfaith Dialogue: Defining the Emerging Fourth Option," *STR* 40.4 (1997): 394.

5. Barth, *Romans* 96–97.

35). As Krister Stendahl has said, we must once and for all get rid of the idea "so totally absent from Romans" that "salvation means we win and others become like ourselves."[6] It is necessary to tell the story right. Salvation means that God will win, and we shall all be the better for it.

Insiders

If none of us has any standing before God save on the basis of God's justice and God's mercy, what does that imply about our relationships among ourselves, within the fellowship of Christian faith? Paul's address to the Romans took not merely the form of a protreptic, but also that of a "family letter," because he regarded those he was addressing not merely as a collection of individuals, but also as a household, God's household, and therefore inextricably bound to each other even if they disagreed with or disliked each other.

For Paul, proclaiming and hearing the gospel led directly to forming communities "in Christ"—communities of the new age, which had begun with the Messiah's victory. In short, the gospel led to the church (12.1–5). Therefore the important question for Paul about behavior was always not, "Does this square well with your conscience?" but, "Does this serve to build up your brothers and sisters in the community?"—and *especially* is this the case, if you happen to consider your brothers and sisters to be weaker than you? (14.1–15.13). And in any case, "Who are you to pass judgment on someone else's household slave?" (14.4).

The ancients, and presumably Paul among them, were as well aware as we are of the violence of the world (see 2 Corinthians 11.24–25). Rome itself was a frightening, violent city.[7] Yet Paul thought it possible for believers to create among themselves what François Bovon has called "zones of peace"[8]—"caring for one another with brotherly and sisterly affection" (12.10).

The apostle's insistence in Romans 12–15.13 (and notably at 14.1–15.13) on continuing fellowship in the church among groups who evidently differed widely among themselves in a range of significant matters of faith and practice continues to challenge not only the behavior of Christians toward each other *within* congregations, communities, and denominations, but also the feeble ecumenism that marks all major Christian denominations in their relationships toward each other at the end of the twentieth century.

What, for example, of table fellowship? Peter refused table fellowship with baptized but uncircumcised gentiles at Antioch (Gal. 2.11–21)—and his refusal was understandable enough, when we consider just how dramatically such fellowship required the Jewish followers of Jesus to adapt. Yet Paul was furious. With what biting irony, then, would Paul have addressed those who continue to insist on a divided table among Christians who confess the same Triune God, recite the same

---

6. Krister Stendahl, *Final Account: Paul's Letter to the Romans* (Minneapolis: Fortress Press, 1995), 44.

7. On Roman violence, see T. P. Wiseman, *Catullus and His World: A Reappraisal* (Cambridge: Cambridge University Press, 1985), 5–10.

8. François Bovon, "The Child and the Beast: Fighting Violence in Ancient Christianity," *HDB* 27.4 (1998): 16.

ecumenical creeds, hold in reverence the same Scriptures, and celebrate the same sacraments of Baptism and Eucharist? While we may grant differences in denominational understanding of those sacraments, yet in the same breath we must also confess those differences to be so subtle that it takes a trained theologian to understand them. C. S. Lewis's observation (although he applied it only to the internal politics of the Church of England) remains true: that it was the devil's work when there was division over the sacrament between those who could not actually have stated the difference between Aquinas's, Calvin's, and Hooker's eucharistic theologies in any way that would hold water for two minutes. To create and sustain such division remains the devil's work, whoever does it—however exalted their office or pious their pretensions or beliefs.

During the twentieth century the major denominations took a major step forward—instead of abusing each other, they began to treat each other as "brothers and sisters," albeit "separated." There remains for the twenty-first century a logical next step. Brothers and sisters may disagree, but that does not stop them sometimes eating together. Brothers and sisters may live in separate houses and have quite different life styles, but even that does not stop them eating together on occasion. And so long as they eat together, they may take what time they need to come to a common understanding of the meaning of their fellowship. On the other hand, for so long as they will not eat together, the world must be forgiven if it thinks that essentially they are not in love, in fellowship, or in a family—and the world must also be forgiven if it does not take seriously much that they say, *particularly* when they presume to speak on love, fellowship, or family. The Christians' divided tables are a stumbling block and a scandal in the way of those for whom Christ died. The Christians' divided tables are a denial of the gospel. So, as Karl Barth said, the Epistle to the Romans "waits."

Hope

Protreptic is more than just exhortation to a way of living: protreptic bases exhortation on a perception of how the world is, and how it will be. Others have looked at the world and seen endless flux, endless progress, or utter meaninglessness. Paul, as Luther said, looked "with his sharp, discerning, apostolic eye" and saw everywhere "the holy and beloved cross."[9] To be sure, anyone who looks at the world and does not see everywhere its wounds is evidently not really looking. It is, however, as Ellen Bradshaw Aitken has said, "the nature of the church to attend to such wounds, including those in its own life, in order to recognize and to proclaim that they are joined to Jesus' wounds, to the life of the crucified one."[10]

In that joining, and in our tending those wounds in Jesus' name, Paul was aware that something happened. "For you did not receive the spirit of slavery to fall back into fear, but you have received the Spirit of adoption, through whom we cry 'Abba! Father!' The same Spirit bears witness in support of our spirit that we are children of

---

9. Cited in Barth, *Romans* 307.
10. Ellen Bradshaw Aitken, "A Rogation Procession," *STR* 40.4 (1997): 381.

God, and if children, then also heirs, heirs of God and co-heirs with Christ, given that we suffer with him, in order that we may be glorified with him" (Romans 8.15–17).

That is how the world is now. Already we have received "the first fruits" (8.23). And what of the world as it will be?

Always, Paul says, there was hope. "For the creation waits with eager longing for the revealing of the sons and daughters of God. For the creation was subjected to futility (not of its own will, but because of the one who subjected it) in hope" (8.19–20). Paul's hope is not then concerned just with individual wholeness, nor just with the church, nor even (if I have understood him correctly) just with humankind. Paul's hope is for "the creation." Paul's hope involves an order of joy, justice, and courtesy that shall compass the universe. Only so will be fulfilled the promise that paradise is to be restored (Isa. 11.6–9). Only so will be fulfilled Scripture's assurance that God has a covenant with the creation older than the covenant with the church and older than the covenant with Israel—a covenant with "every living creature of all flesh that is upon the earth" (Gen. 9.16; compare Gen. 9.8–17, Ps. 36.5–9). Only so will humankind's betrayal of the created order finally be made right (Rom. 8.21–23).

This hope gives meaning to the enterprise of faith. For Paul, those who are in fellowship with Christ are, virtually by definition, those who live in hope (Rom. 5.2, 8.24–25). Such hope ("eschatology") is not a belief beside other beliefs, to be thought of when there is leisure from more pressing matters. Hope springs directly from the Old Testament promise, is affirmed and clarified in the death and resurrection of Christ, and so undergirds and gives direction to all other belief and all other action. Because we have hope, it is worthwhile *now* engaging in the creative subversion that is Christian witness, going from the Liturgy into the world to be "faithful witnesses of Christ our Lord"—as the various eucharistic orders of the various communions all demand of us, in one way or another. Because we have hope, it is worthwhile *now* engaging in the apparently hopeless task of trying to create zones of peace, justice, and courtesy in the church and in the world. We do not have two lives, one transitory and one eternal, but *one* life, which was designed from the beginning to be eternal life in Jesus Christ our Lord. Therefore it is already "high time for you to awake out of sleep. For salvation is nearer to us now than when we first believed" (13.11).

Or, as Paul reminded the Corinthians on another occasion, "in the Lord, your labor is not in vain" (1 Cor. 15.58). He was talking, as it happened, about resurrection. The last thing to be said (at least from the present point of view) is that hope overcomes death. Such hope assures us, Paul says, that death cannot finally separate us from the love of God that is in Christ Jesus our Lord (Rom. 8.38–39). Even here, however, Paul does not speak merely of individual hope, "because the creation itself will be set free from the bondage of corruption and obtain the liberty of glory of the children of God . . . for God has confined all to disobedience, that he may have mercy on all" (8.21, 11.32). Even here we are directed, essentially, to think of the hope of the other.

> O the depth of the riches and wisdom and mercy of God! How unsearchable are his judgements and how inscrutable are his ways! (11.33)

For this, too, the Epistle to the Romans "waits."

General Bibliography

Primary Sources

THE BIBLE

The English translation of the Bible here used as a basis is the RSV, although I have freely made changes where either clarity or accuracy seemed to require them. There is at present, however, no satisfactory translation into English of those parts of the Septuagint that are based upon the Hebrew: therefore I have had to make my own.

Behind my references to Scripture in the original languages or in versions other than English lie the following editions:

French Bible (BJ): *La Sainte Bible: traduit en français sous la direction de L'École Biblique de Jérusalem*. Paris: Les Éditions du Cerf, 1961.

Greek New Testament (Nestle-Aland 27): Eberhard Nestle and Erwin Nestle, with Barbara Aland, Kurt Aland, Johannes Karavidopoulos, Carlo M. Martini, and Bruce M. Metzger, *Novum Testamentum Graece*. 27th edition. Stuttgart: Deutsche Bibelgesellschaft, 1984.

Greek Old Testament (LXX): Alfred Rahlfs, ed., *Septuaginta: Id est Vetus Testamentum graece iuxta LXX interpretes*. Stuttgart: Deutsche Bibelgesellschaft; Athens: Ἡ Ἑλληνικὴ Βιβλικὴ Ἑταιρία, 1936.

Hebrew Scriptures, Masoretic Text (MT): K. Elliger and W. Rudolph, *Biblia Hebraica Stuttgartensia*. Stuttgart: Deutsche Bibelstiftung, 1966–67.

Italian Bible (BEP): A. Girlanda, P. Gironi, F. Pasquero, G. Ravasi, P. Rossano, and S. Virgulin, eds., *La Bibbia: nuovissima versione dai testi originali*. Milan: Edizioni Paoline, 1987.

Latin Bible (Vg): Boniface Fischer, John Gribomont, H. F. D. Sparks, and W. Thiele, *Biblia Sacra: iuxta Vulgatam Versionem*. Stuttgart: Deutsche Bibelgesellschaft, 1969.

OTHER ANCIENT SOURCES

Adam and Eve, Life of [Apocalypse] (Greek), *Life of* (Latin). Greek text in D. A. Bertrand, *La vie grecque d'Adam et Eve*. Recherches intertestamentaires, 1. Paris: Maisonneuve, 1987. Latin text in J. H. Mozley, "The Vitae Adae." *JTS* 30 (1929): 121–49. Translation by L. S. A. Wells, revised by M. Whittaker. In Sparks, *Apocryphal Old Testament*, 141–67.

"Ambrosiaster." *Ad Romanos* [*Exposition of Romans*]. Text in CSEL 81.1

Apollinarius. *To Taesis*. Text and translation in A. S. Hunt and C. C. Edgar, *Select Papyri*. Vol. 1. *Private Affairs*, 302–5. LCL. London: Heinemann; New York: Putnam's: 1932.

Appianus. *The Civil Wars*. Text and translation in Horace White, *Appian's Roman History*. 4 vols. LCL. London: Heinemann; New York: Macmillan, 1912–13. Translation in John M. Carter, *Appianus of Alexandria: The Civil Wars*. London: Penguin Books, 1996.

Apuleius. *Metamorphoses*. Text and French translation in Donald Struan Robertson and Paul Vallette, *Apuleius: Les Metamorphoses*. Collection des universités de France. Paris: Les Belles Lettres, 1940–46. Also Los Altos, California: Packard Humanities Institute, 1991 (CD Rom) [taken from original, Paris: Les Belles Lettres, 1940–46]. Translation in Patrick Gerard Walsh, *Apuleius Lucius: The Golden Ass*. WC. Oxford: Oxford University Press, 1995 [1994].

Aquinas. *Summa Theologica*. Text in Petrus Caramello, *S. Thomae Aquinatis Doctoris Angelici Summa Theologiae*. Turin: Marietti, 1952. Translation in *St. Thomas Aquinas: Summa Theologica*. Trans. Fathers of the English Dominican Province. 5 vols. Westminster, Maryland: Christian Classics, 1981.

Aristotle. *Nicomachean Ethics*. Text in Ingram Bywater, *Aristotelis Ethica Nicomachea*. Oxford: Clarendon Press, 1959 [1894]. Text and translation in H. Rackham, *The Nicomachean Ethics*. LCL. Cambridge, Massachusetts: Harvard University Press; London: Heinemann, 1934. Translation in Sir David Ross, *The Nicomachean Ethics of Aristotle*. WC. London: Oxford University Press, 1954 [1925].

———. *Poetics*. Text in D. W. Lucas, ed., *Aristotle: Poetics*. Oxford: Oxford University Press, 1959. Text and translation in Ingram Bywater, *Aristotle: On the Art of Poetry*. Oxford: Clarendon Press, 1909.

———. *Politics*. Text in William David Ross, *Politica Aristotelis*. Oxford: Clarendon Press, 1962. Text and translation in Harris Rackham, *Aristotle: Politics*. LCL. London: Heinemann; New York: Putnam's 1932.

———. *Rhetoric*. Text in W. D. Ross, *Aristotelis Ars Rhetorica*. Oxford: Clarendon Press, 1959. Text and translation in John Henry Freese, *Aristotle: The "Art" of Rhetoric*. LCL. Cambridge, Massachusetts: Harvard University Press; London: Heinemann, 1926.

Assumption of Moses. See *Testament of Moses*.

Augustine. *Against Julian*. Text in J.-P. Migne, *Patrologia Latina* 44. Paris: 1865, cols. 641–874. Translation in Matthew A. Schumacher, *Saint Augustine Against Julian*. New York: Fathers of the Church, 1957.

———. *Contra duas Epistolas Pelagianorum* [*Against Two Letters of the Pelagians*]. Text in CSEL 60.421–570; William Bright, *Select Anti-Pelagian Treatises of St. Augustine and the Acts of the Second Council of Orange*. Oxford: Clarendon Press, 1880.

———. *The Literal Meaning of Genesis*. Text and French translation in P. Agaësse and A. Solignac, *La Genèse au sens littéral en douze livres*. 2 vols. Bibliothèque Augustinienne: Œuvres de Saint Augustin 48–49. Paris: Desclée de Brouwer, 1972. Translation in John Hammond Taylor, S. J., ed. and trans., *St. Augustine: The Literal Meaning of Genesis*. Ancient Christian Writers 41. 2 vols. New York: Newman Press, 1982.

———. *Propositions on the Epistle to the Romans and Unfinished Commentary on the Epistle to the Romans*. Texts in CSEL 84, 3–52, 145–81. Texts and translation in Paula Fredriksen Landes, *Augustine on Romans: Propositions from the Epistle to the Romans, Unfinished Commentary on the Epistle to the Romans*. Texts and Translations 23. Early Christian Literature Series 6. Chico, California: Scholars Press, 1982.

———. *The Spirit and the Letter*. Text (with French translation and notes) in P. Agaësse and A. Solignac, *Bibliothèque augustinienne: Oeuvres de saint Augustin*. Vols. 48–49 (Paris,

1972). Translation in John Burnaby, *Augustine: Later Works*. Library of Christian Classics 8. London: SCM Press; Philadelphia: Westminster Press, 1955.

Aurelius Dius. *To Aurelius Horion*. Oxyrhynchus Papyri 1296. Text and translation in A. S. Hunt and C. C. Edgar, *Select Papyri*. Vol. 1. *Private Affairs*, 343–345. LCL. London: Heinemann; New York: Putnam's, 1932.

Cassius Dio Cocceianus. *Roman History*. Text and translation in Earnest Cary, on the basis of the version by Herbert Baldwin Foster, *Dio's Roman History*. 9 vols. LCL. London: Heinemann; New York: Macmillan, 1914–27.

Cato, Marcus Porcius ("Cato the Censor"). *Origines*. The text is lost, but fragments have survived; for these see Martine Chassignet, *Marcus Porcius Cato: Les origines: (fragments)*. Paris: Les Belles Lettres, 1986. Also Hermann W. G. Peter, ed., *Marcus Porcius Cato: Origines*. Los Altos, California: Packard Humanities Institute, 1991 (CD Rom) [taken from original, Leipzig: Teubner, 1914].

Catullus. *Poems*. Text in D. F. S. Thompson, ed., *Catullus: A Critical Edition*. Chapel Hill, North Carolina: University of North Carolina Press, 1978. Also in Robinson Ellis, *Catulli Carmena*. Oxford: Clarendon Press, 1904.

Chairas. *To Dionysius the Physician*. PMert. 1.12. Text and translation in John L. White, *Light from Ancient Letters*, 145. Philadelphia: Fortress Press, 1986.

Chariton. *Callirhoe*. Text and translation in G. P. Goold, *Chariton: Callirhoe*. Cambridge, Massachusetts: Harvard University Press, 1995.

Chrysostom. *Homilies on the Epistle to the Romans*. Text in Migne, *Patrologiæ* 60.391–682.

Cicero. *Against Piso*. Text in Albert C. Clark, *M. Tulli Ciceronis Orationes*. 6 vols. Oxford: Clarendon Press, 1901–11. Text and translation in N. H. Watts, *Cicero: The Speeches*. LCL. London: Heinemann; New York: Putnam's, 1931.

———. *Haruspicum responsis*. Text in Alfred Klotz and Fritz Schöll, *M. Tulli Ciceronis scripta quae manserunt omnia*. Vol. 8. Leipzig: Teubner, 1919.

———. *Letters to His Friends*. Text in D. R. Shackleton Bailey, *Cicero: Epistulae ad Familiares*. 2 vols. Cambridge: Cambridge University Press, 1977. Translation in D. R. Shackleton Bailey, *Cicero's Letters to His Friends*. 2 vols. Harmondsworth, Middlesex: Penguin Books, 1978.

———. *On Behalf of Milo*. Text in Albert C. Clark, *M. Tulli Ciceronis Orationes*. 6 vols. Oxford: Clarendon Press, 1901–11. Text and translation in N. H. Watts, *Cicero: The Speeches*. LCL. London: Heinemann; New York: Putnam's, 1931.

———. *On Invention*. Text and translation in H. M. Hubbell, *Cicero: De Inventione, De Optimo Genere Oratorum, Topica*. Cambridge, Massachusetts: Harvard University Press; London: Heinemann, 1944.

[———.] *To Herennius*. Text and translation in Harry Caplan, *[Cicero] ad C. Herennium de Ratione Dicendi (Rhetorica ad Herennium)*. LCL. Cambridge, Massachusetts: Harvard University Press; London: Heinemann, 1954.

Claudia Severa. *To Sulpicia Lepidina*. Text and translation in A. K. Bowman and J. D. Thomas, "New Texts from Vindola," in *Brittania* 18 (1987): 125–42. Also in Alan K. Bowman, *Life and Letters on the Roman Frontier: Vindolanda and Its People*, 127. London: British Museum Press, 1994; New York: Routledge, 1998.

Clement of Alexandria. *The Rich Man's Salvation*. Text and translation in G. W. Butterworth, *Clement of Alexandria*. LCL. Cambridge, Massachusetts: Harvard University Press; London: Heinemann, 1982.

Clement of Rome. *1 Clement*. Text and translation in Kirsopp Lake, *The Apostolic Fathers*. Vol. 1. LCL. London: Heinemann; Cambridge, Massachusetts: Harvard University Press, 1912.

Columella. *On Agriculture*. Text and translation in E. S. Forster and Edward H. Heffner, *Lucius Junius Moderatus Columella: On Agriculture*. 3 vols. LCL. Cambridge, Massachusetts: Harvard University Press; London: Heinemann, 1941–55.

Cyprian. *Thasci Caecili Cypriani ad Quirinum: Testimoniorum Libri Tres* [*T. C. Cyprian to Quirinius: Three Books of Testimonies*]. Text in CSEL 3.1, 35–184.

Cyril of Jerusalem. *Mystagogical Catecheses*. Text and translation in F. L. Cross, ed., R. W. Church, trans., *St. Cyril of Jerusalem's Lectures on the Christian Sacraments: The Procatechesis and the Five Mystagogical Catecheses*. London: SPCK, 1966.

Dead Sea Scrolls. Text and translation in James H. Charlesworth, ed., *The Dead Sea Scrolls: Hebrew, Aramaic and Greek Texts with English Translations*. 10 vols. in progress. Tübingen: Mohr (Siebeck); Louisville, Kentucky: Westminster/John Knox Press, 1994–. Translation in Geza Vermes, *The Dead Sea Scrolls in English*. Fourth edition. London: Penguin Books, 1995.

Deferential Greetings to a Patron. Text and translation in G. H. R. Horsley, *New Documents Illustrating Early Christianity: A Review of the Greek Inscriptions and Papyri Published in 1976*. North Ride, New South Wales: Macquarie University, 1981.

Demeter, Hymn to. Text and translation in Helen P. Foley, *The Homeric Hymn to Demeter*. Princeton, New Jersey: Princeton University Press, 1994.

"Demetrius." *On Style*. Text, and translation by Doreen C. Innes based on W. Rhys Roberts, in Stephen Halliwell, Donald Russell, and Doreen C. Innes, eds., *Aristotle, Poetics; Longinus, On the Sublime; Demetrius, On Style*. LCL. Cambridge, Massachusetts: Harvard University Press, 1995.

Dio Chrysostom. *Discourses 4: On Kingship*. Text and translation in J. W. Cohoon, *Dio Chrysostom*. Vol. 1. LCL. London: Heinemann; New York: Putnam's, 1932.

———. *Discourses 77/78: On Envy*. Text and translation in H. Lamar Crosby, *Dio Chrysostom*. Vol. 5. LCL. Cambridge, Massachusetts: Harvard University Press; London: Heinemann, 1951.

Diogenes Laertius. *Lives of Eminent Philosophers*. Text in H. S. Long, *Diogenis Laertii Vitae Philosophorum*. 2 vols. Oxford: Clarendon Press, 1964. Text and translation in R. D. Hicks, *Diogenes Laertius: Lives of Eminent Philosophers*. 2 vols. LCL. Cambridge, Massachusetts: Harvard University Press; London: Heinemann, 1950 [1925].

Dionysius of Halicarnassus. *Letter to Gnaeus Pompeius, First Letter to Ammaeus, Second Letter to Ammaeus*. Text and translation in Stephen Usher, *Dionysius of Halicarnassus: The Critical Essays*. Vol. 2. LCL. Cambridge, Massachusetts: Harvard University Press; London: Heinemann, 1985.

———. *Roman Antiquities*. Text and translation in Edward Spelman, revised by Earnest Cary, *The Roman Antiquities of Dionysius of Halicarnassus*. 7 vols. Cambridge, Massachusetts: Harvard University Press; London: Heinemann, 1990 [1937–50].

1 (Ethiopic Apocalypse of) Enoch. Text and translation in Michael A. Knibb, in consultation with Edward Ullendorff, *The Ethiopic Book of Enoch: A New Edition in the Light of the Aramaic Dead Sea Fragments*. 2 vols. Oxford: Clarendon Press, 1978. Translation by Michael A. Knibb. In Sparks, *Apocryphal Old Testament*, 169–319.

Epicharmus. The works are lost, but fragments have survived: for text see George Kaibel, *Comicorum Graecorum Fragmenta*, vii, 88–138. Berlin: Weidmann, 1958.

Epictetus. *Discourses*. Text and translation in W. A. Oldfather, *Epictetus*. 2 vols. LCL. London: Heinemann; New York: Putnam's, 1926–28. Translation in Christopher Gill, *The Discourses of Epictetus*. Translation by Elizabeth Carter (1758), revised by Robin Hard. Everyman. London: Dent, 1995.

Euripides. *Bacchae*. Text and translation in Arthur S. Way, *Euripides*. Vol. 2. LCL. Cambridge, Massachusetts: Harvard University Press; London: Heinemann, 1912.

————. *Medea*. Text and translation in Arthur S. Way, *Euripides*. Vol. 4. LCL. Cambridge, Massachusetts: Harvard University Press; London: Heinemann, 1912.

————. *Orestes*. Text and translation in Arthur S. Way, *Euripides*. Vol. 2. LCL. Cambridge, Massachusetts: Harvard University Press; London: Heinemann, 1912.

Eusebius of Caesarea. *Demonstrationis Evangelicae*. Text in William Dindorf, *Eusebii Caesariensis Opera*. Vol. 3. Leipzig: Teubner, 1867.

Galen. *On the Pulse* and the fragment of the *Summary of Plato's Republic*. Text and translation of cited passages in R. Walzer, *Galen on Jews and Christians*, 14–16. London: Oxford University Press, 1949.

Heracles. *To Musaeus*. Text and translation in B. R. Rees, *Papyri from Hermopolis and Other Documents of the Byzantine Period*, 1–2. Graeco-Roman Memoirs 42. London: Egypt Exploration Society, 1964. Translation in Stanley K. Stowers, *Letter Writing in Greco-Roman Antiquity*, 156. LEC. Philadelphia: Westminster Press, 1986.

Heraclitus Stoicus. *Quaestiones Homericae*. Text in Franz Oelmann, *Heracliti Quaestiones Homericae*. BSGRT. Leipzig: Teubner, 1910.

Heraklas. *To Horos and Tachonis*. Text and translation in Robert A. Kraft and Antonia Tripolitis, "Some Uncatalogued Papyri of Theological and Other Interest in the John Rylands Library," *BJRL* 51 (1968): 137–63; G. H. R. Horsley, *New Documents Illustrating Early Christianity*, 51–52. New South Wales, Australia: Macquarie University, 1981.

To Herennius. See [Cicero].

Homer. *Iliad*. Text in Thomas W. Allen, *Homer Ilias*. Oxford: Clarendon Press, 1931. Text and translation in A. T. Murray, *Homer: The Iliad*. 2 vols. LCL. Cambridge, Massachusetts: Harvard University Press; London: Heinemann, 1944.

Horace. *Carmen Saeculare*. Text in Daniel H. Garrison, *Horace: Epodes and Odes, A New Annotated Latin Edition*. Norman: University of Oklahoma Press, 1991.

————. *Satires*. Text in Edward C. Wickham, *Horace: The Satires, Epistles, and De arte poetica*. Oxford: Clarendon Press, 1903. Text and translation in H. Rushton Fairclough, *Horace: Satires, Epistles, Ars Poetica*. LCL. Cambridge, Massachusetts: Harvard University Press; London: Heinemann, 1939.

Josephus. *Against Apion, The Jewish War*, and *Jewish Antiquities*. Text and translation in H. St. J. Thackeray, Ralph Marcus, Allen Wikgren, and L. H. Feldman, *Josephus*. 10 vols. LCL. Cambridge, Massachusetts: Harvard University Press; London: Heinemann, 1926–65.

Jubilees. Ethiopic text in R. H. Charles, *The Ethiopic Version of the Hebrew Book of Jubilees*. Oxford: Clarendon Press, 1895. Hebrew fragments in M. Baillet, J. T. Milik, and R. de Vaux, *Les 'Petites Grottes' de Qumran. Discoveries in the Judaean Desert*, 3. Oxford: Clarendon Press, 1962. Translation by R. H. Charles, revised by C. Rabin. In Sparks, *Apocryphal Old Testament*, 1–139.

Julius Victor. *The Art of Rhetoric*. Text in C. Halm, ed., *Rhetores Latini Minores*. Leipzig: Teubner, 1863. Text and translation (by Jerome Neyrey, S.J.) of 27 (*On Letter Writing*) in Abraham J. Malherbe, *Ancient Epistolary Theorists*, 62–65. SBLSBS 19. Atlanta, Georgia: Scholars Press, 1988.

Justin. *Apologia Maior*. Text in Miroslav Marcovich, ed., *Iustini Martyris Apologiae pro Christianis*. Patristische Texte und Studien 38. Berlin: de Gruyter, 1994.

Juvenal. *Satires*. Text and translation in G. G. Ramsey, ed. and trans., *Juvenal and Persius*. LCL. London: Heinemann; Cambridge, Massachusetts: Harvard University Press, 1918.

Livy. *From the Founding of the City*. Text in R. S. Conway, C. F. Walters, S. K. Johnson, and A. H. McDonald, *Titi Livi Ab Urbe condita*. Oxford: Clarendon Press, 1914–. Text and translation in B. O. Foster, F. G. Moore, Evan T. Sage, A. C. Schesinger, and R. M. Geer (General Index), *Livy*. 14 vols. Publication varies among Cambridge,

Massachusetts: Harvard University Press; New York: G. P. Putnam's; London: Heinemann, 1919–59.

Lucan. *Civil War*. Text in A. E. Housman, ed., *M. Annaei Lucani Belli Civilis Libri Decem*. Cambridge, Massachusetts: Harvard University Press, 1926. Text and translation in J. D. Duff, *Lucan (Pharsalia)*. LCL. London: Heinemann; New York: Putnam's, 1928.

Lucian. Text in M. D. McLeod, *Luciani Opera*. 4 vols. Oxford: Clarendon Press, 1972–80. Text and translation in A. M. Harmon, K. Kilburn, and M. D. MacLeod, *Lucian*. 8 vols. LCL. Cambridge, Massachusetts: Harvard University Press; London: Heinemann, 1967–79.

3 Maccabees. Text and translation in Moses Hadas, *The Third and Fourth Books of Maccabees*. New York: Harper, 1953. Translation by H. Anderson. In Charlesworth, *Old Testament Pseudepigrapha* 2, 509–29.

4 Maccabees. Text and translation in Moses Hadas, *The Third and Fourth Books of Maccabees*. New York: Harper, 1953. Translation by H. Anderson. In Charlesworth, *Old Testament Pseudepigrapha* 2, 531–64.

Marcus Aurelius. *Meditations*. Text and translation in Arthur Spenser Loat Farquharson, ed. and tr., *ΜΑΡΚΟΥ ΑΝΤΩΝΙΟΥ ΑΥΤΟΚΡΑΤΟΡΟΣ ΤΑ ΕΙΣ ΕΑΥΤΟΝ The Meditations of the Emperor Marcus Antoninus*. 2 vols. Oxford: Clarendon Press, 1944.

Martial. *Epigrams*. Text and translation in D. R. Shackleton Bailey, *Martial: Epigrams*. LCL. 3 vols. Cambridge, Massachusetts: Harvard University Press, 1993.

Martyrdom of St. Polycarp. Text and translation in Kirsopp Lake, *The Apostolic Fathers*. Vol. 2. LCL. London: Heinemann; Cambridge, Massachusetts: Harvard University Press, 1913.

Mekilta de-Rabbi Ishmael. Text and translation in Jacob. Z. Lauterbach, *Mekilta de-Rabbi Ishmael*. 3 vols. Philadelphia: Jewish Publication Society of America, 1933.

Mishnah. Text and translation in Philip Blackman, *Mishnayoth*. 6 vols. Gateshead: Judaica Press, 1983. Translation in Herbert Danby, *The Mishnah*. Oxford: Clarendon Press, 1933.

Odes of Solomon. Syriac text and translation in James H. Charlesworth, *The Odes of Solomon: The Syriac Texts*. Oxford: Clarendon Press, 1973; reprint, Texts and Translations 13, Missoula, Montana: Scholars Press, 1978. Translation by J. A. Emerton. In Sparks, *Apocryphal Old Testament*, 683–731. Translation by James H. Charlesworth. In Charlesworth, *Old Testament Pseudepigrapha* 2, 725–71.

Origen. *Commentary on St. Paul's Epistle to the Romans*. The complete work has been lost, but considerable fragments have been preserved, as well as an evidently not-entirely-reliable Latin translation by Rufinus. Text and French translation of Greek fragments pertaining to Romans 3.5–5.7 in Jean Scherer, *Le Commentaire d'Origène sur Rom. III.5–V.7 d'après les extraits du papyrus n°88748 du Musée du Ciare et les fragments de la Philocalie et du Vaticanus gr. 762: Essai de reconstitution du texte et de la pensée des tomes V et VI du "Commentaire sur L'Épîre aux Romains."* Cairo: Institut Français d'Archéologie Orientale, 1957. Text of further fragments in A. Ramsbotham, "The Commentary of Origen on the Epistle to the Romans," Part 1 in *JTS* 13 (1911–12) 209–24, Part 2 in *JTS* 13 (1911–12) 357–68, and Part 3 in *JTS* 14 (1912–13) 10–22. Rufinus's Latin translation (*Origenis Commentaria in epistolam b. Pauli ad Romanos*) in Migne, *Patrologiæ* 14.837–1292.

Ovid. *Metamorphoses*. Text and translation in Frank Justus Miller, *Ovid: Metamorphoses*. Vol. 1 (revised G. P. Goold). LCL. Cambridge, Massachusetts: Harvard University Press, 1977. Vol. 2. London: Heinemann; Cambridge, Massachusetts: Harvard University Press, 1916.

Passion of Saints Perpetua and Felicity. Texts (Latin and Greek) and French translation in Jacqueline Amat, *Passion de Perpétue et de Felicité. suivi des Actes.* SC 417. Paris: Les Éditions du Cerf, 1996.

Paulus Fabius Maximus. [*To the Corporation of Greek Citizens*]. Text in Dittenberger, *Inscriptiones*, 2.458.

Philo. Text and translation in F. H. Colson and G. H. Whitaker, *Philo.* 10 vols with 2 supp. vols. LCL. Cambridge, Massachusetts: Harvard University Press; London: Heinemann, 1968–81.

Plato. *Lysis.* Text in John Burnet, *Platonis opera.* Vol. 3. Oxford: Clarendon Press, 1968 [1903]. Translation in W. R. M. Lamb, *Plato.* Vol. 5. LCL. London: Heinemann; New York: Putnam's, 1932 (revised) [1925].

———. *Phaedo.* Text in John Burnet, *Platonis opera.* Vol. 1. Oxford: Clarendon Press, 1967 [1900]. Translation in David Gallop, *Plato: Phaedo.* WC. Oxford: Oxford University Press, 1993 [1975].

———. *Republic.* Text in J. Burnet, *Platonis Opera.* Vol. 4. Oxford: Oxford University Press, 1967 [1900]. Translation in Desmond Lee, *Plato: The Republic.* Second edition, revised. Harmondsworth, Middlesex: Penguin Books, 1987.

———. *Statesman.* Text in J. Burnet, *Platonis Opera.* Vol. 1. Oxford: Oxford University Press, 1967 [1900]. Translation in J. B. Skemp, *Statesman.* London: Routledge and Kegan Paul, 1952.

Pliny the Younger. *Letters.* Text in R. A. B. Mynors, *Pliny: Letters I–X.* Oxford Classical Text. Oxford: Oxford University Press, 1963. Translation in Betty Radice, *The Letters of Pliny the Younger.* Harmondsworth, Middlesex: Penguin Books, 1963.

———. *Panegyricus.* Text and translation in Betty Radice, *Pliny: Letters and Panegyricus.* Vol. 2. LCL. Cambridge, Massachusetts: Harvard University Press; London: Heinemann, 1969.

Plutarch. *Moralia.* Text in W. Nachstädt, W. Sieveking, J. B. Tichener, and C. Hubert, *Plutarchi Moralia.* 4 vols. Leipzig: Teubner, 1971. Text and translation in Frank Cole Babbit, W. C. Helmbold, Philip H. De Lacy, Benedict Einarson, P. A. Clement, H. B. Hoffleit, E. L. Minar, Jr., F. H. Sandbach, H. N. Fowler, L. Pearson, and H. Cherniss, *Plutarch's Moralia.* 16 vols. LCL. Cambridge, Massachusetts: Harvard University Press, 1927–. Translation of selections in Donald Russell, *Plutarch: Selected Essays and Dialogues.* WC. Oxford: Oxford University Press, 1993.

———. *Parallel Lives.* Text in Konrat Ziegler and Hans Gärtner, *Plutarchi Vitae parallelae.* BSGRT. 4 vols. Leipzig: Teubner, 1969–80. Text and translation in Bernadotte Perrin and James Wilfred Cohoon, *Plutarch's Lives.* 11 vols. LCL. London: Heinemann; Cambridge, Massachusetts: Harvard University Press, 1914–26.

Polybius. *Histories.* Text in Theodor Büttner-Wobst, *Polybii historiae.* 4 vols. 1893–1905. Text and translation in W. R. Paton, *Polybius: The Histories.* 6 vols. LCL. Cambridge, Massachusetts: Harvard University Press; London: Heinemann, 1922–27.

Psalms of Solomon. Greek text in Oscar von Gebhardt, Ψαλμοὶ Σολομῶντος: *Die Psalmen Salomo's zum ersten Male mit Benutzung der Athoshandschriften und des Codex Casanatensis herausgegeben.* Leipzig: Hinrichs, 1895; Herbert Edward Ryle and M. R. James, ΨΑΛΜΟΙ ΣΟΛΟΜΩΝΤΟΣ. *Psalms of the Pharisees, commonly called the Psalms of Solomon.* Cambridge: Cambridge University Press, 1891; also in Rahlfs, *Septuaginta* 2, 471–89. Translation by S. P. Brock. In Sparks, *Apocryphal Old Testament,* 649–82.

Pseudo-Philo, *Biblical Antiquities.* Text and French translation in Daniel J. Harrington, Jacques Cazeaux, Charles Perrot, and Pierre-Maurice Bogaert, *Pseudo-Philon, Les Antiquités Bibliques.* SC 229–30. Paris: Les Éditions du Cerf, 1976. Translation by D. J. Harrington. In James H. Charlesworth, *Old Testament Pseudepigrapha* 2, 298–377.

Quintillian. *Institutio Oratoria.* Text and translation in H. E. Butler, *The Institutio Oratoria of Quintillian.* 4 vols. LCL. London: Heinemann; New York: Putnam's, 1920–22.

Qumran. See Dead Sea Scrolls.

Seneca. *Letters.* Text and translation in Richard M. Gummere, *Seneca ad Lucilium epistulae morales.* 3 vols. LCL. London: Heinemann; New York: Putnam's, 1920.

———. *Moral Essays.* Text and translation in John W. Basore, *Seneca: Moral Essays.* 3 vols. London: Heinemann; New York: Putnam's, 1928–35.

———. *Phaedra* [or *Hippolytus*]. Text and translation in Frank Justus Miller, *Seneca's Tragedies.* 2 vols. LCL. Second edition revised. 1917.

Sibylline Oracles. Text in Johannes Geffcken, *Die Oracula sibyllina.* Die griechischen christlichen Schriftsteller 8. Leipzig: Hinrichs, 1902 [reprint: Leipzig: Zentral-Antiquariat der Deutschen Demokratischen Republik, 1967; New York: Arno Press, 1979]. Translation by J. J. Collins. In Charlesworth, *Old Testament Pseudepigrapha* 1, 318–472.

Sophocles. *Philoctetes.* Text and French translation in Alphonse Dain and Paul Mazon, *Sophocle,* vol. 3, 10–66. Paris: Les Belles Lettres, 1967 [1960]. Text and translation in Hugh Lloyd-Jones, *Sophocles: Antigone, The Women of Trachis, Philoctetes, Oedipus at Colonus.* Cambridge, Massachusetts: Harvard University Press, 1994.

Suetonius. *Lives of the Caesars.* Text and translation in J. C. Rolfe, *Suetonius.* 2 vols. LCL. Cambridge, Massachusetts: Harvard University Press; London: Heinemann, 1979 [vol. 1, 1913; vol. 2, 1914].

Stobaeus. *Anthologies.* Text in Curtius Wachsmuth and Otto Hense, eds., *Ioannis Stobaaei Anthologii.* 5 vols. plus appendix. Berlin: Weidmann, 1884–1923.

Tacitus. *Agricola.* Text in R. M. Ogilvie and Ian Richmond, *Cornelii Taciti: De Vita Agricolae.* Oxford: Clarendon Press, 1967. Text and translation in Sir William Peterson and Maurice Hutton, *Tacitus: Dialogus, Agricola, Germania.* LCL. London: Heinemann; New York: Putnam's, 1914.

———. *The Annals.* Text in C. D. Fisher, ed., *Cornelii Tacitii Annalium ab excessu Diui Augusti Libri.* Oxford: Clarendon Press, 1906. Text and translation in Clifford H. Moore and John Jackson, *Tacitus, The Histories, The Annals.* LCL. 4 vols. Cambridge, Massachusetts: Harvard University Press; London: Heinemann, 1931–37.

———. *The Histories.* Text and translation in Clifford H. Moore and John Jackson, *Tacitus, The Histories, The Annals.* LCL. 4 vols. Cambridge, Massachusetts: Harvard University Press; London: Heinemann, 1931–37.

Talmud. Text and translation in A. Zvi Ehrman, *The Talmud with English Translation and Commentary.* Jerusalem: El-Am, 1965–. Translation of Babylonian Talmud in Isidore Epstein, *The Babylonian Talmud.* London: Soncino Press, 1961.

Targum, Neofiti 1. Deuteronomy. Text and translation by Martin McNamara and Michael Maher. In Alejandro Díez Macho, *Neophyiti 1: Targum Palestinense ms de la Biblioteca Vaticana.* Vol. 5: *Deuteronomio.* Madrid: Consejo Superior de Investigaciones Cientificas, 1978.

Tertullian. *Against marcion.* Text and translation in Ernest Evans, *Tertullian Adversus Marcionem.* 2 vols. Oxford: Clarendon Press, 1972.

Testament of Moses. Text in Johannes Tromp, *The Assumption of Moses: A Critical Edition with Commentary.* Leiden: Brill, 1993. Also, with a French translation, in Ernest-Marie Laperrousaz, *Le Testament de Moïse (généralement appelé "Assomption de Moïse").* Semetica: Cahiers publiés par l'Institut d'Études sémetiques de l'Université de Paris, 19. Paris: Libraire d'Amerique et d'Orient, 1970. Translation by R. H. Charles, revised by J. P. M. Sweet. In Sparks, *Apocryphal Old Testament,* 606–16. Translation by J. Priest. In Charlesworth, *Old Testament Pseudepigrapha* 1, 919–34.

Testaments of the Twelve Patriarchs. Text in Marinus de Jonge, H. W. Hollander, H. J. de Jonge, and Th. Korteweg, *The Testaments of the Twelve Patriarchs*. Pseudepigrapha veteris testamenti Graece 1. Leiden: Brill, 1978. Translation by Marinus de Jonge. In Sparks, *Apocryphal Old Testament*, 515–600. Translation by H. C. Kee. In Charlesworth, *Old Testament Pseudepigrapha* 1, 775–828.

Theodore of Mopsuestia. *In Epistolam Pauli ad Romanos commentarii fragmenta*. Text in *Theodori Mopsuestini in epistolam Pauli ad Romanos commentarii fragmenta* in Migne, *Patrologiæ*, 66.787–876.

Theodoret of Cyrrhus. *Interpretatio Epistolae ad Romanos*. Text in Migne, *Patroligiæ*, 82.43–226.

Theon. *Prgymnasmata*. Text in Leonard Spengel, *Rhetores Graeci*, 59–130. Leipzig: Teubner, 1854. Text and translation in James R. Butts, *The Progymnasmata of Theon: A New Text with Translation and Commentary*. Claremont: Claremont Graduate School, 1986.

Thucydides. *History of the Peleponnesian War*. Text in Henry Stuart Jones, *Thucydidis Historiae*. 2 vols. Oxford: Clarendon Press, 1942 (revised). Text and translation in Charles Foster Smith, *Thucydides*. 4 vols. LCL. London: Heinemann; Cambridge, Massachusetts: Harvard University Press, 1919–23.

Tyconius. *Book of Rules*. Text and translation in William S. Babcock, ed., *Tyconius: The Book of Rules*. Texts and Translations 31. Early Christian Literature Series 7. Atlanta, Georgia: Scholars Press, 1989.

Virgil. *Aeneid*, I. Text in R. G. Austin, ed., *P. Vergili Maronis Aeneidos Liber Primus*. Oxford: Clarendon Press, 1971.

The Wanderer. Text in Anne L. Klinck, ed., *The Old English Elegies: A Critical Edition and Genre Study*, 75–78. Montreal and Kingston: McGill-Queen's University Press, 1992.

Xenophon. *Memorabilia*. Text in Edgar C. Marchant, *Xenophontis opera omnia*. 5 vols. Oxford: Clarendon Press, 1985 [1900–20]. Text and translation in Edgar C. Marchant, *Xenophon: Memorabilia and Oeconomicus*. LCL. Cambridge, Massachusetts: Harvard University Press; London: Heinemann, 1965 [1923].

Secondary Sources

COMMENTARIES ON THE EPISTLE TO THE ROMANS

Barrett, C. K. *A Commentary on the Epistle to the Romans*. BNTC. London: Black, 1962 (corrected edition) [1957].

Barth, Karl. *The Epistle to the Romans*. Edwyn C. Hoskyns, trans. London: Oxford University Press, 1933. (ET: *Der Römerbrief*. Bern: Bäschlin, 1919.)

———. *A Shorter Commentary on Romans*. D. H. van Daalen, trans. London: SCM, 1959. (ET: *Kurze Erklärung des Römerbriefes*. Munich: Chr. Kaiser Verlag, 1956.)

Byrne, Brendan, S.J. *Romans*. Sacra Pagina Series, Vol. 6. Collegeville, Minnesota: Liturgical Press, 1996.

Calvin, Jean. *Commentary on the Epistle of Paul the Apostle to the Romans*. Text in T. H. L. Parker, ed., *Commentarius in epistolam Pauli ad Romanos*. Studies in the History of Christian Thought 22. Leiden: Brill, 1981. My page references are to the English translation in R. Mackenzie, ed. and trans., *The Epistles of Paul the Apostle to the Romans and the Thessalonians*. Calvin's Commentaries 8. Edinburgh: Oliver and Boyd, 1960.

Chrysostom, John. *Homilies on the Epistle to the Romans*. See Primary Sources.

Cranfield, C. E. B. *A Critical and Exegetical Commentary on the Epistle to the Romans*. Vol. 1. *Introduction and Commentary on Romans I-VIII*. ICC. Edinburgh: Clark, 1985 (first edition, 1975).

———. *A Critical and Exegetical Commentary on the Epistle to the Romans.* Vol. 2. Commentary on Romans IX–XVI and Essays. ICC. Edinburgh: Clark, 1983 (first edition, 1979).

Dodd, C. H. *The Epistle of Paul to the Romans.* London: Hodder and Stoughton, 1932.

Dunn, James D. G. *Romans.* WBC 38. 2 vols. Dallas, Texas: Word Books, 1988.

Fitzmyer, Joseph A., S.J., *Romans: A New Translation with Introduction and Commentary.* AB 33. New York: Doubleday, 1993.

Johnson, Luke Timothy. *Reading Romans: A Literary and Theological Commentary.* New York: Crossroad, 1997.

Käsemann, Ernst. *Commentary on Romans.* Geoffrey W. Bromiley, trans. Grand Rapids, Michigan: Eerdmans, 1980. (ET: *An Die Römer* [fourth edition] Tübingen: Mohr [Siebeck], 1980.)

Lagrange, M.-J. *Saint Paul: Épitre aux Romains: Études Bibliques.* Reprint. Paris: Librairie Lecoffre, J. Gabalda et Cie., 1950 (1916).

Leenhardt, F-J. *The Epistle to the Romans. A Commentary.* Harold Knight, trans. London: Lutterworth Press, 1961. (ET: *L'Épître de saint Paul aux Romains.* CNT 6. Neuchâtel: Delachaux et Niestlé, 1957.)

Lietzmann, H. *An die Römer.* HNT 8. Tübingen: Mohr (Siebeck), 1933 (first edition, 1906).

Luther, Martin. *Lectures on Romans.* Text in Johannes Ficker, *Die Scholien: Epistola ad Romanos.* In *D. Martin Luthers Werke: Kritische Gesamtausgabe (Weimarer Ausgabe).* Vol. 56. *Der Brief an die Römer,* 157–528. Weimar: Hermann Böhlaus Nachfolger, 1938. My page references are to the translation in Wilhelm Pauck, *Luther: Lectures on Romans Newly Translated and Edited.* LCC 15. London: SCM Press, 1961.

Moo, Douglas J. *The Epistle to the Romans.* NICNT. Grand Rapids, Michigan: Eerdmans, 1996.

Nygren, Anders. *Commentary on Romans.* Carl C. Rasmussen, trans. Philadelphia: Muhlenberg Press, 1949. (ET: *Pauli brev till Romarna.* Tolkning av Nya Testamentet, 6. Stockholm: Svenska Kyrkans Diakonistyrelses Bokförlag, 1944.)

Origen. *Commentary on the Epistle to the Romans.* See Primary Sources.

Rhys, Howard. *The Epistle to the Romans.* New York: Macmillan, 1961.

Sanday, W., and A. C. Headlam, *A Critical and Exegetical Commentary on the Epistle to the Romans.* ICC. Edinburgh: Clark, 1895.

Stuhlmacher, Peter. *Paul's Letter to the Romans: A Commentary.* Scott J. Hafemann, trans. Louisville, Kentucky: Westminster/John Knox Press, 1994.

Theodore of Mopsuestia. *Commentary on the Epistle to the Romans.* See Primary Sources.

STUDIES, PAPERS, AND MONOGRAPHS ON THE EPISTLE TO THE ROMANS, OTHER THAN COMMENTARIES

Adams, Edward. "Abraham's Faith and Gentile Disobedience: Textual Links between Romans 1 and 4." *JSNT* 65 (1997): 47–66.

Aletti, Jean-Noël. "The Rhetoric of Romans 5–8." In Stanley E. Porter and Thomas H. Olbricht, eds., *The Rhetorical Analysis of Scripture: Essays from the 1995 London Conference,* 294–308. JSNTSS 146. Sheffield, England: Sheffield Academic Press, 1997.

Aune, David. "Romans as a *Logos Protreptikos.*" In Karl P. Donfried, ed., *The Romans Debate: Revised and Expanded Edition,* 278–96. Peabody, Massachusetts: Hendrickson, 1991.

Aus, R. D. "Paul's Travel Plans to Spain and the 'Full Number of the Gentiles' of Rom. xi 25." *NovT* 21 (1979): 232–62.

Bell, Richard H. *No one seeks for God: An Exegetical and Theological Study of Romans 1.18–3.20,* WUNT 106. Tubingen: Siebeck Mohr, 1999.

Betz, H. D. "The Foundation of Christian Ethics According to Romans 12:1–2." In P. E.

Devenish and G. L. Goodwin, eds., *Witness and Existence: Essays in Honour of Schubert M. Ogden*, 55–72. Chicago: University of Chicago Press, 1989.

Black, David Allen. "The Pauline Love Command: Structure, Style, and Ethics in Romans 12.9–21." *FilNeot* 2 (1989): 3–22.

Bowers, W. P. "Jewish Communities in Spain in the Time of Paul the Apostle." *JTS* 26 (1975): 395–402.

Boyarin, Daniel. *A Radical Jew: Paul and the Politics of Identity*. Berkeley: University of California Press, 1994.

Brändle, Rudolf, and Ekkehard W. Stegemann. "The Formation of the First 'Christian Congregations' in Rome in the Context of the Jewish Congregations." In Karl P. Donfried and Peter Richardson, eds., *Judaism and Christianity in First-Century Rome*, 117–27. Grand Rapids, Michigan: Eerdmans, 1998.

Branick, Vincent P. "The Sinful Flesh of the Son of God (Rom. 8:3): A Key Image of Pauline Theology." *CBQ* 47 (1985): 246–62.

Brawley, Robert L. "Multivocality in Romans 4." In *Society of Biblical Literature 1997 Seminar Papers*, 284–305. Atlanta, Georgia: Scholars Press, 1997.

Brooten, Bernadette. "'Junia . . . Outstanding among the Apostles' (Romans 16.7)." In L. Swidler and A. Swidler, eds., *Women Priests: A Catholic Commentary on the Vatican Declaration*, 141–44. New York: Paulist Press, 1977.

———. "Patristic Interpretations of Romans 1.26." In E. A. Livingston, ed., *Studia Biblica XVIII*, 287–91. Kalamazoo, Michigan: Cistercian Publications, 1985.

Bryan, Christopher. *Way of Freedom: An Introduction to the Epistle to the Romans*. New York: Seabury Press, 1975.

Calvert, N. L. "Abraham and Idolatry: Paul's Comparison of Obedience to the Law to Idolatry in Galatians 4.1–10." In C. A. Evans and J. A. Sanders, eds., *Paul and the Scriptures of Israel*, 225–35. JSNTSup. 83. Sheffield, England: JSOT Press, 1992.

Cambier, J. *L'Évangile de Dieu selon l'Épître aux Romains: Exégèse et théologie biblique*. Vol. 1. *L'Évangile de la justice et de la grace*. Studia Neotestamentica, Studia 3. Bruges: Desclée de Brouwer, 1967.

Campbell, Douglas A. "False Presuppositions in the ΠΙΣΤΙΣ ΧΡΙΣΤΟΥ Debate: A Response to Brian Dodd," *JBL* 116 (1997): 713–19.

———. *The Rhetoric of Righteousness in Romans 3.21–26*. JSNTSup 65. Sheffield, England: Sheffield Academic Press, 1992.

———. "Romans 1:17—A *Crux Interpretum* for the Πίοτις Χριοτοῦ Debate," *JBL* 113 (1994): 265–85.

Caragounis, Chrys C. "From Obscurity to Prominence: The Development of the Roman Church between Romans and 1 Clement." In Karl P. Donfried and Peter Richardson, eds., *Judaism and Christianity in First Century Rome*, 245–79. Grand Rapids, Michigan: Eerdmans, 1998.

Cervin, Richard S. "A Note Regarding the Name 'Junia(s)' in Romans 16.7." *NTS* 40.3 (1994): 464–70.

Christoffersson, O. *The Earnest Expectation of the Creature: The Flood-Tradition as Matrix of Romans 8, 18–17*. Stockholm: Almqvist, 1990.

Cipriani, Settimio. "ΚΤΙΣΙΣ: creazione o genere umano?" *RB* 44.3 (1996): 337–40.

Clarke, A. D. "The Good and the Just in Romans 5:7." *TynBul* 41 (1990): 128–42.

Cranfield, C. E. B. "The Significance of *dia pantos* in Romans 11.10." In *SE* 2.1 (1964), 546–50.

Derrett, J. Duncan M. "'You Abominate False Gods; but Do You Rob Shrines?' Rom 2.22b." *NTS* 40.4 (1994): 558–71.

Dinter, P. E. *The Remnant of Israel and the Stone of Stumbling in Zion According to Paul (Romans 9–11)*. Ph.D. dissertation, Union Theological Seminary, 1980.

Dodd, Brian. "Romans 1:17—A *Crux Interpretum* for the Πίοτις Χριοτοῦ Debate?" *JBL* 114 (1995): 470–73.

Donfried, Karl P., ed. *The Romans Debate: Revised and Expanded Edition.* Peabody, Massachusetts: Hendirckson, 1991.

Elliott, N. *The Rhetoric of Romans: Argumentative Constraint and Strategy in Paul's Dialogue with Judaism.* JSNTSup 45. Sheffield, England: JSOT Press, 1990.

Finamore, Steve. "The Gospel and the Wrath of God in Romans 1." In Christopher Rowland and Crispin H. T. Fletcher-Lewis, eds., *Understanding, Studying, and Reading: New Testament Essays in Honour of John Ashton,* 140–45. JSNTSS 153. Sheffield, England: Sheffield Academic Press, 1998.

Fitzmyer, Joseph A. S.J. "The Consecutive Meaning of ΕΦ'Ω in Romans 5.12." *NTS* 39.3 (1993): 321–39.

Gagnon, Robert A. J. "The Meaning of ὙΜΩΝ ΤΟ ἈΓΑΘΟΝ in Romans 14:16," *JBL* 117.4 (1998): 675–89.

Gamble, Harry. *The Textual History of the Letter to the Romans: A Study in Textual and Literary Criticism,* Texts and Documents 42. Grand Rapids, Michigan: Eerdmans, 1977.

Giglioli, A. *L'oumo o il creato? Κτίσις in s. Paolo.* Studi biblici 21. Bologna: EDB, 1994.

Gillman, Florence Morgan. "Another Look at Romans 8.3: 'In the Likeness of Sinful Flesh.'" *CBQ* 49 (1987): 597–604.

Grenholm, Cristina. "The Process of the Interpretation of Romans." In *Society of Biblical Literature Seminar 1997 Papers,* 306–36. Atlanta, Georgia: Scholars Press, 1997.

Guerra, Anthony J. *Romans and the Apologetic Tradition: The Purpose, Genre, and Audience of Paul's Letter.* SNTSMS 81. Cambridge: Cambridge University Press, 1995.

Hays, Richard. "Have We Found Abraham to Be Our Forefather According to the Flesh? A Reconsideration of Romans 4:1." *NovT* 27 (1985): 251–70.

Hooker, Morna D. "Adam in Romans 1." *NTS* 6 (1959–60): 297–306.

———. "A Further Note on Romans 1." *NTS* 13 (1966–67): 181–83.

———. "ΠΙΣΤΙΣ ΧΡΙΣΤΟΥ." *NTS* 35 (1989): 321–42.

Jewett, Robert. "Ecumenical Theology for the Sake of Mission: Romans 1:1–17+15:14–16:24." In David M. Hay and E. Elizabeth Johnson, eds., *Pauline Theology.* Vol. 3. *Romans,* 89–108. Minneapolis: Fortress Press, 1995.

———. "Paul, Phoebe, and the Spanish Mission." In Jacob Neusner, Ernest S. Frerichs, Peter Borgen, and Richard Horsely, eds., *The Social World of Formative Christianity and Judaism: Essays in Tribute to Howard Clark Kee,* 142–61. Philadelphia: Fortress Press, 1988.

———. "Romans as an Ambassadorial Letter." *Interpretation* 36 (1982): 5–20.

Johnson, E. Elizabeth. "Romans 9–11: The Faithfulness and Impartiality of God." In David M. Hay and E. Elizabeth Johnson, *Pauline Theology.* Vol. 3. *Romans,* 211–39. Minneapolis: Fortress Press, 1995.

Johnson, Luke Timothy. "Romans 3.21–6 and the Faith of Jesus." *CBQ* 44 (1982): 77–90.

Jolivet, Ira J., Jr. "An Argument from the Letter and Intent of the Law as the Primary Argumentative Strategy in Romans." In Stanley E. Porter and Thomas H. Olbricht, eds., *The Rhetorical Analysis of Scripture: Essays from the 1995 London Conference,* 309–34. JSNTSS 146. Sheffield, England: Sheffield Academic Press, 1997.

Karris, Paul. "Romans 14.1–15.13 and the Occasion of Romans." In Karl P. Donfried, ed., *The Romans Debate: Revised and Expanded Edition,* 65–84. Peabody, Massachusetts: Hendrickson, 1991.

Käsemann, Ernst. "Principles of Interpretation of Romans 13." In *New Testament Questions of Today,* 196–216. Philadelphia: Fortress Press, 1969.

Keck, Leander E. "The Function of Romans 3.10–18: Observations and Suggestions." In

J. Jervall and Wayne A. Meeks, eds., *God's Christ and His People: Studies in Honour of Nils Alstrup Dahl*, 141–57. Oslo: Universitetsforlaget, 1977.

Lampe, Peter. "The Roman Christians of Romans 16." In Karl P. Donfried, ed., *The Romans Debate: Revised and Expanded Edition*, 216–230. Peabody, Massachusetts: Hendrickson, 1991.

La Piana, George. "La Primitiva Comunità Cristiana di Roma e L'Epistola ai Romani," *Ricerche Religiose* 1 (1925): 209.

Lincoln, Andrew T. "From Wrath to Justification: Tradition, Gospel, and Audience in the Theology of Romans 1.18–4.25." In David M. Hay and E. Elizabeth Johnson, eds., *Pauline Theology*. Vol. 3. *Romans*, 130–59. Minneapolis: Fortress Press, 1995.

Lyonnet, S. "Le sens de ἐφ ' ᾧ en Rom 5,12 et l'exégèse des Pères grecs." *Biblica* 36 (1955): 436–56.

Moxnes, Halvor. "Honor, Shame, and the Outside World in Paul's Letter to the Romans." In Jacob Neusner, Ernest S. Frerichs, Peter Borgen, and Richard Horsely, eds., *The Social World of Formative Christianity and Judaism: Essays in Tribute to Howard Clark Kee*, 207–18. Philadelphia: Fortress Press, 1988.

Peterman, G. W. "Romans 15.26: Make a Contribution or Establish Fellowship?" *NTS* 40 (1994): 457–63.

Piper, John. "The Demonstration of the Righteousness of God in Romans 3:25, 26." *JSNT* 7 (1980): 2–32.

Räisänen, Heikki. "Paul, God, and Israel: Romans 9–11 in Recent Research." In Jacob Neusner, Ernest S. Frerichs, Peter Borgen, and Richard Horsely, eds., *The Social World of Formative Christianity and Judaism: Essays in Tribute to Howard Clark Kee*, 178–206. Philadelphia: Fortress Press, 1988.

Romaniuk, K. "Was Phoebe in Romans 16.1 a Deaconess?" *ZNW* 81(1990): 132–34.

Sampley, J. Paul. "Romans in a Different Light: A Response to Robert Jewett." In David M. Hay and E. Elizabeth Johnson, eds., *Pauline Theology*. Vol. 3. *Romans*, 109–29. Minneapolis: Fortress Press, 1995.

Stowers, Stanley K. *The Diatribe and Paul's Letter to the Romans*. SBLDS 57. Chico, California: Scholars Press, 1981.

———. "Ἐκ πίστεως and διὰ τῆς πίστεως in Romans 3.30." *JBL* 108 (1989): 665–74.

———. "Paul's Dialogue with a Fellow Jew." *CBQ* 46 (1984): 707–22.

———. *A Rereading of Romans: Justice, Jews, and Gentiles*. New Haven: Yale University Press, 1994.

Suggs, M. Jack. "'The Word is Near You': Romans 10:6–10 with the Purpose of the Letter." In W. R. Farmer, C. F. D. Moule, and R. R. Niebuhr, eds., *Christian History and Interpretation: Studies Presented to John Knox*, 289–312. Cambridge: Cambridge University Press, 1967.

Talbert, C. H. "The Pauline Love Command: Structure, Style, and Ethics in Romans 12.9–21." *FilNeot* 2 (1989): 3–22.

———. "Tradition and Redaction in Romans xii.9–21." *NTS* 16 (1969–70): 83–93.

Thielman, Frank. "The Story of Israel and the Theology of Romans 5–8." In David M. Hay and E. Elizabeth Johnson, eds., *Pauline Theology*. Vol. 3. *Romans*, 169–95. Minneapolis: Fortress Press, 1995.

Walters, James C. *Ethnic Issues in Paul's Letter to the Romans: Changing Self Definitions in Earliest Roman Christianity*. Valley Forge, Pennsylvania: Trinity Press International, 1993.

Ward, Roy Bowen. "Why Unnatural? The Tradition behind Romans 1:26–27." *HTR* 90.3 (1997): 263–84.

Wedderburn, A. J. M. "Adam in Paul's Letter to the Romans." *Studia Biblica 1978*, vol. 3, *JSNTSup* (1980): 413–30.

Wuellner, Wilhelm. "Paul's Rhetoric of Argumentation in Romans: An Alternative to the Donfried-Karris Debate over Romans." *CBQ* 38 (1976): 330–51; reprinted in Karl P. Donfried, ed., *The Romans Debate: Revised and Expanded Edition*, 128–146. Peabody, Massachusetts: Hendrickson, 1991.

Yinger, Kent L. "Romans 12:14–21 and Nonretaliation in Second Temple Judaism: Addressing Persecution within the Community." *CBQ* 60.1 (1998): 74–96.

GENERAL

Aitken, Ellen Bradshaw. "τὰ δρώμενα καὶ τὰ λεγόμενα: The Eucharistic Memory of Jesus' Words in First Corinthians." *HTR* 90.4 (1997): 359–70.

———. "A Rogation Procession." *STR* 40.1 (1997): 379–82.

Auden, W. H. *For the Time Being*. London: Faber and Faber, 1946.

Baeck, Leo. "Romantic Religion." In Walter Kauffmann, ed. and trans., *Judaism and Christianity: Essays by Leo Baeck*, 189–292. New York: Atheneum, 1970.

Barnett, Paul. *The Second Epistle to the Corinthians*. NICNT. Grand Rapids, Michigan: Eerdmans, 1997.

Barr, James. "'Abba, Father' and the Familiarity of Jesus' Speech," *Theology* 91 (1988): 173–79.

Barrett, C. K. "Shaliach and Apostle." In E. Bammel, C. K. Barrett, and W. D. Davies, eds., *Donum Gentilicium: New Testament Studies in Honour of David Daube*, 88–102. Oxford: Clarendon Press, 1978.

Bartchy, S. S. *First Century Slavery and the Interpretation of 1 Corinthians 7:21*. SBLDS 11. Missoula, Montana: Scholars Press, 1973.

Barth, Karl. *Church Dogmatics*. 4 vols. Trans. G. T. Thomson, T. F. Torrance, G. W. Bromiley, et al. Edinburgh: Clark; New York: Scribner's, 1936–69. (ET: *Die kirchliche Dogmatik*. Vol. 1.1. Christian Kaisar Verlag, 1932. Vol. 1.2, et seq. Zürich: Evangelischer Verlag A.G., 1939–68.)

Barth, Marcus. *Ephesians: Introduction, Translation and Commentary on Chapters 1–3*. AB 34. New York: Doubleday, 1974.

———. "The Faith of the Messiah." *HeyJ* 10 (1969): 363–70.

Bash, Anthony. *Ambassadors for Christ: An Exploration of the Language of the New Testament*. WUNT 92. Tübingen: Mohr (Siebeck), 1997.

Battle, Michael. *Reconciliation: The Ubuntu Theology of Desmond Tutu*. Cleveland, Ohio: Pilgrim Press, 1997.

———. "The Ubuntu Theology of Desmond Tutu." In Leonard Hulley, Louise Kretschmar, and Luke Lungile Pato, eds., *Archbishop Tutu: Prophetic Witness in South Africa*, 93–105. Cape Town: Human and Rousseau, 1996.

Bauckham, Richard. *The Theology of the Book of Revelation*. New Testament Theology. Cambridge: Cambridge University Press, 1993.

Baumann, Richard A. *Women and Politics in Ancient Rome*. London: Routledge, 1992.

Baumgärtel, Friedrich. See Schweizer, Eduard, and Friedrich Baumgärtel.

Behm, J. "μορφή, μορφόω, μόρφωσις, μεταμορφόω." In *TDNT* 4.742–59.

Berger, Klaus. *Formegeschichte des Neuen Testament*. Heidelberg: Quelle and Meyer, 1984.

———. "Hellenestische Gattungen im Neuen Testament." In *ANRW* 25.2 (1984), 1031–1432.

Bertram, Georg. See Grundmann, Walter, and Georg Bertram.

Best, Ernest. *The Temptation and the Passion: The Markan Soteriology*, SNTSMS 2. Second edition. Cambridge: Cambridge University Press, 1990.

Beyer, Hermann W. "διακονέω, διακονία, διάκονος." In *TDNT* 2.81–93.

The Book of Common Prayer and Administration of the Sacraments and other Rites and Ceremonies of the Church according to the use of the Church of England [1662].

Boswell, John. *Christianity, Social Tolerance, and Homosexuality: Gay People in Western Europe from the Beginning of the Christian Era to the Fourteenth Century*. Chicago: University of Chicago Press, 1980.

Bovon, François. "The Child and the Beast: Fighting Violence in Ancient Christianity." *HDB* 27.4 (1998): 16–21.

Bowerstock, Glen W. *Fiction as History: Nero to Julian*. Berkeley: University of California Press, 1994.

Bowman, Alan K. *Life and Letters on the Roman Frontier: Vindolanda and Its People*. London: British Museum Press, 1994; New York: Routledge, 1998.

Bradley, K. R. *Discovering the Roman Family*. New York: Oxford University Press, 1991.

Breuggemann, Walter. *Theology of the Old Testament: Testimony, Dispute, Advocacy*. Minneapolis: Fortress Press, 1997.

Brooten, Bernadette. *Women Leaders in Ancient Synagogues*. Brown Judaic Studies 36. Chico, California: Scholars Press, 1982.

Bruce, F. F. *The Epistle of Paul to the Galatians: A Commentary on the Greek Text*. NIGTC. Exeter: Paternoster Press, 1982.

Bryan, Christopher. "Holy Traditions and Scholarly Inquiries." *STR* 37.1 (1993): 3–8.

———. "The Preachers and the Critics: Thoughts on Historical Criticism." *ATR* 74.1 (1992): 37–53.

———. *A Preface to Mark: Notes on the Gospel in Its Literary and Cultural Settings*. New York: Oxford University Press, 1993.

———. "Who is Heard?" *STR* 42.1 (1998): 3–5.

Bultmann, Rudolf. *Der Stil der paulinischen Predigt und die kynisch-stoische Diatribe*. FRLANT 13. Göttingen: Vandenhoeck and Ruprecht, 1910.

———. "πιστεύω, πίστις, πιστός, κτλ.." In *TDNT* 6.174–82, 197–228.

Burridge, Richard A. *What Are the Gospels? A Comparison with Graeco-Roman Biography*. SNTSMS 70. Cambridge: Cambridge University Press, 1992.

Burton, Ernest de Witt. *A Critical and Exegetical Commentary on the Epistle to the Galatians*. ICC. Edinburgh: Clark, 1921.

Caird, G. B. *The Language and Imagery of the Bible*. London: Duckworth, 1980.

Cairns, Douglas L. *Aidōs: The Psychology and Ethics of Honour and Shame in Ancient Greek Literature*. Oxford: Clarendon Press, 1993.

Calvert, N. L. "Abraham and Idolatry: Paul's Comparison of Obedience to the Law to Idolatry in Galatians 4.1–10." In C. A. Evans and J. A. Sanders, eds., *Paul and the Scriptures of Israel*, 221–37. JSNTSup. 83. Sheffield, England: JSOT Press, 1992.

Cambier, J. *L'Évangile de Dieu selon l'Épître aux Romains: Exégèse et théologie biblique*. Vol. 1. *L'Évangile de la justice et de la grâce*. Studia Neotestamentica, Studia 3. Bruges: Desclée de Brouwer, 1967.

Carpenter, Rhys, Charles H. Morgan, Oscar Broneer, and Robert L. Scranton. *Ancient Corinth: A Guide to the Excavations*. Sixth edition. Athens: American School of Classical Studies at Athens, 1954.

Cohen, Boaz. *Jewish and Roman Law: A Comparative Study*. New York: Jewish Theological Seminary of America, 1966.

Collange, Jean-François. *L'Épître de Saint Paul aux Philippiens*. Neuchâtel: Delachaux et Niestlé, 1973.

Collins, John N. *Diakonia: Re-interpreting the Ancient Sources*. New York: Oxford University Press, 1990.

Conzelmann, Hans, and Walther Zimmerli. "χαίρω, χαρά, συγχαίρω, χάρις, κτλ.," in *TDNT* 9.359–402.

Cranfield, C. E. B. *The Gospel According to Saint Mark*. CGTC. Cambridge: Cambridge University Press, 1972.

Cullmann, Oscar. *The State in the New Testament*. New York: Scribner's, 1956.

Danker, Frederick W. *Benefactor: Epigraphic Study of a Graeco-Roman and New Testament Semantic Field*. St. Louis: Clayton, 1982.

Dante Alighieri. *Commedia*. Text in Anna Maria Chiavacci Leonardi, ed., *Dante Alighieri: Commedia*. 3 vols. Milan: Arnoldo Mondadori, 1991–. Text and translation in John D. Sinclair, *The Divine Comedy of Dante Alighieri*. 3 vols. New York: Oxford University Press, 1939.

Daube, David. "Alexandrian Methods of Interpretation and the Rabbis." In *Festschrift H. Lewald*, 27–44. Basel: Helbing and Lichtenholm, 1953.

———. "Rabbinic Methods of Interpretation and Hellenistic Rhetoric." *HUCA* 22 (1949): 259–65.

Davies, W. D. *Paul and Rabbinic Judaism*. London: SPCK, 1978.

Dodd, C. H. "ἱλάσκεσθαι, Its Cognates, Derivatives and Synonyms in the Septuagint." In *JTS* 32 (1931): 352–60.

———. *The Bible and the Greeks*. London: Hodder and Stoughton, 1935.

Donne, John. *Meditations upon Emergent Occasions* 17. In John Booty, ed., *John Donne: Selections from Divine Poems, Sermons, Devotions, and Prayers*, 271–73. CWS. New York: Paulist Press, 1990.

Downing, F. Gerald. "À bas les Aristos. The Relevance of Higher Literature for the Understanding of the Earliest Christian Writings." *Novum Testamentum* 30.3 (1988): 212–30.

Dumont, Louis. *Essays on Individualism: Modern Ideology in Anthropological Perspective*. Chicago: University of Chicago Press, 1986.

Dunn, James D. G. *Jesus, Paul, and the Law: Studies in Mark and Galatians*. London: SPCK; Louisville, Kentucky: Westminster/John Knox Press, 1990.

———. "Once More, ΠΙΣΤΙΣ ΧΡΙΣΤΟΥ." In E. H. Lovering, ed., *Society of Biblical Literature 1991 Seminar Papers*, 730–44. Atlanta, Georgia: Scholars Press, 1991.

Edwards, Douglas E. *Religion and Power: Pagans, Jews, and Christians in the Greek Near East*. New York: Oxford University Press, 1996.

Fishbane, Michael. *Biblical Interpretation in Ancient Israel*. Oxford: Clarendon Press, 1985.

———. "Inner Biblical Exegesis: Types and Strategies of Interpretation in Ancient Israel." In Geoffrey H. Hartmann and Sanford Budick, eds., *Midrash and Literature*, 19–37. New Haven: Yale University Press, 1986.

Fitzgerald, J. T. "Virtue/Vice Lists." In *ABD* 6.857–69.

Fitzmyer, Joseph A. "Abba and Jesus' Relation to God." In R. Gantoy, ed., *À cause de l'Évangile: Études sur les Synoptiques et les Actes offertes au P. Jacques Dupont, O.S.B. à la occasion de son 70e anniversaire*, 15–38. LD 123. Paris: Les Éditions du Cerf, 1985.

Foerster, Werner. See Fohrer, Georg, and Werner Foerster.

Fohrer, Georg, and Werner Foerster. "σῴζω, σωτηρία, σωτήρ, σωτήριος." In *TDNT* 7.965–1023.

Fowler, Alistair. *Kinds of Literature: An Introduction to the Theory of Genres and Modes*. Oxford: Clarendon Press, 1982.

———. "The Life and Death of Literary Forms." In Ralph Cohen, ed., *New Directions in Literary History*, 77–105. London: Routledge and Kegan Paul; Baltimore, Maryland: John Hopkins University Press, 1974.

Frye, Northrop. *Northrop Frye on Shakespeare*. Robert Sandler, ed. New Haven: Yale University Press, 1986.

Fuller, Reginald H. *The Foundations of New Testament Christology.* New York: Scribner's, 1965.

Furnish, Victor Paul. *The Love Command in the New Testament.* London: SCM Press; Nashville: Abingdon, 1972.

———. *II Corinthians.* AB 32a. Garden City, New York: Doubleday, 1984.

Gager, John G. *The Origins of Anti-Semitism: Attitudes Toward Judaism in Pagan and Christian Antiquity.* Oxford: Oxford University Press, 1983.

Garrett, Susan R. *The Temptations of Jesus in Mark's Gospel.* Grand Rapids, Michigan: Eerdmans, 1998.

Gaston, Lloyd. *Paul and the Torah.* Vancouver: University of British Columbia Press, 1987.

Giardina, Andrea, ed. *The Romans.* Lydia G. Cochrane, trans. Chicago: University of Chicago Press, 1993. (ET: *L'uomo romano.* Rome: Editori Laterza, 1989.)

Gilbert, W. S. *The Mikado: or The Town of Titipu.* Kalmus Vocal Scores 6181. Melville, New York: Belwin Mills Publishing, no date.

Glucker, John. *Antiochus and the Late Academy,* Hypomnemata 56. Göttingen: Vandehoeck and Ruprecht, 1978.

Goodman, Martin. *Mission and Conversion: Proselytizing in the Religious History of the Roman Empire.* Oxford: Clarendon Press, 1994.

Greer, Rowan A. See Kugel, James L., and Rowan A. Greer.

Grundmann, Walter, and Georg Bertram. "καλός." In *TDNT* 3.536–56.

Guillet, Jacques, S.J. "The Role of the Bible in the Birth of the Church." In Charles Kannengiesser and Pamela Bright, dirs., *The Bible through the Ages.* Vol. 1. Paul M. Blowers, ed. and trans., *The Bible in Greek Christian Antiquity,* 34–48. Notre Dame, Indiana: University of Notre Dame Press, 1997. (Based on Claude Mondésert, ed., *Bible de tous les temps.* Vol. 1. *Le monde grec ancien et la Bible.* Paris: Éditions Beauchesne, 1984.)

Gundry, Robert H. *Sōma in Biblical Theology: With Emphasis on Pauline Anthropology,* SNTSMS 29. Cambridge: Cambridge University Press, 1976.

Gutbrod, W. "νόμος," B 1–D III 3. In *TDNT* 4.1036–85.

Hackforth, R., and B. R. Rees. "Letters, Greek." In *OCD,* 598–99.

Hall, Edith. *Inventing the Barbarian: Greek Self-Definition through Tragedy.* Oxford: Clarendon Press, 1989.

von Harnack, Adolf. "Über die beiden Recensionem der Geschichte der Prisca und des Aquila in Act. Apost. 18,1–27," *SPAW* (1900): 2–13.

Havelock, Eric A. "Oral Composition in the Oedipus Tyrannus of Sophocles." *NLH* 16 (1984): 175–97.

Hays, Richard B. *Echoes of Scripture in the Letters of Paul.* New Haven: Yale University Press, 1989.

———. "ΠΙΣΤΙΣ and Pauline Theology." In *SBL 1991 Seminar Papers,* 714–29.

Hengel, Martin. *Between Jesus and Paul: Studies in the Earliest History of Christianity.* J. Bowden, trans. London: SCM Press, 1983.

———. *The Charismatic Leader and His Followers.* James C. G. Greig, trans. Edinburgh: Clark, 1981.

———. *Judaism and Hellenism: Studies in Their Encounter in Palestine During the Early Hellenistic Period.* John Bowden, trans. 2 vols. London: SCM Press, 1974.

———. *The Zealots: Investigations into the Jewish Freedom Movement in the Period from Herod I to 70 A.D.* David Smith, trans. Edinburgh: Clark, 1989. (ET: *Die Zeloten: Untersuchungen zur Jüdischen Freiheitsbewegung in der Zeit von Herodes I. bis 70 n. Chr.* Leiden: Brill, 1976 [revised (1961)].)

Herron, R. W., Jr. "The Origins of the New Testament Apostolate." *WTJ* 45 (1983): 101–31.

Hill, D. "Greek Words and Hebrew Meanings: Studies in the Semantics of Soteriological Terms." *MSSNTS* 5. Cambridge: Cambridge University Press, 1967.

Hinks, D. A. G. "*Tria Genera Causarum.*" CQ 30 (1936): 170–76.

Hirsch, E. D. *Validity in Interpretation.* New Haven: Yale University Press, 1974.

Holmberg, Bengt. *Paul and Power: The Structure of Authority in the Primitive Church as Reflected in the Pauline Epistles.* Coniectanea Biblica, New Testament Series 11. Lund: CWK Gleerup (LiberLäromedal), 1978.

Hooker, Morna D. *The Gospel According to Mark.* London: Black, 1991.

Hooker, Richard. *A Learned Sermon of the Nature of Pride.* In W. Speed Hill, ed., *The Folger Library Edition of the Works of Richard Hooker.* Vol. 5, 309–61. Cambridge, Massachusetts: Belknap Press of Harvard University Press, 1990.

Hübner, Hans. *Law in Paul's Thought.* J. C. G. Greig, trans. Edinburgh: Clark, 1984. (ET: *Das Gesetz bei Paulus. Ein Beitrag zum Werden der paulinischen Theologie.* FRLANT 119, Heft. Göttingen: Vandenhoeck and Ruprecht, 1978.)

Hughes, Robert Davis, III. "Christian Theology of Interfaith Dialogue: Defining the Emerging Fourth Option." STR 40.4 (1997): 383–408.

Hultgren, A. J. "The *Pistis Christou* Formulation in Paul." NovT 22 (1980): 148–63.

Innes, Doreen C. See Kennedy, George A., and Doreen C. Innes.

Janzen, J. Gerald. "Habakkuk 2:2–4 in the Light of Recent Philological Advances." HTR 73.1–2 (1980): 53–78.

Johnson, Luke Timothy. *Discernment and Decision Making in the Church.* STR 39.4 (1996): 351–84.

Jolivet, Ira J., Jr. "An Argument from the Letter and Intent of the Law as the Primary Argumentative Strategy in Romans." In Stanley E. Porter and Thomas H. Olbricht, eds., *The Rhetorical Analysis of Scripture: Essays from the 1995 London Conference,* 309–34. JSNTSS 146. Sheffield, England: Sheffield Academic Press, 1997.

de Jonge, M. "The Earliest Christian Use of *Christos.* Some Suggestions." NTS 32 (1986): 321–43.

Jordan, Mark C. "Ancient Philosophic Protreptic and the Problem of Persuasive Genres." In *Rhetorica* 4 (1986): 309–33.

Julian of Norwich. *Showings.* In Edmund Colledge, O.S.A., and James Walsh, S.J., eds. and trans., *Julian of Norwich: Showings.* CWS. New York: Paulist Press, 1978.

Kennedy, George A. "Language and Meaning in Archaic and Classical Greece." In George A. Kennedy, ed., *The Cambridge History of Literary Criticism,* vol. 1, 78–91. Cambridge: Cambridge University Press, 1989.

———. *New Testament Interpretation through Rhetorical Criticism.* Chapel Hill: University of North Carolina Press, 1984.

Kennedy, George A., and Doreen C. Innes. "Hellenistic Literary and Philosophic Scholarship." In George A. Kennedy, ed., *The Cambridge History of Literary Criticism,* vol. 1, 201–19. Cambridge: Cambridge University Press, 1989.

Kent, John Harvey. *Ancient Corinth: A Guide to the Excavations.* Athens: American School of Classical Studies at Athens, 1954.

Klassen, W. "Kiss (NT)." In ABD 4.89–92.

Kleinknecht, Hermann. "νόμος," A 1–4. In TDNT 4.1022–35.

Koch, Dietrich-Alex. *Die Schrift als Zeuge des Evangeliums: Untersuchungen zur Verwendung und zum Verständnis der Schrift bei Paulus.* BHT 69. Tübingen: Mohr (Siebeck), 1986.

Koch, K. "צדק, sdq, to be communally faithful, beneficial." In TLOT 2.1046–62.

Koester, Helmut. "φύσις, φυσικός, φυσκῶς." In TDNT 9.251–77.

———. "The Community of the New Age: Paul's Letters as a New Political Theology for Christian Community," HDB 27.4 (1998): 24–26.

———. *Introduction to the New Testament.* Vol. 2. *History and Literature of Early Christianity.*

New York: de Gruyter, 1982. (Translated from *Einführung in das Neue Testament*, chs. 7–12. Berlin: de Gruyter, 1980.)

Koskenniemi, Heikki. *Studien zur Idee und Phraseologie des griechischen Briefes bis 400 n. Chr.*, Annales Academiae scientiarum fennicae, Series B. 102.2. Helsinki: Suomalainen Tiedeakatemia,1956.

Kramer, W. G. *Christ, Lord, Son of God.* B. Hardy, trans. London: SCM Press, 1966.

Kugel, James L. *Traditions of the Bible: A Guide to the Bible As it Was at the Start of the Common Era.* Cambridge, Massachusetts: Harvard Univerity Press, 1998.

Kugel, James L., and Rowan A. Greer. *Early Biblical Interpretation.* LEC. Philadelphia: Westminster Press, 1986.

Lamarche, Paul, S.J. "The Septuagint: Bible of the Earliest Christians." In Charles Kannengiesser and Pamela Bright, dirs., *The Bible through the Ages.* Vol. 1. Paul M. Blowers, ed. and trans., *The Bible in Greek Christian Antiquity*, 15–33. Notre Dame, Indiana: University of Notre Dame Press, 1997. (Based on Claude Mondésert, ed., *Bible de tous les temps.* Vol. 1. *Le monde grec ancien et la Bible.* Paris: Éditions Beauchesne, 1984.)

La Piana, George. "Foreign Groups at Rome during the First Centuries of the Empire." *HTR* 20 (1927):183–403.

Lane, William L. "Roman Christianity during the Formative Years from Nero to Nerva." In Karl P. Donfried and Peter Richardson, eds., *Judaism and Christianity in First Century Rome*, 196–244. Grand Rapids, Michigan: Eerdmans, 1998.

Lausberg, Heinrich. *Handbook of Literary Rhetoric: A Foundation for Literary Study.* David E. Orton and R. Dean Anderson, eds. Matthew T. Bliss, Annemiek Jansen, and David E. Orton, trans. Leiden: Brill, 1998. (ET: *Handbuch der literarischen Rhetorik. Eine Grundlegung der Literaturwissenschaft.* Second edition. Ismanig bei München: Max Heuber Verlag, 1973 [1960].)

Levens, R. G. C. "Letters, Latin." In *OCD*, 599.

Lewis, C. S. *A Preface to Paradise Lost.* London: Oxford University Press, 1942.

Levison, John R. *Portraits of Adam in Early Judaism: From Sirach to 2 Baruch.* Sheffield, England: JSOT Press, 1988.

Liebermann, Saul. *Hellenism in Jewish Palestine.* New York: Jewish Theological Seminary, 1962.

Liedke, G., and C. Petersen, "תּוֹרָה, *Tôrâ:* instruction." In *TLOT* 3.14.

Lightfoot, J. B. *Saint Paul's Epistle to the Philippians.* Reprint of fourth edition with additions and slight alterations. London: Macmillan, 1885.

de Lubac, Henri. *Medieval Exegesis.* Vol. 1. *The Four Senses of Scripture.* Mark Sebank, trans. Grand Rapids, Michigan: Eerdmans; Edinburgh: Clark, 1998. (ET: *Exégèse médiévale*, 1: *Les quatre sens de l'écriture.* Paris: Aubier, 1958.)

Lührmann, Dieter. "Freundschaftsbrief trotz Spannungen: Zu Gattung und Aufbau des Ersten Korintherbriefs." In Wolfgang Schrager, ed., *Studien zum Text und zur Ethik des Neuen Testaments: Festschrift zum 80. Geburtstag von Heinrich Greeven*, 298–315. BZNW 47. Berlin: de Gruyter, 1986.

Luther, Martin. *Lectures on Galatians.* In Jaroslav Pelikan and Walter A. Hansen, eds., *Luther's Works.* Vol. 26. *Lectures on Galatians (1535) Chapters 1–4.* Saint Louis, Missouri: Concordia, 1963.

Lyall, F. "Roman Law in the Writings of Paul—Adoption." *JBL* 88 (1969): 458–66.

Lytle, Guy Fitch, III. "Elegies in the Resurrection." *STR* 40.3 (1997): 279–98.

———. "Friendship and Patronage in Renaissance Europe." In F. W. Kent, Patricia Simons, and J. C. Eade, *Patronage, Art, and Society in Renaissance Italy*, 47–61. Oxford: Clarendon, 1987.

MacMullen, Ramsay. "Roman Attitudes to Greek Love." *Historia* 31 (1982): 484–502.

———. "Women in Public in the Roman Empire." *Historia* 29 (1980): 208–18.

Maier, H. O. "The Household in the Ancient World." In *The Social Setting of the Ministry as Reflected in the Writings of Hermas, Clement, and Ignatius*, 15–28. Waterloo, Ontario: Wilfred Laurier University Press, 1991.

Malherbe, Abraham. "Ancient Epistolary Theorists." *Ohio Journal of Religious Studies* 55 (1977): 3–77. Reprinted with minor revisions as SBLSBS 19. Atlanta, Georgia: Scholars Press, 1988.

———. *Moral Exhortation: A Greco-Roman Source Book*. LEC. Philadelphia: Westminster Press, 1986.

Malina, Bruce J. *The New Testament World: Insights from Cultural Anthropology*. Lousiville, Kentucky: Westminster/John Knox Press, 1993.

———. "Understanding New Testament Persons." In Richard L. Rohrbaugh, ed., *The Social Sciences and New Testament Interpretation*, 41–46. Peabody, Massachusetts: Hendrickson, 1996.

Malone, Dumas. *The Sage of Monticello*. Boston: Little, Brown, 1981.

Marmorstein, Arthur. *The Doctrine of Merits in the Old Rabbinical Literature*. Revised. 3 vols. in one. New York: Ktav, 1968 [vol. 1 first published, 1920; vol. 2, 1927; vol. 3, 1937].

Martin, Dale B. *Slavery as Salvation: The Metaphor of Slavery in Pauline Christianity*. New Haven: Yale University Press, 1990.

Martin, J. Louis. *Galatians*. AB 33a. New York: Doubleday, 1997.

Martin, Luther H. "The Anti-Individualistic Ideology of Hellenistic Culture." *NUMEN* 41.2 (1994): 118–40.

Martin, Ronald. *Tacitus*. London: Bristol Classical Press, 1994 (corrected).

Marxsen, Willi. *Introduction to the New Testament: An Approach to Its Problems*. G. Buswell, trans. Philadelphia: Fortress Press; Oxford: Blackwell, 1968.

Matera, Frank J. *Galatians*. SPS 6. Collegeville, Minnesota: Liturgical Press, 1992.

Meecham, H. G. "The Use of the Participle for the Imperative in the New Testament." *ExpTim* 58 (1946–47): 207–8.

Meeks, Wayne A. *The First Urban Christians: The Social World of the Apostle Paul*. New Haven: Yale University Press, 1983.

Michaelis, Wilhelm. *Der Brief des Paulus an die Philipper*. THNT 11. Leipzig: Deichertsche Verlagbuchhandlung, 1935.

Momigliano, Arnaldo. *Studies in Historiography*. London: Weidenfeld and Nicolson, 1966.

Montevecchi, Orsolina. "Una donna 'prostatis' del figlio minorenne in un papiro dell IIa." *Aegyptus* 61 (1981): 103–15.

Monti, Joseph. *Arguing about Sex: The Rhetoric of Christian Sexual Morality*. Albany, New York: State University of New York Press, 1995.

Moxnes, Halvor. "Honor and Shame." In Richard L. Rohrbaugh, ed., *The Social Sciences and New Testament Interpretation*, 19–40. Peabody, Massachussetts: Hendrickson, 1996.

Munck, Johannes. *Paul and the Salvation of Mankind*. Frank Clarke, trans. London: SCM Press, 1959. (ET: *Paulus und die Heilsgeschichte*. Aarhus: Universitetsforlaget, 1954.)

Munday, Anthony, et al.; revised by Henry Chettle, Thomas Dekker, Thomas Heywood, and William Shakespeare. *Sir Thomas More: A Play*. In Vittorio Gabrieli and Giorgio Melchiori, eds., *Sir Thomas More: A Play*. The Revels Plays. Manchester, England: Manchester University Press, 1990.

Murphy-O'Connor, Jerome. *St. Paul's Corinth: Texts and Archaeology*. Good News Studies 6. Wilmington, Delaware: Glazier, 1983.

Mussner, Franz. *Tractate on the Jews: The Significance of Judaism for Christian Faith*. Leonard Swidler, trans. London: SPCK; Philadelphia: Fortress Press, 1984.

Neusner, Jacob. *Judaism in the Beginning of Christianity.* London: SPCK, 1984.
———. *Method and Meaning in Ancient Judaism: Third Series.* Atlanta, Georgia: Scholars Press, 1981.
———. *What Is Midrash?* Philadelphia: Fortress Press, 1987.
Neusner, Jacob, Ernest Frerichs, Peter Borgen, and Richard Horsely, eds., *The Social World of Formative Christianity and Judaism: Essays in Tribute to Howard Clark Kee.* Philadelphia: Fortress Press, 1988.
Nissinen, Martti. *Homoeroticism in the Biblical World: A Historical Perspective.* Kirsi Stjerna, trans. Minneapolis: Fortress Press, 1998.
North, J. Lionel. Review of Bash, *Ambassadors for Christ.* JTS 49.1 (1998): 278–81.
Oepke, Albrecht. "διώκω." In *TDNT* 2.229–30.
Panzini, Alfredo. *Il bacio di Lesbia.* Milan: Montadori, 1937.
Paranuk, H. Van Dyke. "Oral Typesetting: Some Uses of Biblical Structure." *Biblica* 62 (1981): 153–68.
———. "Transitional Techniques in the Bible." *JBL* 102.4 (1983): 525–48.
Parry, Milman. "The Historical Method in Literary Criticism." In Adam Parry, ed., *The Making of Homeric Verse: The Collected Papers of Milman Parry*, 408–13. New York: Oxford: Oxford University Press, 1987. Reprinted from *HAB* 38 (1936): 778–82.
Pedersen, Johannes. *Israel: Its Life and Culture.* London: Oxford University Press, 1926.
Petersen, C. See Liedke, G., and C. Petersen.
Pfeiffer, Rudolph. *History of Classical Scholarship from the Beginning to the End of the Hellenistic Age.* Oxford: Oxford University Press, 1968.
Pierce, C. A. *Conscience in the New Testament.* London: SCM Press, 1955.
Pokorný, Petr. "The Temptation Stories and Their Intention," *NTS* 20 (1973–74): 115–27.
Porter, Stanley E. "Paul of Tarsus and His Letters." In Stanley E. Porter, ed., *Handbook of Classical Rhetoric in the Hellenistic Period, 330 B.C.–A.D. 400*, 533–86. Leiden: Brill, 1997.
Quell, Gottfried, and Gottlob Schrenk. "δίκη, δίκαιος, δικαιοσύνη, δικαιόω, κτλ." In *TDNT* 2.174–225.
Rahner, Karl. *Theological Investigations* 6. London: Darton, Longman, and Todd, 1969.
Räisänen, Heikki. *Paul and the Law.* WUNT 29. Tübingen: Mohr (Siebeck), 1983; Philadelphia: Fortress Press, 1986.
Rees, B. R. See Hackforth, R., and B. R. Rees
Reese, J. M. *Hellenistic Influence on the Book of Wisdom and Its Consequences.* Rome: Pontifical Biblical Institute, 1970.
Ringgren, Helmer. *The Faith of Qumran: Theology of the Dead Sea Scrolls.* Emilie T. Sander, trans. Expanded edition. New York: Crossroad, 1995.
Robinson, H. Wheeler. "Corporate Personality in Ancient Israel." In P. Volz, F. Stummer, and J. Hempel, eds., *Werden und Wesen des Alten Testaments: Vorträge gehalten auf der Internationalen Tagung Alttestamentlicher Forscher zu Göttingen vom 4.–10. September 1935.* Beihefte zur Zeitschrift für die Alttestamentliche Wissenschaft, 66. Berlin: Alfred Töpelmann, 1936. Reprinted in John Reumann, ed., H. Wheeler Robinson, *Corporate Personality in Ancient Israel*, 1–20. Facet Books, Biblical Series 2. Philadelphia: Fortress Press, 1964.
Rossano, Pietro. "L'Ideale del bello (καλός) nell'etica di S. Paolo." In *SPCIC* 2.373–82.
Rouffiac, Jean. *Recherches sur les caractères du grec dans le Nouveau Testament d'après les Inscriptions de Priène.* Paris: Leroux, 1911.
Salom, A. P. "The Imperatival Use of the Participle in the New Testament." *AusBR* 11 (1963): 41–49.
Sanders, E. P. *Paul and Palestinian Judaism: A Comparison of Patterns of Religion.* London: SCM Press; Philadelphia: Fortress Press, 1977.

————. *Paul, the Law, and the Jewish People.* London: SCM Press; Philadelphia: Fortress Press, 1983.

Sandmel, Samuel. *Philo's Place in Judaism: A Study of Conceptions of Abraham in Jewish Literature.* Cincinnati: Hebrew Union College Press, 1956.

Schechter, Solomon. *Aspects of Rabbinic Theology.* London: Macmillan, 1909.

Schneider, Johannes. "ὁμοίωμα." In *TDNT* 5.191–98.

Schoenberg, M. W. "*Huiothesia*: The Word and the Institution." *Scripture* 15 (1963): 115–23.

Schrenk, Gottlob. "ἱεροσυλέω, ἱερόσυλος." In *TDNT* 3. 255–57.

————. See Quell, Gottfried, and Gottlob Schrenk.

Schüssler-Fiorenza, Elizabeth. *In Memory of Her: A Feminist Reconstruction of Christian Origins.* New York: Crossroad, 1983.

Schweizer, Eduard. *The Good News According to Mark.* Donald H. Madvig, trans. Richmond: John Knox Press, 1970. (ET: *Das Evangelium nach Marcus. Das Neue Testament Deutsch,* neues Göttinger Bibelwerk, 1. Göttingen: Vandenhoeck and Ruprecht, 1967.)

Schweizer, Eduard, and Friedrich Baumgärtel, "σῶμα, σωματικῶς, κτλ.," in *TDNT* 7.1024–85.

Shakespeare, William. *Coriolanus.* In R. B. Parker, ed., *The Tragedy of Coriolanus.* The Oxford Shakespeare. Oxford: Clarendon Press, 1994.

————. *Macbeth.* In Rex Gibson, ed., *Macbeth.* Cambridge: Cambridge University Press, 1993.

————. *Much Ado About Nothing.* In F. H. Mares, ed., *Much Ado About Nothing.* Cambridge: Cambridge University Press, 1988.

————. See Munday, Anthony, et al.

Sherwin-White, A. N. *Roman Society and Roman Law in the New Testament.* Oxford: Clarendon Press, 1963.

Sissa, Giulia. "The Sexual Philosophies of Plato and Aristotle." In Georges Duby and Michelle Perrot, gen. eds., *A History of Women in the West.* Vol. 1. Pauline Schmidt Pantel, ed., *From Ancient Goddesses to Christian Saints,* 46–81. Arthur Goldhammer, trans. Cambridge, Massachusetts: Belknap–Harvard University Press, 1992. (ET: *Storia delle Donne in Occidente.* Vol. 1. *L'Antichità.* Rome: Laterza e Figli, 1990.)

Souilhe, Joseph. *Épictète Entretiens.* Collections des universites de France. Paris: Société d'édition "Les belles lettres," 1975.

Spicq, C., O. P. *Agapè dans le Nouveau Testament: Analyse des textes.* 3 vols. Paris: Gabalda, 1958–59.

Stählin, Gustav. "φιλέω, καταφιλέω, φίλημα." In *TDNT* 9.118–46.

Stamm, J. J. "גאל, *g;';l.*" In *TLOT* 1.288–96.

————. "פדה, *pdh.*" In *TLOT* 2.964–76.

Stanley, Christopher D. *Paul and the Language of Scripture: Citation Techniques in the Pauline Epistles and Contemporary Literature.* SNTSMS 74. Cambridge: Cambridge University Press, 1992.

Staveley, Eastland Stuart. "*Provocatio.*" In *OCD,* 892–93.

Stendahl, Krister. *Final Account: Paul's Letter to the Romans.* Minneapolis: Fortress Press, 1995.

————. "Qumran and Supersessionism—and the Road Not Taken." *PSB* 19.2 (1998): 134–41.

Stirewalt, Martin Luther, Jr., "The Form and Function of the Greek Letter-Essay." In Karl P. Donfried, ed., *The Romans Debate: Revised and Expanded Edition,* 147–71. Peabody, Massachusetts: Hendrickson, 1991.

Stoebe, H. J. "רחם, *rhm,* to have mercy." In *TLOT* 3.1225–30.

Stowers, Stanley K. "The Diatribe." In David E. Aune, ed., *Greco-Roman Literature and the New Testament: Selected Forms and Genres,* 71–83. SBLDS 2. Atlanta, Georgia: Scholars Press, 1988.

————. *Letter Writing in Greco-Roman Antiquity.* LEC. Philadelphia: Westminster Press, 1986.

Talmon, Shemaryahu. "Textual Study of the Bible—A New Outlook." In Frank Moore Cross and Shemaryahu Talmon, eds., *Qumran and the History of the Biblical Text,* 321–400. Cambridge: Harvard University Press, 1975.

Tate, J. "On the History of Allegorism," *CQ* 28 (1934): 105–14.

Thébert, Yvon. "The Slave." In Andrea Giardina, ed., *The Romans,* 138–74. Lydia G. Cochrane, trans. Chicago: University of Chicago Press, 1993. (ET: *L'uomo romano.* Rome: Editori Laterza, 1989.)

Theissen, Gerd. *Psychological Aspects of Pauline Theology.* Trans. John P. Galvin. Philadelphia: Fortress Press, 1987. (ET: *Psychologische Aspekte paulinischer Theologie.* FRLANT 131. Göttingen: Vandenhoeck and Ruprecht, 1983.)

————. *The Social Setting of Pauline Christianity.* Edinburgh: Clark, 1982.

Thomas, Yan. "The Division of the Sexes in Roman Law." In Georges Duby and Michelle Perrot, gen. eds., *A History of Women in the West.* Vol. 1. Pauline Schmidt Pantel, ed., *From Ancient Goddesses to Christian Saints,* 83–137. Arthur Goldhammer, trans. Cambridge, Massachusetts: Belknap–Harvard University Press, 1992. (ET: *Storia delle Donne in Occidente,* vol. 1, *L'Antichità.* Rome: Laterza e Figli, 1990.)

Thraede, Klaus. *Grundzüge griechisch-römischer Brieftopik,* Monographien zur klassischen Altertumswissenschaft 48. Munich: Beck, 1970.

de Tocqueville, Alexis. *Democracy in America.* Phillips Bradley, ed., Henry Reeve, trans., Francis Bowen, rev., 2 vols. New York: Knopf, 1945. (ET: *De la démocratie en Amérique.* Paris: Gosselin, 1835.)

Tutu, Desmond. "Where Is Now Thy God?" Address at Trinity Institute, New York, January 8, 1989.

Veyne, Paul. "Humanity." In Andrea Giardina, ed., *The Romans,* 342–69. Lydia G. Cochrane, trans. Chicago: University of Chicago Press, 1993. (ET: *L'uomo romano.* Rome: Editori Laterza, 1989.)

————. "The Roman Empire." In Philippe Ariès and Georges Duby, eds., *A History of Private Life.* Vol. 1. Paul Veyne, ed., *From Pagan Rome to Byzantium,* 5–234. Arthur Goldhammer, trans. Cambridge, Massachusetts: Harvard University Press, 1987. (ET: *Histoire de la vie Privée.* Vol. 1. *De l'Empire romain à l'an mil.* Paris: Editions du Seuil, 1985.)

Vos, J. S. "Die Hermeneutische antinomie bei Paulus (Galater 3.11–12 Römer; 10.5–10)." *NTS* 38 (1992): 254–70.

Vriezen, Theodorus Christiaan. *An Outline of Old Testament Theology.* Second edition, revised and enlarged. Oxford: Oxford University Press, 1970.

Walbank, W. "Polybius." In T. A. Dorey, ed., *Latin Historians,* 39–63. New York: Basic Books, 1966.

Walsh, P. G. "Livy." In T. A. Dorey, ed., *Latin Historians,* 115–42. New York: Basic Books, 1966.

Warren, Austin. See Wellek, René, and Austin Warren.

Watson, Francis. *Paul, Judaism, and the Gentiles: A Sociological Approach.* SNTSMS 56. Cambridge: Cambridge University Press, 1986.

Watson, N. M. Review of J. A. Ziesler, *Meaning of Righteousness in Paul.* In *NTS* 20 (1974): 217–28.

Wellek, René, and Austin Warren. *Theory of Literature.* Third edition. Harmondsworth, Middlesex: Penguin Books, 1963.

Wells, Colin. *The Roman Empire.* Second edition. Cambridge, Massachusetts: Harvard University Press, 1992.

Westerholm, Stephen. "*Torah, Nomos,* and Law: A Question of 'Meaning'", *SR* 15 (1986): 327–36.

Westermann, Claus. "כבד, kbd, to be heavy." In *TLOT* 2.590–602.

———. "עֶבֶד, 'ebed, servant." In *TLOT* 2.819–32.

White, John L. "Ancient Greek Letters." In David Aune, ed., *Greco-Roman Literature and the New Testament: Selected Forms and Genres*, 85–105. SBLSBS 21. Atlanta, Georgia: Scholars Press, 1988.

———. *Light from Ancient Letters*. Philadelphia: Fortress Press, 1986.

White, Victor, O.P. "Guilt: Theological and Psychological," in Philip Mairet, ed., *Christian Essays in Psychiatry*, 155–76. New York: Philosophical Library, 1956.

Williams, Charles. *The Place of the Lion*. London: Faber and Faber, 1931.

Winger, M. *By What Law? The Meaning of Νόμος in the Letters of Paul*. Atlanta, Georgia: Scholars Press, 1992.

Winter, Bruce M. *Seek the Welfare of the City: Christians as Benefactors and Citizens. First-Century Christians in the Graeco-Roman World*. Carlisle, England: Paternoster Press; Grand Rapids, Michigan: Eerdmans, 1994.

Wiseman, T. P. *Catullus and His World: A Reappraisal*. Cambridge: Cambridge University Press, 1985.

Wright, N. T. *Christian Origins and the Question of God*. Vol. 1. *The New Testament and the People of God*. Second edition. London: SPCK, 1993.

———. *The Climax of the Covenant: Christ and the Law in Pauline Theology*. Second edition. Minneapolis: Fortress Press; Edinburgh: Clark, 1992.

———. *What Saint Paul Really Said: Was Paul of Tarsus the Real Founder of Christianity?* Oxford: Lion; Grand Rapids, Michigan: Eerdmans, 1997.

Wyschogrod, Michael. "The Impact of Dialogue with Christianity on My Self-Understanding as a Jew." In Erhard Blum, Christian Macholz, and Ekkehard W. Stegemann, eds., *Die Hebräische Bibel und ihre zweifache Nachgeschichtei, Festschrift für Rolf Rendtorff zum 65 Geburtstag*, 725–36. Neukirchen-Vluyn: Neukirchener Verlag, 1990.

Ziesler, J. A. *The Meaning of Righteousness in Paul: A Linguistic and Theological Inquiry*. SNTSMS 20. Cambridge: Cambridge University Press, 1972.

Zimmerli, Walther. See Conzelmann, Hans.

Index of Holy Scripture

Old Testament
Genesis
1.1–3, 118
1.2, 156, 157
1.4, 143
1.6–9, 68
1.10, 143
1.12, 143
1.18, 143
1.21, 143
1.25, 143
1.26–27, 154
1.26–28, 78
1.27–28, 88
1.28, 75
1.31, 143
1–3, 82–83
2.18–25, 88
3.5, 78, 83
3.13, 142
3.14-19, 178
3.17, 151
4.12, 125
6.3, 157
6.17, 156
6.19, 156
9.8–17, 238
9.26, 170
12.2–3, 75
12.3, 103
12.3, 117
13.15, 117
15.1–20, 169
15.5, 118
15.6, 62, 115, 117
16.1–6, 160
17.1–9, 170
17.2, 6–8, 75

17.5, 117
17.8, 117
18.10, 160
18.17–19, 154
19.15, 136
21.12, 160
22.12, 154
22.16, 154
22.16–18, 75
15.23, 160
26.3, 75
26.5, 49
26.24, 75
35.11, 75
46.28, 48
48.3–4, 75
Exodus
2.24, 170
4.21, 161
4.22, 169
4.22–23, 148
6.6, 104
9.16, 161
12.25, 170
12.16, 170
12.49, 49
13.5, 170
14.13, 75
14.15, 183
14.31, 62
16.7, 169
16.10, 169
16.28, 49
19.5, 170
19.6, 136
20.17, 141
21.2, 57
21.32, 57

22.29 (LXX 22.28), 152
23.7, 116
23.19, 152
24.1–8, 170
25.17, 112
25.19–22 (LXX 25.18.22), 104
29.30–31, 161
31.17, 104
32.11–12, 191
32.13, 191
32.30–33.16, 161
32.32, 159, 164
33.18–22, 84
33.19, 161
34.7, 136
35.12, 104
36.24–25, 136
37.6–9, 104
38.21, 211
Leviticus
4.3, 146
4.14, 146
4.35, 146
5.3, 102
5.15, 101
5.17, 102
11.44–45, 136
15.31, 136
16.2–15, 104
16.14–16, 104
16.21, 136
18.5, 141, 168, 172, 173, 174, 175
19.2, 136
19.18, 207, 208
20.25–26
22.32–33
26.41, 96

263

Numbers
7.89, 104
15.17–21, 180
15.30, 142
15.31, 102
16.22, 157
18.12, 152
25.1–18, 167
Deuteronomy
4.8, 49, 70
5.21, 141
6.4, 106
6.24, 141
7.8, 104
7.25–26, 95
10.16, 96
10.17, 93
14.1, 148
18.4, 152
27.26, 42, 46
28.15–68, 95
29.1–31.13, 170
29.4, 178
30.6, 96
30.10, 49
30.11–14, 168–69, 173
30.15, 148
30.16, 141
31.16–21, 95, 141
31.29, 141
32.21, 177, 179
32.43, 215
32.46, 49
33.21, 152
Joshua
1.7, 49
1.24, 49
13.5, 75
22.27, 170
24.26, 49
Judges
13.5, 75
20.16, 101
1 Samuel (LXX 1 Kingdoms)
12.22, 177
2 Samuel (LXX 2 Kingdoms)
7.12, 170
7.16, 170
12.1–13, 205
12.7–8, 209
13.18, 210
23.5, 170, 189
1 Kings (LXX 3 Kingdoms)
2.3, 49
10.5, 210
12.1, 182
19.10, 178
19.14, 178
2 Kings (LXX 4 Kingdoms)
17.13
18.12

2 Chronicles
33.10–16, 96
Job
7.2, 57
10.8–9, 162
19.20, 156
31.16–22, 35
Psalms
2.7, 61
18.50 (LXX 17.50), 215
19.1–4 (LXX 18.1–4), 77
19.5 (LXX 18.5), 176
25.2, 20 (LXX 24.2, 20), 68
25.6–7 (LXX 24.6–7), 93
31.19 (LXX 30.20), 93
31.24, 117
32.1–2 (LXX 31.1–2)
33.6 (LXX 32.6), 68, 157
35.3 (LXX 34.3), 75
36.5–9, 238
45.5, 48
50.16–18, 21–22 (LXX
     49.16–18, 21–22), 95
51.1, 6 (LXX 50.1, 6), 98
51.12 (LXX 50.12), 157
51.12–14 (LXX 50.12–14),
     152–53
51.13, 61
51.19 (LXX 50.19), 157
56.10–11 (LXX 55.10), 154
62.13 (LXX 61.13), 93
69.10 (LXX 68.10), 214
69.22–23 (LXX 68.22–23),
     179
69.25 (LXX 68.25), 122
69.29, 164
72.9 (LXX 71.9), 224
76.9–11a (LXX 75.8–10),
     77
78.51 (LXX 77.51), 152
79.6 (LXX 78.6)
85.9–10 (LXX 84.9–10)
86.5 (LXX 85.5), 93
89.4–5 (LXX 88.4–5), 170
94.14 (LXX 93.14), 177
96.2 (LXX 95.2), 60
100.5 (LXX 99.5), 93
105.36 (LXX 104.36),152
106.20 (LXX 105.20), 79,
     142
106.30–31, 167
107.10–11 (LXX 106.10–
     11), 97
117.1 (LXX 116.1), 215
119.6 (LXX 118.6), 67
119.68 (LXX 118.68), 93
132.11 (LXX 131.11), 170
143 (LXX 142), 100
147.19–20 (LXX 147.8–9),
     97
149.5–9, 167

Proverbs
3.4, 202
3.35, 80
6.13, 48
8.22–31, 76
11.16, 80
Ecclesiastes (Qohelet)
1.2, 151
1.14, 151
25.24, 101
Isaiah
1.29, 67, 68
1.11–17, 195
2.3, 224
8.14, 166
9.6, 121
10.16, 80
10.22–23, 164
11.1, 215
11.2, 157
11.6–9, 151
11.12–13, 238
21.2, 75
22.18, 80
24.5, 49
27.9, 182
27.13, 183
28.16, 68, 175
28.22, 164
28.16, 166
29.16, 162
40.5, 156
40.9, 60
40.13–14, 184
42.6–7, 94
43.19–21, 151
45.1–3, 209
45.9–13, 162
45.21, 70
45.23, 212
49.1–6, 154
49.3, 57
49.18, 212
50.7–8, 68
50.7–9, 155
51.11, 104
52.5, 95
52.7, 60, 176
52.15, 223
53.1, 176
53.4, 68
53.10, 146
55.10–11, 68
55.12–13, 151
59.20–21, 182
59.21, 183
60.1–11, 224
60.6, 60
61.1–2, 157
61.10, 210
63, 77

63.3–10, 104–105
63.10–11, 61
63.17, 161
64.8, 162
65. 1–2, 177
66.10–14, 224
66.15–16, 98
Jeremiah
1.5, 154
2.11, 79
2.36, 68
3.23, 75
4.4, 96
4.10, 159
7.25, 57
9.9, 68
9.23–24, 106, 122
9.25–26 (LXX 9.24–25),
   95–96, 96
18.1–12, 162
27.4–7, 209
29.7, 39, 207
31.31–37, 170
32.33, 189
32.23, 49
Ezekiel
11.19, 157
18.21, 126
22.15, 136
36.27, 157
36.17–20, 95
36.25, 136
37.1–14, 157
37.5, 156
44.7–9, 96
Daniel
1.3–16, 211
2.18–23, 189
2.27–30, 189
2.47, 189
4.37, 66
7.1–27, 76
9.11, 182
Hosea
1.10, 164
2.1, 164
2.23, 164
4.7, 80
5.10, 122
6.6, 195
Joel
2.28 (LXX 3.1), 156
2.32 (LXX 3.5), 175
3.1, 122
3.5, 60
3.12, 98
Amos
3.2, 93
5.21–24
Jonah
4.8, 156

Micah
4.2, 224
Habakkuk
1.1–2.5, 70
2.4, 62, 70–71, 165
2.16, 80
Zechariah
12.10, 122
Malachi
1.2–3, 161
2 [4] Esdras
14.9, 76
Tobit
13.8–11, 224
Judith
8.11–27, 73
Wisdom of Solomon, 25
1.4, 136
1.16, 136
2.23–24, 82, 101
5.20, 181
5.22, 181
6.1–11, 209
11.23, 93
12.7, 148
12.8–11, 93
12.20–22, 93
12.21, 148
13.1–5, 78
13.1–9, 78
14.22–26, 79
14.27, 79
15.7, 162
16.10, 148
16.21, 148
16.26. 148
17.1, 144
18.13, 148
18.22, 169
19.6, 148
Sirach (Ecclesiasticus)
1.9, 122
3.10, 80
5.13, 80
7.29–30, 210
10.4, 209
17.11, 76
17.11–14, 141
18.11, 122
19.20, 76
24.1–34, 76
24.9, 152
29.6, 80
31.5–11, 35
33.13, 162
35.13, 93
38.34, 76
38.1–11, 76
44.11, 169
44.19–21, 114–15
44.21, 117

Baruch
3.29–32, 169
Prayer of Manasseh, 96
2 [4] Esdras 7.119, 106
1 Maccabees
1.43, 170
1.49, 136
1.62–63, 123
2.19, 170
2.22, 170
2.44, 136
2.51–52, 115
2 Maccabees, 15, 16
1.1–10a, 15
1.10b–2.18, 15
2.19–23, 16
2.19–32, 15
2.26, 17
2.28, 17
8.15, 169

New Testament
Matthew
5.16, 39
5.17, 171
5.44, 202
6.24, 57
10.40, 64
18.21–35, 32
22.21, 207
25.44–45, 199
26.10–12, 143
Mark
1.12–13, 82
8.33, 147
8.34–35, 149
9.23, 163
9.37, 64
10.20, 47
10.45, 185
12.10, 166
12.17, 207
12.26, 178
14.6, 143
14.37, 149
Luke
3.38, 82
6.13, 64
8.3, 39
9.48, 64
12.16–20, 35
12.42–46, 57
14.13–14, 35
14.32, 65
19.42, 163
20.25, 207
John
5.30–36, 64
6.39–40, 64
6.62, 163
8.34, 136

John (*continued*)
　7.16–18, 64
　17.18, 64
　17.20–23, 202
Acts
　2.27, 122
　4.11, 166
　4.18–19
　5.29, 40–41
　6.1, 199
　7.19, 170
　9.5–6, 61
　9.13–15, 61
　9.15, 185
　10.30–48, 235–36
　13.13, 61
　13.14–51, 218
　14.1–7, 218
　14.4–14, 64
　15.3, 224
　16.14–15, 39
　18.1–3, 226
　18.7–15, 218
　18.15, 27
　18.18, 226
　18.25, 200
　18.26, 226
　23.9, 163
　24.25, 90
　26.24–25, 201
Romans (main discussions are
　　indicated in **bold italic**)
　1.1, 64, 195
　1.1–15, 19, **57–64**
　1.2, 17, 42, 45, 67, 122
　1.5, 65
　1.5–6, 218
　1.6–8, 185
　1.7, 66, 232
　1.9, 190
　1.10, 74
　1.11–12, 224
　1.12, 46
　1.13, 31, 65, 218
　1.15, 64
　1.16, 64, 166, 190
　1.16–17, **67–71**
　1.16–4.25, 19–20, **67–119**,
　　165
　1.17, 42, 165
　1.18, 150
　1.18–21, 127
　1.18–32, **77–82, 82–83**,
　　104, 150
　1.18–3.20, 145
　1.20, 203
　1.21, 146, 150, 212
　1.22, 203
　1.23, 84, 142
　1.24, 74, 196
　1.25, 151

　1.26, 74
　1.26–27, **84–89**
　1.27, 74
　1.22–31, 88
　1.28, 196
　1.29–32, 25
　1.32, 88, 203
　2.1, 214
　2.1–3.20, **91–102**
　2.3, 91
　2.7, 74
　2.10, 74
　2.12, 127
　2.12–16, 208
　2.12–17, 46
　2.15, 214
　2.17, 74, 121
　2.17–29, 49
　2.23, 74
　2.24, 42
　2.29–3.4, 23
　3.1–2, 88
　3.4, 42
　3.6, 47
　3.10, 42
　3.10–19, 46
　3.12, 89
　3.19, 46
　3.20, 46, 83, 88, 127, 139
　3.21, 17, 42, 45, 46, 49, 215
　3.21–22, 46, 173
　3.21–31, **102–13**
　3.22, 59, 83
　3.23, 83, 84, 88, 89, 121,
　　129, 139, 150, 151
　3.23–24, 142
　3.24, 89, 122
　3.24–26, **107–108**, 112
　3.25, **112–113**
　3.26, 70, 108
　3.27, 46, 74, 121, 146
　3.29–30, 175
　3.30, 96, **113–114**, 190
　3.31, 17, 42, 45, 47, 173,
　　174
　4.1, **118–19**
　4.1–25, **114–118**, 174
　4.2, 74
　4.3, 42
　4.7, 139
　4.13, 170
　4.15, 46, 127, 139
　4.16, 31
　4.16–22, 170
　4.17, 42
　4.23, 42
　4.23–24, 54
　4.25, 139
　5.1, 59
　5.1–5, 150
　5.1–21, **120–28**

　5.1–11.36, 20, **120–93**
　5.2, 74
　5.3, 74, 106
　5.3–4, 90, 152
　5.5, 74, 112
　5.11, 74, 106
　5.12, **128–29**, 150
　5.12–14, 83
　5.12–21, 83, 101
　5.13, 46, 49
　5.14, 139
　5.15, 59, 151
　5.15–16, 63, 139
　5.15–21, 150
　5.17, 59
　5.18–19, 129
　5.20, 46, 83, 139
　5.20–21, 133
　5.21, 59
　6.1–8.39, **137–59**
　6.4, 195
　6.5, **137–38**
　6.6, 158
　6.14, 139
　6.16, 59
　6.17–18, 231
　6.21, 74
　6.23, 63
　7.1, 31
　7.1–23, 46
　7.1–8.39, **138–55**
　7.7–11, 46, 49
　7.7–25, 47, 90, 101, 127
　7.12, 127
　7.15, 88
　7.21, 36
　7.23, 46
　7.24, 158
　8.3, 47, 112
　8.3–27, 157
　8.4, 173
　8.8, 156
　8.10, 158
　8.11, 158
　8.12, 31
　8.13, 158
　8.14–16, 157
　8.14–17, 31
　8.17, 204
　8.18, 139
　8.18–25, 96
　8.19–20, 238
　8.21–23, 238
　8.36, 42
　8.38–39, 238
　8.39, 123
　9.1–3, 191
　9.1–10.10, **159–69**
　9.1–11.36, 20, **159–93**
　9.4, 46
　9.4–5, 97, **169–70**

9.5, 59, **170–71**
9.6, 191
9.13, 42
9.17, 42
9.20, 91
9.21, 74
9.27–10.21, 191
9.30–31, 46
9.33, 42, 74
10.1, 31
10.2–5, 47
10.4, 17, 20, 42, 45, **168,
      171–72**
10.5–10, **168, 172–75**
10.9, 175
10.11, 42, 74
10.11–11.32, **175–83**
10.13, 170
10.15, 42
11.1–24, 191
11.2, 42
11.8, 42
11.11–12, 139
11.13, 178, 218
11.13–14, 218
11.13–32, 218
11.15–16, **187–88**
11.20, 190
11.23,190
11.25, 63, **188–89**, 191
11.25–26, 190
11.25–32, 191
11.26, 42, **189–93**
11.27, 139
11.28, 191
11.29, 63
11.30–31, **193**
11.32, 20, 89, 192, 235, 238
11.33, 238
11.33–36, 193
12.1, 31, 59, 158, 231
12.1–2, **194–96**
12.1–5, 158, 236
12.1–15.13, 21, **194–221**
12.3, **200–201**
12.3–13, **196–200**
12.5, 32
12.6, 32, 63
12.7, 185
12.10, 31–32, 74, 236
12.14–13.7, 81
12.14–13.14, **201–208**
12.14–21, 133
12.17, 158
12.19, 42
13.1–11, **204–208**
13.3, 39, **206–7**
13.3–4, 40
13.4, 185, 210
13.7, 74
13.8, 40

13.11, 238
13.11–14, 96
13.14, 59
14.1, 212
14.1–15.13, 22, 158, **211–
      17**, 219, 236
14.4, 32, 63, 89, 236
14.8, 59
14.10, 31
14.11, 42
14.14, 88
14.15, 31
15.1, 219
15.3, 42
15.4, 42, 54
15.5, 217
15.6, 59
15.7, 27, 185
15.7–12, 218
15.9, 42
15.14–16.23, 21, **222–233**
15.14–33, **222–225**
15.16, 211
15.17, 74
15.21, 42
15.22, 83
15.23–24, 27
15.25, 185, 199
15.27, 185
15.29, 63
15.30, 31
15.31, 185
15.35, 182
16, 219
16.1, 185
16.1–2, **33–34**, 38, 40,
      225–26
16.3, 218, 219
16.3–5, 39, 220
16.3–16, **226–30**
16.3–26, 31
16.5, 188
16.7, 64
16.10, 220
16.11, 218, 220
16.17, 31
16.17–20, 14, **230–31**
16.21–23, **232–33**
16.23, 39
16.25, 189
16.26, 62

1 Corinthians, 3
1.1, 64, 65
1.3, 66
1.11, 39
1.19, 42
1.21–25, 66
1.22–25, 27
1.30, 67, 168
1.31, 106, 122
2.1, 189

2.7, 189
2.8, 208
2.11–13, 157
3.5, 185
3.30, 189
4.1, 189
6.3, 208
6.15, 158, 197
6.20, 139
7.2–6, 88
7.2, 10–11, 88
7.22–23, 59
8.1–10, 216
8.9–13, 158
9.10, 54
9.19–21, 46
9.19–25, 218
10.1, 63, 170
10.11, 54
10.15–22, 216
10.19, 216
10.28, 158
11.3–24, 195
11.14–15, 80
11.17–34, 158
11.20–29, 200
11.26, 189
11.27, 189
12.1, 63
12.5, 197
12.12–27, 197
12.27, 197
13.2, 189
14.1, 198
14.2, 189
14.26–40, 195
15.3–4, 42
15.5–7, 64
15.8–10, 61
15.9, 64, 167, 196, 201,
      203
15.9–11, 61
15.20, 188
15.21, 101
15.21–22, 83
15.22, 78, 83, 128
15.22–23, 61
15.24, 208, 232
15.33, 232
15.43, 80, 152
15.45–50, 101
15.51, 189
15.58, 238
16.3, 33
16.6, 224
16.15, 188
16.19, 226–27
16.20, 230

2 Corinthians, 3
1.1, 64, 65
1.2, 66

2 Corinthians (*continued*)
1.3, 194
1.8, 63
1.16, 224
1.22, 180
2.14–3.18, 65
3.1–2, 33
3.6, 185
3.7–11, 84
3.9, 65
3.14, 173
4.4, 154
4.4–6, 84
4.6, 118
5.5, 152
5.6, 158
5.16–17, 168
5.18, 61, 121
5.19–20, 65, 66
5.21, 146, 153
6.4, 185
6.8, 80
7.23, 84
8.13–14, 224
9.5, 163
9.11–14, 185
10–13, 66
11.3, 83, 101
11.13, 142
11.15, 185
11.23, 185
11.23–29, 153
12.2, 158
12.8–9, 170
12.9–10, 66
13.7, 159
13.9, 159
13.10, 181
13.12, 230
Galatians
1.1, 64
1.1–2, 13
1.4, 139
1.6–9, 27
1.10, 57
1.12, 185
1.13, 47, 201, 203
1.13–14, 166, 167
1.13–16, 61
1.16, 218
1.14, 46
1.23, 203
2.7–9, 218
2.11–21, 236
2.14–16, 97
2.16, 108
2.20, 108, 138, 139
3.2, 156, 180
3.8, 42, 46, 49, 174
3.10, 46

3.11, 70
3.11–14, 174
3.13, 139
3.13–14, 103
3.16–29, 170
3.17, 46
3.19, 47
3.22, 42, 46, 108
3.23–24, 47
3.26–28, 149
3.27–29, 229
4.3–6, 149
4.4, 146
4.6, 157
4.21–31, 46
4.29, 203
4.30, 42
5.4, 27
5.6, 199
5.11, 203
5.19–20, 156
5.23, 90, 156
5.24, 156
6.10, 31
6.11–18, 14
6.12, 203
6.17, 57, 58, 212
Ephesians
1.9, 189
1.20–23, 208
2.3–4, 163
2.13–16, 173
2.19, 31
3.3, 189
3.10, 208
3.12, 108
5.32, 189
6.12, 208
6.19, 189
Philippians, 3
1.1, 13, 57
1.2, 66
1.20, 158
1.27, 108
2.1, 194
2.5, 64, 136
2.10–11, 212
2.12–13, 196
2.25, 210
2.29, 226
3.3, 156
3.3–9, 47
3.5–6, 166, 167
3.6, 46, 167, 203
3.9, 108
3.19, 231
3.21, 152
4.2, 39
4.3, 164
4.8–9, 202

Colossians
1.15–18, 208
1.24, 185
1.24–27, 223
1.26, 189
1.27, 189
2.2, 189
2.9–10, 208
4.3, 189
1 Thessalonians, 3
1.1, 66
4.11–12, 40
4.13, 63
5.14, 40
5.23, 157
5.26, 230
2 Thessalonians
2.7, 189
3.6–13, 40
3.17–18, 14
1 Timothy
1.12–13, 61
2.9, 201
2.13–14, 82
3.9, 189
3.16, 189
2 Timothy
2.8, 61
3.16, 53
Titus
1.13
Philemon, 3
3, 66
Hebrews
4.15, 146
9.5, 104
10.38, 70
1 Peter
2.4, 166
2.12, 202
2.12–15, 39, 39–40
2.13, 209
2.13–14, 206
3.15–16, 4
3.22, 208
4.4, 26
5.14, 230
2 Peter
2.19, 136
1 John
4.9, 123, 146
Revelation
1.1, 57
3.5, 164
7.3, 57
13.1–18, 206
17.8, 164
19.5, 57
20.12, 164
20.15, 164

Index of Other Ancient Authors and Sources

"Ambrosiaster"
Ad Romanos, 219–20
Apollinarius
To Taesis, 30
Apollonius
To Sarapion, 33
Appianus
Civil Wars, 157–58
Apuleius,
Metamorphoses, 57, 125, 230
Aristotle
Nichomachean Ethics, 89, 123, 143
Poetics, 18
Politics, 49, 210
Protrepticus, 19
Rhetoric, 21, 200
Arrian
To Lucius Gellius, 22
Augustine
Confessions, 19
Contra duas Epistolas Pelagianorum, 124, 128
Literal Meaning of Genesis, 52
Against Julian, 213–14
Marriage and Concupiscence, 86
Propositions on Romans, 148, 170
Spirit and Letter, 70, 113, 123
Aurelius Dius
To Aurelius Horion, 31

2 Baruch
3.9–4.4, 76
30.1, 76
78.2, 67

Cassius Dio
Roman History, 129, 220
Cato
Origins, 44

Catullus
Poems, 116
Chairas
To Dionysius the Physician, 30
Chariton
Callirhoe 44, 85, 184
Chrysostom
Homilies on Romans, 61, 86, 147, 148, 151,
163, 170, 171, 178, 195, 198, 199, 202,
211, 213–14, 228, 229
Cicero
[To Herrenius], 21, 62, 67, 120
Hortensius, 19
Invention, 53
On Behalf of Milo, 85
Philippics, 85
Claudia Severa
To Sulpicia Lepidina, 12–14, 15, 29
Clement of Alexandria
Rich Man's Salvation, 47
Clement of Rome
1 Clement, 209
Columella
On Agriculture, 180
Cyprian
Ad Quirinium, 99
Cyril of Jerusalem
Catecheses 137, 138

Dead Sea Scrolls. See Qumran
"Demetrius"
On Style, 16, 18, 71
Didache
11.3–6, 64
Dio Chrysostom
Discourses, 22, 23, 25, 51, 113
Diogenes Laertius
Lives of Eminent Philosophers 19, 129, 143, 155

Dionysius of Halicarnassus
  Letter to Gnaeus Pompeius, 15, 16
  First and Second Letter to Ammaeus, 15, 16
  Roman Antiquities, 113, 131, 181
Dius
  To Aurelius Horion, 31

1 *Enoch*
  62.11
Epicharmus, 122
Epictetus, 22
  Discourses, 5, 23, 24, 25, 40, 87, 89–90, 90–
    91, 92, 123, 126, 131, 136, 144, 155,
    156, 195
Euripides
  Medea, 73, 143
  Orestes, 152
Eusebius
  Demonstratio Evangelica, 171

Florentinus
  Digest, 57

Galen, 19
  On the Pulse, 27
  Summary of Plato's Republic, 27, 90

Heracles
  To Musaeus, 33
Heraclitus Stoicus
  Quaestiones Homericae, 151
Heraklas
  To Horos and Tachonis, 30
Herodotus
  Histories, 64, 152
Homer
  Iliad, 157, 178
  Odyssey, 24
Horace
  Art of Poetry, 18
  Carmen Saeculare, 73
  Odes, 74, 123
Hymn to Demeter, 188

Jerome
  In Michaeam, 43
Josephus
  Against Apion, 84, 85, 86, 201
  Antiquities, 53, 64, 65, 69, 115, 147, 175, 184,
    223, 228
  Jewish War, 36, 53, 59, 75, 90, 225
Jubilees
  1.22–25, 148
  1.23, 96
  3.23–25, 101
  3.28–32, 82
  3.30–31, 76
  15.25–27, 76
  19.15–31, 76
  19.21, 117
  22.10–14, 76

Justin
  Apologia Maior, 230
Juvenal
  Satires, 36

Letter of Aristeas, 80, 84, 90
Life of Adam and Eve, 101
Livy
  From the Founding of the City, 131
Lucan
  Civil War, 43–44
Lucian of Samosata
  Alexander the False Prophet, 62
  Demonax, 188–89
  Icaromenippus, 184
  Nigrinus, 15, 16, 19, 26, 67
  Parasite, 19, 67
  Passing of Peregrinus, 15, 16
  Tyrant, 32
Lucius Apuleius
  Metamorphoses, 57

3 *Maccabees*
  2.31, 231
  4.14, 170
  7.11, 231
4 *Maccabees*
  1.1–6, 201
  1.30–32, 201
  5.33–35, 90, 126
  5.35, 170
  7.16–19, 155–56
  17.16, 170
  18.1–2, 139
Marcus Aurelius Antoninus
  Meditations, 181
Martial
  Epigrams, 36, 37, 40, 73, 230
Martyrdom of Saint Polycarp, 15, 16, 17
Mekilta, 117
Midrash Rabbah
  Exod. 21.8, 183; 30.22, 175
Mishnah
  'Abot 1.1, 4
  Ber. 5.5, 64
  Sanh. 4.5, 125; 10.1, 182,
  Sota 9.15, 122
  Toharot, 166
Moses, *Testament of*, 231

Origen, 19
  Commentary on Romans, 112, 113, 139–40, 142,
    146, 153, 170, 181, 187, 202, 211, 224
Ovid,
  Art of Love, 87
  Metamorphoses, 143, 144

Passion of Saints Perpetua and Felicity, 90, 123
Philo of Alexandria
  On Abraham, 84, 85, 86, 115, 170, 175
  Allegorical Interpretation, 155

Cher., 104, 170, 223
Flaccus, 36, 75, 181
Flight, 104
Giants, 155
Husbandry, 19, 178
Legum Allegoria, 233
Moses, 65, 104
Sacrifices of Abel and Cain, 25
Special Laws, 76, 96, 139, 175, 181
Virtues, 78, 115, 231
Philon of Larissa, 19
Philostratus
Letters, 44
Plato
Apology, 24
Laws, 49
Lysis, 47
Phaedo, 200
Republic, 71, 95, 131, 200
Statesman, 184
Timaeus, 86
Pliny the Younger
Pangyricus, 22, 230
Letters, 13, 26, 35, 36, 73, 222
Plutarch
Alexander, 223
Aratus, 129
Cimon, 129
Consolation to My Wife, 14, 16, 29, 32, 62
Coriolanus, 131
Curiosity, 22, 24, 129
On Exile, 157
Intelligence of Animals, 32
Numa, 157
Of Love, 85
On Marriage, 15, 17, 73, 87
Oracles in Decline, 69, 77
Pericles, 156
Quiet of Mind, 16
On Moral Virtue, 144
Reply to Celotes, 125, 155
Romulus, 210
Table Talk 5, 155
Talkativeness, 22
Virtues in Women, 73, 90
Polybius
Histories, 156
Psalms of Solomon, 59, 93
Pseudo-Demetrius
Epistolary Types, 31, 33, 34
Pseudo-Philo
Biblcial Antiquities, 117

Quintilian
Institutio Oratoria, 21, 22, 47, 90, 120, 140, 142, 145

Qumran, 59, 61, 70, 96, 99, 100, 101, 127, 142, 162, 189, 203, 224

Seneca
Letters, 25–26, 123, 132
Moral Essays, 36
Phaedra, 142, 143, 145
Solomon, Odes of
11.1–3, 96
Sophocles
Antigone, 72
Philoctetes, 101–102
Stobaeus
Anthologies, 19
Suetonius
Caligula, 73
Claudius, 220
Nero, 205
Tiberius, 230
Sybelline Oracles, 80, 84

Tacitus
Agricola, 44
Annals, 63, 85, 205, 207
Histories, 81
Targum
Neophyti I, 202
Talmud (Babylonian)
'Abod. Zar. 3b, 4
'Abod. Zar. 4b, 4
B. Mes. 5, 128
B. Qam. 38a, 175
Sabb. 31a, 207; 151a, 134
Sanh. 59a, 175; 98a, 182
Tertullian
Against Marcion, 70
Theodore of Mosuesta
Commentary on Romans, 113–14, 150, 170, 187
Theodoret of Cyrrhus
Interpretatio Epistolae ad Romanos, 171, 211
Theon
Progymnasmata, 140
Thucydides
Peleponnesian War, 52, 178, 201
Tosephta
Sanh. 7.11, 50
Twelve Patriarchs, Testaments of the
T. Simeon, 59
T. Levi, 61, 76
T. Judah, 59
T. Benjamin, 182
Tyconius
Book of Rules, 50

Virgil
Aeneid, 43–44

Xenophon
Memorabilia, 201

Index of Authors and Sources between 1000 and 1850

Aquinas, Thomas, 237
  Summa Theologica, 52, 102
Austen, Jane
  Pride and Prejudice, 37

Book of Common Prayer (1662), 101, 210

Calvin, John, 237
  Commentary on Genesis, 52
  Commentary on Romans, 114, 147–48,
      156, 172, 186–87, 187–88,
      201–202, 230
Chaucer, Geoffrey
  Romaunt of the Rose, 71

Dante Alighieri
  Commedia, 71, 81–82
Donne, John
  Meditations upon Emergent Occasions,
      131

Hooker, Richard, 237
  Sermon on Pride, 131

Jefferson, Thomas, 204
Julian of Norwich
  Showings, 192, 235

Kyd, Thomas
  Spanish Tragedy, 11–12

Luther, Martin, 237
  Lectures on Galatians, 103
  Lectures on Romans, 171, 177–78

Munday, Anthony, and others
  Sir Thomas More, 209–10

Pearl, 71

Shakespeare, William
  Corialanus, 131, 210
  Hamlet, 11–12, 71
  Macbeth, 72
  Much Ado About Nothing, 71
  Sir Thomas More: see Munday, Anthony, and
      others
Southey, Robert
  Thalaba the Destroyer, 101

de Tocqueville, Alexis, 130, 132

Wesley, Charles, 192
Wood, Robert
  Essay on the Genius of Homer, 51

Index of Modern Authors and Sources

Adams, Edward, 83, 118
Aitken, Ellen Bradshaw, 54, 237
Aletti, Jean-Noël, 140
Auden, W. H., 133
Aune, David, 18, 19, 28

Baeck, Leo, 205
Balch, David L., 40, 41
Barnett, Paul, 65
Barr, James, 149
Barrett, C. K., 64, 119, 147, 176, 199, 215
Bartchy, S. S., 58
Barth, Karl, 6, 58, 70, 72, 77, 91, 112, 145, 149,
    150, 164, 168, 172, 174, 178, 181, 183,
    187, 188, 213, 223, 232, 235, 237, 238
Barth, Marcus, 110, 172
Bash, Anthony, 65–66
Battle, Michael, 132
Bauckham, Richard, 206
Baumgärtel, Friedrich, 159
    Baumann, Richard A., 38
Behm, J., 195–96
Bell, Richard H., 83
Bengel, J. A., 223
Berger, Klaus, 28
Bertram, Georg, 143
Best, Ernest, 82
Betz, H. D., 196
Beyer, Hermann W., 184
Black, David Alan, 199
Bloom, Harold, 5
Boswell, John, 84
Bovon, François, 150, 236
Bowers, W. P., 226
Bowerstock, Glen W., 44
Bowman, Alan K., 12, 15
Boyarin, Daniel, 221
Bradley, K. R., 32
Brändle, Rudolf, 221
Branick, Victor P., 146
Brawley, Robert L., 92

Breuggemann, Walter, 49, 69
Brodie, Sir Benjamin, 101
Broneer, Oscar, 233
Brooten, Bernadette, 86, 229
Bruce, F. F., 172, 174
Bryan, Christopher, 3, 18, 50, 82
Bultmann, Rudolf, 22, 25, 197
Burton, Ernest de Witt, 174, 218
Byrne, Brendan, 6, 79, 87, 129, 136, 146, 173,
    197, 223

Caird, G. B., 111
Cairns, Douglas L., 75, 110
Cambier, J., 104, 108
Calvert, N. L., 118
Campbell, Douglas A., 108, 110
Caragounis, Chrys C., 221
Carpenter, Rhys, 233
Cervin, Richard S., 228
Cipriani, Settimio, 150
Clarke, A. D., 124
Cohen, Boaz, 53
Coleridge, Samuel Taylor, 5
Collange, Jean-François, 108
Collins, John N., 184, 185
Cranfield, C. E. B., 6, 47, 61, 63, 64, 66, 81,
    104, 106, 107, 110, 112, 115, 119, 124,
    129, 137, 145, 146, 147, 151, 152, 159,
    162, 163, 166, 168, 171, 172, 175, 177,
    179, 182–83, 185, 187, 188, 195–96, 201,
    211, 214, 218, 223, 229
Cristoffersson, Olle, 150
Cullmann, Oscar, 208

Danker, Frederick W., 34, 40
Daube, David, 50
Davies, W. D., 221
De Lacy, Philip H., 15
Derrett, J. Duncan M., 95
Dodd, Brian, 110
Dodd, C. H., 48, 49, 50, 81, 111, 123

Donfried, Karl P., 15, 17, 18
Downing, F. Gerald, 15, 18
Dumont, Louis, 129, 130
Dunn, James D. G., 6, 11, 47, 106, 109, 110,
    115, 119, 169, 172, 173, 211, 224–25, 225,
    231–32

Edgar, C. C., 15
Edwards, Douglas E., 44, 204
Einarson, Benedict, 15
Elliott, John H., 40

Finamore, Steve, 77
Fishbane, Michael, 43
Fitzgerald, John T., 29
Fitzmyer, Joseph A., 6, 18, 64, 83, 98, 99, 104.
    106, 107, 110, 119, 129, 134, 145, 149,
    161, 166, 173, 187, 190, 211, 218, 230
Fowler, Alistair, 12
Fuller, Reginald H., 146
Frye, Northrop, 72
Furnish, Victor Paul, 65, 208, 216

Gamble, Harry, 21, 29, 211, 217
Gager, John, 189–90
Gagnon, Robert A. J., 211
Garrett, Susan R., 82
Gaston, Lloyd, 189
Giglioli, A., 150
Gilbert, W. S., 68
Gilchrist, Gilbert F., 133
Gillman, Florence Morgan, 146
Girard, René, 77
Glucker, John, 28
Greer, Rowan A., 43, 52
Grenholm, Cristina, 6
Grundmann, Walter, 143
Guerra, Anthony J. 18, 19, 28, 204
Guillet, Jacques, 54
Gundry, Robert H., 159
Gutbrod, W., 48

Hachforth, R. H., 14
Hall, Edith, 91
von Harnack, Adolf, 228
Havelock, Eric, 120
Hays, Richard B., 5, 43, 92, 110, 119
Headlam, A. C., 119, 160, 171, 173, 195, 227, 229
Hengel, Martin, 26, 76, 167
Herron, R. W., 64
Hill, D., 111
Hinks, D. A. G., 28
Hirsch, E. D., 12
Hollander, John, 43
Holmberg, Bengst, 41, 185
Hooker, Morna D., 79, 82, 83, 110
Horsely, G. R. H., 15, 41, 111
Hübner, Hans, 47, 167
Hughes, Barbara, 162
Hughes, Robert Davis, 235
Hultgren, A. J., 110
Hunt, A. S., 15

Innes, Doreen C., 71

Janzen, J. Gerald, 70–71
Jewett, Robert, 39, 226, 231
Johnson, E. Elizabeth, 166
Johnson, Luke Timothy, 89, 110, 204
Jolivet, Ira J., 28, 53
Jordan, Mark D., 19, 28, 201

Karris, Paul, 216
Käsemann, Ernst, 6, 59, 83, 107, 119, 140, 146,
    147, 148, 153, 171, 173, 182, 187, 204,
    216, 231
Keck, Leander E., 99
Kennedy, George A., 21, 71
Kinneavy, James L., 62
Klassen, W., 230
Kleinknecht, Hermann, 49–50
Koch, Dietrich-Alex, 17, 71
Koester, Helmut, 158, 198, 200
Krafft-Ebbing. von, 84
Kugel, James L., 43, 53, 174
Koskenniemi, Heikki, 14

Lagrange, M.–J., 119, 147, 193
Lamarche, Paul, 43, 50
Lampe, Peter, 21, 29, 221, 227, 228
Lane, William L., 205, 217, 221
La Piana, George, 217, 219, 220
Lapide, Pinchas, 48
Lausberg, Heinrich, 140
Leenhardt, F.-J., 188
Leonardi, Anna Maria Chiavacci, 5
Lewis, C. S., 5, 11
Liebermann, Saul, 50
Liedke, G., 48
Lightfoot, J. B., 228, 229
Lincoln, Andrew T., 28
Lord, Albert Bates, 25
de Lubac, Henri, 71
Luck, Ulrich, 200
Lyall, F., 149
Lyonnet, S., 128, 129
Lytle, Guy Fitch, 29, 37, 135

MacMullen, Ramsey, 38, 85
Maier, H. O., 32–33
Malherbe, Abraham, 14, 19, 28, 29
Malina, Bruce J., 74, 125
Marmorstein, Arthur, 183
Martin, Dale B., 58
Martin, Luther H., 125
Martin, Ronald, 44
Martyn, J. Louis, 110, 174, 218
Mason, Hugh J., 233
Matera, Frank J. 110, 174, 218
Marxsen,W., 18
Meecham, H. G., 199
Meeks, Wayne A. 39, 41, 85
Michaelis, Wilhelm, 108
Momigliano, Arnaldo, 52
Montevecchi, Orsolina, 38, 41

Monti, Joseph, 89
Moo, Douglas, 6, 11, 18, 64, 106, 110, 115, 119, 172, 173, 190, 231
Morgan, Charles H., 233
Morris, L., 111
Moxnes, Halvor, 74, 81
Moule, C. F. D., 109, 128
Munck, Johannes, 218
Murphy O'Connor, Jerome, 39, 41,
Mussner, Franz, 189
Mynors, R. A. B., 15

Neusner, Jacob, 166, 167
Nissinen, Martti, 84, 85
North, J. Lionel, 65
Nygren, Anders, 69

Oepke, Albert, 203
Ogilvie, R. M., 44

Panzini, Alfredo, 5
Paranuk, H. Van Dyke, 120
Parry, Milman, 25, 51
Pedersen, Johannes, 125
Peterman, G. W., 225
Petersen, C., 48
Pfeiffer, Rudolph, 71
Pierce, C. A., 94
Piper, John, 107
Pokorný, Petr, 82
Porter, Stanley E., 28

Quell, Gottfried, 69

Radice, Betty, 15, 37
Rahner, Karl, 103, 234
Räisänen, Heikki, 46, 146, 191
Rees, B. R., 14
Reese, J. M., 29
Reinhartz, Adele, 49
Reumann, John, 130
Rhys, Howard, 119, 149
Richmond, Ian, 44
Ringgren, Helmer, 59
Robinson, H. Wheeler, 129–30
Rossano, Pietro, 143, 202
Rouffiac, Jean, 38
Russell, Donald, 15

Sampley, J. Paul, 231
Sanday, W., 119, 160, 171, 173, 195, 227
Sanders, E. P., 46, 47, 167, 190–91, 208, 218
Sandmel, Samuel, 118
Sayers, Dorothy, 5
Schechter, Solomon, 48
Schoenberg, M. W., 149
Schoeps, Hans Joachim, 48, 49
Schneider, J., 146
Schrenk, Gottlob, 69, 95
Schweizer, Eduard, 82, 159
Scranton, Robert L., 233

Sherwin-White, A. N., 206
Sissa, Giulia, 114
Smyth, Herbert Weir, 109, 128
Souilhe, Joseph, 28
Spicq, Ceslas, 64, 66, 69, 83, 84, 208
Stählin, Gustaf, 230
Stambaugh, John E., 40, 41
Stamm, J. J., 104
Stanley, Christopher D., 44–45
Staveley, Eastland Stewart, 206
Stegemann, Ekkehard W., 221
Stendahl, Krister, 59, 189, 236
Stirewalt, Martin Luther, 15–18
Stoebe, H. J., 66, 194
Stowers, Stanley K., 14, 18, 28, 29, 91, 92, 110, 113, 119, 139–40, 142, 144, 218
Suggs, M. Jack, 169

Talbert, C. H., 199
Talmon, Shemaryahu, 45
Tate, J., 71
Thébert, Yvon, 58
Theissen, Gerd, 141, 233
Thielman, Frank, 141
Thomas, J. David, 15
Thomas, Yan, 38
Turner, Nigel, 109
Tutu, Desmond, 133

Veyne, Paul, 32, 34, 40–41, 204
Vorgrimler, Herbert, 234
Vos, J. S., 174, 175
Vriezen, Theodorus Christiaan, 84

Walbank, F. W., 52
Walsh, P. G., 52
Walters, James C., 211–212, 220
Ward, Roy Bowen, 86, 87
Warren, Austen, 12
Watson, Francis, 217
Watson, N. M., 69
Wellek, René, 12
Wells, Colin, 205
Westermann, Claus, 84
Westerholm, Stephen, 49
White, John L., 14, 15, 32
White, Victor, 102
Williams, Charles, 5, 52
Winger, Michael, 97, 141, 146
Winter, Bruce M., 39, 40, 41, 124, 233
Wiseman, T. P., 85, 236
Wright, N. T., 47, 54, 76, 106, 127, 146, 167, 168, 174, 221
Wright, Rebecca Abts, 71
Wuellner, W., 21, 28
Wyschogrod, Michael, 96

Yinger, Kent L., 203

Zerwick, Maximilian, 128
Ziesler, J. A., 69

Index of Subjects

Abraham, 47, 62, 114–18, 119
Adam, 77, 82–83, 129, 151
  community of, 121, 124, 126–28,
    134
  Israel in, 83, 100, 129, 142
  last, 127
adikia, 81
Adoption, 149
akrasia, 89, 143
Ambassadorial language, 65–66
Ambiguity, 71–72, 109–110
Amicitia, 29
Apostle, 60, 64–66
apostolos and cognates, 64–66
Aquila. *See* Prisca
Aristobulos, 227–28
Augustus, 205
Authorities, the, 204–205, 208–209
  instituted by God, 209–10

Baptism, 134
Bar Kochba. *See* Bar Kosiba
Bar Kosiba, 59
Benefactor, benefaction, 35. *See also* Patron,
    patronage
Beneficium. *See* Patron, patronage
Boasting, 121–22, 223
Body, 148, 157–59, 197
  of Christ, 158–59, 197–98
Book of Life, 164

Calvin, 186–87
charis, 61, 66, 198
charisma, 63, 198
Christ, 59–60
  "in Christ," 124, 126–28
  "end" of the Law, 168, 171–2
  as God, 170–71
"Christians," 221

Church. *See also* Church, in Rome
  body of Christ, 158–59, 198–99
  ecumenism, 236–37
  as household of God, 31–32, 62–63, 226, 236
  principles for life in, 196–200
  and non-believers, 201–10
  and state, 204–10
Church, in Rome, 27, 63–64, 217–21
  ethnic composition, 61, 217–21
  house churches, 220–21
  origins of, 219–21
  "strong" and "weak," 211–15, 215–17
Circumcision
  outward and inward, 95–96
  purpose of, 116
Claudius, 228
Clean and unclean, 136–37
Cliens, clientela. *See* Patron, patronage
Collection for Jerusalem, 185, 224–25
Commedia, 71, 81–82
Conscience, 94
Corporate personality, 129
Creation
  creation story, 78–79, 82–83
  healing of creation, 75, 127, 136–37
  and sin, 78–79, 101, 124, 126–28
Criticism
  critical method, 4–6
  historical criticism, 4–6, 50–53
  literary criticism, 4–6
  See also Genre; Greco-Roman Letters; *ktisis*

Dia. *See* ek
diakonia and cognates, 34, 65, 184–86, 205–206
Diatribe, 22–25
dikaiōsis, dikaiosunē and cognates, 69–70, 76–77,
  126
doulos, 57
doxa, 80, 83–84

Ecumenism, 236–37
egkrateia, 82, 89–91, 139, 142, 143, 144, 196, 214
eiper, 147
eirēnē, 61, 66, 125
ek, 106, 113–114
eph'hō[i], 124, 128–29
epithumia, 141
Endurance, 152, 152
euaggelion, 60
Epideictic rhetoric, 21–22
Erastus, 232–33
Eschatology
    future, 151–55, 238
    inaugurated, 60–61, 136–37, 138, 151–52
exousiai, 204–205, 208–209
Expiation. *See* Propitiation

Faith, and cognates, 62, 68–69, 70–72, 105,
    165–66
    "measure of," 197
Familia, 29
Family, Greco-Roman, 29, 32, 33
Family letters, 29–32
First fruit, 152
Flesh, 138, 155–56
Foreknowledge, 154
Fullness, 179–80, 182

Genre, 11–12, 25
Gentiles, 106, 116–18, 164, 165, 180
Gift, 63, 198
Glory, 80, 83–84
God
    Christ as, 170–71
    faithfulness of, 97–98, 159–84
    foreknowledge, 154, 163–4
    and gentiles, 106, 116–18, 164, 165
    grace of, 61, 66, 135
    and Israel, 159–84
    justice of, 105, 234–25
    mercy of, 161, 164
    patience of, 93, 105, 163
    wrath of, 77, 163
Gospel, 60–61, 67–68
Granville, Lord, 52
Grace, 61, 66, 135, 198
Greco-Roman letters, 12–14
    letters of commendation, 33
    family letters, 29–32, 236
    letter essays, 15–18

Hadrian, 205
hamartia and cognates, 100–102
    peri hamartias, 146
haparchē, 152
Herod the Great, 227
hilastērion, 104, 107, 112
Holism, 129
Holy of Holies, 104
homoiōma, 146
Homosexuality, 84–89

Hong Kong club, 36–37
Honor and shame, 67–68, 70, 72–74
Hope, 151–55, 238
House church, 220–21
Household. *See* Family, Greco-Roman
huiothesia, 149, 152, 159
hupomenē, 122

Individualism, 129–33
Interfaith dialogue, 235–36
Israel
    in Adam, 83, 100, 129, 142
    privileges, 169–70
    remnant, 164–65
    salvation of all, 175–84, 186–87
    unbelief of, 159–69
Ius gladii, 206

Justice, and cognates, 46, 69–70, 76–77, 105,
    234–35
    God's, 105, 234–25
    "saving" and "retributive," 70, 76–77
Justification. *See* Justice

kalos, 143
kashrut, 211, 213
ktisis, 78, 150

latreia, 170, 195
Law, 45–50, 127, 142–43, 144
    end of, 171–72
    of faith, 105–106, 146
    Israel and, 159, 166–69
    Paul and, 45–47
    works of, 100, 105–106, 146
leitourgos, 207, 210–11, 223
Letters of Commendation, 33
Letter Essays, 15–18
logikos, 195
logizomai, 115–16

Macbeth, 72
Medea, 143–44
Mercy, God's, 161
Mercy Seat, 104, 112
Messiah, 59–60
The Mikado, 68
Moderation, 196–97, 200–201
Monotheism, 106, 234–35
Ministry, 184–86, 198–99
Much Ado About Nothing, 71
mustērion, 181, 188–89
Mystery, 181, 188–89

Narcissus, 228
Nations. *See* Gentiles
Nero, 205, 207, 220
nomos, 45, 48–50,106

oiketēs, 63
oikia, 29
oiktirmos, 194–95